HERE, THERE AND EVERYWHERE
THE BEATLES

HERE, THERE AND EVERYWHERE

THE BEATLES

NANCY J. HAJESKI

THUNDER BAY
P·R·E·S·S

SAN DIEGO, CALIFORNIA

Thunder Bay Press
An imprint of the Baker & Taylor Publishing Group
10350 Barnes Canyon Road, San Diego, CA 92121
www.thunderbaybooks.com

Publisher: Peter Norton

Moseley Road Inc., www.moseleyroad.com
President: Sean Moore
General Manager: Karen Prince
Editorial Director: Lisa Purcell
Art Director: Tina Vaughan
Production Director: Adam Moore

Picture and memorabilia research: Duncan Youel, Sean Moore, Nancy Hajeski
Art Direction and Design: Duncan Youel and Philippa Baile at OilOften Graphic Design
www.oiloften.co.uk
Editorial Director: JoAnn Padgett

Library of Congress Cataloging-in-Publication Data
Hajeski, Nancy J., 1951-
    Beatles : here, there, and everywhere / Nancy J. Hajeski.
        pages cm
    Includes bibliographical references and index.
    ISBN-13: 978-1-62686-088-9 (hardcover : alk. paper)
    ISBN-10: 1-62686-088-2 (hardcover : alk. paper)
1. Beatles. 2. Rock musicians--England--Biography. I. Title.
    ML421.B4H315 2014
    782.42166092'2--dc23
    [B]

4003741

Printed in China

14 15 16 17 18 6 5 4 3 2 1

Opposite: The Beatles pose in profile for a group portrait, circa 1967.
Front cover: Top, portraits of the Beatles, from *A Hard Day's Night* U.K. movie poster, 1964; bottom, silhouettes of the Beatles from the soundtrack album sleeve of their 1965 movie, *Help!*
Back cover: From top to bottom, the Beatles perform at the Majestic Theatre, Birkenhead, in April 1963; the Beatles' historic appearance on *The Ed Sullivan Show* on February 9, 1964; a publicity shot of the Beatles for *Our World*, the first global TV transmission by satellite, on June 25, 1967; the Beatles and their entourage pose for a photograph at the Maharishi's retreat in Rishikesh, India, in February 1968.

HERE, THERE AND EVERYWHERE
THE BEATLES

INTRO THE MAGICAL MYSTERY FOUR | 08

01 LIVERPOOL | 10
Gateway to the World | Postwar Blues | American Rock and Roll Rhythm |
John Lennon | Paul McCartney | George Harrison | Stuart Sutcliffe | Pete Best

02 HAMBURG | 28
Roughing It on the Reeperbahn | Raving Up Live | Astrid, Klaus, and Jürgen |
Soul Mates and the Deportation Blues

03 ROCKING IT UNDERGROUND: THE CAVERN | 38
Clubland | A Cellar on Mathew Street | Hamburg and a Record Contract | Stuart's
Twilight in Germany | Brian Epstein | A Significant Request | The Decca Tapes

04 ABBEY ROAD STUDIOS: THE EARLY SIXTIES | 54
EMI Studios | Breaking New Ground | George Martin: The Perfect Complement | Recording
Prodigy | Goodbye, Pete | Ringo Starr | "Love Me Do" | "Please Please Me" | Album on the Fly

05 IN THE PUBLIC EYE | 74
Mr. Epstein's School of Deportment | Closing the Bedroom Door | "Love, Love, Love" | Songs for
Other Voices | SPOTLIGHT: Instruments of the Early Years

06 LONDON | 86
The Coolest Crucible | London Digs | London After Dark | With the Beatles | On Tour: Great
Britain and Sweden | The Beatles Show | SPOTLIGHT: Merchandising the Mersey Beat

07 AMERICA | 108
Tough Times and Musical Doldrums | Hitting the Top of the American Pop Charts |
The Promoter and the Impresario | "All Beatles, All the Time!" | Beatlemania | Press Darlings |
SPOTLIGHT: The British Invasion Unleashed

08 ON THE SILVER SCREEN | 128
A Hard Day's Night | A New Name | Making the Album | Australian and American Tours |
Meeting Bob Dylan | Beatles for Sale | Help! | Making the Album | Shea Stadium: The Wall
of Noise | U.S. Fanzines | The King Meets the Boys

09 A NEW MOOD: ABBEY ROAD IN THE MID-SIXTIES | 150
Playing the Palace | Rubber Soul | Revolver | Studio Staff "We can do magic" | SPOTLIGHT:
The Capitol Albums—Tampering with Success

10 ON THE WORLD STAGE | 166
Feeling Grim on the Pacific Rim | The John and Jesus Controversy | The End of the Long
and Winding Road | The Support Staff | SPOTLIGHT: Instruments of the Middle Years

23

59

108

145

158

11 BEATLES IN PRIVATE | 178

Domestic Arrangements | John and Cynthia Lennon at Kenwood | Paul McCartney and Jane Asher in London | George and Pattie Harrison at Kinfauns | Ringo and Maureen Starkey at Sunny Heights | Brian Epstein in Belgravia | SPOTLIGHT: On Vacation

12 BEATLES IN DISGUISE | 188

Free at Last | The Celebrity Cover | *Sgt. Pepper*'s Legacy | Maharishi Magnetism | Mr. Epstein's Ethics | A Shocking Loss | *Magical Mystery Tour* | On Retreat in Rishikesh

13 APPLE CORPS | 208

Taking a Bite of the Apple | The Apple Bites Back | Apple Subsidiaries

14 ABBEY ROAD: THE LATE SIXTIES | 218

Emotional Escapades | Animated Antics: *Yellow Submarine* | The Great White | Ringo Loses the Beat | Mixed Reviews and Apolitical Views | Vindicated By the Charts | SPOTLIGHT: Instruments of the Later Years

15 FINALE | 232

Get Back: The Making of *Let It Be* | Last Licks: Up on the Roof | *Abbey Road*: Crossing Over | The Cover Story | SPOTLIGHT: Hit Singles, England and America

16 COMING APART | 244

"Breaking Up Is Hard to Do" | "Baby, You're a Rich Man" | "Oh, Yoko" | Unfinished Paintings | "Without You"

17 JOHN LENNON: SOME TIME IN NEW YORK CITY | 256

Bed Peace, Hair Peace | Deportation Blues, Part II | Beautiful Boys: Julian and Sean | *Double Fantasy* | Darkness at the Dakota | The Song Is Over

18 PAUL McCARTNEY: MULL OF KINTYRE | 270

Lovely Linda | Period of Adjustment | Wings Over the World | Macca's Back | Paul Plays On

19 GEORGE HARRISON: IN THE MATERIAL WORLD | 282

George Unchained | With Pattie at Friar Park | Bangladesh | Olivia and Dhani | "All things must pass away . . ."

20 RINGO STARR: SUNSHINE LIFE FOR ME | 294

Troubled Times | A Little Help from His Friends | The All-Stars | The Hip Elder Statesman of Rock

21 ROCK ON: THE BEATLES' LEGACY | 304

The Beatles' Legacy | Homage to the Band | Multimedia

AFTERWORD | 310

BEATLES BIBLIOGRAPHY | 314

INDEX | 316

CREDITS AND ACKNOWLEDGMENTS | 319

THE MAGICAL MYSTERY FOUR

"How is it possible that four men whom I have never met, one of whom died 18 years before I was even born and another who died when I was still watching *Dora the Explorer,* had such a life-changing impact on me? How is it possible that this song written by and for people I will never hope to know well at all, elicits such tears? Why do I love them so much? Because they are there for me, and for you, and for us all . . . "

APPLESNACKS5, "Here Today" YouTube video

How did they do it?

That is the question every Beatles fan asks at some point. How did a rag-tag band from a bombed-out British city become so hugely popular, so widely influential, and so enduring?

The odds had to be stacked against four self-taught musicians making even a ripple in the entertainment cosmos, let alone carving out a nine-year performing career, especially in a business where longevity is most often measured in weeks or months . . . or piffling years . . . rarely in decades. Yet these four managed to sustain eight years of consistently strong recordings, eventually pumping out hit after hit and album after world-changing album, and many decades since of chart-busting and poll-topping popularity. (The sales and chart statistics surrounding them are fairly staggering—a growing collection of "Mosts" and "Bests," "fastests" and "highests.") It is no stretch to say that the Beatles became, collectively, the biggest entertainment phenomenon the world has seen to date. The band maintained such preeminence in the music industry—even

after it ceased to exist—that its status has not ever been challenged, let alone surpassed.

Beyond the music, how did four unsophisticated urban lads with limited educations end up shaping the fashions, perceptions, and ideologies of one generation in the mid-60s—when art and culture and a thousand new concepts virtually exploded from every thoroughfare in London, a movement that the Beatles, depending on sources, either jump-started or quickly became part of—and then go on molding major aspects of the culture for each successive generation? What was it that made them so pervasive and earned them such adulation?

No one—neither music critics nor fans—is quite sure how they did all this. Not even the Beatles themselves. (Paul has often kidded around, saying they were a "pretty good" garage band.) Maybe it was their ability to not only read the zeitgeist, but also to alter it. Or perhaps it was because they were ridiculously proficient at writing songs that entwined themselves around our brain stems and infiltrated our souls. They may

have claimed that their lyrics rarely had the deeper meaning we so desperately sought, but then all good poets insist that what they write is straightforward . . . and all good poets know it for a lie.

There is no denying there was stage presence and personal charisma there nearly from the start. And before long, an ambitious manager, one who parlayed their Merseyside mystique into outright mythos. And then a savvy, avuncular producer . . . who taught them his whole bag of studio tricks. At first, the public knew only what the men behind the scenes decided they should know. The foursome's glib comebacks, hurled like pub darts during press conferences, left the scribes even more bemused than they were by Bob Dylan's intentional obfuscations. The reporters knew the Beatles were clever, but they only rarely got wise to the disdain behind the quips. But it was there, in the comments and the music, a bit of bitter with the sweet, a little sneer in the sincere. It lent even their occasionally trite musical compositions depth and pungency.

Yet for the most part the Beatles

Left: The Beatles perform "All You Need Is Love" on *Our World*, the first live satellite uplink performance broadcast to the world on June 25, 1967 in London, England.

played along with the charade, pretending to have a gloss and a glamour they did not precisely possess, somehow understanding that England needed them to be that exact thing, at that exact time: a symbol of promising youth awakened during a dark period, as though the poppy fields of Flanders and the shores of Dunkirk had brought forth these standard-bearers of another gilded generation that would undo all the previous despair of wars and deprivation. And, oh!—when they sang and played, those dark memories did indeed fade away, and spirits soared higher than . . . well, the White Cliffs of Dover. Their music seemed to offer a universal benediction to all, like a touch on the forehead by Jove.

Ultimately, England's embrace could not contain them. Their music spread to Europe, then America, and before long, it seemed the whole world was chanting along with every Liverpudlian refrain. They became, inevitably, the lightning rods of their era—inventive and derivative, eclectic and experimental, but always accessible. They ended up as almost

everyone's beau ideal. (They may have been the rock and roll band all the teenage girls crushed on, but they were also the one the moms and kid brothers liked.)

And there was something more that set the Beatles apart, a trait they shared with creative types from an earlier era—that wherever they lived or traveled, they stayed attuned to their surroundings. Liverpool and the Mersey Beat shaped much of their music, as well as America, in the form of the rollicking rhythmic music favored by both white and black teens. The red-light district of Hamburg honed them as performers. A move to London gave them access to other rock and rollers, as well as exposure to live jazz and Caribbean influences. India offered them a retreat for a short time and exotic Eastern tempos soon crept into their sound.

Even as mature, solo performers, their output rarely flagged, and once again their environment affected them—Paul, reflective and domestic in Scotland; John, besieged and primal in New York; George, transcendental in the meditation room at Friar

Park; Ringo, twanging it up in Nashville or taking in the mellow Mediterranean sun. They soaked up influences along with the sights and sounds of their chosen havens, and they continued to produce personal, entertaining, relevant music from decade to decade—not due to pressure from the fan machine or their own brand of competition, but for the sheer pleasure of it. Because that was what they did.

How they did it, on the other hand, is a question that remains without a definitive answer.

Suffice to say the Beatles possessed talent, drive, curiosity, adaptability, a powerful camaraderie, a fluid creative instinct that kept them in the vanguard of new trends, and a keen sense of their surroundings. Yet there is still some elusive alchemy that remains beyond our comprehension to explain the long, long shadow they cast. Perhaps this is why we can never let them go, because that mystery tweaks us every time we hear them sing . . . and we realize we were born with that music inside us.

"LIVERPOOL I LEFT YOU, SAID GOODBYE TO MADRYN STREET;
I ALWAYS FOLLOWED MY HEART, AND I NEVER MISSED A BEAT.
DESTINY WAS CALLING, I JUST COULDN'T STICK AROUND.
LIVERPOOL I LEFT YOU, BUT I NEVER LET YOU DOWN."
RINGO STARR, *LIVERPOOL 8*

CHAPTER ONE
LIVERPOOL

"SHIPS, SHIPS AND SHIPPING EVERYWHERE."
NOVELIST ALBERT SMITH

Gateway to the World

"Besides, of all the sea-ports in the world, Liverpool, perhaps, most abounds in all the variety of land-sharks, land-rats, and other vermin, which make the hapless mariner their prey . . . And yet, sailors love this Liverpool; and upon long voyages to distant parts of the globe, will be continually dilating upon its charms and attractions, and extolling it above all other seaports in the world. For in Liverpool they find their Paradise . . . and one of them told me he would be content to lie in Prince's Dock till he *hove up anchor* for the world to come."

HERMAN MELVILLE, *Redburn* (1849)

Above: The Liverpool skyline, circa 1950, shows Liverpool Cathedral on the horizon rising above the varied rooftops of the city. Liverpool suffered the second worst bombing blitz during World War II after London, and many damaged sections of the city were not rebuilt for years.

Preceding pages: December 8, 1926, the Cunard liner RMS *Mauretania* arriving at Liverpool docks. A fleet of tugboats are nosing her into position.

"LIVERPOOL IS SECOND ONLY TO LONDON IN MY HEART."

CHARLES DICKENS, 1842

Liverpool lies on the eastern shore of the Mersey Estuary, which runs into the Irish Sea. When seen from the open water, the city presents a profile of stately Victorian edifices, sleek high-rise apartments, and towering office buildings. From this perspective, Liverpool nearly recaptures her past glory—when 19th-century trade from the West Indies, Ireland, and Europe brought her wealth that at times exceeded that of London, and when her custom house was the largest contributor to the British Exchequer.

Home to invention and innovation as well as humane institutions, the city pioneered the development of the commercial railroad, the city tram, the ferry, and the skyscraper, and offered the first school for the blind, and the first societies for the protection of children and animals. Described in 1851 as the "New York of Europe," Liverpool catered to the wealthy and powerful and was the port of registry for the ill-fated luxury liner, RMS *Titanic*, and her sister ships, RMS *Olympic* and HMHS *Britannic*.

Throughout most of the first half of the twentieth century, Liverpool maintained her status as England's "second city." The docks expanded to include the 1901 Stanley Dock Tobacco Warehouse—at one time the world's largest building in area, which today remains the largest brickwork building—and the Three Graces of the Pier Head: the Royal Liver Building, the Cunard Building, and the Port of Liverpool Building. In the service sector, the city's commerce was fueled by the banking, finance, and insurance industries.

In the 1920s and 30s a great number of inner-city families were relocated to suburban "council" housing estates in order to "improve their standard of living," a foretaste of the urban renewal that would ruin the character of many Merseyside neighborhoods in the 1950s. But overall, the city remained a thriving, bustling center of industry and trade . . . at least until the late 1930s, when a dark cloud gathered to the East and England was drawn into war.

FabFact

Denizens of Liverpool are also known as "Scousers" and speak with a "Scouse" accent; the word derives from "scouse," a type of local stew.

Right: The three stately "grand dames" of the Liverpool waterfront—the Royal Liver Building, the Cunard Building, and the Port of Liverpool Building—stood as a symbol of the city's commercial history and elevated stature in 1925. But then financial depression and the German blitz during World War II reduced Liverpool to a shell of its former self.

"WE WERE A SAVAGE LITTLE LOT, LIVERPOOL KIDS, NOT PACIFIST OR VEGETARIAN OR ANYTHING. BUT I FEEL I'VE GONE BEYOND THAT, AND THAT IT WAS IMMATURE TO BE SO PREJUDICED AND BELIEVE IN ALL THE STEREOTYPES."

PAUL McCARTNEY

Naturally, Liverpool was of great strategic importance during World War II. With its eleven miles of quays, the seaport offered anchorage to multinational naval and merchant ships, and provided England's main link with American arms shipments and supplies. Merseyside dockworkers would eventually handle 90 percent of the war materials brought into the county. Liverpool was also the site where the plans for the North Atlantic Defense were developed. The sad result of the city's noble wartime effort was that this proud "gateway to the world" received the worst bombing, second only to London, from the German Luftwaffe with a final death toll of more than 3,000 people. During a three-month period in 1940, heavy bombing raids occurred

fifty times, and in May 1941 seven straight nights of bombardment left much of the city in rubble. That same year a visiting Winston Churchill observed somberly, "I see the damage done by the enemy attacks, but I also see . . . the spirit of an unconquered people."

The fighting ended in 1945, but for Liverpool, as for many other industrialized cities in Great Britain, the aftermath was grim. Britannia may have won the war, but she appeared to be losing the peace. The country's resources were depleted by five years of conflict— economists estimate one quarter of the nation's entire wealth had been used up resisting German invasion. The 1941 Lend-Lease support program from the United States, which allowed England

to continue importing American aircraft and other armaments when their financial reserves were almost gone, ceased in 1945. Furthermore, the Anglo-American loan of 1946, which did help restore some economic stability, was geared more toward overseas expenditures than boosting the reforms of the newly elected Labour Party at home. While some resource rationing continued after the war, including gasoline and clothing, the financial situation soon grew so bad that bread rationing was instituted from 1946 to 1948, a measure that had not been taken during the war.

While America flourished and expanded economically during the early 1950s, Great Britain, weighted down with a massive war debt and low morale from

"I mean, I was born the day war broke out, but I don't remember all the bombs though they did actually break up Liverpool, you know. I remember when I was a little older, there were big gaps in all the streets where houses used to be. We used to play over them."

RINGO STARR

the continued rationing of such staples as meat, butter and cheese, was barely marking time. Many cities still bore deep scars from the German bombing blitz, and entire neighborhoods lay in ruins and had yet to be rebuilt. Children were so inured to military conflict as a part of their daily lives that all they ever played were war games—some even using army surplus machine guns with the firing pins removed. Movie studios continued to produce war films. As America began its long history of conspicuous consumption, many Britons were still leading lives of deprivation, fear, and uncertainty.

"AS GOOD AS ANY MAN"

If there was one positive aspect of the war, it was that it had begun to erode England's centuries-old barriers of class. After fighting shoulder-to-shoulder with the gentry, the yeoman—or "common man"—began to believe that he was the equal of anyone. Yet in spite of these early cracks in the class system, attitudes of rigid conformity and an emphasis on respectability still prevailed in much of the country throughout the 1950s, a "dreariness of public behavior," as Indian writer Nirad Chaudhuri observed.

Eventually this tension between the "haves," who desired to maintain the status quo and the "want-to-haves" would come to a head—in strikes, protests, and riots. In popular culture this rebellion was fomented by literature's "angry young men," working-class playwrights and authors like John Osborne, Harold Pinter, and Kingsley Amis, who peddled dissatisfaction; by youthful, edgy actors such as Albert Finney, Tom Courtney, Richard Harris, and Rita Tushingham, who represented the views of a disaffected generation; and by a brash new brand of dance music that blasted tradition and shattered boundaries, something the teenagers over in America called rock and roll.

Opposite: Even as late as 1954, much of Liverpool still had not been rebuilt after the German bombings. Here, children play near a wasteland in one of the city's slums.

Above: Just after the war, in 1947, a group of boys play soccer during recess in a rubble-strewn field beside a damaged church in a bombed-out neighborhood of Liverpool.

"From the year dot, when King John filled out the birth certificate, Liverpool has been the gateway between England and the World."
LOYD GROSSMAN

Liverpool during the early 1950s still bore the terrible effects of the war, so the civic focus was on rebuilding. The city's plans for urban renewal, however, included an unpopular restructuring of the city center and, incomprehensibly, the destruction of many of the town monuments that had survived the blitz. The plan further replaced older, entrenched neighborhoods with massive tracts of low-rent estate or council housing— either small, attached homes or multistoried apartments similar to American project housing. The result was an increasingly dulled-down landscape of poverty and apathy amid newly decaying slums. Gangs eventually formed, made up of tough teenagers and angry young adults, eager to fight and let off steam . . . and as a result many bars and music clubs hired burly waiters who doubled as bouncers, a set of brass knuckles hidden in their pockets.

THE RIGHT STUFF

This city on the downward slide seemed an unlikely place to produce an innovative musical movement like the Mersey beat, let alone a quartet of young men so talented and relentlessly up-

tempo that they would help to lift England out of the doldrums, both psychologically and financially. But to be fair, in spite of its flawed urban reconstruction and general air of defeat, Liverpool still had several positive things going for it.

Of primary relevance was the character of the Liverpudlians themselves. Joseph Conrad wrote in "Youth" (1902): "That crew of Liverpool hard cases had in them the right stuff. It's my experience they always have."

The men and women of Merseyside were entrepreneurial by nature: their city was not a center of manufacturing, it expedited the output of others . . . and Liverpudlians always took their cut as goods passed through their hands. They were canny wheeler-dealers, charming opportunists, and, occasionally, loudly extroverted eccentrics. Yet there was a darker side to the Scouse spirit, one that carried a chip on its shoulder and felt hard done by whenever the dockside economy faltered. It was then that their most valuable trait came to the fore—a plucky resilience of the sort that can only be found in cultures that once knew great glory . . . and aspired to reclaim

it ever after. Somehow, against so many odds, the beleaguered people of Liverpool still believed that a golden future lay before them.

Another plus for the city was that Liverpool, for all its financial woes, was still a major seaport. Merchant marines from all over the globe converged on the dockside neighborhoods whenever their ships were at anchorage, and Americans, called the "Cunard Yanks," were especially welcomed.

REVOLUTIONARY CARGO

Along with ordinary cargo from the United States, something else, something slightly subversive, was arriving at those docks. The ships' crews brought American LP records and 45s ashore—including "race" records by black performers and others—rare properties the locals were eager to bargain for. It wasn't long before the young people of Liverpool were dancing with uninhibited abandon to the raw, powerful sounds of Chuck Berry, Little Richard, Fats Domino, and Roy Orbison, and singing along to the sweet harmonies of the Shirelles, Smokey Robinson and the Miracles, and Buddy Holly and the Crickets. Called "beat" music by the locals, it lit a spark in that dreary port town . . . soon boys were practicing guitar in their bedrooms, girls were using hairbrushes for microphones, and makeshift bands began to spring up, playing in church basements all over the city. This in turn led to the rise of shilling-admission dances held in small public halls, supplying these fledgling groups with a stage and an audience. More groups formed, more live music venues cropped up, until Liverpool became the center of the new beat music craze.

A MUSICAL MELTING POT

British popular music in the mid 1950s, dance bands, brass or military bands, and the broad, bawdy tunes of the British music hall tradition (cousin to America's Vaudeville) was in transition to swing, middle-of-the-road pop, and the folk- and jazz-based rhythms of skiffle—which had begun in America in the 1920s and was revived to became a craze in England by Lonnie Donegan. His debut recording, a cover of Lead Belly's "Rock Island Line," became a monster hit.

Skiffle bands typically included homemade instruments, washboards, jugs, the tea-chest bass, and kazoos, in addition to guitars and drums. In Liverpool, skiffle and beat intermingled with an additional ingredient— the plaintive lyrics and melodic tunes of Irish folk music. It was these traditions, these local flavors, blending with the gospel, blues, and rock and roll that teens heard on their American records that gave birth to the Mersey Beat . . . and inspired the music of two teenage boys who met at a church fair.

Opposite: Chuck Berry in a recording session, circa 1956.

Top: A crowd of mostly teenagers and young adults line up at the Gaiety Cinema in Manchester, England, to view the 1956 American film *Rock Around the Clock*, which featured the pulsating music of Bill Haley and the Comets.

Above: The Shirelles—Beverly Lee, Doris Coley (top), Shirley Owens (seated), and Addie "Micki" Harris—were a highly influential girl group that scored in the late 1950s and 1960s with hits like "Dedicated to the One I Love," "Will You Love Me Tomorrow?" and "Mama Said."

John Lennon

John Lennon once admitted that he was the boy the other kids' parents, including Paul McCartney's father, warned them to stay away from. He seemed to relish the role of prankster and troublemaker. Yet in spite of his low marks in school, his teachers' complaints over his disruptive behavior, and the parental warnings, there was something about him—a swift, sly intelligence coupled with a cheeky attitude and cocky charm—that marked him as special to anyone who really cared to look. He also possessed a measure of what some might call natural leadership or even star quality. Not surprisingly, he knew it, but in those early days in Liverpool he was still just a legend in his own mind.

John Winston Lennon was born to Julia and Alfred Lennon on October 9, 1940. His father, a merchant seaman who was often at sea, was only a vague figure to his little boy, and he ended up going AWOL in February 1944. When he returned six month later, Julia was pregnant with another man's child and refused Alfred's offer to look after them. Julia's sister Mimi Smith then stepped in and became John's guardian. Mimi always had the boy's welfare at heart, but she was starchy and strong-minded and brooked little opposition. Compared to the compliant Julia, she must have seemed imposing to the boy.

When John was six, his father returned unexpectedly and took him on a trip to the resort town of Blackpool—with the secret intention of carrying him away to New Zealand. But Julia, suspicious of Alfred's abrupt reappearance, had followed them. An argument ensued, and Alfred demanded that John choose between the two of them. He twice chose his father, but when Julia started to walk away, he cried for her.

LIFE AT MENDIPS

John spent the remainder of his youth living with Mimi and her husband George at Mendips, a semidetached house in Woolton. Mimi remained distant toward the child, but at least his Uncle George showed him some affection and even taught him to play the harmonica. At 11, John began to visit his mother's home in Liverpool, where she lived with her common-law husband and John's two half sisters. Julia kept him distracted and entertained, playing Elvis Presley records and teaching him chords on the banjo. When he was 16, she loaned him £5, about $7.50, for an inexpensive Gallotone Champion guitar, providing he keep it at her place—they both knew Mimi did not support his ambition of becoming a musician. John was 17 when Julia died after being struck by a car while walking home from Mendips. The tragedy would affect him in ways he could not yet calculate.

It was not surprising that John, never a stellar student to begin with, failed his GCE O-Levels (requirements for a Certificate of Education taken at age 16). His one saving grace was his artistic talent; he'd even self-published a magazine at school called the Daily Howl featuring his droll cartoons. He was admitted to Liverpool College of Art only after both his aunt and headmaster interceded on his behalf. This was

> ## "NOTHING REALLY AFFECTED ME UNTIL I HEARD ELVIS. IF THERE HADN'T BEEN AN ELVIS, THERE WOULDN'T HAVE BEEN THE BEATLES."
> JOHN LENNON

where he met future wife Cynthia Powell before being expelled—for disrupting classes and ridiculing teachers—a year prior to graduation.

THE QUARRYMEN

John had been playing in a skiffle band since the age of 15. While at the Quarry Bank High School, he formed the Quarrymen with himself and Eric Griffiths on guitar, John's best mate Pete Shotton on the washboard, Shotton's friend Bill Smith on tea-chest bass and Smith's friend Rod Davis on banjo. Early rehearsals were conducted at Shotton's house, until his mother, weary of the noise, sent them out to the air-raid shelter in the back garden. Early on Bill Smith left and was replaced by another of John's friends, Len Garry. When Garry couldn't make rehearsals, a young man named Ivan Vaughan sat in. Colin Hanton, a drummer with his own kit, completed the lineup.

After the group's second official gig, the St. Peter's Church Rose Queen garden fête on July 6, 1957, Ivan Vaughan introduced John to another young musician named Paul McCartney, ablaze in his signature white sports jacket. The two immediately began talking about rock and roll music, and Paul demonstrated some tunings and sang a few songs. John was impressed because Paul not only played the guitar well and possessed a clear tenor voice, he knew the lyrics to many of the American songs John loved . . . but could never figure out the words to. Within two weeks, Paul was invited to join the group. Paul agreed, but only after he'd attended scout camp and gone on a family vacation in Yorkshire. Although Paul's father disapproved of John, he did allow the band to practice in the front room of the family home.

Paul's debut with the Quarrymen, on October 18, 1957, was not auspicious. He missed his cue on the instrumental, "Raunchy," and bumbled the performance. Paul appeared so crestfallen, John bit back his usual snide comments. Paul made up for this gaffe when he later played John the song he'd composed after the death of his mother, "I've Lost My Little Girl." John was astonished and impressed.

Opposite: Young John Lennon with his mother Julia, 1949, in the garden of Aunt Mimi's Liverpool home, Mendips. To date, this is the only known photograph of John with his mother. It was taken by John's cousin, Stanley Parkes.

Top: Elvis Presley, a son of Memphis, Tennessee—shown here performing in the mid-1950s—came to represent the essence of American rock and roll to many young Britons.

Above: November 23, 1957. Paul, John, and the other Quarrymen present a unified look in sports jackets and string ties as they perform a skiffle number at the New Clubmoor Hall in Norris Green, Liverpool—where Paul had made his Quarrymen debut five weeks before.

Paul McCartney

proved to be a good student, being one of only three out of ninety students who passed the 11-plus exams (tests for secondary school placement taken at age 11) at Joseph Williams Junior School. This allowed him to attend the prestigious Liverpool Institute, or Inny, putting him on track to attend university. While on the bus one day he met fellow Inny student—and guitarist— George Harrison, who was a year younger. The two fell into an easy camaraderie, brought together by their keen interest in American rock and roll music.

Paul's Dad, a trumpet player who had formed the Jim Mac Jazz Band during the 1920s, still kept a piano in the front parlor. Paul learned to play it by ear, and when his father gave him a trumpet, he eventually traded it for a Framus Zenith acoustic guitar, an instrument that, he explained to his dad, would allow him to play

"LIVERPOOL MADE ME WHAT I AM—IT KEPT MY FEET ON THE GROUND."
PAUL McCARTNEY, 2002

Paul McCartney possessed an upbeat and charismatic personality; he was certainly not the self-effacing type. Yet he got along with fellow Beatle and composing partner, John Lennon, for more than a decade in spite of the latter's tendency to insist on being the center of attention. It speaks more to Paul's level of diplomacy than to John's sweet nature that the partnership ended

up being as prolific and enduring as it was. It surely helped, in the end, that they were best mates.

James Paul McCartney was born at Walton Hospital on June 18, 1942. His mother, Mary, was a nurse/midwife, and his father, James McCartney, was a wartime volunteer firefighter—who was out on a call and missed the birth. Paul's younger brother, Michael, was born two years later. Paul

and sing. Initially it was difficult for the left-handed Paul to work the chords, but after seeing a poster of leftie Slim Whitman playing with reversed strings, Paul followed suit. It wasn't long before he'd composed his first song, "I Lost My Little Girl," on the guitar.

SOLACE IN MUSIC

When Paul was 14, his mother died suddenly of an embolism

"**When we were starting off as kids, just the idea of maybe going to do this as a living instead of getting what we thought was going to be a boring job, was exciting.**"
PAUL McCARTNEY

following breast cancer surgery, a loss that later enabled him to empathize with John Lennon, whose own mother died when he was 17. As Lennon would do, Paul let the music he loved—American rhythm and blues and especially the songs of Little Richard— fill the painful gap in his life. He even sang Little Richard's raucous hit, "Long Tall Sally," as his first public performance at a holiday camp talent show.

At 15, Paul attended a church fair at St. Peter's in Woolton and enjoyed listening to some local lads, the Quarrymen, perform their rollicking blend of rock and roll and skiffle. A friend, Ivan Vaughan, introduced him to the band after the gig and he spent some time hanging out with John Lennon. When the offer to join the band fell into his lap, Paul didn't hesitate to accept. Unhappy with the Quarrymen's haphazard guitar playing, however, he suggested that John invite Paul's schoolmate George to join them. While George wasn't a charmer like Paul, or an amusing cut-up like John, he did have one thing going for him—"he could play the guitar just like ringing a bell."

Top: Paul (foreground) and his younger brother Mike pose for the camera during their summer vacation in Wales, in 1948.

Above: Paul McCartney with his father Jim and brother Mike, in the garden of the McCartney family home, Forthlin Road, circa 1960.

George Harrison

As a boy, George Harrison was seriously into guitars, sketching different makes and models in his notebooks during class. When he grew older, his musical tastes ran to swing, jazz, and blues artists like Cab Calloway, Hoagy Carmichael, Django Reinhardt, and Big Bill Broonzy. Then came a day when he rode his bike past a neighbor's house and heard Elvis Presley's "Hound Dog" blaring from its windows. His interest immediately shifted to American rock and roll. His record collection expanded apace with albums and 45s representing Motown, the Delta blues, and Memphis soul.

George Harrison was born at home in the Wavertree section of Liverpool on February 25, 1943, to Louise and Harold Harrison. He had one sister, Louise, and two brothers, Harry and Peter—all of them sharing a cold, terraced house with an outhouse at the end of the garden. Fortunately, when George was six, the family moved to a less-primitive government-subsidized house in Speke. His dad, a bus conductor, had once worked as a steward for the White Star Line (of *Titanic* fame) and his mother was a shop assistant. It was she who encouraged George to follow his interest in music, insisting that her only desire was that her children be happy. George's dad was less enthusiastic, but when the boy turned 13, his father bought him a Dutch Egmond flat-top guitar. A family friend taught him to play such traditional tunes as "Sweet Sue" and "Dinah," and before long George had formed a skiffle group, The Rebels, with his brother and a friend.

After scoring well on his 11-plus entrance examinations, George

"The front room was never used. It had the posh lino and a three-piece suite, was freezing cold and no-one ever went in it. We huddled together in the kitchen, where the fire was, with the kettle on, and a little iron cooking stove."

GEORGE HARRISON, on his first home

was accepted into the Liverpool Institute, where he met Paul McCartney. They quickly became friends. Paul recalls that George was cocky and self-assured at school, at ease with himself and others. After Paul joined the Quarrymen, he convinced John to let George try out for lead guitar. George auditioned at Rory Storm's Morgue Skiffle Club, but John felt that the 14-year-old George, who looked about ten at the time, was too young. Paul arranged a second audition atop a double-decker bus. George played a spirited rendition of the popular instrumental "Raunchy" for John and won him over. The band allowed George to "sit in" until he was 15, at which time he became a legitimate member of the group.

With this consolidation, the singing, strumming, and composing core of something much larger and more profound had now finally fallen into place.

Opposite: The Silver Beatles (including Stuart Sutcliffe, far left, and Johnny Hutchinson standing in on drums) audition for the impresario Larry Parnes in May 1960, displaying their intense, animated stage manner—and three admirable quiffs.

Top: George, John, and Paul pose in relaxed mode by the back door of Paul's house in Forthlin Road.

Right: In 1954, a youthful George Harrison strikes a pose with his first guitar, a sunburst-top, beginner's model acoustic Egmond. The guitar is now owned by an anonymous collector and is estimated to be worth $800,000.

"AS A STUDENT, STUART WAS PRECISELY THE OPPOSITE OF JOHN, BECAUSE HE WAS WORKING HIMSELF TO DEATH, TOTALLY DEDICATED. HE WASN'T EATING PROPERLY AND DIDN'T HAVE MUCH TO DO WITH GIRLS. HIS WORK WAS ALL-IMPORTANT TO HIM."

CYNTHIA LENNON

Though not an inspired musician like his bandmates in the Quarrymen, Stuart Sutcliffe had good looks and a decent singing voice. At a time when Paul was still a baby-faced teen, Stu had the cool and the charisma to draw girls and women to the edge of the stage whenever he crooned "Love Me Tender."

Stuart Sutcliffe was born June 23, 1940, in Edinburgh, Scotland. In 1943, his civil servant father, Charles, moved the family to Liverpool to help with war work, while his mother, Millie, taught at a nursery school.

As a boy Stuart had shown an aptitude for art and so after completing his academic qualification exams, he began attending the Liverpool Art Institute. There he met John Lennon through a mutual friend and they were soon inseparable pals.

Stuart was a star at the college, a talented sketch artist and painter who helped John improve his drawing skills. In return,

Opposite: Stuart Sutcliffe performs with the band at the Top Ten Club in Hamburg. In spite of applying himself to the bass guitar, he never really mastered it. Painting would always remain his first passion.

John invited him to be part of his band. Stu had recently sold a painting for £65, about $100, and intended to use the money for art supplies, but John convinced him to buy a Hofner President bass guitar instead. Sutcliffe was not without a musical background—he'd sung in a local church choir, had taken piano lessons since the age of nine, and played bugle in the Air Training Corps. His father had even taught him some guitar chords. But even though he eventually got the hang of the electric bass, his playing remained flat.

Still, that didn't matter, because he was now part of a bona fide rock and roll band, currently called the Silver Beatles (after a stint as Johnny and the Moondogs and the Silver Beetles). It was Stuart who shared an afternoon at the Renshaw Hall bar with John and his girlfriend, Cynthia Powell, thinking up new names for the group. John eventually decided on the Beatals (again, riffing on the name of Buddy Holly's group, the Crickets and incorporating the word 'beat' because that was the type of music they played). He later changed it to the Beatles, because the earlier version sounded too French.

Once the group started getting regular paying gigs, Stuart also made himself useful by organizing their bookings. It was as if he knew he had to make up somehow for his lack of ability on the bass.

"One April evening in 1960, walking along Gambier Terrace by Liverpool Cathedral, John and Stuart announced: 'Hey, we want to call the band the Beatles.'"

PAUL McCARTNEY

FabFact

John Lennon, never one to shrink from rewriting his own history, claimed he had a vision at the age of twelve, when he saw a man on a flaming pie who said "You are Beatles with an 'a.'" "And so we were," John insisted.

Pete Best

"THE TOGETHERNESS, THE CAMARADERIE, THE CHEMISTRY, THE CHARISMA: YOU NEVER SAW ONE OF THE BEATLES BY HIMSELF."

PETE BEST, ON THE BAND

Sometimes a person has a brush with history . . . and history moves on. This was the case with Pete Best, an early band member of the Beatles, although not one destined to share their fame or wealth. His association with them lasted long enough, however, that he has become an enduring part of their legend.

Randolph Peter Best was born November 24, 1941, in Madras, India. In 1945 his family relocated to Liverpool, where his mother, Mona, opened the Casbah Coffee Club in the basement of the family's large house—with money she won on a long-shot racing bet. It became an increasingly popular spot for the teens of Liverpool, eventually growing to one thousand members. John's early Quarrymen played there, as did Pete's own group, the Black Jacks.

On May 10, 1960, the band, now the Silver Beetles, auditioned with Larry Parnes for a chance to tour as the backing group for Billy Fury. An awkward Stuart, however, embarrassed by his lack of skill, played the gig facing backward. Parnes was annoyed by this and offered the band the job without Sutcliffe. John vehemently refused. Instead they were given a May tour backing Elvis clone Johnny Gentle in Scotland.

Meanwhile, as the club scene in the city expanded, a local entrepreneur named Allan Williams opened the Jacaranda on Slater Street. It became one of the hottest clubs in Liverpool. Before long Williams was putting bands together, arranging tours, and organizing dances in church and town halls. He also found some work for John and Stu—painting a mural in the ladies room of the club.

Williams did eventually find the Beatles some local work, though he always maintained they were worthless. After their Parnes' tour with Johnny Gentle, the Beatles still had no reliable full-time drummer. Their semiregular drummer, Tommy Moore, a thin, sensitive man, was often a no-show. He also found John's crude humor— usually at Moore's expense— distressing. Williams found the whole lot of them unprofessional and a pain in his backside.

Williams, meanwhile, had met wealthy German club owner Bruno Koschmider in London. The German felt the Mersey Beat bands might do well in his home country, and so Williams began hiring out his English bands to clubs in Hamburg. William's initial export, Derry and the Seniors, was a big success on the Reeperbahn in Hamburg's red-light district, also known as the "mile of sin."

Now, Koschmider wanted a group for one of his lesser venues, the Indra Club. Williams immediately thought of another of his powerhouse groups, Rory Storm and the Hurricanes. Alas, they were booked at a holiday camp. Instead, Williams decided to send Bruno his least favorite clients— the Beatles. After Williams gained approval from their guardians, John, Paul, George, and Stuart were set to go . . . except for one thing—they had no drummer. This offer of a paid gig working abroad coincided with one of Tommy Moore's truancies. The Beatles scouted around and settled upon Pete Best from the Casbah. He was a decent drummer, time was running out, and so they offered him the job, which—after an audition for Williams—he accepted.

Williams knew he wasn't doing the Beatles any favors by sending them to the rough German seaport—they were a bunch of kids not even out of their teens. Then again they were Scousers, possessing, he hoped, the resiliency and grit of most other Merseysiders. He had no idea he was casting the boys into a fire that would test them, tax them, and eventually temper them into something unique and enduring.

Opposite bottom: John snapped this shot of Stuart, Paul, George, and Pete—along with Allan and Beryl Williams and Lord Woodbine—at the British Commonwealth War Graves Cemetery at Arnhem in the Netherlands. The group had stopped off for a break while driving to Hamburg in August 1960. They later visited a music shop in the town, where John shoplifted a mouth organ.

"WE WERE AT OUR BEST WHEN WE WERE PLAYING IN THE DANCE HALLS OF LIVERPOOL OR HAMBURG. THE WORLD NEVER SAW THAT."
PETE BEST

Left: Drummer Pete Best never adopted the shaggy Beatles' haircut; he preferred to retain his lofty pompadour.

"I MIGHT HAVE BEEN BORN IN LIVERPOOL BUT I GREW UP IN HAMBURG."
JOHN LENNON

CHAPTER TWO

HAMBURG

"WE GOT BETTER AND BETTER AND OTHER GROUPS STARTED COMING TO WATCH US."

PAUL McCARTNEY

Hamburg, the second largest city in Germany and second largest port in Europe after Rotterdam, remained a major transportation hub after the war. A media and industrial center, it was as much of a melting pot as Liverpool had been during its heyday.

The Reeperbahn, circa 1960, was the tawdry heart of Hamburg's red-light district, which after dark presented a visual and aural cacophony fit to rend the soul. The first assault on the senses, flashing neon lights projecting from the façades of bars and clubs—oversized women's torsos or cocktail glasses outlined in garish hues of red, blue and green—soon gave way to the discordant music

Above: The port of Hamburg, 1960.

Previous pages: The Beatles onstage at the Indra Club during their first weeks in Hamburg, August 1960. Pale sports jackets worn with dark, pipe-stem trousers was the first Beatles' Hamburg "look."

of competing bar bands blaring into the street, overlaying the calls of hustlers and the noise of the crowd: sailors, soldiers, young men and old surging along the pavement, seeking entertainment . . . music, drinks, drugs, prostitutes . . . seeking some diversion or temporary oblivion.

Into this maelstrom of immorality came five cocky young Englishmen, thinking themselves tough Liverpool Teddy boys, not willing to admit the reality, that they were untried, unsophisticated provincials, practically lambs to the slaughter.

They had been booked into the Indra Club by Bruno Koschmider for a limited engagement, which could be increased depending upon their success on stage (and their ability to stay alive and intact on this avenue of iniquity).

That first night after their arrival in the St. Pauli quarter, they took the stage at the Indra following a sultry dance by the alluring and popular Conchita, a transvestite stripper. The jaded, drunken audience, an older crowd than the Beatles were used to, was not impressed by the group's cool, laid-back style. Bruno harangued them afterward for being so lackluster and insisted they "Mach schau!" or "Make a show!"—or it was back to Liverpool for them all.

The next night John offered patrons his silliest routines, using his cruel school pantomimes of the lame or disabled, and the audience

quickly warmed up to them. Soon all five were cavorting on stage, aping old men or gays, knocking each other about, and daring to make fun of the Nazis. John even played one night in his underwear with a toilet seat around his neck. (These routines might have been the bizarre genesis of the scrubbed-clean Marx Brothers' antics seen in their first two films.)

BEATLES' BOOT CAMP

For a band used to playing sets of an hour or so, the musical demands of the Indra were extraordinary: five, six, seven hours a night, nearly nonstop, like rock and rock boot camp hell. It was a classic case of whatever doesn't kill you makes you stronger, because the band tightened up immeasurably in Hamburg, growing slicker and sharper on stage and gaining endless endurance. Their introduction to "Prellies" (Preludin) through fellow performer Tony Sheridan might have helped them maintain the frantic pace. Although John and Paul were working on their own songs in Germany, their level of confidence wasn't high enough to permit the band to play most of them. Instead, they fed the crowd a diet of popular tunes and American rock and roll classics. Still, in spite of their considerable arsenal of songs, the band had trouble filling up those long, endless sets. Standard three-minute numbers began to expand, the songs swelling to twenty minutes or longer, similar

to the way Ray Charles discovered the power of the extended riff when he'd had to stretch "What'd I Say?" to fulfill his contractual stage time.

If the working hours were grueling, the living conditions were possibly worse—the five teens were meant to sleep in an airless, windowless storeroom, next to the ladies' loo and behind the screen in the Bambi Kino porn cinema. So in addition to the squalor and the smell, there was a constant soundtrack of escalating adult activity.

The Beatles' first sojourn in Hamburg was akin to that nightmare spring break vacation, the one that college kids look back on fondly . . . because they grew so close to each other, enduring the shared tortures of sunburn, tourist tummy, and heatstroke from the broken air conditioner. The Beatles survived their trial by fire, and they all grew up—as opposed to matured—rapidly while living on the "mile of sin."

Above The Grosse Freiheit at night in the early 1960s. This was one of the main streets off the Reeperbahn. The Beatles began their Hamburg learning curve by playing the Indra, **left**, before, over the next two years, moving on to the Kaiserkellar, Top Ten, and finally, The Star-Club. With the exception of the Top Ten, all these clubs were on the Grosse Freiheit. The Bambi Kino digs were also just at the end of the street.

"YOU'D BETTER PULL YOUR SOCKS UP BECAUSE RORY STORM AND THE HURRICANES ARE COMING IN, AND YOU KNOW HOW GOOD THEY ARE. THEY'RE GOING TO KNOCK YOU FOR SIX."
ALLAN WILLIAMS

When the Indra Club was closed due to a noise complaint, Bruno switched the Beatles to his youth-oriented club, The Kaiserkeller. Unfortunately, it had recently been taken over by a gang of hitters, the German version of rockers. Yet here, finally, was an audience the Beatles understood. With this crowd, the band didn't need so many silly antics or slapstick routines to amuse the customers, and so they returned to their preferred style of playing, remotely cool, sometimes cheeky, the music increasingly powerful. (Although Bruno did still rail at them to "Mach schau!")

When Rory Storm and the Hurricanes, another client of Williams, came to play at the Kaiserkeller, they and the Beatles enjoyed a genial rivalry. Storm's drummer, fellow Liverpudlian Ringo Starr, seemed an amiable bloke, and the Beatles formed a budding acquaintance with him.

As the Beatles' popularity increased, young women—mostly strippers and whores—began flocking to the erstwhile bedrooms of boys they called the peedles. Bacchanalia became the order of the day and the lads were never

"I didn't like the look of Rory's drummer myself. He looked the nasty one, with his little grey streak of hair. But the nasty one turned out to be Ringo, the nicest of them all."
GEORGE HARRISON

loath to entertain two or more frauleins per night. There were several pregnancies as a result, one ending in an abortion at John's insistence, another creating a persistent paternity suit against Paul that he later had dismissed after two negative blood tests.

While for the most part, these were well-brought up young men who were not inclined toward any crime

more serious than shoplifting, they were also the product of an opportunistic culture . . . and when their finances grew worse than usual, there are tales that John sometimes resorted to "rolling" a drunken sailor. They had seen a hard world in Liverpool, but they were now seeing and experiencing a seedy, vice-ridden, immoral world in Hamburg. Whether they might have been further sullied

by their time there is debatable, and ultimately moot. Because someone, a young woman, herself no stranger to the exotic, took them under her wing and carried them out of those dark alleyways.

Opposite: The Beatles began to hit their stride in Hamburg once they got used to the long hours, the miserable accommodations, and the constant come-ons from strippers and drunken female fans.

Top: Showman extraordinaire, Rory Storm (left), was the leader of the Hurricanes. Their drummer was Ringo Starr, second right, and **inset**.

"IT WAS LIKE A MERRY-GO-ROUND IN MY HEAD, THEY LOOKED ABSOLUTELY ASTONISHING . . . MY WHOLE LIFE CHANGED IN A COUPLE OF MINUTES. ALL I WANTED WAS TO BE WITH THEM AND TO KNOW THEM."

ASTRID KIRCHHERR, ON MEETING THE PRE-FAME BEATLES

Just as there were mod and rocker factions in Liverpool, in Hamburg there were also similar cultural divides among young adults. The hitters, like the Beatles, wore slicked-back hair, tight rolled jeans, and long pointy winklepicker shoes. The exis (short for existentialists) were more cerebral, academic or artistic middle-class kids who dressed in black leather but with an artistic flair, the boys combing their hair down into side-swept bangs.

The exis were often the targets of the hitters, so it was unusual for an exis to come into the Kaiserkeller at night. But this particular young man, Klaus Voorman, had just had a heated row with his longtime girlfriend, and wandered in for a drink to cool down.

What he saw on stage that night—the pounding, raw rock and roll of the Beatles—left him breathless. He hurried back to tell his girlfriend, Astrid Kirchherr, and their close friend, Jürgen Vollmer, about this amazing discovery, these wild British rockers. As avant-garde art students and strict jazz fans, the other two were understandably skeptical. When they returned to the club later that week, however,

and saw the Beatles in person they all became equally smitten. The Beatles now had a devoted fan club of three glamorous young Germans, who came to see them night after night. Before long, they were all hanging out together.

Astrid was appalled by their living conditions and one day, after a photo shoot, insisted on bringing them to her mother's house for some real home-cooked food. She took them to her bedroom, which was papered in silver foil and had all-black furnishings and tree branches hanging from the ceiling. Another time Klaus showed them his distinctive artwork for albums and liner notes, while Jürgen shared his portfolio of moody photographs.

The Beatles had that muscular Liverpool disdain for anything remotely effete or "poufy" yet they were as taken with this artsy trio as the Germans were with them. Perhaps it wasn't so surprising that fellow art students Stuart and John found them appealing, but Paul, George and Pete were also intrigued.

EARLY TRANSFORMATION

Both Astrid and Jürgen were skilled photographers, and the pictures they took chronicling the Beatles' evolution in Hamburg resulted in images that were crisp and incisive, yet frequently haunting. Astrid recalled that before meeting her, the Beatles had not been into wearing leather. But under her sartorial influence they were soon sporting edgier clothing—and later, on subsequent visits, leather pants and motorcycle jackets and fancy, tooled cowboy boots.

She altered Stuart's appearance in one other way, eliminating his greased-back pompadour and re-creating the shaggy bangs she and her friends wore. The other Beatles rejected this look at first as too "girly," but when John and Paul traveled to Paris to visit

Vollmer, who had moved there for photography work, he convinced them to copy the style. George, naturally followed suit, once they were reunited in Germany. So it was out with Elvis and in with Exis . . . for everyone but Pete. This new "shaggy" haircut would set the Beatles apart from almost every other band in England.

Opposite, top: The Beatles share the stage with Tony Sheridan at the Top Ten Club, shortly before George Harrison was deported from Germany, in November 1960.

Opposite, below: Klaus Voorman, Astrid Kirchherr, and Stuart Sutcliffe suitably dressed for the Hamburg Art School Carnival in 1961.

Above, left: Jürgen Vollmer, the third of the Hamburg "Exis" befriended by the Beatles.

Above, right: George, Paul, and John pose on a Hamburg roof in their leathers and cowboy boots, in a rare piece of Beatles' memorabilia from the Beatles Museum in Hamburg.

"Just recently I have found the most wonderful friends, the most beautiful looking trio I have ever seen. I was completely captivated by their charm. The girl thought I was the most handsome of the lot."

STUART SUTCLIFFE, on Astrid and friends

"IT WAS LIKE ONE OF THOSE FAIRY STORIES."
PETE BEST ON STUART AND ASTRID'S LOVE AFFAIR

Even though Astrid spoke almost no English, she enjoyed spending time with the Beatles, who were always full of fun and up for a lark. They in turn seemed to find in her a clever, worldly, free-spirited sister of sorts. But this mutually platonic bubble soon burst when Astrid realized she was falling in love with Stuart. She began using her camera as an excuse to stay close to him, under the guise of taking candid photos of the band.

Stuart was not immune to the presence of the pretty, bohemian blonde and soon returned her feelings. He asked her German friends about her taste in books and films and art in order to know her better. The two became engaged in November 1960 and exchanged rings in the traditional German manner.

BEATLES MINUS ONE

In late October 1960, the Beatles jumped at the chance to make more money at the upscale Top Ten Club—and stay in better digs—even though this meant disregarding their contract with Koschmider. Bruno was so angry at their defection, he reported seventeen-year-old George Harrison to the authorities for working while underage—even though he had been the one employing him. George was quickly deported.

When Paul and Pete went back to the Bambi Kino to pack up their stuff, they hung a condom on the concrete wall, as a message to Koschmider, and set it on fire. Bruno again trumped them, by having McCartney and Best held by the local police and questioned

for attempted arson. Pete and Paul were deported, Lennon had his work permit revoked, and Stuart, who had been sick with a cold when this all went down, later borrowed money from Astrid to fly home.

Timing-wise, the Beatles' ejection from Germany was not a total disaster. The band knew they were ready now to go out and conquer new worlds, or in their case, old worlds—their former stomping grounds in Liverpool. But this time they knew they would no longer be the warm-up act at the shilling-entry dances. No, they believed they were returning home like heroes, having survived and thrived on the Continent. As it turned out, they would end up playing in Liverpool's most popular nightclub, the Cavern. But it would be for a series of less-glamorous lunchtime gigs; the Cavern showcased only jazz acts at night.

While the Beatles often spoke of how those grueling nights in Hamburg bonded them as a group

and improved their stagecraft and showmanship exponentially, other transplants from England shared similar experiences. Acts like Gerry and the Pacemakers, the Swinging Blue Jeans, the Searchers, King Size Taylor, and the Dominoes all maintained that Hamburg had been a transformative experience for them.

Opposite: One of a series of portraits capturing Astrid and Stuart in a pensive mood, taken by Jürgen in April 1961. By this point they were both sporting the signature short "exis" haircut with sideswept, feathered bangs. **Above, left:** Astrid's portrait of a smouldering George Harrison complete with shaggy bangs and black leather jacket.

Above and Below: Two more Liverpool bands working the Hamburg scene alongside the Beatles were The Searchers (above) and Gerry and the Pacemakers (below). Both went on to achieve national fame back home in England during the huge rise in popularity of the Mersey Beat.

> "WELL IT'S FUN OF COURSE. WE'RE HAVING A FAB TIME. BUT IT CAN'T LAST LONG. ANYWAY, I'D HATE TO BE OLD. JUST IMAGINE IT. WHO WOULD WANT TO LISTEN TO AN 80-YEAR-OLD BEATLE?"
> JOHN LENNON

CHAPTER THREE
ROCKING IT UNDERGROUND:
THE CAVERN

Clubland

In the late 1950s and early 1960s, with the craze for skiffle and the influx of American rock and roll gradually transforming into the Mersey Beat, Liverpool was soon home to more than 300 bands and at least 200 music venues, including pubs, clubs, lounges, dance halls, and coffee bars.

Toxteth—or Liverpool 8 as it was called—the poor, Bohemian neighborhood where Ringo Starr grew up, boasted 20 clubs alone that offered various musical and adult entertainments. Among the most popular were the Sierra Leone, the Silver Sands, the Nigeria, and the Somali Club. The names reflect the international flavor of these clubs, where immigrants banned from whites-only establishments created their own musical havens. (The Nigeria is one of the few remaining relics of that once-thriving scene.) Most of these alternative clubs were open to patrons and performers of all ethnicities, creating a melting pot of sounds and musical styles, and subsequently drawing crowds from far outside the city.

HOTTEST SPOTS IN TOWN

In the other neighborhoods of Liverpool, small, intimate clubs that once catered to merchant marines by offering American lounge tunes or steel drum bands were now beset by kids clamoring to hear their own loud, raucous brand of music. Many owners had no choice but to comply. These small clubs were later augmented by large dockside warehouse spaces, where teens and adults could groove to the Liverpool sound en masse.

Above, right: Paul sits on the stage at the Cavern, December 8, 1961.

Previous pages: The Beatles play the Cavern in August, 1962.

Several former club owners still clearly recall those early days. Australian Stan Pierce, cofounder of the Boomerang Club, a coffee, snack, and music bar on Duke Street, relates that his place started out as a jazz venue. Then his partner convinced him rock and roll bands would bring in more revenue. It worked like a charm—until other nearby clubs followed suit. Pierce cited his main competition from the late 1950s to 1960 as the Kinkajou, another coffee bar on Duke Street, and Jacaranda on Slater Street, which was the first club venture for Allan Williams, the man who eventually handled the Beatles' early gigs and sent them to Hamburg. Pierce was forced to close his club due to repeated police warnings over rowdy patrons, but his partner reopened it months later as the Zodiac.

Roy Adams, a former bouncer and the last owner of the original Cavern, recalled many of the most popular 1960's clubs in his book *Hard Nights: My Life in Liverpool's Clubland*: the Harlequin in Church Street, the Basement Club in Mount Pleasant, the Checquers Club and the Blue Angel in Seel Street, the Pyramid in Temple Street, the Chelsea Reach in New Brighton,

Shorrocks Hill Country Club in Formby, Toad Hall in Ainsdale, Kingsway in Southport, and Gatsby, Revolution, and the Cavern Club in Mathew Street down near the docks in the warehouse district.

It was the latter space, a subterranean series of barrel vaults connected by open arches, that soon became the hottest club in the Merseyside. The decor was clearly not a factor—the dank interior featured rows of straight-backed chairs and a crude stage with a backdrop simulating dungeon walls; the club even had its own distinctive odor—a melange of disinfectant, human sweat, cigarettes, and the scent of fruit wafting down from the produce markets up above. But there was something potent about the energy down in that red-lit cellar, whenever a band was onstage cranking the music up and out and driving the overheated audience into a frenzy of dancing until they looked like highly articulated marionettes. It was sublime. And it was here the Beatles came when they returned from Hamburg, to this "cellar full of noise," where they were able to continue the journeyman phase of their evolution.

MODS AND ROCKERS

"I do not live in the past by any means and there is much to be said for the present day but it will never match the absolute excitement of the sixties."

JOHN WATERS, Mod spokesman

Scotland Road was another area of Liverpool that developed its own flavor and was home to numerous pubs. Originally the coaching road that ran north from the city center, during the middle-to-late 1800s, Scotland Road welcomed several waves of immigrants including the Irish and the Italians. By 1964 it had become the notorious home turf of two warring gangs, the mods and the rockers. The mods arose out of the working class, but they emulated the upper classes in dress and manner. Boys wore tailored suits, fitted trousers, pointy shoes and rode motor scooters. Mod girls aimed for an androgynous waif effect, with cropped hair, pale lips, and overly made-up eyes.

Mods preferred American jazz music, rhythm and blues, and of the newer British bands, opted for bluesy groups like the Rolling Stones, the Yardbirds, the Kinks, and the Small Faces. But mods were no strangers to violence, as was shown by the destructive stage antics of the their favorite rock group, the Who.

Rockers, also from the working class, worshipped at the altar of Elvis Presley and Roy Orbison. They outfitted themselves in tight blue jeans, black leather jackets adorned with studs and chains, and biker boots. They flouted authority, rode souped-up Triumph or Norton motorcycles (and eschewed alcohol or drugs), and relished their bad boy image. As for actual clashes between the two groups, the media claimed they were frequent and fierce, but in reality their "wars" amounted to little more than malicious mischief—broken store windows, smashed trash bins, and the like.

Stylistically, both groups were influential to the Beatles' stage appearance. Pre-Brian Epstein, the boys were strictly rockers with their Astrid-influenced leathers—in spite of their brushed-down bangs. But after Brian put them into couture suits, they could easily be taken for mods. Their music also began to transform around this time, incorporating more blues influences and even Latin rhythms.

Left, from top to bottom: Rockers liked their leather black and their bikes big and noisy, yet most avoided alcohol or drugs; A bobby strong-arms a troublemaking rocker; A group of Mods arrive in Brighton for the Bank Holiday weekend; Mods were famous for their flashy Italian motor scooters and upper-class togs.

"WE PROBABLY LOVED THE CAVERN BEST OF ANYTHING. WE NEVER LOST OUR IDENTIFICATION WITH THE CROWD AND WE NEVER REHEARSED ANYTHING. WE WERE PLAYING TO OUR OWN FANS WHO WERE LIKE US."
GEORGE HARRISON

Imagine . . .

The white lights of the stage darken, while the eerie red wall lights continue to cast a dim glow in the vaulted space.

Imagine . . .

The youthful audience perches on the edges of their hard wooden chairs, anticipating the moment, the divine instant, when four lanky, leather-clad young men will appear from off to one side and race up the steps to the stage. Now . . . this is it! Here they come! Electric guitars swiftly plugged in, the drummer barely seated before he begins the snare beat, and three singers approach the microphones.

Just imagine . . .

Holding your breath, waiting for the song to start, reeling from the reverb of those first chords, knowing exactly what is coming next, but clinging to that precise moment because the anticipation feels so good, far too good to rush.

It's a pity the original building that housed the Cavern was demolished in 1974. How the faithful would have adored returning to that subterranean tabernacle, that Temple of Rock, relished sitting on those hard chairs, all the while trying to re-create the iconography—John perfecting his snake-head singing stance, Paul offering a boyish wink along with his vocals, George managing a shy smile over some nimble fretwork, or Ringo shaking his head so hard in pure joy that his hair bounces upward like a crazy fringe.

It was initially turned into a carpark, that hallowed site,

although a few of the original lower vaults were reclaimed for use by the new Cavern, which opened across the street from the original club in 1976. It in turn became Revolution, then Eric's, which showcased new wave bands like Elvis Costello and the Attractions.

The Cavern Club's original owner in 1957 was Alan Sytner, who intended it to be a jazz venue similar to the Parisian underground club, Le Caveau. The Quarrymen actually played the Cavern on January 16, 1957; they auditioned for the spot by performing for Sytner's father at the Childwell Golf Club (and earned £15 by passing around the hat). The night of their debut they were told to play skiffle only, and when John began singing "Don't Be Cruel," Sytner, in a move displaying a complete lack of prescience, sent him a note that read "Cut out the bloody rock and roll." It's no wonder the lads stayed away for more than four years.

By the time the Beatles proper played there, starting in February 1961, the owner was Ray McFall, and since the club was still geared to jazz, rock and roll bands were booked over lunchtimes only. Initially the group was earning £3 15 shillings, about $6.50, per appearance. Eventually as the Beatles's popularity increased, they played occasional night-time gigs. Many fans still look back on those days, when office girls could run to the Cavern and watch the Beatles during their lunch hour, or when couples would steal one last kiss before DJ Bob Wooler signaled the end of the evening by playing Bobby Darin's "I'll Be There."

"**He managed to give off this attitude of not caring two hoots, but deep down I know he did. He loved every minute.**"
BOB WOOLER, Cavern DJ, on John Lennon

Opposite, top and bottom: A patient queue at the Cavern Club, 1964; Girls had no problem dancing with other girls at the Cavern. Here, two stylish female patrons show off a new trend—dress pants for women.

Top: John, Paul, and Pete giving it their all on the Cavern stage.

Above, left: Many of the friendships formed by Beatles fans at the Cavern lasted for decades.

Above, right: Cilla Black (left), was a Cavern regular before being discovered by Brian Epstein.

From March 27 to July 2, 1961, the Beatles—now that George Harrison was officially of age—returned to Hamburg, where they again played the Top Ten Club and shared the bill with Tony Sheridan. Sheridan recalled that the management put them up in a spare Dickensian dormitory over the club, where they slept in narrow bunk beds and had to wash their own linens.

It was with Sheridan, who asked them to be his backing group, that the Beatles cut their first record. The recording session would be under the aegis of Bert Kaempfert, the Geman bandleader who would soon have a number of American hits, including "African Beat" and "Swingin' Safari." Kaempfert was

Top, left and right: British guitarist Tony Sheridan got to know the Beatles in Hamburg and the boys sometimes played as his backing band. Producer Bert Kaempfert heard them playing together and arranged a recording session; Polydor released the resulting single, "My Bonnie"/"The Saints," under the name Tony Sheridan & the Beat Brothers. Pictured is the original pressing, with slow intro in German.

producing Sheridan's record for the German branch of the Polydor label.

Sheridan and the boys drove to Hamburg–Harburg, to the Friedrich-Ebert-Halle, an auditorium. There the Beatles recorded six songs with Tony, including "My Bonnie," an up-tempo number based on the Robert Burns poem, and a B-side, "The Saints." The band also recorded "Cry for a Shadow" and "Ain't She Sweet" on their own. Once the session was over, Kaempfert signed them all to a one-year contract.

When "My Bonnie"/"The Saints" was released in West Germany, it charted under the name Tony Sheridan and the Beat Brothers. It turned out that Polydor didn't like the name Beatles and asked them to change it on the release. "We went along with it," Paul explained with a shrug. "It was a record."

Decca issued the single in England in January 1962 (now attributed

to the Beatles, possibly due to Brian Epstein's influence) and in America, but in limited quantities.

The Beatles had a bit more spending money this time around in Hamburg and so replenished their tattered wardrobes in the port city's eclectic shops, buying leather jackets, leather pants, and tooled cowboy boots. Astrid took photos of them posing moodily in their new gear, like British versions of James Dean.

The Beatles were about to head back to Liverpool, when Stuart announced he was leaving the group. He wanted to stay in Hamburg with Astrid, he said, and was considering a return to art school. John couldn't believe his mate was abandoning him after all this time, while Paul, who was called upon to take over the role of bass player, was not exactly thrilled. It ultimately proved to be a happy solution, however. Paul

could keep time and drive the bass line in a way Stuart never could.

WELCOME HOME

When the Beatles returned from Hamburg in July 1961, with Paul now manning the Hofner bass, the Cavern arranged a welcome home celebration. Liverpool was already beginning to acknowledge the importance of these soon-to-be hometown heroes.

Eventually the Cavern started to offer rock and roll at night. Overall, the Beatles played 292 dates there from February 9, 1961, to August 3, 1963. After 152 lunchtime performances—fan favorites, even

though the Beatles treated them like rehearsals—their last noon show was on February 3, 1963.

Their final evening show turned into a mob scene. John lost a jacket sleeve just passing the queue—and had to stitch it back on. When the power cut, Paul vamped—singing an acoustic version of "When I'm Sixty-Four." The bill featured five other bands, and the place was so crowded that when Faron's Flamingos went on, band members collapsed and had to be carried outside. But, as Bob Wooler recalled of that final gig, "the Beatles were very professional: there was no larking around and they got on with it."

Above: Stuart Sutcliffe, John Lennon, and George Harrison perform at the Top Ten club in Hamburg, during the Beatles' engagement there from March to July 1961. Stu left the band and stayed on in Hamburg with Astrid when the Beatles returned home to Liverpool in July.

FabFact

A video from 1962 of the band at the Cavern playing "Some Other Guy" is the earliest film of the Beatles performing live and the only film of them playing at the Cavern. The sound and picture quality are muddy, but the energy is there in spades.

"MAKE YOUR DECISION. YOU EITHER DIE WITH HIM OR GO ON LIVING."
JOHN LENNON'S ADVICE TO ASTRID KIRCHHERR, *JOHN WINSTON LENNON*

It had been difficult for Stuart Sutcliffe to part ways with the band. He'd started out as John's close friend and mentor from art school well before John asked him to join the Beatles, and he would always be grateful for John's attempt to include him in his world. And even though Stuart suspected that Paul was at times jealous of his relationship with John, Paul and he had become mates during those rough days in Hamburg. Stuart knew he would miss them all, but he didn't see any other solution.

It was clear to him that music was not, nor ever would be, his forte or his passion. It was the study of art that compelled him. And it would be just as easy, he reasoned, to enroll at the Hamburg College of Art where Astrid lived, as go back to Liverpool.

Stuart applied and was accepted to the college, receiving a postgraduate scholarship. He started classes in June 1961, and one of his instructors, a Scot named Eduardo Paolozzi, would go on to become a celebrated pop artist. Paolozzi called Stuart one

of his best students, even though his style was more aligned with abstract expressionism. It was clear to Stuart he'd made the right decision in leaving the Beatles.

UNCERTAIN DIAGNOSIS

Occasionally Stuart suffered terrible headaches, but he wasn't that concerned. After all, he was working hard at his painting and at making Astrid happy. Together they explored Hamburg and spent every available moment together. He sometimes suspected the head pains might be caused by a beating he'd gotten outside Lathom Hall after a performance in January, when he'd been thrust, head-first, into a brick wall.

Then in February 1962, he collapsed in an art class and had to leave school. Afterward Astrid's family, suspecting a brain tumor, convinced him to undergo two brain scans, but nothing suspicious showed up. He then saw two specialists who could find nothing wrong with him. Yet the headaches increased in intensity, until by March he was actually suffering fits and temporary blindness. Sutcliffe had been on bed rest for two weeks when he suffered his final collapse on April 10. Astrid raced home from her studio after a frantic phone call from her mother, and held Stuart during the ambulance ride to the hospital. He died in her arms before he was even admitted.

An autopsy showed that his death was the result of cerebral paralysis caused by bleeding in the right ventricle of the brain. It is likely this was caused by either an aneurism or an arteriovenous malformation, both congenital disorders.

The next day, the Beatles returned to Hamburg to play at the Star Club. Astrid met them at the airport with the terrible news of Stuart's sudden death. They were all stunned, but John, as he had done after the death of his uncle, gave way to hysterical laughter, shocking Astrid and his mates. The truth was, he had no other way of coping with his distress. Later, while the Beatles were still in Hamburg, Jürgen Vollmer took several photos of John in Stuart's art studio. John's pain and sense of loss are there in

"MY ALTER EGO ... A SPIRIT IN HIS WORLD ... A GUIDING FORCE."
YOKO ONO ON JOHN'S RELATIONSHIP WITH STUART

every frame. In the midst of his silent grief, John must have been wondering why the people who were most important to his life, who supported his creativity— Julia, Uncle George, now Stuart— were taken away from him.

After Stuart's death, Astrid, Klaus and Jürgen remained in touch with the Beatles over the years, finding connection in their shared memories of their friend. Klaus would go on to create the cover of *Revolver* and played bass guitar

with both John and George. Though few of Stuart's paintings remain, the Walker Art Gallery in Liverpool owns "Hamburg Painting no. 2," "Self-portrait" (in charcoal), and "The Crucifixion."

Opposite Stuart at first seemed very pleased with his decision to continue his art studies in Hamburg, where he could spend his free time with Astrid. But before many months had passed, he began suffering from mysterious headaches that forced him to leave school.

Above: This portrait of Astrid shows Stuart's ability to capture a mood in spite of his abstract-expressionist style.

Brian Epstein

"THE BEATLES WILL BE BIGGER THAN ELVIS!"
BRIAN EPSTEIN, 1961

"I felt like an old man by the time I reached 21."
BRIAN EPSTEIN

Above: Brian Epstein—dapper, affable, and a bit neurotic—always maintained he wanted to accomplish something memorable in the field of show business. Little did he suspect that the musical entity he helped create would end up changing the world.

Brian Epstein, the Fab Four's star-making manager and agent, was called the Prince of Pop and the Fifth Beatle by the press. An artistic young man who could never seem to find his true niche, he'd been a data entry clerk in the Royal Army Corps, worked in a furnishing shop, and managed several family-run retail stores. Yet his greatest desire was to leave his mark on the world, preferably in the realm of entertainment.

Brian Samuel Epstein was born on September 19, 1934, in Liverpool, to Harry and Queenie Epstein, a prosperous Jewish couple. Harry's family had been in the retail furniture business for two generations, with a large store, I. Epstein and Sons, on Walton Road. When their store expanded to selling appliances and musical equipment they renamed it NEMS, for North End Music Stores. Known for their liberal credit arrangements for cash-strapped customers, NEMS was where Paul McCartney's father bought the family piano.

An indifferent student, often labeled "lazy," Brian passed through a series of boarding schools, eventually spending two years at Weekin College (a high school) in Shropshire. He was then set up as an apprentice in the family business, despite pleading with his father in a long letter to be allowed to study fashion design.

Eventually his family realized that Brian was in some emotional distress, and they followed his psychologist's advice and made arrangements for him to leave

Liverpool. He enrolled in the Royal Academy of Dramatic Arts in London, where he lasted for three terms before returning home—he hated student life—and was then assigned to the record department of the NEMS music store on Great Charlotte Street. Intent on finally proving his mettle, Brian worked hard to make the store one of the largest retail music outlets in the north of England. When a new NEMS store opened on Whitechapel, he

was the obvious choice to manage it. Somehow this sensitive young gay man not only managed to survive in the jackbooted warrens of the city, Epstein now found himself at the very center of the thriving Liverpool music scene.

One of the music publications Brian displayed at NEMS was a local paper called *Mersey Beat*. The cover of the second issue showcased the Beatles. Brian Epstein had to have known about

them, not only from *Mersey Beat* (touted in the magazine as Liverpool's big band), but also from the numerous street posters touting their appearances in the city. Yet his interest in them was not properly piqued until an actual order came into the store.

Above: The second NEMS store was located on Great Charlotte Street just beyond the tailor shop, Alexandre. After Brian Epstein was put in charge of the music department, he turned it into the major retail music outlet in the north of England.

"I WAS IMMEDIATELY STRUCK BY THEIR MUSIC, THEIR BEAT, AND THEIR SENSE OF HUMOUR ON STAGE—AND, EVEN AFTERWARDS, WHEN I MET THEM, I WAS STRUCK AGAIN BY THEIR PERSONAL CHARM. AND IT WAS THERE THAT, REALLY, IT ALL STARTED."

BRIAN EPSTEIN, RECALLING THE BEATLES AT THE CAVERN

Alistair Taylor, who would later witness the signing of the historic first contract between Epstein and the Beatles, was at first taken aback by the stage show. He observed " . . . these four horrible young men on stage, dressed in black leather trousers, black jackets, smoking, drinking and making noise," but amended, " . . . they were charismatic and exciting . . . I thought they were sensational . . . diabolical, but magic."

At the end of their set, Paul announced they would perform one of their own songs, and the band launched into "Hello, Little Girl." Impressed, Taylor thought to himself, "If they can write songs as good as that . . . "

Brian frequently claimed he did not have any interest in the Beatles until someone named Raymond Jones came into the store and specifically asked for the single they'd made backing Tony Sheridan. Epstein then contacted *Mersey Beat* publisher Bill Harry for some background on the group.

Brian's personal assistant, Alistair Taylor, recalls it a bit differently in *The Beatles Book* (1997): "The truth is . . . we were being asked for 'My Bonnie,' but no one actually ordered it. Brian would order any record once we had a firm request for it. I thought we were losing sales and I wrote an order in the book under the name Raymond Jones . . ."

On November 9, Epstein and Taylor made arrangements— through Bill Harry—with Ray McFall to watch the Beatles perform at the Cavern (as a music VIP in Liverpool, Epstein was able to skip the long queues outside). Epstein, no great fan of rock and roll, was nevertheless impressed by the energy of their performance, amused by their good-natured antics, and later, in their closet-sized dressing room, won over by their peculiar brand of naughty charm. Cheeky George even quipped, "And what brings Mr. Epstein here?"

Epstein and Taylor discussed the performance over lunch at the Peacock, concerned that the boys were rough material, but agreeing that there was something there. "I think they're tremendous!" Brian exclaimed at one point, and as the two were leaving the restaurant, he grabbed his assistant's arm and sputtered eagerly, "Do you think I should manage them?"

Brian became a regular at the Beatles' noontime shows, and finally met with the group at NEMS

Above: The leather-clad Beatles (who had given up the Edwardian dandy "Teddy boy" look while in Hamburg) rock hard in front of the Cavern's signature "dungeon" wall.

MERSEY BEAT

Above: Bill Harry had been a college chum and former flatmate of John Lennon's and so was always happy to include articles about the Beatles in his hometown music magazine, *Mersey Beat.*

on December 3, with the intention of offering them a management contract. Paul was delayed, apparently by taking a bath, but George advised an upset Brian, "He may be late, but he'll be very clean." John brought along Bob Wooler from the Cavern, anxious for his take on Brian, and, typical for John, introduced the DJ as his dad.

Brian had already cleared the way with their former manager, Allan Williams, who, disgruntled over some money issues, famously advised Epstein not to touch the group "with a barge pole." But Brian was not to be dissuaded. During that first meeting, when they revealed that they had no manager, he told them that with everything that was going on, "someone ought to be looking after you." The boys must have thought it a good idea, because after the guardians of the three underage members—Harrison, McCartney and Best—had given their consent, the Beatles signed a five-year contract with Brian Epstein on January 24, 1962, allowing him 25 percent of their gross income.

First issued on July 6, 1961 (exactly four years after John and Paul met at the St. Peter's Church fair), the music magazine was the brainchild of Bill Harry, John Lennon's Liverpool Art College classmate and former flatmate of both John and Stuart Sutcliffe. Oddly, Harry intended the title to refer to a policeman's "beat" and not beat music. *Mersey Beat* covered the Liverpool area and focused on the tastes of younger club attendees and concertgoers. This was a startling concept—most mainstream music publications run by older businessmen told young fans what to like. Harry's magazine reflected local taste rather than dictating it.

Not surprisingly, considering his connection to both John and Stuart, Bill Harry frequently promoted the Beatles and made sure fans got plenty of photos and interviews. Such a steady stream of free publicity appearing at this pivotal moment in their careers was invaluable.

In August 1961, Brian Epstein began writing a column for the paper: "Stop the World—and Listen to Everything in It."

Harry still produces an online version of the magazine including a site that contains a gold mine of archival material—old editions covering the early Liverpool scene and featuring numerous articles about the Beatles as well as contributions by individual members of the band.

Top: Early editions of *Mersey Beat,* "Merseyside's own entertainments paper."

"HE SAID, 'THEY ARE FOUR BOYS AND I'D LIKE TO MANAGE THEM. IT WOULDN'T TAKE ANY LONGER THAN TWO HALF DAYS AT A TIME, IT'S JUST SORT OF A PART-TIME OCCUPATION.' HE SAID IT WOULD NEVER INTERFERE WITH BUSINESS."

QUEENIE EPSTEIN

When Brian formed NEMS Management Enterprises, as a result of his recent acquisition, his parents were understandably concerned, fearful that he was off again following yet another "shiny, new" venture. He promised them his time commitments to the Beatles would be minimal and that he would not neglect his duties at the store. (It probably rankles many aspiring pop performers with full-time managers that Brian was able to propel the Beatles to superstardom as a "part-time" endeavor.)

Brian immediately began to smarten up their look—switching the black leather jackets to sweaters and ties, reducing their unruly stage antics, and injecting some discipline into their performances, which would often start and stop at random. Yet he didn't tamper too much with the formula; he understood that their fans enjoyed the onstage banter and their firecracker style of launching full-tilt into a song. He curried favor with the local news media, "charming and smarming them" as Lennon called it, to get his group some column space, while Bill Harry at *Mersey Beat* continued to laud the band. When Brian booked them into better area clubs, they saw a slight rise in their income.

Brian's main order of business was to land them a record deal. Before the band had even signed his contract, he'd already made numerous trips to London, trying to wangle a contract from the major labels—Columbia, Philips, Pye, and Oriole, but to no avail. Mike Smith of Decca had at least come to the Cavern to see the band live. He offered them an audition in London on January 1, 1962. The producer would be Tony Meehan, the former drummer of Cliff Richard's backup group, the Shadows. (The Beatles later discovered it was Brian, not Decca, who paid for Meehan's services.)

By all accounts—and the audition tape still exists—the band was having something of an off day. According to Pete Best, severe hangovers from celebrating the New Year had something to do with it. Paul's voice (he performed most of the lead vocals) sounds nasal. Brian's play list bypassed their hard rocking fan favorites and trotted out hoary old chestnuts like "Bésame Mucho" and "The Sheik of Araby," and allowed just three of their own compositions. Critics agree that the only song on the tape that wasn't a pale vestige of the Beatles' high-energy sound was John doing his sneering rendition of "Money (That's What I Want)."

Mike Smith ultimately rejected the group, further informing Brian, in what has come to be one of rock's legendary miscalculations, that guitar bands were on the way out and that the Beatles had no future in show business. Decca decided to sign another "band for the ages," Brian Poole and the Tremeloes, who'd auditioned the same day as the Beatles.

Never one to put all his eggs in one basket, Brian had also contacted Ron White, an executive at EMI, while courting Decca. White put him in touch with three of their four record producers . . . and all three turned him down. The fourth producer, an oboist in charge of EMI's classical music and comedy label, Parlophone, was away on vacation.

A LITTLE COMEDY LABEL

Deeply dismayed by so much rejection, yet buoyed up by the Beatles' endless faith in themselves, Brian brought the audition tape to EMI's HMV store on Oxford Street to have it transferred to 78 rpm acetate discs, which he could more easily promote to producers. It was here that Brian got his first real break. Jim Foy, a disc-cutter at HMV, told Brian he really liked the Beatles's tape. He sent Brian to Sid Coleman, the head of EMI's record publishing division, Ardmore and Beechwood. Coleman also liked the tape, so he arranged a meeting for Brian with George Martin of Parlophone—the very same EMI producer who had been away.

The timing couldn't have been better—George Martin had been looking for a way to get on the rock and roll bandwagon. He wanted to expand his Parlophone catalog, which at the time consisted of classical and baroque music, cast albums of musical plays, and comedy recordings, including *The Goon Show*, an early comedy troupe featuring Peter Sellers, Peter Cook, Spike Mulligan and Jonathan Miller. Martin was having trouble finding a band he believed could guarantee him a hit song or two.

According to Brian, when he and George met at the EMI studios on February 13, 1962, Martin was not very keen on signing his boys. Epstein claimed he had to threaten to boycott EMI's records at the NEMS stores in order to get the contract. Martin insists that he was carried away by Brian's enthusiasm and his conviction that the Beatles would become major recording stars.

Whatever wheeling and dealing took place behind the scenes, the upshot was that an agreement was reached between the two men at the EMI Studio on May 8, 1962. Brian at once sent a telegram to the Beatles in Hamburg: "Have secured recording contract with EMI's Parlophone label. 1st recording date set for June 6th."

While this might have been cause for great jubilation among the boys, the contract itself was paltry: The Beatles were to receive one British penny, about $0.15, per record in royalties (among the four of them that came to a pitiful farthing each), and a half penny for singles sold outside the United Kingdom. (Brian also neglected to tell them that George Martin had not yet signed anything.)

Still, as Paul had said to ameliorate the shame of having their name changed on the Tony

Above: Parlophone producer George Martin, looking to break away from classical music, comedy recordings, and Broadway musicals, was in search of a promising rock and roll band when the Beatles came his way. At the time, he wasn't sure they had the potential to create hit songs.

Sheridan single, "It was [for] a record." This time around, however, they wouldn't be the Beat Brothers or some other name a producer preferred. This time they would be recording as themselves—as the Beatles.

FabFact...

Just prior to the release of "Love Me Do," Brian signed Lennon and McCartney to a three-year NEMS music publishing contract. He also scooped up a number of other Liverpool artists and signed them to management contracts: Gerry and the Pacemakers, Billy J. Kramer and the Dakotas, the Fourmost, Tommy Quickly, and, his only female act, Cilla Black.

"IN THE EARLY SIXTIES, WHOEVER HAD A HIT SINGLE WOULD TRY TO MAKE THE NEXT RECORD SOUND AS CLOSE TO IT AS POSSIBLE—BUT WE ALWAYS TRIED TO MAKE THINGS DIFFERENT. THINGS WERE ALWAYS DIFFERENT, ANYWAY—IN JUST A MATTER OF MONTHS WE'D CHANGED IN SO MANY WAYS THERE WAS NO CHANCE OF A NEW RECORD EVER BEING LIKE THE PREVIOUS ONE."

GEORGE HARRISON, *ANTHOLOGY*

CHAPTER FOUR

ABBEY ROAD STUDIOS:
THE EARLY SIXTIES

"Some of the most defining sounds of the twentieth century were created within the walls of the Abbey Road Studios. English Heritage has long recognized the cultural importance of Abbey Road—it contains, quite simply, the most famous recording studios in the world which act as a modern day monument to the history of recorded sound and music. The listing of the building is a welcome acknowledgment of the contribution the studios have made to our musical heritage, and we hope that in some form, they can continue to play a role in inspiring the musicians of the future"

SIMON THURLEY Chief Executive of English Heritage

Above: This 1970 shot of Studio Two at Abbey Road, complete with grand piano, shows the enormous scope of the rooms.

Previous pages: The Beatles between takes in Studio Two, Abbey Road on July 1, 1963, during the recording session for "She Loves You." This photo is one of a series made that day by the British photographer Terry O'Neill; The background shows the Vox AC30 amplifier, the Beatles' amplifier of choice.

> ## "I HAVE VISITED STUDIO TWO, THE HOLY OF HOLIES WHERE THE BEATLES WORKED THEIR MAGIC, AND TO ME IT SEEMED AS FULL OF WONDER . . . AS ANY CATHEDRAL."
>
> JOHN HARRIS, IN THE *GUARDIAN*, FEBRUARY 2010

The EMI Recording Studios lie at No. 3 Abbey Road, St. John's Wood, in London. It was here the Beatles recorded most of their music and also where, during any down time, they created new material or worked out the details of songs in progress.

Originally a nine-bedroom Georgian townhouse built in 1830, the elegant building was first converted to apartments, then taken over in 1931 as studio space by the Gramophone Company—which would later evolve into EMI. Pathé made a newsreel of the opening, featuring Sir Edward Elgar conducting the London Symphony Orchestra inside one of the soaring studio spaces. Several nearby buildings were also part of the studio complex and used to house visiting musicians.

The building currently boasts a white, two-story facade with tidy gray trim. Although the studio is often referred to as Abbey Road, it was not until the eponymous Beatles' album appeared that the name stuck. In 1970, Abbey Road became the studio's official name.

In 1958, well before the Beatles showed up, the studio had already been home to a music milestone when Cliff Richard and the Drifters recorded Ian Samwell's "Move It"— what many consider to be the first rock and roll record made outside the United States—in Studio Two. Originally "Move It" was intended to be the B-side of Richards' new single, a remake of the American hit, "Schoolboy Crush," but when TV producer Jack Good heard the Samwell track, he insisted Richard sing it on his show, *Oh Boy!* And just like that, "Move It" became the A-side. The song not only reached number two on the charts, it propelled Richard into pop music stardom and six decades of creating British hit songs.

Although the Beatles put No. 3 Abbey Road on the map, during the 1960s the studio was also home to Pink Floyd, the Zombies, the Hollies, and the Beatles' proteges, Badfinger. More recently Red Hot Chili Peppers, Sting, Oasis, Leona Lewis, Lady Gaga, and Kylie Minogue, among many others, have recorded there.

CREATING BLOCKBUSTER SCORES

In 1980, Abbey Road branched out into movie scoring when Anvil Post Production needed a new scoring stage after the famous Korda Studios were shut down and then demolished. Anvil and Abbey Road formed a partnership that lasted until 1984. Composer John Williams conducted the London Symphony there for all but the first of the six *Star Wars* films. Although Howard Shore recorded the music for the three *Lord of the Rings* films with the London Philharmonic Orchestra at Walford Town Hall, the scores were all mixed at Abbey Road. James Horner, composer for the two highest-grossing films of all time, *Titanic* and *Avatar*, uses the studio as his base whenever he is recording in England.

In 2009, the studio came under threat from building developers. Happily, the British government stepped in to protect the space and granted the studio English Heritage Grade II status. This designation means that the site is "of special interest and warrants every effort to preserve it."

For a detailed close-up look into the actual studios, complete with views of control rooms and mixing boards, go to http://www.abbeyroad.com, their official website.

Above: In 1933, violin prodigy Yehudi Menuhin poses with composer Sir Edward Elgar on the steps of the Abbey Road studio just after recording Elgar's violin concerto.

"EVERYBODY'S BORN KNOWING ALL THE BEATLES LYRICS INSTINCTIVELY. THEY'RE PASSED INTO THE FETUS SUBCONSCIOUSLY ALONG WITH ALL THE AMNIOTIC STUFF. THEY SHOULD BE CALLED 'THE FETALS.'"

JOHN HANNAH, *SLIDING DOORS* (1998)

Before they ever entered a sound studio (and thereafter throughout the balance of their recording careers), the Beatles were determined to do things differently, not only in regard to how their music was produced, but also as to how the finished product was presented to the public. It's well known that John was no fan of the pop music machine, but the other three were likely as balky about being "handled" like rubes or having their sound "cleaned up" or their records marketed as novelties. They might have come across on stage as music's answer to *The Goon Show*, but they were deadly serious when it came to the integrity of their music and their songs.

In spite of their lack of experience, the Beatles did not remain cowed for long by the intricacies of the recording process. Quite

the opposite, in fact. They were eager to learn about sound recording and all the tricks of the audio engineer's trade. They soon developed firm ideas about what they wanted the outcome of their efforts to be in both album content and packaging—ideas that would break new ground for the pop music industry.

SOMETHING NEW

The Beatles were able to implement a few of these changes right from the start; others would require the band to have a bit more clout with the Parlophone label:

• **Powerhouse song selection:** At the time, many pop music albums consisted of one or two hit singles patched together with a bunch of throwaway "filler" songs— traditional ballads, covers of pop favorites, show tunes, novelty numbers, etc. The Beatles wanted

every song they recorded to count and to have hit potential—which a great many did. (Although Parlophone—unlike most American labels—had a habit of leaving hit singles off albums, they did expect at least one or two album tracks to also become popular.)

• **Specific song order:** The Beatles carefully arranged the sequence of songs on all but their earliest albums to achieve maximum impact with the listener. Unfortunately, because Capitol typically culled songs from the Parlophone albums in order to create money-making compilations from them, this listening order was rarely preserved on the American releases.

• **Printed lyrics:** The Beatles first did this with *Sgt. Pepper*, printing the album's lyrics on the back cover. It soon became the industry standard, lyrics appearing either

Opposite and above: Another two of Terry O'Neill's iconic pictures of the Beatles taken at Abbey Road during the "She Loves You" recording session of July 1, 1963.

on the back or inside gatefold cover or on the record liner.

• **Making a statement or setting a mood with the cover:** Again, prior to the Beatles, most contemporary music albums used cheesy stock photos or stilted posed shots of the singers or groups. The Beatles soon tired of traditional portrait covers and began to influence the design. *Rubber Soul* did not even feature their names on the cover, just a distorted upward shot of a dazed-looking band guaranteed to proclaim that the Beatles were definitely into weed. Unfortunately on the cover of the American release, *Yesterday and Today*, the boys went too far; the photo of them wearing butcher aprons amidst a pile of doll body parts was a serious miscalculation. The albums were quickly recalled, and a bland image of the band posed around a

travel trunk was pasted over the offensive photo. Later releases simply had the trunk cover.

• **Creating a Mystique:** Eventually, the Beatles began to create little mysteries within their songs or in their album art, offering cryptic sound effects and images that remain unexplained. For instance, who was the Walrus? What did all those celebrities on *Sgt. Pepper* signify? This intentional confusion is partially responsible for the "Paul is dead," phenomenon, a time when fans, using clues from the music or cover art, began to suspect that Paul had been killed in a car crash and replaced with a look-alike. It wasn't hard to buy into the paranoia, not when distorted snippets of recorded conversation were easily misconstrued as "I buried Paul" or "Paul's dead, miss him, miss him"; or seeing Paul's "double"

walking barefoot on the cover of Abbey Road, indicating that he was the deceased (Paul simply liked to go barefoot in the studio); or the "fake" Paul in a tux, wearing the only black rose, the symbol of death, in *Magical Mystery Tour*. The likeliest explanation for all those audio and visual stumpers is that the band members, no strangers to LSD, were simply playing with their listeners' heads (and perhaps even feeding into the myth of Paul's demise as an inside joke—definitely John's speed).

In light of this unknown band wanting to try out all these new ideas, the Beatles were fortunate in their record producer. George Martin, in spite of his classical music training and upper-class background, sensed that he ought to give these "wild boys" their heads a bit. He reasoned he could always rein them in if they got too unruly. Meanwhile, it would be interesting to see what they came up with. He quickly gathered that they were sponges for information, eager to learn about the mixing console, the tape decks, and the various tools audio engineers used to enhance output.

Eventually they won him over completely . . . to the point that when they needed some circus music on "Being For the Benefit of Mr. Kite" (on *Sgt Pepper*), George Martin found them some real calliope recordings. And when the resultant mix proved too ordinary, Martin instructed his engineer to cut up the tape, throw the pieces into the air and then splice them together at random. It was as though the older the Beatles got, the more youthful and daring their producer grew.

George Martin: The Perfect Complement

"I REMEMBER WELL THE VERY FIRST TIME I HEARD A SYMPHONY ORCHESTRA. I WAS JUST IN MY TEENS WHEN SIR ADRIAN BOULT BROUGHT THE BBC SYMPHONY ORCHESTRA TO MY SCHOOL FOR A PUBLIC CONCERT. IT WAS ABSOLUTELY MAGICAL."
GEORGE MARTIN

Above: George Martin in Abbey Road, circa 1966.

Opposite, above: One of the first group portraits of the Beatles with Ringo, taken in the fall of 1962.

Opposite, below: The cavernous Studio Two accommodates a full orchestra, circa 1970.

In 1999, George Martin toured America and reminisced about working with the Beatles in a talk with video elements called *The Making of Sgt. Pepper*. For almost two hours he entertained the crowds in auditoriums and symphony halls, his rich, cultured voice rising and falling effortlessly without a hint of hesitation or an awkward pause. His fond recollections from those sessions with the Beatles at Abbey Road were crystal clear and so vividly presented, it seemed as though he might fly back to London, drive to EMI, and find them all waiting in Studio Two.

George Henry Martin was born January 3, 1926, in Highbury, London. He had no formal musical training as a boy, he just grew up "feeling music and naturally making music." After teaching himself to play the family piano, he soon began composing his own material. By the time he was fifteen he, like John Lennon, had formed his own band, the Four Tune Tellers. But, unlike John, he started making a decent amount of money with it.

During the Second World War, Martin served in the Fleet Air Arm, a part of the Royal Navy, becoming a pilot and commissioned officer.

At times he went up as an aerial observer, requiring him to sit in an open cockpit and communicate with the pilot through a tube. In an aerodrome interview conducted by Paul McCartney for the documentary *Produced by George Martin*, he demonstrated to the former Beatle how he was wired to the fuselage so that he wouldn't fall out if the plane inverted. Apparently after that harrowing experience, working with the brash, early Beatles was a cakewalk.

HOOKED ON PRODUCING

Martin returned from the service at age 21 with no marketable skills. A music professor friend advised him, based on his youthful compositions, to study music. The professor arranged an audition for Martin at the Guildhall School of Music and Drama, and the young man was accepted as a composition student. He also took up the oboe (tutored by Jane Asher's mother, Margaret, of all people), so he could earn extra money by sitting in with various orchestras.

While he was working a day job at the music department of the BBC, Martin received a note from the EMI Studios on Abbey Road. They wanted him, as a classically trained musician, to help their record chief, Oscar Preuss, with the recording of baroque music for the Parlophone label. He took the job, not knowing what to expect, but soon found he'd become "hooked" on producing. Eventually his duties expanded to include to arranging, conducting, composing, and audio engineering, as he tackled not only classical but also jazz, pop, and comedy recordings.

"When I first met the Beatles in 1962, I didn't think much of their songs at all. But they learned so quickly how to write a hit. They were like plants in a hothouse. They grew incredibly fast."

GEORGE MARTIN, *Jazzwax*, September, 2012

"I'M A PERSON WHO GETS BORED QUITE EASILY AND I DON'T LIKE DOING THE SAME THING OVER AND OVER AGAIN."

GEORGE MARTIN

After five years, Preuss retired, and George was given sole responsibility for Parlophone, making him the youngest A&R man at EMI to have his own label, a label that included legends like Stan Getz and Shirley Bassey, as well the popular comedy troupe, *The Goon Show*. "I was in my twenties still," Martin points out. He was sure someone else was going to be sent in from "upstairs" to supervise him. Yet he was left alone, which proved fortuitous for his newest clients from up north, who soon began infecting him with their own particular brand of lunacy.

Not that Martin himself was a square—he already had a track record of supporting bold, new ideas and musical experimentation. Earlier that year he'd recorded a dance single of electronic

music called "Time Beat" (under the clever name Ray Cathode) at the BBC Radiophonics Workshop, and he'd also created a number of "sound pictures" with actors and comedians.

Martin didn't have a big budget for his label, but he had something that was almost better—the liberty to do whatever he felt would work best for the specific needs of each artist or group. In the summer of 1962, he was about to receive what would amount to the most innovative musical gift of his lifetime.

MEETING THE BEATLES

George Martin first met the Beatles in person on June 6, 1962, when they arrived at EMI Studios to make a demo tape, something to give their new producer an idea of their vocal

range and playing ability.

He didn't attend the taping, but came into the control room to listen once the Beatles had finished recording four songs. His first impression was not good, an opinion born out by his engineers: Pete Best's drumming left a lot to be desired, and the songs themselves were, in Martin's own words, "simply not good enough." Martin finally turned to the Beatles and asked them if there was anything they personally didn't like. George Harrison drawled, "Well, there's your tie for a start."

Martin found himself grinning helplessly, drawn immediately under their spell. That was the deciding moment, he always said, when he realized he was actually going to sign them, if only for their quick wit and good humor.

Above: The Goons in 1951. Harry Secombe, Michael Bentine, Peter Sellers, and Spike Milligan in the upstairs of Grafton's pub, where many *Goon Show* scripts were written.

> "We don't want to hang out with him. It's Mrs. Martin we all love. The great Judy. We thought she was the queen, she was so posh."
>
> **RINGO STARR**, in *Produced by George Martin*

Left: George Martin instructs the Beatles on technique during the recording session of March 5, 1963. By the end of the day they had recorded "From Me To You," and laid down "takes" for "Thank You Girl," and "One After 909."

And so one of the most amazing of all musical odysseys began: a group of young men with the talent, drive, and conviction to be "greater than Elvis" and a classically trained producer whose job it would be to make the magic happen. Over and over and over.

George Martin went on to become the Beatles's trusted creative confidante, and, often, their father confessor. Many students of rock and roll would call him the Fifth Beatle, but that is almost a disservice. By necessity, he stood apart from the gang of four. Musically he was their facilitator, their interpreter, the grand manipulator, the man behind the curtain. He was Oz, the Great and Powerful—who abetted this quartet in finding the creativity, heart, and courage to bring their vision home.

Above, right: A posed publicity photograph of the Beatles taken during the March 5, 1963, session.

> "IN THE VERY FIRST SESSIONS, I ALWAYS SAY WE CAME IN THE TRADESMEN'S ENTRANCE."
>
> **PAUL McCARTNEY, IN *PRODUCED BY GEORGE MARTIN***

"THE LAST THING ON MY MIND WAS THAT I WAS GOING TO GET KICKED OUT OF THE BEATLES."
PETE BEST

Above: Pete Best, photographed in the Spider Room at the Casbah, his mother's club in Liverpool.

and come so far with them—it must be taken into consideration that he'd been chosen as a last-minute replacement drummer before their first Hamburg gig. He was not their mate, a fine distinction, but one that carried weight with them. The boys had quickly closed ranks when asked by Larry Parnes to replace Stuart Sutcliffe. They clearly felt no similar loyalty to Pete.

This coolness on their part was somewhat due to Pete's personality. "Mean, moody, and magnificent," the birds at the Cavern labeled him, but those were not exactly ideal qualifications for being a Beatle. John, Paul, and George were all extroverts to some extent (yes, even "quiet" George), all out for a lark, bantering with each other on stage. Pete was an intense, brooding introvert, who rarely emoted or spoke on stage. Female fans spent hours flirting with him from the front row just to see him flash one smile.

And that was another issue—Pete's growing popularity . . . with both sexes. The handsome drummer had just been voted their favorite Beatle by the Liverpool fans, something that rankled both John and Paul. By removing Pete, John would draw attention back to himself, and Paul would get to be the "cute" one.

So John, Paul, and George went to Brian Epstein, told him of their decision, and begged him to handle the unpleasant task. Brian reluctantly agreed, and sent word to Pete that he wanted to see him in his office.

As Pete later explained it, he'd thought nothing of the request.

Once John, Paul, and George learned that George Martin was dissatisfied with Pete's drumming, they decided to make a change. "Please explain to Pete he's being replaced," they agreed to tell Brian. "And then bring in Ringo Starr." They were not going to let anyone keep them from achieving their dream, not when they'd gotten this close. If this sounds callous—considering Pete had experienced the tribulations of Hamburg

He sometimes acted as the band's business manager, and would meet with Brian to go over potential gigs, review fees, etc. "I went in, happy as Larry," Pete recalled. "The last thing on my mind was that I was going to get kicked out of the Beatles." A flustered Epstein couldn't confront him at first; he took a while to get the words out, but finally explained that the other boys wanted Pete out . . . and that arrangements had already been made to bring in Ringo Starr. "That was the bombshell," Best added.

Three weeks later, on September 4, 1962, the Beatles went into the studio to record their first single with Ringo Starr as their new drummer.

CODA

Two and a half years after being replaced by Ringo, Pete Best appeared on the American TV quiz show, *I've Got a Secret*. The guest panelists quickly guessed his secret, that he'd once been part of the Fab Four. He then told host Gary Moore that he'd left voluntarily to form his own group, the All-Stars, because he didn't believe the Beatles were going to have much success. It's an odd rewriting of well-documented history—but his insistence that he left the band freely might simply have been Pete trying to save face. And who could blame him?

Eventually some money from the sale of the Beatles' 1995 *Anthology 1*, which featured early tracks with Pete drumming, went to Best and his family. Estimates of the amount range from £1 to £4 million, about $1.6 to $6.7 million.

Above: Pete behind his drum kit, onstage at the Top Ten Club, on the Reeperbahn in Hamburg, during the Beatles' engagement there from March to July, 1961.

FabFact

Another factor that doubtless affected the band's decision to drop Pete Best was his refusal to adopt the Beatles' haircut, preferring to maintain his slicked-up pompadour. Replacement Ringo Starr, on the other hand, was quick to affect the moptop look, and further enhanced the effect by shaking his head with abandon while he drummed.

Ringo Starr

"RINGO WAS A STAR IN HIS OWN RIGHT IN LIVERPOOL BEFORE WE EVEN MET HIM."
JOHN LENNON

Some music critics claim Ringo Starr rode to fame and glory on the coattails of his fellow Beatles, but around Liverpool and on the Reeperbahn in the early 1960s, he was in great demand as a versatile drummer with a steady beat, one who could fill in anywhere in a pinch. Perhaps his greatest contribution to the Beatles was his ability to (almost) always remain a team player—although if cultural immortality were based on dry wit, charming warmth, and baby-blue puppy dog eyes, Ringo Starr would be a lock.

He was born Richard Starkey on July 7, 1940, in a narrow Victorian row house on Madryn Street, in the poor but artsy Liverpool 8 district. The son of Elsie and Richard Starkey, Ritchie was a frail, sickly child who at age six nearly died of peritonitis after undergoing an appendectomy. After missing nearly a year of school while recovering, Ritchie was barely literate. It took years of home tutoring from neighbor, Marie Maguire Crawford, for him to catch up with his schoolmates. Then he contracted tuberculosis at age twelve . . . requiring

two years in a sanatorium.

It was there, where the medical staff encouraged patients to play music as part of their rehab, that the boy was given a mallet to tap on the cabinet beside his bed. Eventually he began playing drums in the hospital band. When neighbor Crawford gave him a copy of Alyn Ainsworth's "Bedtime for Drums," it cemented the boy's interest. The rigors of rock and roll drumming hardly seemed within the scope of his weakened constitution, but from that time onward, his fate was sealed.

"First and foremost I am a drummer . . . But I didn't play drums to make money. I played drums because I loved them . . . My soul is that of a drummer . . . It came to where I had to make a decision—I was going to be a drummer . . . I didn't do it to become rich and famous, I did it because it was the love of my life."

RINGO STARR, *The Big Beat* (1984)

A NEW DAD

Ritchie's parents divorced and his mother married Londoner Harry Graves in 1953. A kind, gentle man, he exposed the boy to American big band music and singers like Dinah Shore, Sarah Vaughan, and Billy Daniels. It was Graves who gave Ritchie his first kit for Christmas in 1957; it was second-hand, but perfect for a bloke who wanted to play in a skiffle band. Ritchie was soon hired by Al Caldwell's Texans, who were looking for a proper drummer in order to transition from skiffle to rock and roll. The group went through several name changes before settling on Rory Storm and the Hurricanes just before Ritchie began playing with them. Starkey also took the opportunity to create his own stage name, Ringo Starr, not just due to the rings he always wore, but because the name had a country and western flavor to it.

After leaving the sanatorium, Ritchie had done a brief stint working for British Rail—to acquire warm clothes—before becoming an apprentice at an equipment manufacturer. As he recalled in a 2011 *Daily Mail* interview: "I was working in a factory, for Henry Hunt and Sons, a light engineering company. I was an apprentice engineer, which was very big news in our family. But I was also playing with Rory and The Hurricanes, and we got the offer of a three-month gig in Butlin's at Skegness and Pwllheli, so we had to give up our jobs. All my uncles and aunties came over to try and tell me that drumming was OK as a hobby. I had to stand there and defend myself. I said, 'No, I'm a drummer, I'm off.' That's a *Sliding Doors* moment. Some decisions are good."

STARR-TIME

Rory Storm and the Hurricanes became enormously popular in Liverpool and the north of England, and Storm himself was often referred to as Mr. Showman or Mr. Showmanship. It wasn't long before Ringo began to accumulate his share of fans as well. Eventually, the drummer was given his own segment, called "Starr-time," where he would get the solo spotlight and sing two or three numbers.

When Allan Williams sent the Hurricanes to the Kaiserkeller in Hamburg, it was there Ringo first met the Beatles. He even sat in with them a few times when Pete Best was indisposed. But he had no way of knowing this ragtag group of rockers, with their crazy stage antics, odd haircuts, and greaser garb, were one day going to "make a big star" out of him.

Opposite: Ringo with beard, right, and the rest of Rory Storm and the Hurricanes. This photo was probably taken during the Hurricanes' stint at Butlins Holiday Camp in Skegness in the summer of 1962.

Above, right: Ringo, the new Beatle.

"HE WAS, QUITE SIMPLY, THE HEART OF THE BEATLES."
JOHN LENNON

FabFact

When other drummers later tried to duplicate Ringo's sound while covering Beatles' songs—and failed badly—it was because they neglected to keep in mind that Ringo was left-handed (like fellow Beatle, Paul), drumming in reverse order on a right-handed kit.

"Love Me Do"

Right, and center: In 1962, apart from rare trips to Doncaster and Swindon, the Beatles played almost exclusively in Liverpool and on the Wirral. On March 10, they played St. Paul's Presbyterian Church Youth Club, in Birkenhead. The River Boat Shuffle ticket, center, is a rare piece of memorabilia: because of the mix-up with the day and date, the gig was eventually canceled, as on the Friday, the Beatles had prior bookings at the Cavern, and the Majestic Ballroom in Birkenhead.

Below: In 1962, one of Paul's early compositions, "Love Me Do," was chosen as the Beatles' first single. It topped out at number 17 on the U.K. charts, leaving the band and their supporters more than a little disappointed. Two years later the record would redeem itself in America, where it hit number one.

George Martin was still not sure if John and Paul's songs were radio worthy, so once the band went into the studio, he encouraged them to record "How Do You Do It?"—a chirpy, danceable number by Mitch Murray—as their first single. But he also allowed them one shot at using their own material for the A-side. Knowing what was at stake, John and Paul went through more than a hundred possible compositions, including an early version of "When I'm Sixty-Four," looking for the perfect debut song.

They finally decided on "Love Me Do," a bluesy rocker written by Paul during his days at the Liverpool Institute and featuring a lusty, head-on harmonica accompaniment by John. George Martin approved of the song; there was something gritty and "northern" about it, something that was lacking in most of the other bland rock and roll songs playing in Europe and the United Kingdom at the time. It was a love song that sounded more like a pagan mating rite, with its repetitive, insistent lyrics and thumping bass line.

The Beatles recorded both songs, albeit somewhat nervously—they required fifteen takes on "Love Me Do"—which were then mixed and cut. When George Martin listened to the playback, he felt there was something lacking: Ringo Starr was not "locking in" his bass drum with the bass guitar, the prevailing style for pop music and something a pro would have known to do. Martin realized he would have to bring in a studio drummer to redo both songs.

On September 11, session

drummer Andy White showed up at EMI with his own drum kit, and accompanied the three Beatles as they re-recorded "Love Me Do," and "How Do You Do It?" and also set down "P.S. I Love You" (intended for the B-side) and "Please Please Me." Ringo stood by and tapped a tambourine.

There are conflicting reports of what happened to the various recordings. Most likely, the Ringo Starr version of "Love Me Do" was released in England (with the drums mixed light), while the Andy White version was released abroad and used on the group's first album, *Please Please Me.* This version was also released in America, but not until 1964.

White later insisted he was also the drummer on the Beatles' next single, "Please Please Me"—based on the distinctive sound of his own drum kit. Regardless, White received £5, the equivalent of only eight dollars, for his work and an extra dollar for bringing in his kit.

A BOOST FROM BRIAN

"Love Me Do" was released on October 5, and within days had charted. Brian Epstein supposedly bought ten thousand copies for NEMS during the first week, in a common record marketing tactic called "loading" the charts. But the Liverpool fans did their part as well, rushing out in droves to buy the record in support of their local lads, including many teens who didn't even own phonographs. At least they cared; Parlophone, in spite of George Martin's dedicated involvement in its genesis, did little to promote

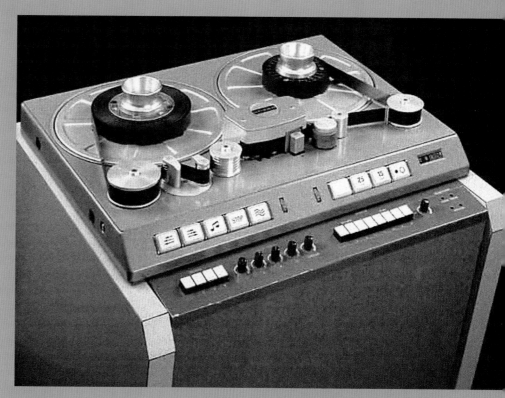

STATE OF THE ART

In 1962 the typical sound studio used four-track tape recorders, necessitating the recording of most songs in one continuous live feed. Some minimal overdubbing, reverb, etc., could be added, but basically what the musicians played was what the listeners heard. Multiple takes were run through and then the best of the bunch was chosen to cut on acetate. In the case of some artists, like the high-energy Beatles, capturing this "live performance" quality on a disc was a real plus.

the single. And the Beatles themselves were unable to promote it, having a prior commitment to play in Hamburg that fall.

Ultimately, in December, the song rose to number 17 on the U.K. chart. Not too shabby for a group most Britons outside of Liverpool had never heard of, a band with a rollicking sound that was still finding its audience. "We were

all pleased for them," recalled Liverpudlian Gerry Marsden of Gerry and the Pacemakers. (Gerry was also pleased, no doubt, because his group later recorded "How Do You Do It?" and took it to number one.) For George Martin and the Beatles, however, it felt like a big let down. They'd been aiming to use John's favorite refrain, "for the toppermost of the poppermost." Number 17 didn't quite cut it.

Fortunately George Martin and the Beatles had already started working on a "bombproof" hit single. This time they'd chosen one of John's songs, "Please Please Me," written while he was living at Aunt Mimi's. He'd been inspired by the early Bing Crosby hit "Please," with its clever opening line of "Please, lend your little ear to my pleas." This lyric naturally appealed to John with his love of all forms of wordplay—homonyms, Spoonerisms, malapropisms, and puns.

John had written the song as a slow-tempo solo, and the band had given it a trial run at the end of the "Love Me Do" session. But George Martin wanted it perked up, with lots of harmonies and a more focused delivery. Otherwise, the boys would be forced to record the backup number—the dreaded Mitch Murray song.

John and Paul worked hard to improve "Please Please Me," ramping up the harmony in homage to their idols, the Everly Brothers, setting John's lone voice in the bridge against the harmonies of Paul and George, until their combined voices broke the tension by melding brightly in the three-part chorus. Martin was so delighted with the result that after the recording session ended he announced from the control room, "Congratulations, gentlemen, you've just made your first number one."

BRIAN SHOPS AROUND

Brian, meanwhile, had been so unhappy with EMI's lackluster efforts on behalf of "Love Me Do," he asked George Martin to recommend a music publisher who could promote this next single more effectively. Martin gave Brian several names, and the one he chose was Dick James. When Brian met with James and played the new single, James responded, "That's a number one record." Brian assured him that if he could help make that prophecy a reality, Brian would offer him a long-term contract. James then called Philip Jones, producer of TV's *Thank Your Lucky Stars*, and played the song for him, gaining the Beatles nationwide exposure on the very next airing of the show.

The deal the two men made, resulting in the creation of Northern Songs, Ltd., would help augment the miserly EMI record contract. Dick James, Brian Epstein, and the Beatles would become wealthy from the publication of the Beatles' songs.

"Please Please Me" was released on January 11, and the public's response was overwhelming. By February 12 the song had hit number one on the singles chart. Everyone in the British music business now sat up and took notice. Just as the Beatles' songs had once exploded from the stage of the Cavern, this record seemed to erupt from radios or turntables, the harmonica and voices coaxing, cajoling, the chorus rising to a falsetto peak worthy of a Roy Orbison or a Little Anthony.

It helped that the Beatles stayed around this time to promote the single, gleefully performing it the day after it debuted—to an audience of snowed-in Britons— on *Thank Your Lucky Stars*. This appearance led to an offer of several national tours by promoter Arthur Howes, which Epstein eagerly accepted.

Oddly, Capitol Records, EMI's American outlet, wanted nothing to do with the record. Their executives felt that these Beatles, these proponents of something called the Mersey beat, were strictly a British novelty geared to quirky British tastes. (There was also a disquieting rumor that the song was referring to a "plea" for oral sex.) Brian licensed the song to Chicago label, Vee-Jay, which released it in February 1963, to little acclaim. It wasn't until the following year, when Beatlemania had swept across the pond to America, that "Please, Please Me" and "Love Me Do" hit the U.S. charts, the former making the top five, the latter going all the way to number one.

Opposite, above: When the Beatles finished recording their second single, "Please Please Me," producer George Martin was so thrilled with the result that he announced from the control booth: "Congratulations, gentlemen, you have just made your first number one."

Opposite, below: Paul and Ringo perform on *Thank Your Lucky Stars.* Note the "antenna" bass drum logo.

MUSIC PUBLISHERS

One thing that songwriters and composers legitimately worry about is that the songs or music they've created (i.e., their intellectual property) are being used without their consent, in a TV commercial, say, or by another artist. To combat this, a musician will assign the copyright for his or her music to a publisher, who then licenses the work, oversees where it is used, and collects royalties for the musician. Music publishers also help promote their clients' work and often find them commissions for original music.

Above: The Beatles sign with music publisher Dick James (left) in Studio Two at Abbey Road during a break in the session to record "She Loves You," on July 1, 1963.

"SO WE WENT IN AND WE DID THE ALBUM IN TWELVE HOURS . . . BECAUSE WE DID EVERYTHING WE'D BEEN DOING ON THE ROAD FOR THE LAST YEAR OR SO, YOU KNOW."
RINGO STARR, ON RECORDING THE BEATLES' FIRST ALBUM

Now Parlophone was finally showing some interest in the Beatles. The head office told George Martin they wanted an album put out as soon as possible to take advantage of the groundswell from "Please Please Me." The LP would include the four cuts from their two singles, and would require another ten songs. With no time for them to hone their older material or write new songs, George Martin brought the boys into the studio on February 11, 1963, and for all intents and purposes recorded one of their live Cavern Club performances—all in three remarkable sessions.

The album, also entitled *Please Please Me*, was released on March 22. The cover, by legendary stage photographer Angus McBean, featured an up-shot (not exactly flattering) of the band leaning over a stairwell inside EMI headquarters in Manchester Square. After this rushed photo session, according to Martin, the Beatles began to request more creative input regarding their covers.

PLEASE PLEASE ME
RELEASED MARCH 22, 1963
(All songs Lennon–McCartney, unless specified)

Side One:

1. I SAW HER STANDING THERE

2. MISERY

3. ANNA (GO TO HIM) (Alexander)

4. CHAINS (Goffin–King)

5. BOYS (Dixon–Farrell)

6. ASK ME WHY

7. PLEASE PLEASE ME

Side Two:

1. LOVE ME DO

2. PS I LOVE YOU

3. BABY IT'S YOU (David–Bacharach–Williams)

4. DO YOU WANT TO KNOW A SECRET

5. A TASTE OF HONEY (Marlow–Scott)

6. THERE'S A PLACE

7. TWIST AND SHOUT (Russell–Medley)

TWICE AS NICE

In May, the album soared to number one on the UK charts, where it remained for 30 weeks, only to be replaced by their second effort, *With the Beatles*. This feat is remarkable not only because the Beatles had consecutive chart toppers, but also because in the 1960s the British album charts were strictly the domain of easy-listening LPs and film soundtracks—a lot of them from America. Apparently the Beatles' radical notion of offering a lot of musical "bang for your buck" was paying off.

Yet, once again, Capitol was nowhere to be found. Most of the cuts from *Please Please Me* appeared in America on Vee-Jay's 1964 release, *Introducing . . . the Beatles*. Capitol finally caught up in 1965, offering the collection as *The Early Beatles*. The original album was not released in America until the Beatles' catalogue was standardized for CD.

CHAPTER FIVE

IN THE PUBLIC EYE

"ONE HAS TO COMPLETELY HUMILIATE ONESELF TO BE WHAT THE BEATLES WERE ... IT HAPPENED BIT BY BIT, UNTIL ... YOU'RE DOING EXACTLY WHAT YOU DON'T WANT TO DO WITH PEOPLE YOU CAN'T STAND—THE PEOPLE YOU HATED WHEN YOU WERE TEN."

JOHN LENNON

Brian Epstein knew instinctively that if the Beatles were going to broaden their fan base, they needed to clean up their act. Of course, the boys balked at this and muttered imprecations about "selling out," and "going com-mehr-cial." Like any tolerant father figure, Brian explained to them that if they wanted to move their careers along, they needed to play the game, and that there was no shame or dishonor about that. Epstein understood, as his band did not, that in order to have clout in the music business, which

they badly wanted, you had to first learn to "come along nicely."

So gone were the lewd stage antics, the chain smoking, the salty language, the crude gestures, the lampooning of the disabled, the elderly, or homosexuals. Gone, as well, were any articles of clothing that could be perceived as ominous—black leather trousers, pointy Cuban shoes, tight jeans, and motorcycle jackets or caps. If left to their own devices, the Beatles might well have initiated the punk look decades before it evolved, but Brian was having

none of that. They had to appear tamed and domesticated, not like tomcats on the prowl. He went so far as to have their signature shaggy haircuts trimmed and shaped by professional stylists.

Even their distinctive northern accents were not sacrosanct. Gerry Marsden, an early Epstein client, recalled Brian instructing all his Liverpudlian performers to speak more slowly and clearly, so they could be understood. "We were Scousers," Marsden explained with a laugh during an interview, and then proceeded to utter a string of rapid-fire syllables only another Scouser could make out. That certainly wasn't going to fly on the BBC.

In his youth, Brian had wanted to become a clothing designer, so his makeover of the Beatles was likely a dream come true. Personally, Brian would have probably preferred the leather-clad Hamburg incarnation of the Beatles, but that was hardly something he would present to the staid British public. If nothing else, he understood his audience.

Still, the Beatles' new look wasn't all Brian's doing by a long shot. Each of the band members was a bit of a dandy, each had an individual sense of style, and so when it became clear the leathers had to go, they hit the stores of Liverpool and London to shop for the latest fashions.

NATTY NOT TATTY

At least Brian didn't have to disguise any problems with their physiques—the Beatles were all slender and, except for Ringo, slightly above average height. They looked particularly good in the prevailing menswear silhouette, the slim-legged trousers and fitted jackets. Brian at first intended to tog them out like Borscht-Belt lounge singers in pastel sports jackets, but sense finally prevailed and, with very vocal input from the boys, he settled on the French-inspired fashion of severely tailored, often

collarless, jackets worn with the popular "drainpipe" trousers over short, elastic-sided boots.

From the start, there was something vaguely military about these outfits, with their frequent use of corded piping, brass buttons, mandarin collars, and epaulettes, to the point that they seem to foreshadow the iconic satin *Sgt. Pepper* uniforms. Even the deep bow Brian schooled them to perform at the end of each set smacked of military precision.

This unifying look, unlike the outfits worn by groups like Rory Storm and the Hurricanes—with the headliner dressed in something dramatic to snag the spotlight and set him apart from his backers— at once identified the Beatles as equals on stage. This concept of equality had also struck George Martin when he first listened to their demo tape . . . hearing three distinct voices but no apparent front man. Unlike Bill Haley and the Comets or Buddy Holly and the Crickets, who featured one "star" vocalist and anonymous backup singers, here were three vocalists who switched the lead on different songs. It has become so common for rock and roll fans to see members of contemporary bands trade vocal leads, that they don't appreciate how unorthodox the Beatles' approach was considered back then.

Opposite: The Beatles pose, somewhat stiffly, soon after Brian put them into tailored suits.

Top: The collarless wool/mohair-blend suits made famous by the Beatles were originally designed by Dougie Millings and most probably inspired by the 1960 "cylinder" suits of Pierre Cardin. Naturally, cheaper knockoffs of the Beatles' clothes were soon flooding stores on both sides of the Atlantic.

Above: In this photoshoot the Beatles play the game and appeal to the sensibilities of young girls, hugging a toy panda. They are backstage at the Manchester Apollo theater, November 20, 1963–and at the height of British Beatlemania.

Previous pages, inset: The last of seventeen appearances at the Majestic Theatre in Birkenhead, on April 10, 1963.

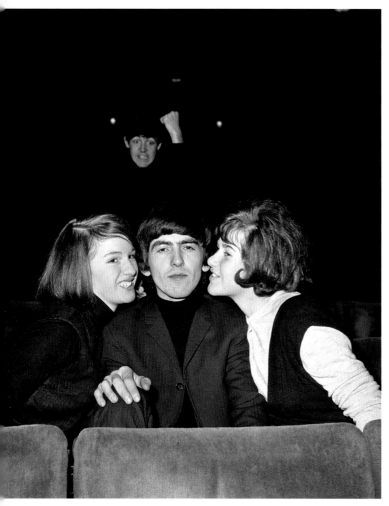

"WE DIDN'T ALL GET INTO MUSIC FOR A JOB! WE GOT INTO MUSIC TO AVOID A JOB, IN TRUTH—AND GET LOTS OF GIRLS."
PAUL McCARTNEY

Above, left: George gets the girls, as Paul McCartney shakes his fist in the background. They're clowning around at the Gaumont Cinema, Doncaster, on December 10, 1963.

Above, right: John and his wife Cynthia wait at Heathrow Airport. He's wearing the Mary Quant hat that sparked a trend.

Brian knew there was another key part of grooming the Beatles for fame (and deflecting the close scrutiny of both fans and the press) and that was keeping their private lives private. Youthful Beatle fans screamed their puppy love for the band, and Brian knew nothing killed a teen crush like a cold dash of reality. So he was determined to keep the fan magazines from discovering anything disagreeable about his boys, most critically that John—the wry, intellectual, funny Beatle who appealed to brainy schoolgirls and college coeds—already had a wife.

John had gotten Cynthia pregnant in 1962 and, to his credit, agreed to marry her, in spite of his numerous misgivings. Cynthia had been pushing for matrimony for some time, and now seemed to be getting her wish. But she might have done better to go it alone or arrange for an adoption. In later interviews she insists that she and John were close, that they'd had a strong marriage, but John played "least in sight" during most of his wife's pregnancy, touring with the band, even performing in Liverpool, while she was holed up at Mendips like a criminal, getting the stink eye from Aunt Mimi.

SWEPT ASIDE

Cynthia understood why John, at this early juncture in his career, needed to feed the fan machine and appear to be available for teen fantasies, but she bitterly resented being swept aside. Even after their son, Julian, was born, John managed to find excuses to stay away from the hospital. To say he was not husband or father material at that point is grossly understating the situation. He'd received very little nurturing himself as a child and so whenever events required him to express real emotion, he either shut down and grew surly or turned everything into a joke.

The other three Beatles, meanwhile, were not living like monks, not with the regular supply of dolly birds being selected by their touring staff and presented to them like bonbons on a dessert cart. Paul even found himself involved in a second paternity suit.

It's a miracle Brian managed to keep these "groupie" romps out of the press (and that the girls themselves didn't go public) and preserve his band's highly sanitized reputation. After the orgies of Hamburg, it might be expected that Paul, George, and Ringo had tired of mindless sex, but this new bevy of willing bed partners were doubtless more attractive, attentive, and adoring than the jaded prostitutes and aging strippers of the Reeperbahn. So the sexual round-robin continued unabated, until, one by one, the three single Beatles tired of the casual couplings and lack of intimacy and found themselves real partners.

Top: Ringo signs his autograph on Beatles' posters.

Above: The secretary of the Beatles Fan Club, Freda Kelly, shown here on on February 14, 1964, is surrounded by the hundreds of valentines sent to the group. Kelly was later featured in the 2013 documentary, *Good Ol' Freda*.

"YOU WERE WILD ONCE, DON'T LET THEM TAME YOU."

DANCER ISADORA DUNCAN

Above: On November 18, 1963 in Lewisham, south London, jubilant Beatles fans hold up their tickets for a Beatles' concert, beside a group of fans being restrained by police, who are still queuing for theirs!

The Beatles possessed enough savvy about the music business to understand a few plain truths. Most critically that, unlike their days as Quarrymen when they attracted fans of both sexes, their current audience was now largely composed of teenage and pre-teenage girls. Brian's taming of the Hamburg tomcats had, in effect, whisked them back to some puerile stage of development, where they were appealing and engaging but not remotely sexy. The androgyny of their long hair and almost feminized nip-waisted suits removed any threat of predation in the minds of young fans.

The second thing the boys understood was that their "little girls" wanted to hear love songs, silly or otherwise. And since John, Paul, and George had cut their teeth on the girl groups of Motown and the crooning love ballads of Bing Crosby and Hoagy Carmichael, they knew the vernacular. "Moon, June, spoon" were all right up their creative alley.

And so John and Paul, and occasionally George, embarked on a songwriting journey during those first few years that attempted to encapsulate every tender, tremulous stage of young love, including: the first meeting—"I Saw Her Standing There"; first physical contact—"I Want to Hold Your Hand," "Just to Dance with You"; the yearning for love—"Love Me Do," "Please Please Me," "I Wanna Be Your Man," "I'll Get You," "Do You Want to Know a Secret?"; the affirmation of love—"PS I Love You," jealousy—"Run for Your Life," "You Can't

Do That"; breaking up—"Don't Bother Me"; and getting back together—"She Loves You."

PLAYING THE GAME

The closest John got to a rebel yell in those days was his raucous version of the Isley Brothers's "Twist and Shout." Just barely a love song, the lyrics tell the love object to "shake it up, baby" which, in retrospect, their millions of female fans certainly did.

This constant focus on love, and especially girlish, giggly, wholly unlusty love, must have been difficult for John, who was aware that many Liverpool mates were accusing him of selling out to the pop music machine. For years his psyche had seethed with unresolved issues and he was beset by personal demons that could have been exorcised to some extent in song. But he squelched his inner voices for the good of the band— and possibly to facilitate his own expectations of oncoming wealth.

Yet it must have grated on him to hear other contemporary artists performing protest songs and songs of raised consciousness or of personal affirmation—Pete Seeger's "Turn, Turn, Turn," or Peter, Paul and Mary's "If I Had a Hammer"—and known that, for the time being, these rich musical lodes were forbidden to him.

When John's true voice did begin to creep into his compositions, it conveyed strained images of alienation, as in "I'm Only Sleeping," ("Everybody seems to think I'm lazy; I don't mind, I think they're crazy.") "A Day in the Life," ("He blew his mind out

in a car . . . A crowd of people just stood and stared."), like a musical journal detailing the angst of his childhood. No wonder that by 1964 John had evolved from putting down Bob Dylan's plaintive, personal narrative songs to envying them deeply.

Paul, on the other hand, seemed fine with the direction of the band's music. He saw himself as an ongoing part of the tradition of songwriting partners, exemplified by the Gershwin brothers, Arlen and Harburg, Lerner and Lowe, and Leiber and Stoller, legends whose stock in trade were love songs, ballads, and novelty numbers. Always happiest when giving the paying customers what they desired, Paul's post-breakup solo compositions remained the most similar to his earlier efforts when compared to those of his bandmates.

George, now going along for the comfortable ride, did eventually grow restless. Sitting at the knees of the masters, as it were, he learned songcraft and brought to it his own tastes, a desire for more bluesy effects combined with an inclusive World Music sound. But in spite of George's oft-dismissed contributions to their early albums, his first recorded song, "Don't Bother Me," is darker and edgier than anything John and Paul were producing, portraying a man in real pain, not exactly a theme geared to teen pop. And with "Taxman," he was the first to tackle a political "message" song, and a few years later offered wry social commentary with "Piggies" on *The White Album*. John should have resented that

"You're always frustrated, you don't have the chance to do a song on the album, like the Beatles did with Ringo and George, or like Led Zeppelin, where everybody was given a chance to contribute. There never is a chance with the Stones."

BILL WYMAN of the Rolling Stones

George was "allowed" these love-free songs, but by *Rubber Soul*, John's psyche was finally out and about—and starting to howl.

The Beatles' vocally idiosyncratic drummer was the one they relied to perform novelty numbers. With a few exceptions—the upbeat love songs "Boys" and "I Wanna Be Your Man"—Ringo was allotted humorous ditties with a country and western lilt, like Carl Perkins' "Honey Don't" or "Matchbox," or childlike Beatles' songs like "Yellow Submarine." Later Ringo was given more mainstream numbers: "With a Little Help from My Friends" on *Sgt. Pepper* or the lovely "Goodnight" from *The White Album*. Ringo would write and record "Don't Pass Me By" for that same album—his own country and western ditty—and "Octopus's Garden"—a novelty number based on his Sardinian vacation—for *Abbey Road*.

"ALMOST EVERYTHING THE BEATLES DID WAS GREAT, AND IT'S HARD TO IMPROVE ON. THEY WERE OUR BACH."

T-BONE BURNETT, SONGWRITER/RECORD PRODUCER

With what seemed like a never-ending succession of Beatles' songs bombarding the airwaves and topping the charts, other singers found it difficult to compete with the mighty Lennon-McCartney hit machine. The obvious answer was to get their hands on one of those foolproof songs and record it. Fortunately, John and Paul were not stingy with their product. And they soon proved their mettle as "songwriters for hire" when the tunes they gave away also became chartbusters. This sideline proved so gratifying to them that Paul once predicted that when the Beatles' fame had run its course, he and John would simply become songsmiths, happily peddling their compositions to others.

Between 1963 and 1964, John and Paul gave away sixteen songs. The first was 1963's "I'll Be on My Way," which went to Brian Epstein's clients, Billy J. Kramer and the

Dakotas, as the B-side for their cover of "Do You Want to Know a Secret." As a follow-up, John wrote "Bad to Me," for Kramer. It hit number one in England and number 9 in the United States (The B-side was another Lennon composition, "I Call Your Name,") a song that predated the Beatles. Lennon didn't like Kramer's version, so the Fab Four recorded it a year later. Kramer also had success with McCartney's "I'll Keep You Satisfied," a song Paul claims he still whistles while gardening.

Here are some of the songs they gave to other artists, many of which became hits:

• "Hello Little Girl," from 1957, was John Lennon's first real song; it was given to another Liverpool group—and good mates of the Beatles—the Fourmost. Their 1963 recording hit number 9 in England. They also recorded Lennon's girl-group homage,

"I'm in Love," which hit number 17 in the United Kingdom.

• Cilla Black started out as the coat check girl at the Cavern, but her ability to belt out a song soon had her up on stage. Brian Epstein's only female client, Black recorded an early Beatles' standard, Paul's "The Love of the Loved," with a brassy Latin beat. It only charted to number 35 in England. She fared better, hitting number 7 in the United Kingdom, with a heavily orchestrated version of Paul's "It's for You." This record, with its departure from the typical Beatles' sound, helped pave the way for "Yesterday."

• "I Wanna Be Your Man," came to the Rolling Stones in pieces. Apparently Paul only gave the chorus to the band's PR agent, Andrew Oldham, but he and John showed up in the studio with the Stones to finish it—in twenty minutes. John reportedly said afterward, "I hope we didn't give away a good one." The song, released November 1, 1963, hit number 12 in England and paved the way for the Stones' decades of success (and inspired the Jagger-Richards writing team, which would go on to pen nineteen songs for other artists in the next two years). The song, with Ringo singing lead, also appeared on *With the Beatles*, which was released three weeks after the Stones' single.

• Peter and Gordon's bouncy debut single, "World Without Love," soared to number one on both sides of the Atlantic in January 1964. Paul had composed the song at sixteen and later happily offered it to his attic mate, Peter Asher. He also wrote the Peter and Gordon hits "Nobody I Know," and "I Don't Want to See You Again." Paul wondered if he could have a hit song without the Lennon-McCartney nameplate, and so the duo released the single "Woman" credited to Bernard Webb. To Paul's relief, the song did very well, even without its pedigree attached.

Perhaps the only nonstarter in this group was "Tip of My Tongue." The Beatles recorded it during

the *Please Please Me* sessions in 1963, didn't like it, and gave it to another of Epstein's singers, Tommy Quickly. It never made the charts and quickly sank from view.

Eventually it occurred to John and Paul that they might be draining their collective think tanks by giving so many songs to the competition. By 1964, John had already shifted his focus to working on writing in his free time, and Paul—who had written the majority of the "gift" songs—restricted himself to one giveaway per year. When he began producing artists for the Beatles new Apple Records label in the later 1960s,

Paul wrote the smash hit "Come and Get It" for Badfinger and penned another winner, "Goodbye," as the follow-up to Mary Hopkin's chartbuster, "Those Were the Days." John also collaborated on David Bowie's megahit, "Fame."

"LENNON AND MCCARTNEY WERE SUPERB COMPOSERS; THEIR SONGS WERE BRILLIANT AND REMAIN BRILLIANT."
MARTIN GOLDSMITH, AUTHOR

FabFact

A boat skipper in the Orkney Islands once told Paul that "Goodbye" was his favorite song. Paul, who had little recollection of writing the song, thought that sounded appropriate. "If you think of it from a sailor's point of view," he said, "it's very much a leaving-the-port song."

Opposite: A Rolling Stones publicity shot from 1963.

Left: Pop duo Peter and Gordon—Peter Asher and Gordon Waller—pose for a portrait in 1965.

Above: Paul with Mary Hopkin, during the Apple Years of the late sixties.

INSTRUMENTS OF THE EARLY YEARS

"FROM 1962 TO 1965, THE GUITAR BECAME THIS ICON OF YOUTH CULTURE, THANKS MOSTLY TO THE BEATLES."

PAT METHENY, AMERICAN JAZZ GUITARIST

Not only did fans want to emulate the Beatles' haircuts, clothing, and boots, the band's more musically inclined followers naturally wanted to duplicate the instruments they played. Fans in the know began tossing around brand names like Rickenbacker, Hofner, Gretsch, Epiphone and Ludwig . . . and sales correspondingly went up for the manufacturers. And of course, when it came time for a particular Beatles' instrument to be repaired, upgraded, or replaced, the manufacturers were happy to perform any service for free. No amount of advertising matched the clout of having a real, live Beatle playing your instruments in front of thousands of potential customers.

A lot of fans assumed the Beatles played German-made instruments, simply because they spent part of their formative years in Hamburg. There was also a prohibitive British tax on electronic equipment imported from America, which enhanced the German-made theory. But the reality was that their favored brands—Rickenbacker, Gretsch, Ludwig—were American companies with German names. Only Paul's Hofner basses were actually made in Europe, in Bubenreuth, Western Germany.

Once the Beatles started making some real money in Hamburg, John decided he needed new guitar. He wanted a Rickenbacker 325, because he'd seen someone playing one on TV and thought it had a nice look. (Ricks were nicknamed "frying pans"

because they had round bodies and long necks.) The one John found in a Hamburg shop was a blond model with the tuning knobs set in white acrylic; eventually he had the body painted black and removed the pick guard. It would become his first signature guitar, the one he used when the Beatles introduced themselves to the world. And when Rickenbacker gave him a new one to replace the original—which was losing parts due to heavy usage—they gave him an exact copy of the old one painted the same black shade. To this day, the company continues to sell the "John Lennon" model in black.

The problem for Paul initially, as a left-handed player, was that he always had to flip over right-handed guitars in order to play. This made an electric guitar look awkward, with the controls up under his arm, instead of below it. Once he officially became the band's bass player, he declined the use of Stu Sutcliffe's right-handed bass, and found a German-made Hofner Violin Bass in the window of a Hamburg music store. The Hofner—which boasted a symmetrical body—became his signature guitar. He soon received a second one from the factory, after the original wore out from those long nights in the Hamburg clubs.

Early in his career, George had played a Futurama, which was a Czech-made Stratocaster knockoff imported by Hofner. George never

found it comfortable to play, so as soon as he got some money, he bought a replacement. Word got around among the other Merseyside bands that the young Beatle was in the market for a new axe, leading to a meeting with a Liverpool man who'd returned from New York years earlier with an American-made Gretsch Duo-Jet. George purchased the second-hand guitar, which he played on the initial singles and albums.

He eventually bought two more Gretsch models—a Country Gentleman and a Tennessean, both of which had been endorsed by Chet Atkins, one of George's guitar heroes. When he sent the original "Gent" in for repairs, and was given a replacement, he liked the new one so much, he used the first one only as a backup, and the replacement became his signature, the one he played throughout the 1964 world tour. Toward the end of the year, however, he switched to the twangier Tennessean model, which he played regularly once the Beatles entered their country-folk rock phase.

ACOUSTIC ACQUISITIONS

Acoustically the Beatles, specifically John and George, started with twin Gibson J160-E acoustic guitars. The "E" designation meant they had pickups and could be plugged into an amp. The Beatles were always careful about their look, and that included their axes, which had to look as sharp as they were. The two

Above: Ringo Starr performs on the set of *A Hard Day's Night* at the Scala Theatre, playing his Ludwig drum kit.

guitars were such look-alikes that the two were accidentally switched. Sadly, John had his (i.e., George's) stolen from a theater where they had been performing in 1963, but he got a new one midway through 1964. Paul purchased a right-handed Epiphone Texan acoustic guitar, most famously used on "Yesterday." Naturally, he flipped it over, so that the pick guard sat on top. George also bought himself a classical-style Jose Ramirez acoustic guitar, which was heard on "And I Love Her" . . . and seen in their first movie.

BLACK OYSTER PEARL

As a youth, Ringo had been forced to play makeshift drums—tin pots, pails, etc.—until his step-dad gave him a secondhand kit. His mother then bought him a set of Premier drums, a popular brand at the time and good enough for the various local groups he joined, including the Beatles. After the band's popularity

increased, Ringo purchased a set of Ludwig drums, in black oyster pearl, at London's Drum City (he'd gone in with Brian intent on a simple black kit, but the black pearl caught his eye). The Beatles' logo on the bass drum, designed by shop owner Ivor Arbiter, changed several times—as did the kit itself—but each time Ringo insisted that the Ludwig name appear above the band's logo. His new drum kit made as much of an impact on the public as the guitars his bandmates were using. Ludwig went into all-day production for a time just to keep up with the demand from wannabe-Beatles who wanted to play a drum kit just like Ringo's. (Pete Best had also been eyeing a set of Ludwig drums for some time, but didn't buy one until after he'd been fired by the group.)

GOING TO ELEVEN

When the Beatles went into the EMI studios for the first time, their

instruments were all first-rate, but their amplifiers were worn out from overuse—fit only for Hamburg gin joints, not the recording of live music in a professional studio. Fortunately, there was a music shop in central London that was an authorized dealer of Vox amps. Vox made their name in England by outfitting the first British bands of the late 1950s. Brian went there and struck a barter deal with the shop's manager, Ken Jennings. Vox would receive unlimited publicity if they would supply the Beatles with equipment, especially guitar amplifiers. Vox agreed to the deal. In fact, they were very accommodating: as the Beatles' concerts got louder from the fans' yelling and screaming, Vox kept upgrading their equipment to handle the increase in volume that the group required. Thus, Vox evolved just as the Fab Four did. This arrangement continued for several years.

Above left from top to bottom: George's 1957 Gretsch Duo Jet guitar fitted with a Bigsby Vibrato and used through the Beatles' early years; Paul's iconic Hofner Model 500/1 "violin" bass guitar; John's 1958 Rickenbacker 325 guitar with added Bigsby Vibrato, and used as his main guitar between 1960 and 1964.

> "LONDON IS THE MOST SWINGING CITY IN THE WORLD AT THE MOMENT."
> DIANA VREELAND, *VOGUE* EDITOR, 1965

CHAPTER SIX

LONDON

> "THERE SEEMED TO BE NO ONE STANDING OUTSIDE THE BUBBLE, AND OBSERVING JUST HOW ODD AND SHALLOW AND EGOCENTRIC AND EVEN RATHER HORRIBLE IT WAS."
> CHRISTOPHER BOOKER, FOUNDER *PRIVATE EYE* MAGAZINE

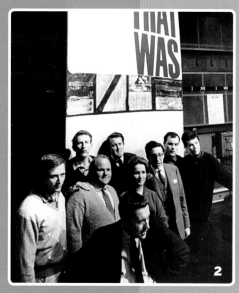

"The thing the Sixties did was to show us the possibilities and the responsibility that we all had. It wasn't the answer. It just gave us a glimpse of the possibility."

JOHN LENNON

Something strange and wonderful began brewing in London during the early 1960s. England was about to shake off her centuries-old mantle of the staid, the hidebound, and the stodgy. A new spirit was set to rise up from those ancient cobbled streets and twisting alleys and break the chains of numbing conformity, a spirit that would eventually touch and enliven much of the civilized world.

No one could argue that for at least two centuries England had been the empress of the planet, with a financial empire that stretched from ocean to ocean to ocean, both north and south of the Equator. But the Second World War had worn her thin, nearly bankrupted her exchequer, exhausted her resources, and left her populace staggering. A decade and a half later, however, the country was finally sensing that a brighter economic future lay ahead of them. This hope, this expectation, helped lay the groundwork for the great revolutionary, evolutionary party that was about to begin.

London remained the cultural hub of the country, but since the war most of the culture had been imported: the music—mainly easy-listening hits and movie soundtracks—from America, fashions from France and Italy, and modern art from the Continent and America. There were a lot of influences coming in, but very few going out. To its young people,

Left: 1) British fashion icon Mary Quant (who first designed the miniskirt and also hot pants) and hairdresser Vidal Sassoon; 2) the team from *That Was The Week That Was*, an influential, satirical TV show; 3) photographer David Bailey; 4) clothes designer Barbara Hulanicki of Biba; 5) painter David Hockney; 6) actress Diana Rigg, who gained stardom in *The Avengers*, a popular British spy show.

England must have seemed sadly square. They were out in the workforce now, many of these older teens and twenty-somethings, and they had disposable incomes to spend on cultural frivolities and fashionable togs . . . if only their country were not so singularly dull.

Then, as if in sync with the downbeat of some unseen conductor's baton, a host of cultural innovators—designers, artists, musicians—in London all unveiled their work within a short span of time, subsequently riffing off each other, challenging each other, trying to surpass each other . . . inspiring an outpouring of spontaneity, individuality, modernity, and optimism in others, the likes of which the world had rarely seen before.

British art schools of the 1950s and 1960s served a very special purpose: they were intended for students who didn't fit the standard academic profile—a John Lennon, say—allowing them to continue their education in an environment of more open-mindedness and creative encouragement than that furnished by the typical British university or polytechnic. While this formula did not work for Lennon, it did help to produce a generation of active iconoclasts who would form the core of the cultural revolution taking place in London.

ART

In the mid-1950s the London-based Independent Group gave birth to Pop Art (so named by British critic Lawrence Alloway) to strike a blow against abstract expressionism, and in the 1960s, this tradition of radicalism was continued by other

> ## "Looking back on it, it was a perfect time, a perfect place, and a perfect education."
> **KIM HOWELLS MP**, on the British art college

British artists like painter David Hockney, sculptor Allen Jones, "formal" artist Patrick Caulfield, conceptual artists Gilbert and George, op-artist Bridget Riley, and pop-artist Peter Blake (who would later design the cover of the *Sgt. Pepper* album).

Yet much of the best art produced there, as in America, was never intended for the public museum or the private gallery, but was meant for the hip youngster on the street—as advertisements for concerts, as wall decor or murals in clubs, and most importantly, as artwork for album covers.

Some representative British covers that rode the zeitgeist during that time include: Martin Sharp's psychedelic dreamscape for Cream's *Disraeli Gears* (1967); the ad-parody photographs by David Montgomery for *The Who Sell Out* (1967); David Anstey's abstract painting on the Moody Blues' *Days of Future Past* (1967); the fantastical art by Hipgnosis for Pink Floyd's *A Saucerful of Secrets* (1968)—only the second group EMI allowed to hire an outside designer, the first being the Beatles; and the flower power intricacies of the Zombies' *Odessey and Oracle* (complete with misspelling) by Terry Quirk (1968).

FASHION

Even in her Victorian heyday, England had never been a fashion hub. For one thing, the damp, chilly climate dictated a sartorial

diet of tartans, tweeds, and worsteds. And that was just in summer . . . There was little chance England would ever rival Paris, Milan, New York, or Tokyo as a mecca of innovative fashion design. Not as long as the women of good families all had their clothing made by the same dreary dressmakers in Mayfair, and the queen set the tone with her starchy dowager suits and matronly hats. But a new queen was about to be crowned, and a new London setting would soon cast Buckingham Palace into the shade as the top tourist destination.

Mary Quant

If there is one obvious disconnect in the footage of the Beatles' early performances, it is the gap between the sharp fashion sense displayed by the young men on stage and the outdated look of the young girls in the audience. The Beatles are togged out in sleek, cutting-edge suits with radical haircuts. The girls, meanwhile, apparently haven't moved beyond the Elvis years—with flip hairdos, cotton blouses with Peter Pan collars, straight, knee-length skirts, and penny loafers. They all look like 1950s sorority sisters, scrubbed clean and hardly as hip as the band they adored. This preppy look was about to change, however.

Previous pages: Picadilly Circus, with its neon signs, neo-classical buildings, and the iconic Shaftesbury Memorial Fountain featuring the statue of Eros, is considered by many to be the heart of London's downtown shopping and entertainment district. The winged statue of Eros was one of the first monuments to be cast in aluminum.

"THAT'S WHAT THE WHOLE SIXTIES FLOWER-POWER THING WAS ABOUT: 'GO AWAY, YOU BUNCH OF BORING PEOPLE.'"

GEORGE HARRISON

Fashion designer Mary Quant opened up her first shop, Bazaar, on the King's Road in 1955 with husband Alexander Plunkett Greene and solicitor Archie McNair. Two years later a second Bazaar debuted. Like the first, it sold trendy clothing—bright knitwear with matching woven stockings, long cardigan dresses, and what Quant called her "mad" lounging pajamas, which she'd designed herself. After the pajamas were licensed by an American clothing manufacturer, Quant decided to design more of her shop's stock. Before long she was setting the style for young, affluent Londoners, most specifically with the scandalous new miniskirt.

Whether or not Quant actually "invented" the miniskirt, she certainly popularized the style in her shops (and reportedly named it, after her favorite car, the Mini Cooper). Her explanation for the skirt's abbreviated hemline was that it allowed a woman to "run for a bus." She's often been quoted as insisting that women's clothing should be both fun and liberating. One thing was certain—with Quant's ascendancy, the age of the staid Mayfair couturier was over.

Her success led the way for other young British designers, who introduced a variety of looks, including many styles that openly threw off tradition and restraint: colored or patterned tights, baby doll dresses, short Victorian dresses with lace collars, caftans, fur vests, gypsy skirts, sheer chiffon blouses, paisley headwraps, poor-boy sweaters, dressy sandals, kitten heels, suede knee boots, picture hats, feather boas, love beads and medallions, go-go boots, space-age A-line mini dresses, capes, unisex pant suits, Nehru jackets, Beatle boots, Italian shoes, velvet Edwardian suits, brocade waistcoats, vintage military jackets, metallic hardware, leather caps, contrasting-collar shirts, and wide, vibrant ties.

Most menswear designers catered to the mods with the "City Gent" look of Italian suits and anoraks, while a few others gravitated to the rockers or "greasers," with their blue jeans, biker boots, and motorcycle jackets. Girls began to wear their hair long and straight, often with bangs; in teased up beehives; or, with the encouragement of hair wizard Vidal Sassoon, lopped off in geometric or asymmetrical cuts. For young men, the shaped Beatle haircut and longish sideburns were the order of the day.

The Street at the Center of the Universe

The fierce creativity surging through London found an outlet in Soho, along a narrow thoroughfare called Carnaby Street. Named after Karnaby House in the late 1600s, the street held small dwellings during the 1700s, was the site of a market in the 1820s, and in 1930 was home to the Florence Mills Social Club, a base for Pan-Africanism. In 1958, after John Stephens opened the boutique, His Clothes, on Carnaby Street, the area was usurped by the young and groovy, who proceeded to open dress shops, interior decor shops, and vintage clothing emporiums. Their earliest customers were people in show business, but the youth of London soon followed in droves.

These boutiques typically had silly or hip names like Granny Takes a Trip, Hung On You, I Was Lord Kitchener's Valet, Kleptomania, Mates, and Ravel in Soho, and Countdown and the Antique Supermarket on Chelsea's King's Road. Hip parents shopped at Gear, which offered trendy children's clothing. Even though Biba, a group of boutiques geared to street people, kept prices low, the wealthy were soon flowing throw their doors. And no matter where in London the cool stores were located, the unwritten rule during daylight hours was to "see and be seen." Shopping became almost as much of a social outlet as clubbing. It wasn't long before the styles and attitudes of these fashion-mad young Londoners had swept across the Atlantic to America—and beyond.

By the mid-1960s, the British had become the leaders of the fashion world, originating styles instead of copying them. They introduced some of the earliest supermodels—Jean Shrimpton, Twiggy, and Penelope Tree—to the world, originated the concept of photographer as celebrity with superstars like David Bailey and Richard Avedon, and created global trends—for bell-bottom

jeans, colored tights, Edwardian blouses, tiered velvet skirts, and ankle boots, for instance—that are still in evidence today.

MUSIC

One of the reasons those teens in Liverpool had been so anxious to get their hands on American records was because the British Broadcasting Company (BBC), their own British radio network, offered so little in the way of popular music.

In the early 1960s, the BBC still had a monopoly over the airwaves in Great Britain, controlling all programming and forbidding commercials. Even though the BBC had been offering the Light Programme (mainstream light entertainment and music) since 1945, the music it showcased was not reflective of the youth market's taste for rock and roll. Fortunately for British teens, there was Radio Luxembourg, which broadcast overnight from the Grand Duchy—using the most powerful privately owned transmitter in the world and bouncing its signal off the ionosphere. Formerly a multilingual commercial station, by 1963 Radio Luxembourg was catering specifically to British teens, featuring both live disc jockeys and prerecorded shows. As a result of the channel not being available until after dark, it was dubbed "208—Your station of the stars."

Offshore Pirate Radio

Then in March 1964, Radio Caroline began daytime broadcasts

"England swings like a pendulum do . . ."
ROGER MILLER

of popular music from a ship anchored four miles off England's southern coast. This "pirate radio" eventually led to a whole fleet of radio ships lying off England and Ireland. In 1967, the Marine Broadcasting Offense Act became law, eliminating the commercials that funded most of the Radio Caroline ships, forcing all but two out of commission. The BBC was then instructed to offer a popular music alternative, and so Radio 1 was born—featuring chart hits by day and more alternative music after 7 PM. Now young Britons could get their fill of Cliff Richard, Adam Faith, and Tommy Steele by day, and blues and modern jazz by night.

WHERE IT ALL CAME TOGETHER

The club scene provided a collective showcase for the endeavors of all these artistic Londoners—there inside those crowded, smoky venues pop-art paintings and psychedelic posters blazed from the walls, the latest fashions made Edwardian dandies of the men

and leather-and-lace gypsies of the women, while the newest pop or rock hits throbbed from the speakers until the dancers blended into one swirling mass beneath the flashing colored lights.

London rapidly became a kaleidoscope world of endless possibilities, offering day- and nighttime frolics—shopping, drinking, dining, clubbing, celebrity watching—with both locals and tourists being drawn to the vintage clothing stores, cutting-edge boutiques, exotic restaurants, and kicky little head shops that lined the hippest streets.

It was into this enriched Petri dish of high-spirited hedonism that the Beatles fell headlong in 1963.

Above, left: Carnaby Street, seen here at Christmas, 1966, was London's fashion hub, a place to see and be seen.

Above, right: Supermodel Twiggy, in 1966, shows off her signature androgynous haircut and exaggerated eyelashes.

Following pages: The Beatles play the Majestic Theatre, Birkenhead, for the final time on Wednesday, April 10, 1963.

London Digs

"I'VE MOVED WITH GREAT RELUCTANCE, ACTUALLY, BECAUSE I LIKE LIVERPOOL AND I LIKE ITS PEOPLE."

BRIAN EPSTEIN, 1964 BBC INTERVIEW

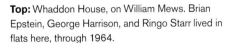

Top: Whaddon House, on William Mews. Brian Epstein, George Harrison, and Ringo Starr lived in flats here, through 1964.

Above, center: John moved from the Green Street flat to 13 Emperor's Gate, with Cynthia and Julian.

Above: 34 Montagu Square in Marylebone. First leased by Ringo, John and Yoko shot the nude cover for *Two Virgins* here, and were also busted here. Jimi Hendrix wrote "The Wind Cries Mary" in the flat.

Top: In their early days in London, the four Beatles shared a flat here, at 57 Green Street, Mayfair.

Above: Brian Epstein sits beside his stereo console at Whaddon House, Knightsbridge, in April 1964. In January 1965 he moved to Chapel Street in Belgravia, not far from Hyde Park Corner. Chapel Street was the scene of many Beatles' parties, significantly the press launch of *Sgt. Pepper* on May 19, 1967, attended by photographer Linda Eastman.

Once the Beatles began regular recording sessions at the Abbey Road studio, it made sense for them to relocate from Liverpool to London. This became an important step in their evolution, for it was there they would complete their education. In the same way they had honed their survival skills and stagecraft in Hamburg, in London they would mingle with trendy, upper-class Londoners, artists, film stars, and other celebrities, and learn the niceties of polite society.

During the summer of 1963, the Beatles moved into the Royal Court in Sloane Square and then into the Hotel President on Russell Square in the artsy, literary neighborhood known as Bloomsbury.

That autumn the four mates found a suite of rooms, Flat L, in an elegant bow-windowed building at 57 Green Street, near Hyde Park, and actually did move in together (reminiscent of the opening scene of *Help!* where the Beatles enter four separate doorways but are then shown sharing one large flat). A short time later, John moved with wife Cynthia and baby Julian to an apartment at 13 Emperor's Gate in Brompton, Knightsbridge.

In late 1963, Brian Epstein moved to the top floor apartment of a six-story brick complex called Whaddon House, which was in upscale Knightsbridge on William Mews near Harrods. George and Ringo were soon sharing a flat in the same building.

MONTAGU SQUARE

A year later, Ringo moved to a two-story apartment—the basement and ground floor of an elegant Regency townhouse at 34 Montagu Square, in the Marylebone district of London. Although he moved out less than a year later, Ringo

retained the lease and offered the place to various friends, including Jimi Hendrix, who composed "The Wind Cries Mary," while living there. When John and Cynthia split up in 1968, she went to live there with Julian—her mother had often stayed there while visiting the Lennons, but they went back to Kenwood three months later, so that John and Yoko could stay there during the recording of *The White Album*. (Neither John nor Yoko was in line for a housekeeping award—any friends who visited remarked on the squalor.) It was there the couple shot the controversial nude cover of *Two Virgins* and on October 18, 1968, it was the site of a police drug raid. Initially, both Lennon and a pregnant Ono resisted opening the doors, fearing it was fans trying to push in. The police eventually recovered 219 grams of hashish in a binocular case; Lennon pleaded guilty and was fined £150, the equivalent of $250. Ono miscarried shortly afterward, and she and John both mourned the loss of their unborn son. John would later also have political reasons for regretting the incident.

AN ATTIC ON WIMPOLE STREET

Paul McCartney found a more personal nest. He had met actress and TV personality Jane Asher, a panelist on *Juke Box Jury*, on April 18, 1963, just prior to a Beatles' performance at the Royal Albert Hall. She'd been sent there to interview the boys for the *Radio Times*. Paul, taken with her lovely face and shining auburn hair, skilfully separated her from his equally smitten bandmates, and the two soon became an item, even though he recognized from the start that she was a "nice" girl.

Her entire family—including her

doctor father, Richard, music professor mother, Margaret, and two siblings, Peter and Clare—welcomed Paul into the family unit. Before long, with her mother's goodwill, he was living in the family's spacious townhouse on Wimpole Street, sharing an attic bedroom with Peter, a talented singer. Jane's mother also tutored Paul on the recorder and gave him music lessons.

Paul at first felt at a disadvantage in a household full of clever, educated professionals who discussed art and literature—and who actually played word games at the dinner table!—but he never tried to bluff and always admitted it when he didn't know something.

He and John wrote "I Want to Hold Your Hand" in the Ashers' basement music room, sitting "eyeball-to-eyeball." The tune for "Yesterday," the song that famously went without real lyrics for years, was composed there, as was "I'm Looking Through You," after a fight with Jane, Paul would later explain.

In September 1963, the couple spent two weeks in Greece with Ringo and future wife, Maureen Cox. Another vacation in the Bahamas spurred Paul to write

"Things We Said Today." Jane was also the inspiration for "And I Love Her," "You Won't See Me," "We Can Work It Out," and "Here, There and Everywhere."

Paul remained with the Ashers for three years, writing a series of hit songs for Peter and Gordon—nerdy-but-adorable red-headed Peter Asher and his sultry-voiced singing partner, Gordon Waller—along the way, before moving with Jane to his own gated house on Cavendish Avenue, in St. John's Wood near the EMI studio.

Even though Jane Asher seemed to furnish Paul with a haven from his frenzied public life, their relationship was not without strife. She was strong-willed and wanted her own career. He was still sleeping around with female celebrities and fans, and being, as he later admitted, a "chauvinist" about the whole fidelity thing. Nevertheless, the other Beatles knew how much Jane meant to Paul and expected him to marry her. But in spite of an engagement in 1967, Paul appeared to be in no rush to settle down.

Top, left: Paul moved from Green Street to the Asher family home on Wimpole Street, W1.

Top, right: In 1966, Paul and Jane moved north to 7 Cavendish Avenue, just around the corner from Abbey Road.

"SIR, WHEN A MAN IS TIRED OF LONDON, HE IS TIRED OF LIFE; FOR THERE IS IN LONDON ALL THAT LIFE CAN AFFORD"

SAMUEL JOHNSON

Left: The Beatles pose for a photograph during a shoot at the Austin Reed tailors' store in Regent Street, London, on July 16, 1963.

The Beatles, no strangers to the club scene in Liverpool, were soon immersed in London's lively nighttime whirl, which consisted of private supper clubs, elite gambling establishments, discotheques, and trendy bars, plus a host of music venues both large and small. The four mates wasted no time in sampling this bounty.

A lucky paparazzo might snap Paul with Jane at dinner, Paul and John with Mick Jagger or George with Eric Clapton at a smoky blues lounge, or Ringo meeting the Monkees for drinks. It was the stuff of fans' daydreams—imagining their Liverpool lads hobnobbing with other rock and roll royalty and sharing candlelit meals with actresses and supermodels. The American teen magazines naturally sanitized these outings for their

nubile readers—all boy-girl encounters were strictly platonic, chiefly so that every fan would believe that her chosen Beatle was waiting for her to give his heart away. This he-and-I-are-fated-to-be-together mentality goes a long way toward explaining the excesses of Beatlemania—tens of thousands of anxious, yearning, hormonal young girls, each one convinced by *Teen Scene* or *Tiger Beat* that she was simply perfect for Paul (or George or Ringo or even John, before his marriage was revealed).

The truth of the boys' nights out lay a little closer to the Hamburg days—booze and birds and pills, and probably a lot of shagging. But many of these London clubs also offered something that beat sex six ways to Sunday—a rare cross-section of music from many

exotic locations around the globe. So the Beatles weren't always on the make; sometimes they just wanted to kick back and listen.

MUSIC OF THE NIGHT

Soho was home to a number of London's best music clubs. The Flamingo offered both R & B and jazz (the subsequent blending of musical cultures here purportedly helped to speed the breakdown of racial prejudice in the country). With top-notch headliners like Rod Stewart, the Byrds, Stevie Wonder, Patti LaBelle, and Jerry Lee Lewis, the club soon became a favorite haunt of the Beatles, as well as the Rolling Stones and Jimi Hendrix. The Marquee Club showcased all the major bands from 1964 onward, including the Rolling Stones, the Yardbirds, Led Zeppelin, the Who, King Crimson, Jethro Tull, Jimi Hendrix, and Pink Floyd. The Moody Blues cut their first hit single, "Go Now," in the garage at the back of the building. The Roaring Twenties on Carnaby Street featured R & B as well as ska music courtesy of the influential Jamaican DJ, Count Suckle.

Tiles, a basement club on Oxford Street that opened in 1966, was a showcase for popular music and catered to mods; another mod hangout, Club Noreik in South Tottenham, offered

dancing and live music by up-and-coming bands, including the Who and Van Morrison. Rocker Cha Cha, as its name implies, catered to rockers, while Samantha's, a basement club near Regent Street, was a popular discotheque.

In spite of this surfeit of venues, the London club scene was "smaller than imagined," according to Peter Noone of Herman's Hermits. He recalls it as an intimate environment where a young fan could ride up the elevator to the Leicester Place Ad Lib Club with John Lennon and end up having the Beatle buy him a drink (which actually happened to Noone). The Ad Lib was also where John and George and their partners decided to flee after a dentist friend laced their coffee with LSD during dinner. The club, known for its strict diet of R & B and soul music, was a favorite with the Stones, the Kinks, and actresses Hayley Mills and Julie Christie. Within a short time, however, it lost its cachet and was replaced by the Scotch of St. James and the Bag O' Nails.

At the very least these club jaunts furnished the Beatles with a steady stream of musical influences—they were never loath to borrow a measure or a riff—and kept their names and faces foremost in the press before they reconvened to record their second album.

Top: A shoeless young woman in a mini-dress enjoys a solo dance at the UFO club, Tottenham Court Road, London, January 31, 1967.

DREAMING UNDERGROUND

During the early- to mid-1960s a counterculture movement began to flourish in and around London, populated by poets, writers, artists, and musicians. American "beats" Allen Ginsberg and William Burroughs were their idols, and the spacey, Syd Barrett-led Pink Floyd was their "house band." Members of this small but select group jammed into the Albert Hall to hear beat poetry readings, danced the night away at the UFO Club, and hung out at Better Books in Charing Cross Road, discussing philosophy, pacifism, and the beat culture. London's underground also became famous for artsy gatherings—nights of music, dancing, and psychedelic drugs—which quickly became a showcase for all that was cutting edge in clothing, jewelry, and self-expression. The movement culminated on April 29, 1967, with the "14-hour Technicolor Dream," a dance and love extravaganza held at the cavernous Alexandra Palace in London. It was organized as a fundraiser for London's underground newspaper, the *International Times*, and featured more than 30 acts—bands, jugglers, dancers, and a performance by Yoko Ono. A mustachioed, tripping John Lennon showed up with Donovan and John Dunbar, the manager of a hip new art gallery, the Indica, which catered to London's avant-garde; it was there that Lennon had met his muse a year earlier. The Technicolor Dream signaled the end of the hardcore underground, as such; it was assimilated into the general scene that encompassed Swinging London and which would soon give way to the worldwide Summer of Love.

Top: Pink Floyd perform with their psychedelic light show at the UFO Club, 1967.

"YOU ALWAYS GET A KICK WHEN A RECORD COMES INTO THE HIT PARADE OR A RECORD HITS NUMBER ONE . . . A RECORD IN THE CHARTS MEANS A GREAT DEAL TO AN ARTIST IN THIS DAY AND AGE."
BRIAN EPSTEIN, 1964

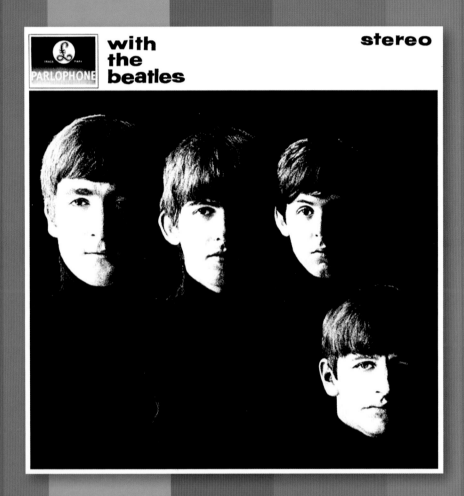

WITH THE BEATLES
RELEASED NOVEMBER 22, 1963

(All songs Lennon–McCartney, unless specified)

Side One:

1. IT WON'T BE LONG

2. ALL I'VE GOT TO DO

3. ALL MY LOVING

4. DON'T BOTHER ME (Harrison)

5. LITTLE CHILD

6. TILL THERE WAS YOU (Willson)

7. PLEASE MR. POSTMAN (Dobbins–Garret–Gorman–Holland–Bateman)

Side Two:

1. ROLL OVER BEETHOVEN (Berry)

2. HOLD ME TIGHT

3. YOU REALLY GOT A HOLD ON ME (Robinson)

4. I WANNA BE YOUR MAN

5. DEVIL IN HER HEART (Drapkin)

6. NOT A SECOND TIME

7. MONEY (THAT'S WHAT I WANT) (Bradford–Gordy)

In July 1963, the Beatles went back into the studio to record their second album for Parlophone. At least EMI gave them more time to prepare than they'd been given for *Please Please Me*, and so the band arrived at Abbey Road with eight original new songs—including a tune composed by George Harrison, "Don't Bother Me"—and a selection of six covers of Motown or R&B standards.

With the Beatles was released on Nov. 22, 1963, and replaced *Please Please Me* at the top of the British album charts. Between the two LPS, the Beatles controlled the top spot for an astonishing total of 51 weeks!

MEET THE BEATLES!

The artsy, chiaroscuro cover portraits, by fashion photographer Robert Freeman, were used on both the British album and Capitol's American release, *Meet the Beatles!* with the latter including a soft blue tint behind the faces.

The Capital album took America by storm. Released January 24, 1964, it offered most of the songs from EMI's *With the Beatles*, including megahit, "I Want to Hold Your Hand," and helped catapult the band into the consciousness of most American kids under age 20 and quite a few of their mothers, as well.

But getting there hadn't been an easy journey—in spite of Brian Epstein and George Martin pleading with EMI for an American release, EMI didn't listen, and the recalcitrant Capitol executives kept

MEET THE BEATLES

RELEASED JANUARY 24, 1964

(All songs Lennon–McCartney, unless specified)

Side One:

1. I WANT TO HOLD YOUR HAND

2. I SAW HER STANDING THERE

3. THIS BOY

4. IT WON'T BE LONG

5. ALL I'VE GOT TO DO

6. ALL MY LOVING

Side Two:

1. DON'T BOTHER ME (Harrison)

2. LITTLE CHILD

3. TILL THERE WAS YOU (Willson)

4. HOLD ME TIGHT

5. I WANNA BE YOUR MAN

6. NOT A SECOND TIME

rejecting any British invasion. EMI president Joseph Lockwood finally listened to Epstein and Martin and sent a deputy to Capitol, ordering them to begin releasing the Beatles' records and start promoting the band in the States.

Vee Jay Records, who had issued the Beatles' early singles in America to a tepid response, dropped their own album, *Introducing . . . The Beatles*, ten days before the Capitol release, hoping to steal Capitol's

thunder. But the competition didn't matter one bit. *Meet the Beatles!* became an industry legend—it topped the pop charts on February 15, 1964, stayed put for eleven weeks and was only dethroned by *The Beatles Second Album*, the first time an artist knocked itself off the top spot.

The songs omitted from *With the Beatles*, exclusively covers— "Please Mr. Postman," "Roll Over Beethoven," "You Really Got a Hold on Me," "Devil in Her Heart," and "Money"—appeared on *The Beatles Second Album*, and the vacancies were augmented here

by "I Want to Hold Your Hand" and its two B-sides, from the UK "This Boy," and from the U.S. "I Saw Her Standing There"—which had already appeared on the British album *Please Please Me*. (Before the advent of the Internet, it would no doubt have taken a Beatles' scholar forever to figure out all the permutations of these British vs. American recordings. Even now only the sharpest audio geeks can manage it.)

A 2003 poll by *Rolling Stone* magazine placed *Meet the Beatles!* at number 59 on their list of the 500 Greatest Albums.

"WE DON'T KNOW THE TOUR SCHEDULE. IT'S NOT UP TO US WHERE WE GO. WE JUST CLIMB INTO THE VAN."
JOHN LENNON

"Who are these guys the Beatles? I try to keep up with the British scene, but I don't know their work."
CHRIS MONTEZ

The Beatles found themselves spending a year on the road in 1963 . . . their appearance on *Thank Your Lucky Stars* having led to the offer of a number of national tours from promoter Arthur Howes. The first tour was arranged in two parts, February 12 through 22 and March 4 through 8, with the Beatles supporting Helen Shapiro, a deep-voiced teen singing sensation.

Shapiro apparently had a bit of a crush on the band and would leave the exclusive "star" section at the rear of the bus to sit up front and chat with them. John and Paul even managed to write "From Me to You" during this tour.

The Beatles then opened for Tommy Roe and Chris Montez in Birmingham, York, and Bristol,

in a tour that ran from March 9 through March 31. American singer Roe was pushing his single, "Sheila," while Montez was promoting two hits, "Let's Dance" and "Some Kinda Fun." When *Please Please Me* hit number one on March 1963, the order of billing changed and the Beatles were now the main attraction. After completing a solo tour

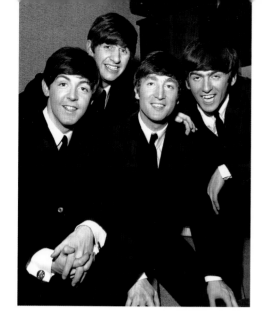

"He'd had so many hit songs and people could sit and listen to him all night. He didn't have to do anything, he didn't have to wiggle his legs, in fact he never even twitched, he was like marble. The only things that moved were his lips—even when he hit those high notes he never strained. He was quite a miracle, unique."

GEORGE HARRISON, Orbison's future bandmate in the Traveling Wilburys

during April, the Beatles then began the Roy Orbison Tour on May 18. They were deeply embarrassed to discover that the roster had again been changed and they were now sharing top billing with one of their most cherished American idols.

Orbison, who was making his first tour of the U.K., was nonplussed at having to share the headliner spot with a band he'd never heard of. The head of his U.S. fan club assured him, however, that it would be great for his career to tour with the Beatles, since they currently had the number one album in England. When Orbison found himself confronted with screaming Beatles fans during the tour, he purposely instructed his bandleader to play so softly that the crowds had to quiet down to hear him. After that, his signature ballads and powerful delivery won them over.

The Beatles also witnessed Orbison writing songs on the tour bus and felt a keen sense of competition to be as good, if not better, than the man who penned "Pretty Woman." It must have worked. According to Paul, "All My Loving" was born on that bus, with the arrangement worked out on a piano at one of the tour venues.

Opposite, far left: John Lennon shares an impromptu dance with singer Helen Shapiro backstage during the recording of TV show *Ready, Steady Go!* in October 1963. The Beatles and Helen had toured together in February and March, 1963.

Opposite, right: The Beatles performing at the Fairfield Halls, Croydon, on April 25, 1963.

Top: A classic Beatles pose, backstage on January 10, 1964.

Above: The Beatles with Roy Orbison (right) and Gerry and the Pacemakers backstage in their dressing room, May 1963. The three acts did a joint British tour through May and June, 1963.

"WE ALWAYS GET DEAD NERVOUS BEFORE WE GO ON STAGE. AND ABOUT NINE TIMES OUT OF TEN WE SUDDENLY FEEL TIRED HALF AN HOUR BEFORE WE GOTTA GET CHANGED. THEN AS SOON AS YOU GO ON, IT'S ALL RIGHT."

JOHN LENNON

Other tours that year included the Summer UK Tour, (June 10 – September 15); Autumn Sweden Tour (October 25 – 29); Autumn UK Tour II (November 1 – December 14), and the Beatles' Christmas Shows in London (December 21 – 31). All together, the band played more than 230 dates in 1963 (often with multiple concerts per day), the same year they released their first number one single and cut their first two albums, *Please Please Me* and *With the Beatles*. Apparently all those long hours and late nights playing in Hamburg had given the band the stamina of Olympians.

By November, the band was no longer sharing billing with anyone. The tour was simply booked as "The Beatles' Show."

The Beatles had become used to touring—hitting small clubs, dance halls, or auditoriums. But as the year progressed and they found themselves booked into much larger venues, something changed. The crowds were now predominately very young girls who screamed and writhed in their seats; some even swooned. When the Beatles played in Sweden, the press wrote: "A couple of Swedish girls who had worked as au pair in England knew how to behave at a pop concert. They yelled, 'We want the Beatles! We want the Beatles!'"

The band actually had an entourage now: road manager and personal assistant Mal Evans—a former doorman at the Cavern—who was also their unofficial bodyguard; and Neil Aspinall, a friend from Liverpool who in sequence became their driver, road manager, personal assistant, and eventually the manager of Apple Corps.

ROYAL COMMAND PERFORMANCE

On November 4, 1963, the Beatles performed at the Prince of Wales Theatre in a command performance for the Queen Mother and Princess Margaret, Queen Elizabeth's mother and younger sister, respectively. There were a total of 19 acts on the bill that night, but everyone agreed that the Beatles were the top draw. They came on seventh and began playing "From Me to You" even before the curtains opened, then shifted their mikes up front, near the edge of the stage. They next performed "She Loves You," and "Till There Was You" (the money shot for all Paul's swooning teenage fans). Then, just before the band launched into "Twist and Shout," John famously asked those in the cheaper seats to clap their hands. "And the rest of you, if you'd just rattle your jewelry," he added. (Epstein had several times cautioned John not to say "your fookin' jewelry.") The press instantly snatched up the remark—another prime example of the Beatles' waggish charm.

FROLICKING AT THE CHRISTMAS SHOW

The Beatles brought 1963 to a close in typical bang-up fashion with a cheerfully zany holiday show. The brainchild of Brian Epstein, the concert was meant to showcase the talent he represented as well as other popular artists, with a grand finale by the jewels in his crown, the Fab Four. That first year the roster included Barron Knights and Duke D'mond, Tommy Quickly, Billy J. Kramer and the Dakotas, Cilla Black, and Rolf Harris. It was held at the lavish, Moorish-style Astoria Theatre in Finsbury Park, London. (Renamed the Rainbow in 1971, it remained a major venue for superstar pop concerts until 1981.)

In between the supporting acts, the Beatles would perform short comedy sketches in an amateurish but endearing—and slightly bizarre—manner. As Tony Barrow, the show's director explained, "The Beatles were never much for rehearsing. That never really mattered as far as songs were concerned, but the fact that they were so bad at doing the sketches was an added extra for the show—it was organized chaos but it was very funny chaos."

From all reports, fans in the audience didn't mind the Beatles' gaffes or their leaden acting, they just kept cheering them on. The production was so well received that the Beatles reprised the show the following year.

"For worried adults we can tell that the first sign that there's a Beatle in the house is that the son is letting the hair grow and spends hours in front of the mirror to get it right."

EXPRESSEN, 1963, Swedish newspaper

Opposite, far left: George and John wait in their dressing room prior to an appearance on Swedish TV in Stockholm, October 1963.

Opposite, right: Queen Elizabeth, the Queen Mother, greets the Beatles after The Royal Variety Show at the Prince of Wales Theatre, London, November 4, 1963.

Above: The Beatles display their comedy antics during the Beatles Christmas Show at the Astoria Finsbury Park, London, on New Year's Eve, 1963.

POP GOES THE BEATLES

In the midst of all this touring, the Beatles also had their own radio show called "Pop Goes the Beatles," which debuted in May 1963. The format was simple—the Beatles played six or seven songs live, bantered with host Lee Peters, and then welcomed a guest artist or band, often mates from Liverpool, like the Searchers or the Hollies. Perhaps the most interesting aspect of the show was that the Beatles performed a wide variety of cover songs, including many by artists that had influenced their own music—Chuck Berry, Carl Perkins, Smokey Robinson, Arthur Alexander, Leiber and Stoller, and Goffin and King.

MERCHANDISING THE MERSEY BEAT

"I've got a business background and probably a reasonable business brain. But I'm no sort of genius."

BRIAN EPSTEIN, 1964 BBC Interview

At times, Brian Epstein's handling of the Beatles' business interests seemed akin to a man stumbling over a pot of gold in the woods and being so taken with the appearance of the pot that he dumped out the gold and simply took the pot home. When Epstein's startling lack of business acumen came to light some years after his death, even the Beatles were shocked. In spite of all the good Brian did for the band, some of the blunders he made were so mind numbing they almost canceled out the positives.

Epstein was the first to admit he had no experience in the music industry as a manager or agent. Yet he took on this dual role with a novice band and apparently never thought to ask anyone in the know for insight or advice. (The one exception being his father, who, to quote Paul, "knew how to run a furniture store.") In light of the Beatles' subsequent massive popularity, it's permissible to think none of his bungling mattered, that they were on the fast track to riches no matter what . . . but the truth is, Brian had set himself up as their driving wheel, often boasting that if he hadn't come along, they would have been quite happy to remain poor and obscure. So, yes, they might have owed him for their fame and success, but in return, he owed them his managerial vigilance.

One of Brian's earliest lapses as a manager involved *The Ed Sullivan Show.* When Colonel Tom Parker booked Elvis Presley on the show in 1956, the foxy old negotiator received a reported $50,000 for three appearances. When Brian booked the Beatles seven years later, he accepted $3,500 per appearance for the whole group. It was like they saw him coming. In this and other negotiations he either didn't do his homework, checking the going rate with other artists, for instance, or he naively trusted that people would be square with him–never a good idea in any business endeavor, let alone in the cutthroat entertainment industry. He might just as well have driven down Oxford Street tossing thousand-pound notes out the window.

Perhaps Brian's worst gaffe as a manager occurred in 1963. As Beatlemania continued to spread, NEMS received increasing requests for the Beatles to endorse products or to lend their names and faces to novelty items. Just prior to the first American tour, Brian finally realized something had to be done. He asked his attorney, celebrity lawyer David Jacobs, to find someone to handle the matter. Jacobs recruited an acquaintance, a Chelsea socialite named Nicky Byrne, to take over the merchandising aspects of NEMS. Byrne agreed to work with Brian but insisted on a 90 percent commission, meaning that the remaining 10 percent of receipts would be split between NEMS, Epstein, and the four Beatles. Epstein, who had no concept of the moneymaking potential

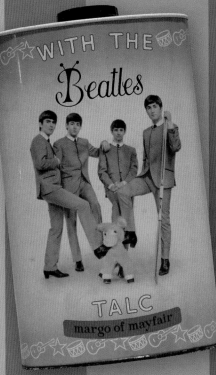

WITH THE Beatles

TALC

margo of mayfair

The Beatles

pencil by number COLOURING SET

PAUL

JOHN

GEORGE

RINGO

Kitfix HOBBY'S LTD

5 NUMBERED READY TO COLOUR PORTRAITS OF JOHN, PAUL, GEORGE, RINGO AND THE GROUP
6 BRILLIANT COLOURED PENCILS

NO PAINTS · NO WATER · NO MESS · ITS SO EASY!

Harrison

WED

MAR

1 7

make a date with the Beatles

JOHN LENNON

GEORGE HARRISON

PAUL McCARTNEY

RINGO STARR

WOW! the BEATLES ARE HERE!

the only AUTHENTIC BEATLE WIG©

Fits All Head Sizes

Mfd. By LOWELL TOY MFG. CORP., BRONX 56, N.Y.

MADE IN U.S.A.

I LOVE PAUL

I'm a

OFFICIAL BEATLES FAN

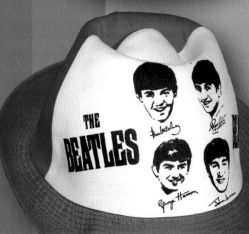

"We did our best; some people have said it wasn't good enough. That's easy to say with 20/20 hindsight but remember that there were no rules. We were making it up as we went along."

ALISTAIR TAYLOR, Brian Epstein's assistant

for brand merchandising on both sides of the Atlantic— once again, he hadn't learned from the Elvis Empire— accepted Byrne's terms. (It has been suggested that Byrne wrote in the 90 percent figure as a joke, knowing Epstein would bargain him down, but Brian simply signed the contract and returned it.) Unfortunately once Brian got to America, and was barraged with endless requests for merchandising and licensing deals, he realized he'd virtually given away the golden goose. He knew he could never reveal this mistake to the Beatles.

Meanwhile, Byrne took over Stramsact in England and set up Selteab (Beatles spelled backwards) in the United States to handle all merchandising and licensing matters. Frenzied retailers began selling everything from Beatles' board games, dolls, clothing, and lunchboxes to clocks, pens, egg cups, bubble gum, and wigs. Perhaps the oddest products were sealed cans labeled "Beatle Breath."

While Brian did renegotiate with Byrne for a 49 percent cut in 1964, he and Byrne became involved in a series of lawsuits and countersuits—Brian sued Byrne over improper accounting, one of Byrne's partners sued him over his extravagant spending, Byrne sued Epstein for damages—all of which took three years to clear up. In the meantime, major retailers canceled orders for millions of dollars in merchandise. It has been estimated these court cases ended up losing the Beatles more than one hundred million dollars in merchandising revenue.

Those early mementos of Beatlemania now fetch top dollar at flea markets, swap meets, on Ebay and at Beatles expos. Many of those kids who grew up with the Beatles lament that at some point they—or their mother—threw out that Beatles lunchbox or that complete set of collector's cards or those four moptop bobbleheads that might be worth a small fortune today.

CHAPTER SEVEN

AMERICA

"The Beatles came to an America that was just peppered with pain."

LUCY BAINES JOHNSON, daughter of President Lyndon Baines Johnson

Above: This famous footage of the Kennedy assassination filmed by eyewitness Abraham Zapruder, shows Jackie Kennedy reaching for the president as he slumps in his seat.

Left: On his third birthday, President Kennedy's son, John Jr., salutes as his father's casket leaves St. Matthew's Cathedral on its way to Arlington Cemetery.

Previous pages: As the Beatles and their entourage descend the steps of Pan Am flight 101 at John F. Kennedy Airport, they greet the screaming fans waiting for them on the observation deck.

Left: West Coast surf music began with twangy instrumentals and gradually evolved into sung ballads and dance songs. The Surfaris, pictured, scored a memorable sixties hit with "Wipe Out."

While America might have bounced back more rapidly than England after World War II and spent much of the 1950s enjoying the fruits of capitalism, during the early 1960s a number of events had damaged the national morale, one of them profoundly. That, of course, was the assassination of young, vibrant, progressive President John F. Kennedy on November 22, 1963. The country was still reeling from the shock as his successor, Lyndon Baines Johnson, took over the reins of the government. The country was also in slow recovery from the worldwide recession of 1958, which raised U.S. unemployment and decimated Detroit, where auto sales fell more than 30 percent.

On the music front, the ebullience of the 1950s, with the hectic rise of rock and roll and the subsequent burgeoning of a teen-centric culture, was fading. Pop music had earlier suffered its own tragedy—the August 1959 plane crash that took the lives of Buddy Holly and the Crickets, Ritchie Valens, and the Big Bopper (J. P. Richardson). Meanwhile, Elvis Presley had left the army a lesser idol; he was now married, and focused on making vapid Hollywood films. Little Richard had found the Holy Spirit

and became a minister, whereas, Jerrry Lee Lewis found a different sort of affirmation and married his 13-year-old cousin. Both were now musical nonstarters.

SURFIN' SAFARIS

The early 1960s did see a new musical genre emerge in America, the Southern California surf sound. Surfing, the Polynesian sport of riding a long, narrow board into shore on the crest of a wave, was growing in popularity throughout the Pacific region from Hawaii to Australia to the beaches of the West Coast. It was natural that musicians would try to emulate the speed, rise, and curl of the really big waves. And so what early proponents called a "wet" sound began to take form, first as an instrumental craze—with hits like "Miserlou" from Dick Dale and the Del-tones (incorporating Arabic and Mexican music into their distinctive sound); the Ventures's "Walk Don't Run"; the Chantays "Pipeline"; and the Surfaris immortal "Wipeout"— that then evolved into surfer-based songs: crooned ballads and up-tempo dance numbers exemplified by the lively guitar work and close harmonies of the Beach Boys and Jan and Dean.

But on the pure rock and roll front, little seemed to be happening. Easy listening had again taken hold of the hit parade, with bandleader Lawrence Welk, the folksinging Highwaymen, piano schlockmeisters Ferrante and Teicher, and country singer Patsy Cline all in Billboard's Top 20 for 1961.

In 1962, it was even worse. Despite the presence of Chubby Checker's "The Twist," Dee-Dee Sharp's "Mashed Potato Time," the Shirelles "Soldier Boy," and Little Eva's "The Loco-Motion" in the year's Top 10, the list also featured Mr. Acker Bilk's tepid "Stranger on the Shore," Bobby Vinton's saccharine "Roses Are Red," and, an unlikely hit, bandleader David Rose's novelty instrumental, "The Stripper." The country's music scene was badly in need of some new energy, something to refuel its enthusiasm and get the teens reinvested in the essence of rock and roll.

America didn't know it yet, but the answer was biding its time on the other side of the Atlantic Ocean, awaiting a proper invitation.

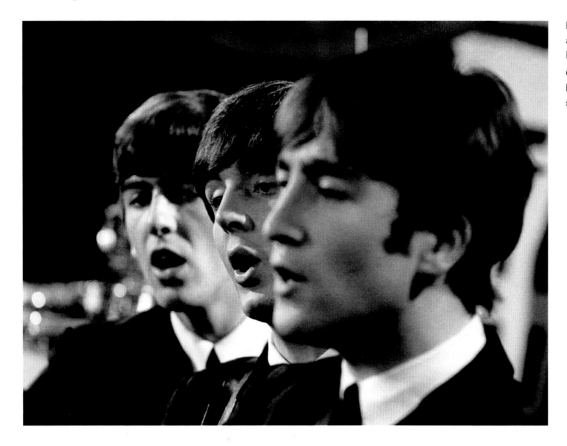

Left: George, Paul, and John perform a three-part harmony to "This Boy" on British TV.

Opposite: The Beatles, in their Dougie Millings suits, recording another British TV show in the fall of 1963.

"THEY WERE DOING THINGS NOBODY WAS DOING. THEIR CHORDS WERE OUTRAGEOUS, JUST OUTRAGEOUS, AND THEIR HARMONIES MADE IT ALL VALID."

BOB DYLAN, *BOB DYLAN* (1973) ANTHONY SCADUTO

Brian Epstein always believed the Beatles would be big in America. Yet for some reason, their British hits didn't go anywhere in that country. In retrospect, this was mainly due to a complete lack of interest by Capitol and poor distribution by Epstein's backup labels, Vee Jay and Swan.

The Beatles next two singles—after "Love Me Do" and "Please Please Me"— were "From Me to You" (released April 12, 1963) and "She Loves You" (released August 23). Both were major hits in England, with the former spending six weeks at number one, alongside the album *With the Beatles,* and the latter song becoming a musical juggernaut that climbed to the

top spot not once but twice. But, again, there wasn't a peep of interest from Capitol in America.

Finally, in November 1963, Brian took Billy J. Kramer and flew to the States to do some promoting and also to take a reading on the mindset of the American rock and roll fan. When Brian returned to London, he told the Beatles he thought the reason for the lackluster response in the United States was because they hadn't yet recorded anything that was right for that market. But he'd listened to a lot of American music while there and now believed that "I Want to Hold Your Hand," which was just about to drop, could be the right song.

As it turned out, he was spot on. While the single, with British advance orders of more than one million, initially only hit number two in England—blocked from the top spot for two weeks by a resurgent "She Loves You"—the real victory was that the record ended up flying off the shelves in America. The stimulus for this surge was that Marsha Albert, a teen from Silver Spring, Maryland, had seen a CBS News piece about the Beatles on Walter Cronkite and contacted DJ Carroll James of WWDC about playing their music. He had a friend send him a copy of the new single from England and after he played it, the station was barraged with approving calls. Before long DJs in Chicago,

and St. Louis were also playing the disc, anticipating the January U.S. release date by weeks.

At first Capitol ordered the radio stations to "cease and desist," but the DJs argued that the record was a smash and could not be contained. Capitol, with its brain finally in the correct and upright position, was forced to acknowledge the Beatles phenomenon, but then realized the 200,00 copies of the record they had allotted for release were not nearly enough. They immediately ordered thousands more, devoting all the machines in two plants to pressing the single. They also moved up the release date to the day after

Christmas, December 26, 1963.

Within three days, a quarter of a millions copies had sold. In New York City, 10,000 copies an hour were streaming out of the stores. The single debuted on the American charts at number forty-five on January 18, 1964, then streaked upward to hit number one on February 1. It remained in that position for seven weeks until it was replaced by, no surprise, "She Loves You."

The Beatles had finally broken into the elusive American market. Even better, now that American listeners began to crave their distinctive, driving music and unique vocal harmonies, the floodgates opened and the band's backlist of British

recordings came pouring into the States. It was a deluge. By April 4 of that year, the Beatles had a firm hold on the top five spots on the Hot 100 chart—with "Can't Buy Me Love," "Twist and Shout," "She Loves You," "I Want to Hold Your Hand," and "Please Please Me"—an industry feat that is unlikely to ever be replicated.

These positive developments—specifically with "I Want to Hold Your Hand"—in late 1963 and early 1964 assured Brian that he had made the right choice for his boys during his fact-finding trip to America—by arranging both a short tour and a major TV appearance for them in February 1964.

"THEY WERE YOUNG GUYS ... THRILLED AT THE RECEPTION GIVEN TO THEM ... AND I GOT THE IMPRESSION THAT THESE ARE LIVERPOOL BOYS, AND THAT IS WHAT THEY'LL ALWAYS BE. ... THEY WERE ALWAYS THE GUYS NEXT DOOR."

SID BERNSTEIN, CONCERT PROMOTER

Top: Promoter Sid Bernstein, who first booked the Beatles into Carnegie Hall and Shea Stadium, eventually became the patron saint of stadium rock.

Above: Carnegie Hall, on 7th Avenue in Manhattan, was best known as a showcase for classical music.

While working as a concert promoter for General Artists Corporation, New Yorker Sid Bernstein kept reading about the Beatles' increasing popularity in England (as a fighter pilot during World War II he'd been stationed in England and grew to love the country). Without hearing a note of their music, Sid decided he wanted to bring them to America. His colleagues thought he was crazy, insisting the Beatles were strictly a local fad. Undeterred, in the spring of 1963, Sid called Brian Epstein at home in Liverpool and told him he wanted to offer the band an American concert tour. "Where?" Brian shot back. Bernstein recalls being nonplussed by the man's directness. Sid then simply named his favorite concert space in his hometown—"Carnegie Hall." Brian took his time deciding, but finally agreed, insisting only that the tour be delayed until 1964, when, he hoped, the band would have broken into the American pop music charts. (Some sources cite that Bernstein did not talk to Brian until November of that year, but Bernstein himself, in numerous interviews before his death in 2013, insisted the initial call was made that spring.)

Bernstein booked two concerts at the venerable music hall for February 12, Lincoln's birthday.

Meanwhile, Brian grappled with the stubborn execs at Capitol Records and got them to agree to release "I Want to Hold Your Hand" in America in mid January (due to fan demand, the release was later moved up to late December). He further convinced them to spend $40,000 to promote the group and their first Capitol album, *Meet the Beatles.* As a result of this publicity—and constant airplay—both Carnegie Hall shows sold out.

Bernstein, who is credited as one of the forces behind the British invasion, would also bring over the Rolling Stones, the Moody Blues, the Kinks, and Herman's Hermits. He would gain additional fame for becoming the first promoter to book rock bands into outdoor sports stadiums.

THE TOAST OF THE TOWN

While passing through Heathrow Airport in the fall of 1963, TV variety show host and entertainment columnist Ed Sullivan witnessed a large crowd of enthusiastic teenage girls greeting four shaggy-haired young men. He quickly discovered the boys were a rock and roll group called the Beatles, coming home from a tour of Sweden. Sullivan, who had helped bring teen idol Elvis Presley to prominence, immediately recognized the "Presley effect" in those frenzied fans. He mentioned the group to his associates, one of whom was London theatrical agent, Peter Pritchard. When the Beatles scored a major success at the London Variety Show, performing before the royal family, Pritchard contacted Brian Epstein. He told him of Ed Sullivan's earlier interest and suggested Brian should meet with the TV host while he was in America the following month.

"**I made up my mind that this was the same sort of mass hit hysteria that had characterized the Elvis Presley days.**"

ED SULLIVAN

Pritchard then set about wooing Sullivan into hiring the Beatles, calling them, "the first long-haired boys invited to appear before the queen." Sullivan apparently called Cronkite, who had done the short TV segment on them, asking about that "English bug group." Cronkite must have said good things, because by the time Brian met the impresario, Sullivan was prepared to offer the band one appearance on his Sunday night TV show and a remote broadcast from Miami. Epstein, hungry for media exposure in America, agreed, but insisted on top billing and the opening and closing spots on both shows. (A third taped performance was later added to the deal.) Sullivan agreed to Brian's requests, no doubt trusting in his own proven ability to target the latest trends.

Epstein must have been exultant as he flew back to London. He managed what was arguably the best live band in the business and now not only would American fans get to see them perform in concert, but also millions of viewers would be able to watch them on one of the most popular TV shows in the country.

Meanwhile, the Beatles were booked for a three-week Parisian tour in early 1964 at L'Olympia Theatre. Even though these concerts had sold out, the Beatles felt a sense of disappointment once the performances began . . . their audience, for a change, was mainly composed of young men who had come to hear the popular "Yeah-Yeahs." George later admitted sheepishly, "We really missed all the girls yelling."

Above: TV variety show host Ed Sullivan had an eye for new talent and put many acts on the map.

"THE WORLD USED US AS AN EXCUSE TO GO MAD."

GEORGE HARRISON

The Beatles landed at JFK Airport on February 7, still unsure of the welcome they'd receive in the States. After all, America was unknown territory for them, a huge country offering lots of musical competition. Cynthia Lennon recalled the group waiting inside the plane after they'd landed, hearing this loud keening noise outside. They all assumed it was a nearby jet readying for takeoff. But, no, what they were hearing were the screams of more than 4,000 Beatles' fans atop the terminal's observation deck.

The band could not know that in the weeks preceding their visit, the local DJs had been promoting the tour with the slogan, "The Beatles Are Coming!" and playing their records almost nonstop. The astonishment the boys displayed as they came down the steps from the Pan Am plane to the tarmac and beheld their legion of fans was palpably genuine.

When Ed Sullivan finally greeted the Beatles in person, he was surely congratulating himself on his flawless timing. By February 9, 1964, the night of the group's TV debut, "I Want to Hold Your Hand" had hit number one, and Beatlemania, with assistance from an eager press, was already spreading from coast to coast. By the time the band took their places on stage, a record 73-million viewers—toddlers, school children, teens, adults, and seniors—had tuned in to watch this longhaired phenomenon from England. It was the largest viewing audience in television history up to that point.

The Beatles did not disappoint, providing two brisk, engaging sets that featured "All My Loving," "Till There Was You," and "She Loves You," followed by "I Saw Her Standing There," and "I Want to Hold Your Hand."

Their appeal was augmented by camerawork that showcased the band as a whole and individually, notably in the close-ups during "Till There Was You," when the Beatles' first names flashed beneath their faces. (John's caption read "Sorry girls, he's married.") The film crew's seamless stream of long shots, close-ups, crowd shots and a move in-and-out view of Ringo taken by a crane camera was especially impressive considering the cameramen couldn't hear the director's instructions over the noise of the fans. By the end of the show—an unquestioned milestone in pop music history—the Beatles had conquered America.

It was now "all Beatles, all the time" on New York AM radio; brash disc jockey Murray the K—who brought John, Paul, and Ringo to the Playboy Club to celebrate after *The Ed Sullivan Show*—soon crowned himself the Fifth Beatle; and thousands of female fans continued to surround the Plaza Hotel, where the boys were staying, requiring the police to bring in mounted patrols and set up barricades.

CARNEGIE HALL

Two days after their smash debut on *The Ed Sullivan Show*, the

"AMERICA: IT'S LIKE BRITAIN, ONLY WITH BUTTONS."
RINGO STARR

Beatles took a train to Washington, DC, for their first official concert in America at the Washington Coliseum. They then went on to play two concerts at Carnegie Hall on February 12. By all reports the band was in great form, but the two 35-minute concerts were neither filmed nor recorded. In retrospect, this seems almost criminal, but Brian apparently didn't have time to work out the details for filming with the various backstage unions.

After their triumph at Carnegie Hall, the Beatles flew to Florida for some rest and relaxation. They would be filming another episode of *The Ed Sullivan Show* while there, but they also took some time off to tour Miami, including a stop at the famous 5th St. Gym to visit heavyweight boxing contender Cassius Clay, who would later reign in the ring as Muhammad Ali. The resulting press photos show five very playful young legends hamming it up for the cameras.

Right: The Beatles joke around with heavyweight boxing contender Cassius Clay (later Muhammad Ali) at his Miami training center, February 18, 1964.

Opposite, left: Exhilarated fans, part of a crowd of 4,000, wave from the observation deck at John F. Kennedy Airport as the Beatles arrive in New York.

Opposite, right: Cynthia Lennon recalled that inside the plane passengers could hear high-pitched squeals outside and assumed it was a nearby jet.

Above, left: New York DJ, Murray the K, allied himself with the Beatles and the British Invasion groups.

Above, right: The conquering heroes perform before 74 million viewers.

Right: The Beatles perform at Carnegie Hall on February 12, 1964.

Ed Sullivan tries to calm the audience of screaming girls as the Beatles appear bemused by the clamor.

"THEY GAVE THEIR MONEY AND THEY GAVE THEIR SCREAMS, BUT THE BEATLES KIND OF GAVE THEIR NERVOUS SYSTEMS."

GEORGE HARRISON, 1995, ON BEATLEMANIA

Above: When the Beatles returned to New York later that year during their U.S. summer tour, the welcome was the same. Here, screaming fans wait outside the Delmonico Hotel hoping to see the Beatles.

Opposite: Police restrain Beatles' fans at Kennedy Airport on their first visit to the United States on February 7, 1964.

When the customers at the Kaiserkeller or the Indra Club in Hamburg shouted for the "Peedles," it was considered normal encouragement. When the girls and boys at the Cavern Club screamed for the Beatles, it was simply acknowledgment from the hometown crowd. But along the way, as the Beatles popularity increased and the venues—and audiences—grew larger, the fans started to become frighteningly out of control: shrieking, moaning, writhing in their seats,

collapsing in tears, and running for the stage or mobbing their idols outside the concert halls.

The term that came to describe this phenomenon first appeared in October 1963. After the Beatles's headline performance on *Val Parnell's Sunday Night at the London Palladium* on October 13, manic fans swamped the band both inside and outside the theater. After TV reporters took note of this mob scene and reported about the hysteria on the nightly news, London's *Daily Mirror* coined the term "Beatlemania" to describe the crowd's frantic behavior.

It was not exactly a new development for the celebrity-loving public, this extreme reaction to artists. During the debut of Ravel's "Bolero" in 1928, the crowd stamped and cheered, while a woman stood up and screamed, "The madman! The madman!" (To which Ravel later responded, "She understands.") Matinee idol Rudolph Valentino caused women to swoon in movie theaters, while crooners like Rudee Vallee and Bing Crosby once held women transfixed.

Yet this all paled when compared to the effect big band singer Frank Sinatra had on his bobby-soxer fans, who wept helplessly and shrieked for "Frankie!" By some reports, the earliest of these overwrought Sinatra fans were audience plants, but the thousands of clamoring girls who followed were not. Elvis Presley continued the tradition, playing, even into podgy middle age, to arenas full of sobbing women. Those über lounge singers Tom Jones and Englebert

Humperdinck likewise became targets for matronly stage-rushers and panty-tossers. The concept had become so widespread, that the composers of Broadway's *Bye Bye Birdie* created a show-stopper, "You Gotta Be Sincere," around the idea of females swooning helplessly when the sexy Presley-clone curled his lip or thrust his hips their way.

NEW HEIGHTS OF HYSTERIA

But in spite of over-the-top reactions to the heartthrobs of the past, the world had never seen anything like Beatlemania. During most concerts, the fans appeared to be afflicted: they leapt about, tore at their hair, fell dazed to the ground, and even lost control of their bladders. The security staff often had to link arms to prevent besotted girls from hurtling onto the stage like crazed long-jumpers. Worst yet, the fans no longer confined themselves to the concert hall or theater; they gathered in surging mobs on the streets and in squares outsides hotels or stations or anywhere a Beatle sighting might take place. They thought nothing of chasing their idols down the streets and assaulting them en masse—to filch a bit of clothing or yank out a lock of hair. When Paul McCartney innocently mentioned during an interview that the band liked jelly babies (jelly beans), the whole band was subsequently pelted with them, almost viciously, for months.

Both the British and American press corps bear some responsibility for fostering this mass hysteria. Without their hyperbolic headlines and slavish devotion to the least detail of

the Beatles' lives, it is doubtful whether the fan adulation would have run so hot or so high. And naturally, the more frenzied Beatlemania grew, the more the press encouraged it, creating a vicious cycle that constantly fed the growing beast.

Ironically, Beatlemania, which had launched the band into breathtaking orbit, was also very much at the root of the band's decision to stop touring. For one thing, the music suffered. The fans' screams so overwhelmed the Beatles's feeble amps in concert that the guitarists could not hear themselves play or sing . . . and Ringo had to watch his bandmates' swaying backsides to keep time. And if the audience couldn't hear the music, why was the band even up there? The group also began to worry about their safety off stage; rowdy crowds sometimes broke through police lines outside theaters, and fans occasionally sneaked into their private suites in hotels. John, specifically, had a fear of being shot while on stage, especially after he made an ill-advised comment about Jesus in an interview and earned the ire of the American Bible belt.

LEGENDARY BILLBOARD STATISTICS

The Beatles can claim the most number one singles of any artist on the Billboard Hot 100 chart with 20. Paul McCartney is credited with the most number one hits (as a songwriter) on the Hot 100—32. George Martin, the Beatles' producer, remains at the top of the list of record producers with the most number one hits—23. The band is also fifth in most Hot 100 entries—72, third in most Top 40 hits—51, third in most Top 10 singles—29, third in most cumulative weeks at number one—59, and second in most consecutive number one hits from 1964 to 1966—6. On April 4, 1964, the Beatles had five songs on the Hot 100 chart, commanding the top five positions.

It's hard not to wince while watching the American press interviewing the Beatles during their first tour there in 1964. The questions are arch and patronizing, and the reporters treat the Beatles as oddities, specimens under the microscope, rather than bona fide entertainers: "Which of you are bald under those wigs?" "What will you do with your lives when this bubble bursts?" "Do you ever get a haircut?" (To which George replied, truthfully, "I had one yesterday.")

Fortunately, the Beatles had already faced a barrage of similarly inane, hair-obsessed questions from the British and European press, and, like the clever autodidacts they were (and with some coaching from Brian) they had developed a number of snappy, yet charming, answers which they now fired back at the American press corps.

"I CAN'T DEAL WITH THE PRESS; I HATE ALL THOSE BEATLES QUESTIONS."
PAUL McCARTNEY

Reporter: "What do you call that haircut?"

Ringo: "Arthur."

Reporter: "How do you find America?"

John: "Turn left at Greenland."

Reporter: "Are you mods or rockers?"

Paul: "We're mockers."

Reporter: "Are you wearing wigs or real hair?"

George: "Our hair's real. What about yours, lady?"

Still, as a result of these attempts to belittle the band, the American press corps came across as mean-spirited, sour, and painfully dated, while the Beatles came across as good sports, witty, and totally hip. Anyone under fifty watching these press conferences was bound to take sides with the British foursome (and wonder why the newspapers and networks were sending these crotchety old fogeys to interview them).

In retrospect, this was the "establishment" trying to rebuff—or demean—the last onslaught of the youth culture, the teen-centric shift that had started in the 1950s with young celebrities like Marlon Brando, James Dean, and Elvis Presley. The Beatles were simply the final nail in the coffin of the adult-based society that had been setting the tone in entertainment, fashion, and a slew of other arenas. There was a new boss in town now.

At least the press gave up gracefully, each reporter or interviewer in turn succumbing to the Beatles' brand of prebaked blarney, delivered as it was with those "adorable" Liverpool accents. The Beatles were soon barraged with requests for live appearances from DJs at major radio stations and from popular TV talk show hosts like Mike Douglas and Dick Cavett, who actually treated the band members with respect and displayed an earnest curiosity about their music and their lives.

Opposite, top: Fresh off the plane, the Beatles are barraged with banal questions from the American press. Fortunately, they were prepared, having already fielded a similar assault in Britain and Europe.

Opposite, below: At another press conference, New York photographer Tony Ray-Jones captured this picture of pop art icon Andy Warhol mingling among the pressmen interviewing the Beatles.

Above: Ed Sullivan examines Paul's Hofner bass, as Brian Epstein looks on. Sullivan helped to popularize the band and their music in the United States.

MISSING PIECES

Brian Epstein had a tremendous instinctive "feel" for the course the Beatles should take in their careers. He never pushed them until he felt the timing was right, and let them make most of their own choices when it came to songs and arrangements. But as their manager/agent, he overlooked one key thing. He forgot about documenting their evolution as a band. Sure, he probably reasoned, if they caught on, their records would always be around . . . but for a man who predicted they would be bigger than Elvis, Brian captured very little of what they created in a permanent medium.

In spite of their ongoing success at the Cavern, only one muddy clip exists of them performing there. Did Brian never think to bring a movie camera along whenever he went there to watch them? After all, he ran a store with a large electronics department. While there are plenty of filmed interviews and press conferences with the band after they became famous, it would have been much more intimate and informative to see the world from their perspective as they made that journey.

It is interesting to note that both of Richard Lester's films, where the Fabs play themselves and not some Hollywood version of a pop star, attempt to do this very thing—show the band trying to cope with their increasing fame—as if filling an unspoken, but very keenly felt, need. The Lindsay-Hogg documentary *Let It Be* goes one step further and furnishes fans with an uncomfortable front row seat during the Beatles' difficult final days.

The British Invasion Unleashed

"THE BRITISH INVASION THIS TIME GOES BY THE CODE NAME BEATLEMANIA."
CBS EVENING NEWS, FEBRUARY 7, 1964

Top, left: The Beatles board the plane at Heathrow for their historic first visit to the United States on February 7, 1964.

Top, right: The Beatles' rivals the Rolling Stones got their big break with a Lennon–McCartney song, "I Wanna Be Your Man."

Above: The Kinks, a quintessentially English band, were part of the original British Invasion, though their antics led to them being banned from visiting the United States for two years.

Opposite, top: The Who, the favorite band of the British mods, evolved into one of the top rock bands in the world—especially after their appearance at the Woodstock Music and Art Fair in 1969.

Just as Brian Epstein had eagerly sought out other artists from Liverpool after signing the Beatles, the American public wanted more, more, more of that British beat after the Fab Four landed—and their pleas were answered when dozens of English groups came bounding across the pond. This "British invasion"—aided and abetted by the prescient Sid Bernstein—introduced America to powerhouse groups like the Rolling Stones, the Kinks, and the Moody Blues, and singer/songwriters like Donovan, who are still composing today. A "second" invasion included the Who, the Zombies, and the Hollies, as well as Cream and the Yardbirds, the latter incorporating a more blues-oriented sound.

The song charts quickly reflected this incursion, and soulful songstress Dusty Springfield was the first Brit to score after the Beatles with "I Only Want to Be With You." In May 1965, every spot in the Hot 100's Top 10 save #2, which went to Gary Lewis and the Playboys' "Count Me In," was held by a British artist. That same year 13 of the 26 songs that hit number one were by British performers, including 1964's "I Feel Fine," by the Beatles. (These same groups were also dominating the airwaves back home in England.) Australia refused to be left out and supplied America with the Seekers, who had two Billboard hits, "I'll Never Find Another You," and Georgy Girl" and the Easybeats, who charted with "Friday on My Mind."

Meanwhile, teen magazines made up feuds between various groups, and the Beatles were often pitted against the Rolling Stones or the Dave Clark Five, while duos like Peter and Gordon would go head to head with Chad and Jeremy in polls.

By the mid 1960s, the demand in America was for everything English, their music, their fashions . . . and even the British flag, the Union Jack, became a beloved motif that could be found on handbags, hats, scarves, wall posters, and even the roofs or door panels of sports cars.

Left: One of the Invasion's few female artists, Dusty Springfield brought her own unique skills to the romantic ballad.

Above: The Animals were another immensely popular British group that mixed rock and blues. Earthy lead singer Eric Burdon (with policeman's hat) guaranteed his rock immortality by growling out their first monster hit, "House of the Rising Sun."

The British Invasion Unleashed

> ## "THE BRITISH INVASION WAS THE MOST IMPORTANT EVENT OF MY LIFE. I WAS IN NEW JERSEY AND THE NIGHT I SAW THE BEATLES CHANGED EVERYTHING."
> STEVEN VAN ZANDT, E Street Band

The British Invasion didn't occur in a vacuum; it went on to internationalize popular music production and opened the minds of many record executives, paving the way for folk rock, roots rock, country rock, glam rock, prog rock, heavy metal, hair bands, world music, ska, reggae, punk, and the garage band movement. It also pushed the counterculture into the mainstream and cemented the influence of the youth culture on America, England, and much of the industrialized world.

Critics complained that the British Invasion destroyed American music trends like the surf sound and the twist, and hurt black and female performers, but Motown, including many girls groups, was as popular as ever at this time, while the blues and folk movement saw the rise of female singers Janis Joplin, Joan Baez, Judy Collins, Buffy St. Marie, Joni Mitchell, and Janis Ian.

By the late 1960s, America had risen up and responded to the British challenge with the drug-fueled sounds of West Coast psychedelic rock—the Doors, Jefferson Airplane, the Grateful Dead, Iron Butterfly, Country Joe and the Fish; folk rock—the Byrds, the New Riders of the Purple Sage, and Poco; avant-guarde artists— Frank Zappa and the Mothers of Invention and Captain Beefheart.

The whole kaleidoscopic decade was capped off in 1969 by an American version of the 14 Hour Technicolor Dream— "3 Days of Peace and Music" known as The Woodstock Music and Art Fair.

During the next decade, rock music would evolve into a genre without national boundaries, with a number of groups boasting members from several countries—the British Fleetwood Mac welcoming American artists Stevie Nicks and Lindsey Buckingham being a case in point.

Above: The Irish band Them, featuring Van Morrison (second from right) had a hit single with "Gloria."

Below, left: Australian folk band the Seekers— featuring female lead singer Judith Durham—had two U.S. hits: "I'll Never Find Another You" and the title song from the movie *Georgy Girl*.

Below, right: Scottish folk singer Donovan was initially hailed as Britain's answer to Bob Dylan, but he soon set himself apart with his mystic, earth-child persona and whispery vibrato.

Opposite, top left: The Easybeats were another Australian group who made it on the British scene before becoming part of the British Invasion.

Opposite, far right: The early lineup of the Moody Blues included Denny Laine (center), later of Wings.

Opposite, center: Billy J. Kramer and the Dakotas.

Opposite, bottom left: Peter and Gordon had a string of top 40 hits—most of them written by Peter's former attic mate Paul McCartney.

Opposite, bottom right: The Zombies appear on Murray the K's show.

CHAPTER EIGHT

ON THE SILVER SCREEN

"A COMIC FANTASIA WITH MUSIC; AN ENORMOUS COMMERCIAL SUCCESS WITH THE DIRECTOR TRYING EVERY CINEMATIC GAG IN THE BOOK."
LESLIE HALLIWELL, BRITISH FILM CRITIC

In post-war America, Hollywood became the refuge of chart-topping singers who had few musical worlds left to conquer, by offering them fresh challenges and new audiences. Bing Crosby, Frank Sinatra, Doris Day, Rosemary Clooney, and Elvis Presley all went on to successful careers in motion pictures. Crosby and Sinatra even netted Oscars for dramatic roles. (Rickie Nelson, on the other hand, was already an actor in his family's long-running TV series, *Ozzie and Harriet*, before he picked up a guitar and became a velvet-voiced singing sensation.)

Influenced by this trend, Brian Epstein turned to the cinema for the Beatles' next project after their initial flush of radio and recording success in England. As their filmed press interviews had proven, the boys were naturals on camera—relaxed, personable, and highly photogenic. So in the fall of 1963, while he was in the States courting new fans for the band, Brian arranged a movie contract with United Artists and signed it on October 29. And for once Brian did a thorough job—the Beatles would actually be allowed some artistic control over the project.

Screenwriter Alun Owen, approved by the Beatles because he was familiar with the Liverpudlian accent, actually followed the band while they were on tour in France, noting their different personalities. The resulting screenplay—for all its madcap hijinks—also shows a darker side of pop music: the Beatles coping with the pressures of fame. The script contained real dialogue that Owen had

"GEORGE, WITH VELVET BROWN EYES AND DARK CHESTNUT HAIR, WAS THE BEST-LOOKING MAN I'D EVER SEEN."

PATTIE BOYD, ON FIRST MEETING GEORGE HARRISON

either heard the boys using or comments gleaned from actual press interviews. As a result, the "characters" had a ring of absolute authenticity to them. A far cry from Elvis Presley posing as a boxer, a convict, a race car veteran, a rodeo cowboy, a native American, or any of his other improbable roles.

The Beatles also chose the director, Richard Lester, from a list furnished by the studio. The young, relatively unknown American transplant to London had worked on British TV with Peter Sellers and was known to the Beatles for his short comedy film, *The Running Jumping & Standing Still Film*, a band favorite.

The seven-week filming began on March 2, 1964, with a six-day shoot aboard a hired train traveling from Paddington Station to Minehead in Somerset, with the balance to be shot at Twickenham Studios. The opening scene in Liverpool, with the crowd of screaming girls running past Paul in disguise, was actually filmed at London's Marylebone Station using real fans.

The Beatles didn't receive their Actor's Equity cards until the morning the shoot began. That first day was memorable for another reason—it was then that George Harrison met Pattie Boyd, a delicate, winsome blond model who had been hired to play a teenage schoolgirl in the movie. George was smitten and jokingly asked her to marry him . . . or at least dine

"**The first we did was the train, which we were all dead nervous in. Practically the whole of the train bit we were going to pieces.**"

JOHN LENNON, 1964, *Anthology*

FabFact

In America, *A Hard Day's Night* received two Academy Award nominations: Alun Owen for Best Screenplay and George Martin for Best Score (Adaptation).

with him. She refused, explaining that she had a boyfriend. But a month later, when Pattie and the other girl extras were called in for some publicity shots, George asked her about the boyfriend and she said she'd "dumped him." He again asked her out for dinner, and they ended up at the exclusive Garrick Club. The date was such a success—in spite of the presence of chaperone Brian Epstein—the two were soon deeply involved.

Opposite: The Beatles run from the police in a rare color still from *A Hard Day's Night.*

Above: Slender, baby-faced Pattie Boyd had the perfect "look" to become a fashion model during the Swinging Sixties. After she was tapped to play a schoolgirl on a train in *A Hard Day's Night,* she met George Harrison and was instantly smitten.

Previous pages: Ringo Starr in his film debut playing . . . Ringo Starr. Only Ringo, of all the Beatles, went on to appear regularly in films; he met his future wife, actress Barbara Bach, while filming *Caveman.*

"WE KNEW IT WOULD OPEN BOTH THE FILM AND THE SOUNDTRACK LP, SO I WANTED A PARTICULARLY STRONG AND EFFECTIVE BEGINNING. THE STRIDENT GUITAR CHORD WAS THE PERFECT LAUNCH."

GEORGE MARTIN

Above: Alun Owen's perceptive plot and writing for the Beatles' characters in *A Hard Day's Night* mirrored the trapped reality of their lives since Beatlemania had hit. Here they are, confined to their hotel suite, as they so often were. In the film, though, they manage to find various modes of escape.

Originally slated to be called *The Beatles* or *Beatlemania*, the film received a proper title when director Lester heard about one of Ringo's famous malapropisms—uttered when he'd left a tough daytime rehearsal to find it was dark out and said, "Well, it's sure been a hard day's, er, night." Lester declared it a perfect fit. (Producer Walter Shenson also takes credit for singling out Ringo's expression as does Paul, who claims they were all sitting around the studio brainstorming, trying to come up with a name and he suggested using Ringo's remark.)

Whatever its genesis, the new name was a go, and with only eight days left before shooting was completed, the movie needed a title song. John composed it in one day, using a poem from one of baby Julian's birthday cards as inspiration.

THE FIRST CHORD

The title song went on to win a Grammy for Best Performance by a Vocal Group, but it is also famous for the brash opening chord that George played on his 12-string Rickenbacker, and which many guitarists have tried to replicate or even identify. George Harrison himself cleared up the mystery during an online interview in February 2001, when he explained that it was an Fadd9—"F with a G on top." Harrison pointed out that John also hit the same chord on his Gibson J-160 six-string, and Paul played a D note on the fifth fret of the A string of his Hofner bass, also enriching the sound.

DOUBLE PREMIERES

The film premiered in London on July 6, 1964—exactly seven years from that first meeting of John and Paul and one day before Ringo's 24th birthday—and quickly became a financial and critical success. This was a happy surprise for the studio, United Artists, whose initial interest in the movie itself had been minimal. *A Hard Day's Night*, filmed in black and white, with a bargain-basement budget, was intended to be an exploitation film, simply a vehicle for all those lucrative songs on the soundtrack. But once again, the Beatles got the last laugh.

On July 10 the movie premiered in Liverpool. More than 200,000 Merseysiders, one quarter of the city, turned out to cheer on their local heroes; the massive crowds lining the parade route and filling Castle Street brought the city to a standstill. Both Paul and John later admitted to some qualms about going back home in such an over-the-top, public way, concerned that their former mates would think they had gotten too big for their breeches or that they had sold out. "Which in a way, we had," John said in 1967.

Despite these later critical

comments, the Beatles appeared to enjoy themselves thoroughly in the film. The same unrehearsed spontaneity and giddy silliness that had made their two Christmas Shows such jolly fun for the audience clearly came through in *A Hard Day's Night*. Teen followers even forgave them for the unflattering portrayal of the crazed fans. Lester had wisely emulated the formula used by Brian Epstein and George Martin before him—simply letting the Beatles be Beatles.

The film ended up kicking off a successful directing career for Lester, whose hits would include *Help!*, *The Three Musketeers* (1973), *Superman II*, and *Robin and Marian*, as well as ushering in a cinematic revival of slapstick comedies, and inspiring *The Monkees* TV show and the looming, as-yet-unrealized entertainment phenomenon called the music video.

Above: One of a series of lobby promo cards from *A Hard Day's Night*, produced for movie theaters, and which, like all Beatles memorabilia, have since become valuable collector's items.

FabFact

United Artists' executives inquired if the group's speaking voices might be dubbed by American actors for the U.S. release of the film. Both the Beatles and Richard Lester said an emphatic *no*.

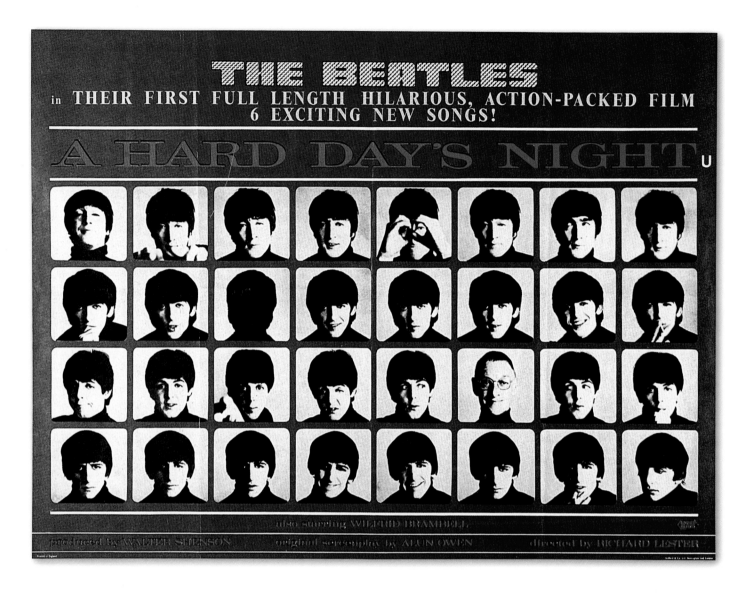

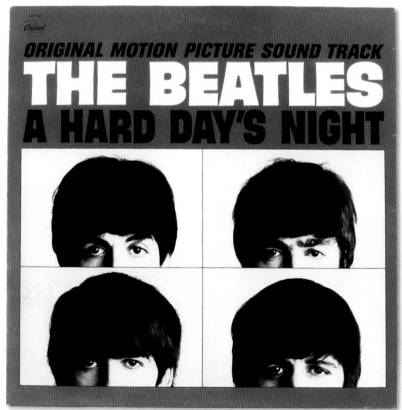

Above: Movie poster for the U.K. release of A Hard Day's Night, with photography by Robert Freeman.

Left: Front cover of the Capitol version of the *A Hard Day's Night* soundtrack album, released in 1980. The original release in the United States was in 1964 on United Artists, the studio that produced the movie.

A HARD DAY'S NIGHT

RELEASED JULY 10, 1964

(All songs Lennon–McCartney)

Side One:

1. A HARD DAY'S NIGHT

2. I SHOULD HAVE KNOWN BETTER

3. IF I FELL

4. I'M HAPPY JUST TO DANCE WITH YOU

5. AND I LOVE HER

6. TELL ME WHY

7. CAN'T BUY ME LOVE

Side Two:

1. ANY TIME AT ALL

2. I'LL CRY INSTEAD

3. THINGS WE SAID TODAY

4. WHEN I GET HOME

5. YOU CAN'T DO THAT

6. I'LL BE BACK

12-STRING FEVER

The novel sound of this album, with George Harrison's ebullient Rickenbacker 12-string chiming throughout, not only influenced the folk-based Byrds to become rock and rollers, it made the Rickenbacker 12-string the guitar of choice for frontman, Roger McGuinn. McGuinn's signature "jingle-jangle" style of playing influenced Tom Petty, another fan of the 12-string, who would later join George Harrison as part of the Traveling Wilburys.

Above: The back cover of the of the Capitol version of the *A Hard Day's Night* soundtrack album.

A Hard Day's Night was the third album the Beatles made for Parlophone. They went into the studio and recorded what was basically a pop album, with no covers, no R & B stylings, just short, peppy songs with catchy lyrics elevated by George Harrison's ringing 12-string guitar. Both the title track and "Can't Buy Me Love" became chart-topping singles on both sides of the Atlantic. Released on July 10, 1964, the album was the first of the Beatles' efforts to be recorded completely on a four-track system, allowing decent stereo mixes at last. It was also the band's only LP to feature Lennon-McCartney compositions exclusively.

FabFact

Vic Flick, the guitarist who played the instrumental version of "This Boy" ("Ringo's Theme") in the film also played the James Bond theme in *Dr. No*.

"I THINK THE BEATLES WERE THE FIRST BAND IN AUSTRALIA TO BE KNOWN AS ARTISTS AS WELL, WHERE THEY DID THE SINGING AND THE WRITING AND THE PLAYING AND EVERYTHING ELSE AT THE SAME TIME."
JOHNNY DEVLIN, SUPPORTING ACT FOR THE BEATLES' AUSTRALIA TOUR

Just months after completing *A Hard Day's Night*, the Beatles went off to visit Australia and New Zealand for the first time. John, Paul, and George flew into Sydney via Hong Kong on June 11, 1964, and were met by a crowd of 2,000 fans at Mascot International Airport. They'd been forced to leave Ringo behind after he collapsed from a serious bout of tonsillitis. A London drummer, Jimmie Nicol, whom George Martin had recently used in a Tommy Quickly session—and who knew the music after drumming on a budget EP of Beatles' covers—was chosen as a replacement until Ringo could fly in. (Loyal George Harrison almost refused to leave on the tour without his pal Ringo.)

In spite of the cold, rainy weather, the Beatles were paraded into town on the back of an open truck. John kept urging the driver to go faster,

but with no luck. Fortunately they'd all had capes made in Hong Kong and quickly pulled them on, but by the time they got to their hotel, the fabric had run and the boys were covered with blue dye.

The crowds in Australia turned out to the biggest the band had ever attracted. In Adelaide, where the Beatles would give their first concert, 300,000 people, more than half the total population, came out to welcome them at their arrival parade. Ringo rejoined the tour after the Adelaide shows and Jimmie Nicol was sent home to England with a sum of money—stories range from £500 to £10,000, about $800 to $16,000—and a gold watch. He later admitted that agreeing to the tour was the worst thing he could have done, giving him a taste for a life he could never again afford.

The Beatles went on to perform in Melbourne, Sydney, New Zealand, and Brisbane to equally enthusiastic crowds.

WHEN LEGENDS COLLIDE: MEETING BOB DYLAN

In August 1964 the Beatles were again touring North America, with 32 concerts slated for 25 cities, starting in San Francisco and ending in New York, and including Las Vegas, Vancouver, Los Angeles, Denver, New Jersey, Philadelphia, Indianapolis, Milwaukee, Chicago, Toronto, Jacksonville, Cleveland, New Orleans, Kansas City, and Dallas.

During the tour's final leg, in New York, they played the Forest Hills Tennis Stadium Music Festival in Queens on August 28 and 29, which had also showcased Barbra Streisand, Joan Baez, Harry Belafonte, Count Basie, Johnnie Mathis, Trini Lopez, Peter Nero, and Woody Allen earlier in the summer.

On August 28, while the Beatles were staying at the Delmonico Hotel in New York City, journalist Al Aronowitz set up a meeting between the band and Bob Dylan. The enigmatic folk singer had not yet achieved worldwide fame, but he was well known on both sides of the Atlantic for his classic protest songs, "Blowin' in the Wind," and "The Times They Are A Changin'." John Lennon had, in fact, gone from mocking

"I'M SO HIGH, I'M ON THE CEILING. ON . . . THE . . . CEILING."
BRIAN EPSTEIN, DURING HIS FIRST POT SMOKING SESSION

Dylan's personal narrative songs to revering his work deeply.

While roadie Mal Evans went out to buy some cheap wine (at Dylan's request), Dylan proceeded to offer the band some pot. "We've never smoked marijuana before," Brian explained sheepishly. Dylan was surprised that they hadn't already been turned on to the drug; he thought the lyrics to "I Want to Hold Your Hand" were "It's such a feeling that my love, I get high." They quickly explained his mistake— the lyric was "I can't hide."

America, circa 1964, might have been evolving into a pot paradise, but England at the time was still a pub culture, where a pint of lager or a scotch and coke (and the occasional Preludin in the Beatles' case) were the preferred

"poison." Dylan quickly rectified this omission in their cultural education by rolling a fattie and handing it to Ringo. Unaware of pot etiquette, Ringo smoked the whole thing. Dylan then instructed them to pass the next one around.

The boys and Brian soon fell into a mood of great hilarity, until Paul begun having a profound vision, taking him from one level of consciousness to the next. He called for a pencil, and when his stoned friends finally found one, he managed to write down his thoughts. The following morning he saw a note that read: "There are seven levels." Paul thought it a lot of nonsense, but later discovered that his stoned insight jibed with several major religions.

Afterward, the Beatles became serious reefer converts, reportedly

lighting up a joint as soon as they awoke in the morning. By the time they were filming *Help!*, the four were stoned most of the time and director Richard Lester recalls a great deal of "giggling" going on during the shoot. As for the Beatles' effect on the American folksinger, Dylan experts liked to cite them as one of the influences that urged him toward a more powerful sound and spurred his conversion to the electric guitar, much to the horror of the Newport Folk Festival in July 1965.

Opposite: Drummer Jimmy Nicol rehearses with the Beatles after stepping in as a substitute while Ringo Starr was in the hospital having his tonsils out.

Above, left: Bob Dylan looks both boyish and pensive in this 1964 portrait.

Above, right: The cover for *The Freewheelin' Bob Dylan*, released by Columbia Records in 1963, features Dylan and his girlfriend Suze Rotolo walking near their Greenwich Village apartment in New York City.

"THEY WERE RATHER WAR-WEARY DURING *BEATLES FOR SALE.* ONE MUST REMEMBER THAT THEY'D BEEN BATTERED LIKE MAD THROUGHOUT '64, AND MUCH OF '63."

GEORGE MARTIN, *THE COMPLETE BEATLES RECORDING SESSIONS*, MARK LEWISOHN

In mid-August 1964, the Beatles went into the studio to begin recording their fourth album for Parlophone. Over a period of three months, until October 26, they sporadically recorded songs for *Beatles for Sale*, which would be released on December 4. With Beatlemania still raging in England, the album hit number one repeatedly during its 46-weeks on the British charts. It held at number one for seven weeks from December 1964 to January 1965 after dethroning *A Hard Day's Night*, hit it again in February for one week and in May for three weeks. (In 1987, the CD release of the album again charted for two weeks.) An American single, "Eight Days a Week," also charted to number one.

The album itself did not appear in America, however, but a close facsimile, *Beatles 65*, did, featuring eight songs from the British LP, along with "I'll Be Back" from *A Hard Day's Night*, and the British single "I Feel Fine" and its B-side. "She's a Woman." *Beatles 65* was released only eleven days after *Beatles for Sale*, and ten days before Christmas. It became the fastest-selling American album of 1964. The six songs from *Beatles for Sale* that were omitted on *Beatles 65* later appeared in America on *Beatles VI*.

The public response to *Beatles for Sale* was typically enthusiastic, but some critics felt the pressure on the Beatles—to do tours, film TV shows, make movies, and record hit albums and singles—was starting to take its toll. The critics observed a general melancholy in the lyrics, and a "weariness" and "cynicism" in the overall production, a sense that Beatles' albums were now nothing more than "products," an interesting commentary considering the LP's title. Perhaps the six cover songs—Paul's energy on "Kansas City" notwithstanding—were responsible for that latter comment, i.e., the band not even bothering to write a decent compliment of songs. The Beatles took heed and rarely fell back on covers after this effort.

JOHN DIGS DEEP

The album did offer one undeniable plus: a fledgling effort from John Lennon to pen something autobiographical, in this case, "I'm A Loser." Up until then, John had kept his past and his personal life out of his music, stating later that he went into a lightweight "pop" mode when he wrote alone or with Paul. But his admiration for angsty narrative poet Bob Dylan, and their recent meeting, must have shaken something loose in John. The result is a harsh, plaintive declaration sung by a shot-down lover that

BEATLES FOR SALE
RELEASED DECEMBER 4, 1964
(All songs Lennon–McCartney unless specified)

Side One:

1. NO REPLY
2. I'M A LOSER
3. BABY'S IN BLACK
4. ROCK AND ROLL MUSIC (Berry)
5. I'LL FOLLOW THE SUN
6. MR. MOONLIGHT
7. KANSAS CITY/HEY-HEY-HEY-HEY (Lieber–Stoller)/(Penniman)

Side Two:

1. EIGHT DAYS A WEEK
2. WORDS OF LOVE
3. HONEY DON'T (Perkins)
4. EVERY LITTLE THING (Holly)
5. I DON'T WANT TO SPOIL THE PARTY
6. WHAT YOU'RE DOING
7. EVERYBODY'S TRYING TO BE MY BABY (Perkins)

Opposite, above: The CD sleeve for 2009's *Beatles for Sale* (Remastered) used Robert Freeman's original cover photo of the band in Hyde Park.

Opposite below: The album cover for Capitol's *Beatles '65* featured the Fabs in four playful shots.

"We got more and more free to get into ourselves. Our student selves rather than 'we must please the girls and make money' . . . 'Baby's in Black' we did because we liked waltz-time . . . and I think also John and I wanted to do something bluesy, a bit darker, more grown-up, rather than just straight pop."

PAUL McCARTNEY

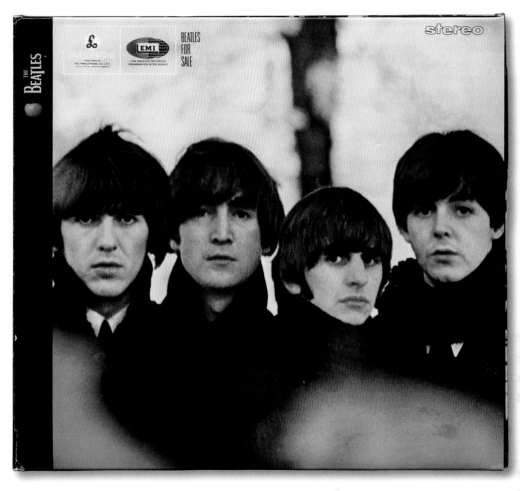

has nothing of June or moon about it. John's primal scream is beginning to emerge from deep, deep down in his psyche.

It is also notable that with the song "Eight Days A Week," the Beatles made one of their earliest forays into audio experimentation; after John and Paul worked for hours to perfect the song's chiming guitar kickoff, the opening ended up being recorded during a separate session and edited in. This opening also presents another Beatles' first—and a pop music oddity—the opening riff is a fade in, as opposed to the traditional pop ending of a fade out.

At the end of October the Beatles received five Ivor Novella Awards from the British Academy of Songwriters, Composers and Authors, indicating that they had, indeed, been accepted by the music establishment of their own country. They would go on to win a total of 15 such awards.

"ABSURD, DELIGHTFUL AND EXUBERANTLY MESSY, *HELP!* IS A PURE PLEASURE TO WATCH."
THE NEW YORK TIMES

After the unexpected success of A *Hard Day's Night*, the Beatles' next film was given the royal treatment by United Artists. No more black-and-white back-alley shots for these lads, this one was filmed in brilliant Eastmancolor and featured location shoots in Austria's scenic Tyrol and the balmy Bahamas. The Beatles intended the film to be an homage to the Marx Brothers' *Duck Soup*, with a bit of a James Bond parody thrown in . . . and it succeeded on both counts. The plot involved Scotland Yard and two demented scientists aiding Ringo after he accidentally ends up wearing the sacrificial ring of a mystical Eastern cult. The use of this comedic cult in the film is a bit ironic considering the Beatles did end up following a mystical Eastern yogi a few years later.

Richard Lester again directed, aiming for another madcap classic, with the Beatles pursued this time not by rabid fans, but by a Keystone Kops version of East Indian thuggees. Compared to *A Hard Day's Night*, this screenplay—by Charles Wood, with a story by Marc Behm—had a relatively involved plot, requiring numerous scenes of the Swami and his henchmen. As a result of this more structured story line, the Beatles felt left out of the creative process. (Director Lester maintained that they were too stoned to contribute much, and the band candidly admitted the movie was shot in a

Left, above: The Beatles film *Help!* at Cliveden House in May 1965. The location played a part in the Profumo affair, a British political scandal that contributed to the downfall of the Conservative government in 1964.

Left, below: The Beatles indulge in some horseplay while filming *Help!*, in Obertauern, Austria, March, 1965.

"haze of marijuana.") Still, John later complained that they ended up as bit players in their own film.

The title had originally been "Eight Arms to Hold You," (with "Eight Days a Week" as the lead-in song), but at some point Richard Lester or Paul McCartney came up with *Help!* and the others liked it. John set to work on a title song and had made a decent start, when Paul showed up at his home to help him finish it. The band recorded the single in four hours on the night of April 13, 1965, with twelve takes in Abbey Road's Studio Two.

During the filming John was going through a rough patch he later called his "fat Elvis" period—because he'd been eating uncontrollably and gaining weight. He later confessed that when he wrote "Help!" he was so depressed and so overwhelmed by the stress of being a Beatle that the song became a genuine cry for help.

The film was released in the United Kingdom on July 29, 1965, to generally positive reviews. Some critics, however, felt the film's bigger budget had cost it the innocence and fun of *A Hard Day's Night*, while others said it "tried too hard to entertain." Still, *Help!* was considered another critical and financial success for the Beatles. As of 2013, the film, which cost $1.5 million to make, had earned more than $12 million in box office receipts and from laserdisc and DVD sales.

Right: In contrast to the snowy Austrian shoot, the boys here enjoy some sun and surf while filming the climax of *Help!* in the Bahamas.

"*Help!* was where we turned on to pot and we dropped drink, simple as that. I've always needed a drug to survive. The others too, but I always had more, more pills, more of everything."
JOHN LENNON

Making the Album

"*Help!* took longer. We had more time. Lots more money and I had to tell the fans to 'get out' in lots of different languages. During the filming, the Beatles discovered marijuana. There was lots of smiling."

RICHARD LESTER,
director, 1965

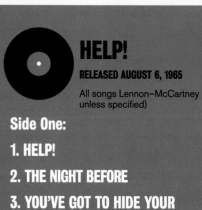

HELP!
RELEASED AUGUST 6, 1965

All songs Lennon–McCartney
unless specified)

Side One:

1. HELP!

2. THE NIGHT BEFORE

3. YOU'VE GOT TO HIDE YOUR LOVE AWAY

4. I NEED YOU (Harrison)

5. ANOTHER GIRL

6. YOU'RE GOING TO LOSE THAT GIRL

7. TICKET TO RIDE

Side Two:

1. ACT NATURALLY (Morrison–Russell)

2. IT'S ONLY LOVE

3. YOU LIKE ME TOO MUCH (Harrison)

4. TELL ME WHAT YOU SEE

5. I'VE JUST SEEN A FACE

6. YESTERDAY

7. DIZZY MISS LIZZY (Williams)

Top: Ringo, George, John, and Paul take a break from filming *Help!*, in Austria.

Above: The Beatles strike random semaphore poses for the cover of *Help!*

Opposite: *Help!* had its royal premiere at the London Pavilion on Shaftesbury Avenue—beneath this extravagant display—on July 29, 1965.

Help! became the fifth British and the tenth American album produced by the Beatles.

A single of the title song was released in America on July 19, 1965, and in England on July 23 and rose to the top of charts in both countries. The British album was released August 6, the American version, with more vivid cover lettering, came out on August 13.

The British album contained fourteen songs; the seven on the A-side were from the film: "Help!" "The Night Before," "You've Got to Hide Your Love Away," "I Need You," "Another Girl", "You're Going to Lose That Girl," and "Ticket to Ride."

The seven songs on the B-side included: "Act Naturally," "It's Only Love," "You Like Me Too Much," "Tell Me What You See," "I've Just Seen a Face," "Yesterday" (the most covered of all Beatles' songs), and "Dizzy Miss Lizzy."

The American soundtrack from Capitol featured the songs from the movie interspersed with Ken Thorne and George Martin's orchestral music from the film (including the use of an Indian sitar). The cover boasted a gatefold sleeve with promotional photos from the film. The album reached number one on September 11 and held that position for nine weeks.

Many Beatles' buffs consider *Help!* the last album of their "early" period, which gave way to a conscious change in content as the band strove for a more creative, free-ranging style and less dependence on American rock and roll standards and cover songs.

OTHER CINEMATIC ENDEAVORS

Throughout their careers as Beatles and even afterward, the members of the band had a keen interest in acting and in the motion picture business in general. In 1966 John played a supporting role in Richard Lester's satirical *How I Won the War*. John would later go on to produce avant-garde movies with his second wife, Yoko Ono, including *Fly*, a nineteen-minute film of a fly walking all over the body of a nude actress.

Ringo Starr, who was friends with *The Goon Show* actor Peter Sellers, appeared with the comedian in the 1969 comedy *The Magic Christian* in a part specially scripted for him by author Terry Southern. Starr also appeared in Frank Zappa's cult film *200 Motels*, in *That'll Be the Day* with David Essex, and in *Son of Dracula* with Harry Nilsson. Ringo met his second wife, Barbara Bach, while they were costarring in the 1981 prehistoric comedy, *Caveman*.

Paul McCartney produced his own film *Give My Regards to Broad Street* in 1984, in which he costarred with Ringo, and had a small part in 1987's *Eat the Rich*. Paul composed a number of film scores, including *The Family Way* in 1966, *Spies Like Us* in 1985, and the hit title song for the 1973 James Bond film, *Live and Let Die*, which he recorded with Wings.

George Harrison took another approach to the movies, initially becoming a producer of the Monty Python film *The Life of Brian* through his friendship with Eric Idle. In addition, Harrison's Handmade Pictures produced *Mona Lisa*, *Time Bandits*, *Shanghai Surprise*, and *Withnail and I*. Harrison also appeared in the Rutles' movie *All You Need Is Cash*—Idle's fond lampoon of the Beatles—playing a reporter standing outside "Rutlecorps." George also composed the music for the dreamlike 1968 film, *Wonderwall*.

Shea Stadium: The Wall of Noise

Above: Two shrieking Beatles' fans attend the historic Shea Stadium gig.

The Beatles set out on a two-week, ten-city American tour in August 1965, in part to create buzz about their upcoming film. Not that they'd exactly been lazing about back home—they had just returned from touring France, Italy, and Spain and attending the London opening of *Help!*

Their first scheduled concert was on August 15 at Shea Stadium in Flushing, Queens. The year-old home of the baseball Mets and football Jets was a circular stadium on Jamaica Bay with an undulating exterior design and four decks of seats rising from the field. Promoter Sid Bernstein had booked the venue, the first time an outdoor sports arena had been used to host a rock concert, and even though stadium officials doubted he could fill all the seats, the tickets sold out

in seventeen minutes. The Beatles received $180,000 for the gig, but Bernstein netted only $6,500.

The warm-up acts—Sounds Incorporated, King Curtis, Brenda Holloway, and the Discotheque Dancers, were introduced by popular disc jockeys Murray the K and Cousin Bruce Morrow. Ed Sullivan, the man who had brought them into American homes the previous year, introduced the Beatles. And when they arrived—in an armored car—and ran across the infield to the stage, the deafening screams of more than 55,000 jubilant fans greeted them. It was the largest crowd they would entertain at a live concert.

The band played a lively set, starting with a rollicking version of "Twist and Shout," then segued

"WHAT I REMEMBER MOST ABOUT THE CONCERT WAS THAT WE WERE SO FAR AWAY FROM THE AUDIENCE..."
RINGO STARR

Opposite, Left and Below: Momentous scenes at Shea Stadium, August 16, 1965. Although a number of fans jumped the barriers and ran across the infield toward the stage, the Beatles continued to perform, trusting in the police and their security forces to keep them safe.

Following pages: This panoramic shot of the crowd at the Beatles' Shea Stadium concert showcases the staggering number of fans who attended.

into "She's a Woman," "I Feel Fine," "Dizzy Miss Lizzy," "Ticket to Ride" and "Everybody's Trying to Be My Baby." They put Ringo center stage with "Act Naturally," followed by "Can't Buy Me Love," "Baby's in Black," touted both their films by playing "A Hard Day's Night," and "Help!" and then finished up with "I'm Down." Even though the band's singing and playing was doctored in the studio for the documentary, *The Beatles at Shea Stadium*, the power and joy of a live Beatles performance still comes across in the film. In spite of the relatively primitive audio set up and the "wall of noise" from the 55,000 fans, the band's many years of playing clubs and touring paid off on this night, perhaps their most famous gig, when they handily won over the crowd with their showmanship and musical chops.

"AT SHEA STADIUM, I SAW THE TOP OF THE MOUNTAIN."
JOHN LENNON

Above: Paul thumbing through one of the many fanzines generated by Beatlemania in the United States. These magazines specialized in features such as "Battle of the British Bands," and "Could You Be the Perfect Beatles Girlfriend?" and offered plenty of photos and gossipy tidbits.

The rest of the American tour went without a hitch, with the band playing to sold-out houses across the country. Just before their final August 31 concert in San Francisco's Cow Palace, the Beatles took a break at the rented Los Angeles mansion of actress Zsa Zsa Gabor, and on August 27 they received an invitation to visit Elvis Presley. Presley—who had been repeatedly critical of the Beatles and who doubtless felt some jealousy over their meteoric rise—finally agreed to a meeting at the behest of his manager Colonel Tom Parker.

Chris Hutchins, a journalist who had been covering the Beatles' tour, got credit for setting up the historic event. Hutchins had interviewed Elvis and sensed his curiosity about the Beatles, so he talked Brian Epstein and Tom Parker into arranging the meeting on Elvis' turf in the exclusive Bel Air section of Beverly Hills. Hutchins also guaranteed there would be no press coverage, not even photographs.

The Beatles were all edgy when they and their staff arrived at Prelsey's home on Perugia

Way, even more so after being introduced to Presley and his beautiful fiancee, Priscilla Beaulieu—and Elvis' entourage, the Memphis Mafia. (John would later nervously lapse into an annoying Inspector Clouseau accent.) Presley finally said jokingly, "Well, if you're just going to sit there and stare at me all night, I'm going to bed." Guitars were eventually passed around and, with Ringo drumming a beat on the coffee table, they played a few Beatles' tunes and some current radio hits. They even spent some time at Elvis' roulette table, which pleased Brian Epstein.

When John asked Elvis why he'd stopped recording rock and roll records, Presley, who

was not happy with either his unchallenging movie career or the middle-of-the-road songs he recorded for those films, promised he would return to rock some day soon. "Well, then we'll start buying your records again," John responded truthfully, not intending to be rude.

After the Beatles left, sometime around 2 AM, John mentioned in the limo that Elvis was stoned. "Aren't we all!" George replied.

Above, left: Palm trees line a street in Beverly Hills, the place where the Beatles finally met their idol, Elvis Presley.

Above, right: Elvis Presley, seen here in 1965, was intrigued by the Beatles' phenomenal rise, so much like his own.

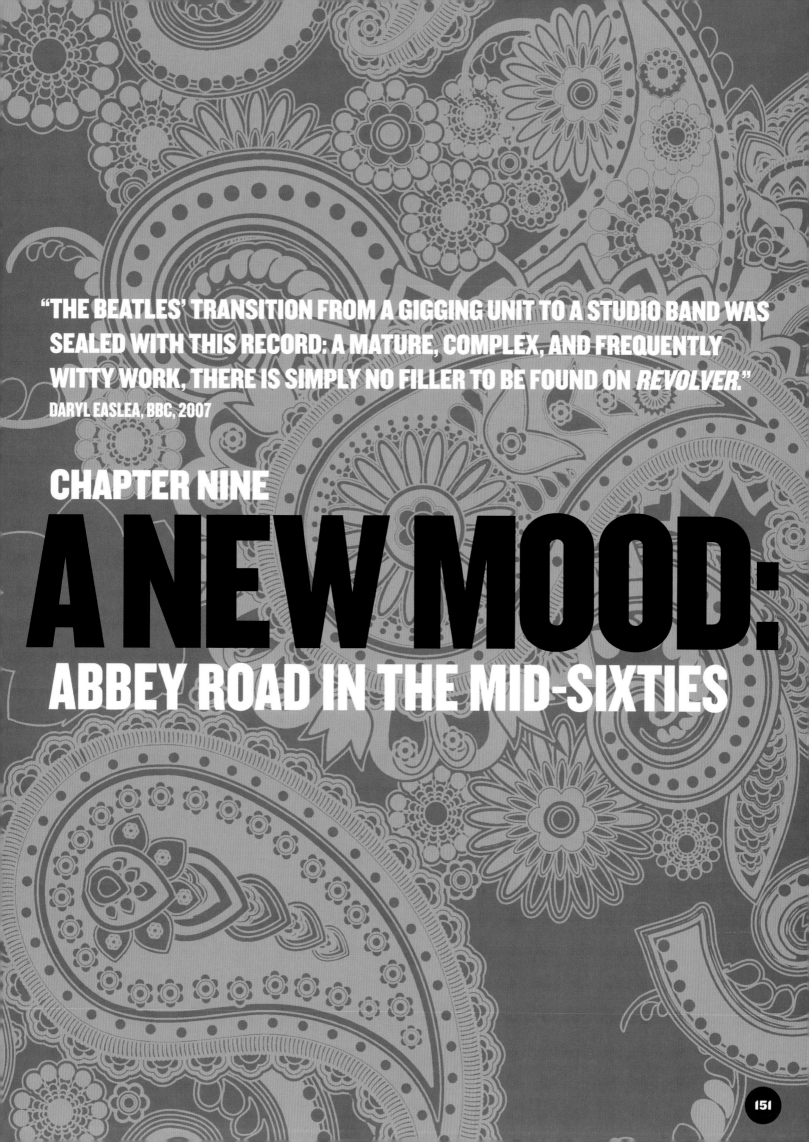

> "THE BEATLES' TRANSITION FROM A GIGGING UNIT TO A STUDIO BAND WAS SEALED WITH THIS RECORD: A MATURE, COMPLEX, AND FREQUENTLY WITTY WORK, THERE IS SIMPLY NO FILLER TO BE FOUND ON *REVOLVER*."
> DARYL EASLEA, BBC, 2007

CHAPTER NINE

A NEW MOOD:
ABBEY ROAD IN THE MID-SIXTIES

"AFTER ALL WE DID FOR BRITAIN, SELLING ALL THAT CORDUROY AND MAKING IT SWING, AND ALL WE GOT WAS A LEATHER MEDAL WITH WOOD AND STRING THROUGH IT!"
GEORGE HARRISON

"IT DOESN'T MAKE ME MORE RESPECTABLE, I'M STILL A SCRUFF."
PAUL McCARTNEY, ON HIS MBE

As 1965 ended, the band went back into the studio to cut a new album. All told, it had been a banner year, with the filming and recording of *Help!*; Ringo's marriage to his sweetheart, Maureen Cox; a European tour; a successful second American tour; a meeting with Elvis Presley; George's engagement to Pattie Boyd . . . and one other thing, a token of appreciation from a very special lady.

When the notices went out from Buckingham Palace announcing Queen Elizabeth's list of MBE recipients for 1965, the Beatles were surely the surprise entry. The MBE, Member of the Most Honorable Order of the British Empire, is a prestigious award bestowed for singular achievements or services rendered to the Crown. It was usually awarded to statesmen, diplomats, members of the military, and other dignitaries, not rock and roll superstars . . . but the Beatles were getting accustomed to breaking down traditions.

Harold Wilson, the new Labour prime minister and a Merseysider himself, had encouraged the queen to bestow the award. He felt the Beatles' contribution to British culture ought to be recognized. As he explained, "I saw the Beatles as having a transforming effect on the minds of youth, mostly for the good. It kept a lot of kids off the streets. They introduced many, many young people to music, which in itself was a good thing. A lot of old stagers might have regarded it as idiosyncratic music, but the Mersey sound was a new important thing. That's why they deserved such recognition." And while the MBE carried with it few privileges—notably, a payment of forty pounds a year and free admission to the Whispering Gallery at St. Paul's Cathedral (which usually cost about a shilling)—it was presented by the queen herself.

Although the Beatles were excited over the recognition—even tough Teddy Boys had to acknowledge notice from the Queen—they were also concerned that this award was too mainstream, that it would ruin their "street cred." Ultimately they decided to accept. Brian, ever class-conscious, doubtless encouraged them in this course. (George supposedly went around telling people the MBE stood for Mr. Brian Epstein.)

The ceremony was held on October 26, 1965, and the Beatles, all "done up proper" in dark suits and ties, dutifully made their way to Buckingham Palace. Rumor claimed they got stoned in the bathroom before the ceremony, but George insisted they were just "having a fag" to calm their nerves. When it was over, the four literally remarked that the queen was very nice, "but she didn't have a lot to say." Paul also reported to the press that the palace was a "keen pad." Both he and George used their medals to decorate their uniforms on the cover of *Sgt. Pepper*, reasoning, no doubt, that if you've got it, flaunt it!

Afterward, many previous recipients of the MBE were offended at what they considered the frivolity of the choice and sent their honors back. At the time, John Lennon responded by pointing out, "Lots of people who complained about us receiving the MBE [status] received theirs for heroism in the war—for killing people . . . We received ours for entertaining other people. I'd say we deserve ours more." John returned his own MBE in November 1969—over England's support of Nigeria in the genocide against Biafra—as a part of his continuing campaign for peace.

Opposite and above: The Beatles display their newly awarded Honours at Buckingham Palace.

Previous pages: As the Beatles' sound matured, their fashion sense also changed. Look-alike "schoolboy" suits were replaced with softer fabrics and finishes—like Paul's suede jacket—paisley-patterned shirts, and a dash of military trappings.

"We're very pleased with the way everything's turned out. We all think it's just about our best LP. I can't wait for it to come out. The sleeve's finished too, and the picture on the front is pretty good!"
GEORGE HARRISON, 1965

Rubber Soul was produced in the late fall of 1965 during four weeks of sustained, dedicated sessions—rather than slapped together between touring breaks as the previous LPs had been. This time around the band had the leisure to construct an album that matched their vision and benefited from their heightened levels of creativity.

With the Beatles' massive capacity for generating revenue, it was not surprising that EMI had adopted a hands-off policy regarding their stars. The band now had unlimited access to the studios and engineers at Abbey Road, paid no fees of any sort, and could come and go as their moods compelled them. This was undreamed-of artistic freedom—and they reveled in it. Abbey Road became their playground, their laboratory, and their center of higher learning (and, eventually, their Thunderdome—where one band enters and four men leave).

A number of things set *Rubber Soul* apart from its predecessors. The songs were less about love and romance and more like observations about relationships, a whole different animal. Jealously, sexism, reverse sexism, impatience, disappointment, betrayal, reassurance—they were all in there. It contained no cover songs, only original material (a formula the band would stick to until "Maggie Mae" appeared on *Let It Be*). Yet it was also an album full of outsider influences, many of them absorbed during their North American Tour. Dylan was there, the Byrds were there, even Brian Wilson's surfer boy harmonies showed up. Listeners caught distinct overtones of folk and R&B, Paul incorporated French cabaret guitar into "Michelle," while John added a Greek taverna feel to "Girl." John also lit a fire with "Norwegian Wood"—and not only due to lyrics hinting at male bad behavior in the face of a liberated woman (what did he actually set on fire?). The song became a significant precursor of the world music movement and introduced the exotic sounds of the Indian sitar to rock fans.

"I think *Rubber Soul* was the first of the albums that presented a new Beatles to the world. Up to this point, we had been making albums that were rather like a collection of their singles and now we really were beginning to think about albums as a bit of art in their own right. We were thinking about the album as an entity of its own and *Rubber Soul* was the first one to emerge in this way."

GEORGE MARTIN

Opposite, left: Robert Whitaker's picture of George relaxing in the Beatles' hotel suite at the Tokyo Hilton Hotel, Japan, during their 1966 tour of Asia.

Opposite, right: The Beatles perform at Alpha Television Studios in Aston, Birmingham, March 1965.

Above: George Martin in 1965.

RAVI SHANKAR—SITAR HERO

In 1965, the Beatles met Byrds' founders Roger McGuinn and David Crosby at Peter Fonda's L.A. home, where they all dropped acid together. It was here that Crosby spoke to George Harrison of his love for Ravi Shankar and Indian sitar music (the Byrds and Shankar shared the same studio). He then showed George some Indian music chords—which McGuinn had been playing on his 12-string to create "raga-rock" numbers like "Why." George was so intrigued, he bought a sitar to experiment with, and first used it on *Rubber Soul*'s "Norwegian Wood."

In June 1966 George actually met Shankar in London, and later that year he and Pattie traveled to Srinagar, India, so that George could study with him for six weeks. Shankar, who wanted to expose more Westerners to his country's music, welcomed the chance to instruct the young Beatle. Meanwhile, both Harrisons became interested in Eastern philosophy and meditation during this trip. George's use of traditional Indian instruments on later Beatles' tracks "Love You To," "Tomorrow Never Knows," "Within You, Without You," and "Inner Light," would help to popularize Indian music, just as Shankar had hoped.

Above: Ravi Shankar displays the classic position for playing the somewhat cumbersome sitar, with its bulbous base and complex fretboard.

"We were getting better, technically and musically. Finally, we took over the studio. In the early days, we had to take what we were given; we didn't know how to get more bass. We were still learning. We were more precise about making this album, and we took over the cover and everything."

JOHN LENNON

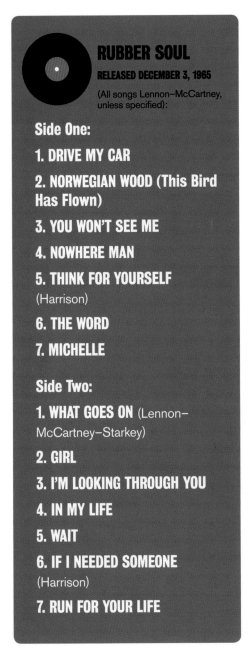

RUBBER SOUL

RELEASED DECEMBER 3, 1965

(All songs Lennon–McCartney, unless specified):

Side One:

1. DRIVE MY CAR

2. NORWEGIAN WOOD (This Bird Has Flown)

3. YOU WON'T SEE ME

4. NOWHERE MAN

5. THINK FOR YOURSELF (Harrison)

6. THE WORD

7. MICHELLE

Side Two:

1. WHAT GOES ON (Lennon–McCartney–Starkey)

2. GIRL

3. I'M LOOKING THROUGH YOU

4. IN MY LIFE

5. WAIT

6. IF I NEEDED SOMEONE (Harrison)

7. RUN FOR YOUR LIFE

Opposite: The cover photo for *Rubber Soul*, seen here on the British release, was first projected onto a piece of white card stock for the Beatles' approval, When the card tilted and the image skewed, the band insisted on replicating that effect on the cover. The distinctive balloon lettering of the title was done by illustrator Charles Front.

For the cover photo, the band had to choose from a series of shots taken by Robert Freeman in John's garden in Weybridge. Paul recalls that Bob visited the band at a friend's flat one night and projected the slides from the shoot onto a piece of white cardboard. When he accidentally tilted the card, distorting the image and elongating their faces, they grew excited. Could he replicate that look in a photo? He told them he could—and the cover with the distinctive skewed perspective was born. Many people felt the image accurately reflected all the changes going on in the Beatles public and private lives. Some fans also describe the album's sound as having a woodsy, mellow, "deep brown" aura, similar to the suede jacket John is wearing on the cover.

According to Mark Lewishohn in *The Beatles' Recording Sessions* (1988), the title came from something Paul kept saying during the recording of "I'm Down." What he'd been repeating was, "Plastic soul, man, plastic soul," which, he explained, was the term black blues musicians used to describe Mick Jagger. "That was Paul's title," John pointed out to *Rolling Stone* in 1970, "meaning English soul."

CRITICAL REACTION

Rubber Soul was released on December 3, 1965, just in time for the Christmas season. It charted in Britain on December 11 and

remained there for an astonishing 42 weeks. On Christmas Day it dethroned *Help!* at the top of the charts and stayed there for eight weeks. Critics couldn't praise it enough—Robert Christgau in *Esquire* lauded it for its "innovation, tightness, and lyrical intelligence" and *Rolling Stone* raved, "they achieved a new musical sophistication and a greater thematic depth without sacrificing a whit of pop appeal." In 2012, *Rolling Stone* voted it number 5 on their list of the 500 Greatest Albums of All Time.

Brian Wilson of the Beach Boys insisted he'd "never heard a collection of songs that were all that good before. It's like a collection of folk songs, and they're all just really, really great songs. And not just about love. They're about a lot of different things, but they all go together, somehow."

Rubber Soul inspired Wilson while he was crafting the Beach Boys' superb concept album, *Pet Sounds*, while *Pet Sounds*, Paul's favorite album of all time, in turn spurred the Beatles to create *Revolver*. But ultimately Wilson couldn't handle this searing level of competition. When he first heard a recording of "Strawberry Fields Forever," his marijuana-clouded brain convinced him he would never be able to equal it, and so he stopped work on a new album he was intending to call *Smile*.

"*RUBBER SOUL* WAS THE POT ALBUM, AND *REVOLVER* WAS ACID. I MEAN, WE WEREN'T ALL STONED MAKING *RUBBER SOUL*, BECAUSE IN THOSE DAYS WE COULDN'T WORK ON POT."

JOHN LENNON

FabFacts

The Beatles originally wanted to record *Revolver* in an American studio, where they could have gotten the raw sound they loved, but they discovered the cost would be prohibitive. Paul later remarked that at least "Eleanor Rigby" benefited from the English studio sessions, since he considered British violinists "better than the American ones."

Klaus Voorman, who drew the *Revolver* cover portraits from memory, received only £40, the equivalent of $65, for his artwork, but he did go on to win a Grammy for Best Album Cover, Graphic Arts, in 1967.

Things never seemed to slow down for the Beatles during this period, and the first half of 1966 was no exception. George and Pattie Boyd were wed in January and went to Barbados on their honeymoon; in March, John spoke to a British teen magazine about the Beatles being "bigger than Jesus," comments that would come back to haunt him that summer. In June, Paul bought a farm on the remote Mull of Kintyre on the southwest coast of Scotland. By then American protesters were burning Beatles' records in anger over John's comments, just as the band was setting out on a tour of the States. During this eventful time—from April to June—the group went into the studio to record a new album, no doubt relieved to be back in the safe and relatively stable environment of Abbey Road.

FRESH SOUNDS

The Beatles really hoped to break out of the studio rut with this album. They wanted the instruments to sound fresh and even foreign, they wanted the British engineers, who had been doing things the same way for decades, to emulate the raw sound quality of American records. And they wanted the

Above, left, Opposite, above, Opposite, below: These informal photos were taken by photographer—and Beatles friend—Robert Whitaker in April and May, 1966, during the *Revolver* sessions at Abbey Road, and at Chiswick House in West London. A black-and-white shot from the series was used on the back cover of the album.

Above right: John was extremely nearsighted but refused to wear glasses in public. After meeting Roger McGuinn of the Byrds, John found a hip solution to his problem by copying McGuinn's tinted prescription "granny" glasses.

LP to have a cohesive feeling; as Paul said, it was intended to "show our versatility rather than a haphazard collection of songs."

John recalled that he and Paul knew they really had to get their act together and come up with some seriously good material. They began collaborating, either at Paul's house in St. John's Wood or at John's home out in Weybridge. Paul noted that he composed songs or bits of melodies in his head during that long drive and, around this time, composed the single "Paperback Writer" while on the way to John's.

Revolver was released on August 8, 1966, to critical and public acclaim. From the guttural countdown on "Taxman" to the droning incantations of "Tomorrow Never Knows," the album was geared to attract attention. "I'm Only Sleeping" and "She Said, She Said" mark the beginnings of John's emerging inner persona winning out over his controlled pop lyrics. Paul creates a mood in minutes with two spectral entries "Eleanor Rigby" and "For No One," pays homage to his muse, Jane Asher, with "Here, There, and Everywhere" and presents another of his signature tributes to rock and roll jubilation with "Got to Get You Into My Life." George managed two goodies, the acerbic "Taxman" and a pleasing up-tempo love song, "I Want to Tell You." In Ringo's playful recording of "Yellow Submarine," it sounds like the Beatles (and the entire staff at Abbey Road) were sitting in a bathtub creating watery sound effects.

"*Revolver* pioneered the idea of a rock album as a singular, complete entity, one that had made the transition from bursts of teenage sugar to a cohesive whole that could be analyzed, dissected, obsessed over, and indulged in—you know, art."

ENTERTAINMENT WEEKLY, 2013

"John, Paul, and I devoted an evening to sifting through an enormous pile of newspapers and magazines for pictures of the Beatles, after which we cut out the faces and glued them all together. Our handiwork was later superimposed onto the line drawing by Klaus Voormann, their old friend from Hamburg."

PETE SHOTTON, *In My Life* **(1983)**

REVOLVER

RELEASED AUGUST 5, 1966

(All songs Lennon–McCartney, unless specified):

Side One:

1. TAXMAN (Harrison)

2. ELEANOR RIGBY

3. I'M ONLY SLEEPING

4. LOVE YOU TO

5. HERE, THERE AND EVERYWHERE

6. YELLOW SUBMARINE

7. SHE SAID SHE SAID

Side Two:

1. GOOD DAY SUNSHINE

2. AND YOUR BIRD CAN SING

3. FOR NO ONE

4. DOCTOR ROBERT

5. I WANT TO TELL YOU (Harrison)

6. GOT TO GET YOU INTO MY LIFE

7. TOMORROW NEVER KNOWS

Revolver's striking black-and-white cover, which instantly became a graphic arts icon, was created by Klaus Voorman, the Beatles' chum from their Hamburg days. A talented artist as well a

guitarist, Voorman managed to convey something puckish and slightly disconcerting in his drawing of the Beatles' faces. The effect is very Art Nouveau, yet almost Asian in essence, like an Aubrey Beardsley illustration of a Japanese woodblock print. The Beatles collectively loved the artwork, but they augmented it by superimposing photo cutouts of themselves over the drawing. When Brian finally saw the finished product and started crying, Voorman was sure he hated it. "No," Brian told him, "This is exactly what we needed. I was worried that this whole thing might not work, but I know now that this is the cover. This LP will work—thank you."

According to Ringo, it was Paul who came up with the name *Revolver*—one early contender was *Abracadabra*, but it had been used already—and since they couldn't come up with anything better, it stuck. Paul dismissed the gun reference, stating that the name simply meant something that went around in a circle.

JOSTLING FOR POSITION

Popular music is a fluid medium, ebbing and flowing with the times. The critics' darling one season might be declared a disaster a few decades on. And fans are harshest

when facing disappointing efforts from the groups they love. As a result of these factors, Beatles albums often find themselves being shuffled in polls like 45s in a Wurlitzer, their status depending on the tastes and attitudes of a given generation. While the supernova *Sgt. Pepper* frequently reigns at the top of radio polls—and *Abbey Road* continues as the sales king—magazine polls often contain surprises. A 2013 issue of *Entertainment Weekly* featuring the Top 100 Albums placed *Revolver* at number one . . . and didn't place *Sgt. Pepper* here, there, or anywhere! Does this mean *Pepper* has lost its zest? Not likely; it's just that pop music continues to be wholly subjective, depending solely on the ear of the beholder.

As long as music maniacs sit up late into the night, the merits of each Beatles album will be assessed and argued, while critics discover new favorites or new ways to trash old favorites—to the point that one person's (or critic's) cherished LP might never top a published list. For example, fans from the early 1970s insist that *The White Album*, with its wide range of flavors and textures, provided a thrill not unlike the bombshell effect of *Sgt. Pepper*—overwhelming and hugely satisfying. Yet subsequent generations found much to criticize. Many listeners consider it simply a collection of interesting solo efforts that anticipated the breakup of the band, and rarely place it high in polls. So the elevation of *Revolver* to this lofty position in *EW* must have been gratifying for the album's legion of fans, who were doubtless ecstatic to see it finally getting its due.

"WE WOULD SAY, 'TRY IT. JUST TRY IT FOR US. IF IT SOUNDS CRAPPY, OK, WE'LL LOSE IT. BUT IT MIGHT JUST SOUND GOOD.' WE WERE ALWAYS PUSHING AHEAD: LOUDER, FURTHER, LONGER, MORE, DIFFERENT."

PAUL McCARTNEY

George Martin is rightfully hailed as one of the most innovative music producers of all time. His work with the Beatles is unmatched in terms of giving his stars the right measure of guidance and freedom they needed to excel in the studio. But even Martin couldn't do it alone. His engineers worked alongside him to embellish, amplify, and augment the Beatles' music in ways that had never been tried before. Sometimes they ran the instruments directly into the board rather than through the amplifiers, which was a mortal sin by EMI's strict standards. They did it anyway, and made musical history . . .

NORMAN SMITH

If anyone could be credited with making the Beatles' records sound as crisp today as when they were recorded, that honor must go to Norman Smith. He was known for carefully placing the studio microphones in front of each instrument so that they wouldn't bleed into each other, i.e., the guitars wouldn't be picked up by the drum mikes, etc. Fortunately, Smith had had many years' experience running the board for Cliff Richard and the Shadows, who were the first beat group in England to dominate the charts, starting in the late 1950s. Smith enjoyed working with the Beatles and eventually engineered

nearly 100 of their songs. John Lennon, who had a nickname for practically everyone, called him Normal Norman, due to his relaxed nature and unhurried manner.

Smith's stint as George Martin's engineer proved so successful, he was promoted to producer at EMI in 1965. He soon began to work with a young art-house band named Pink Floyd and eventually brought them to prominence. He also produced one of the first rock concept albums, the Pretty Things *S.F. Sorrow* in 1968.

And it was Norman "Hurricane" Smith himself who hit the charts in both the United Kingdom and the United States with his self-penned 1972 single, "Oh, Babe (What Would You Say)." He continued writing, producing, and engineering music for himself and others before retiring— only returning to the world of pop music to attend the New York and Chicago versions of The Fest for Beatles' Fans in 2007. He died a year later, just after his eighty-fifth birthday.

GEOFF EMERICK

Geoff Emerick was only 15 when he began working for EMI; at age 20 he replaced Norman Smith as the Beatles' chief engineer. He had worked with them some years earlier—and had been fortunate enough to be present at the first

THE SOUND GARDEN

recording session of the brand-new Beatles lineup that included Ringo Starr—but now he was to be George Martin's right-hand man in the studio. Beginning with *Revolver*, he helped engineer the sound that would make the Beatles studio pioneers and alter the ways pop music was recorded. (It helped that the Beatles each had a Brenell tape recorder at home, so they could capture their new ideas and reworks on acetate before arriving at Abbey Road.)

Emerick was as much an innovator in the studio as Martin. One trick of his involved recording John through a Leslie cabinet speaker, which is what gave the voice track on "Tomorrow Never Knows" its ethereal sound. Lennon wanted to sound like the "Dalai Lama chanting on a hilltop." He also worked with Lennon on *Sgt. Pepper*'s complex "Being For the Benefit of Mr. Kite" to get the circus music so realistic you might be able to "taste the sawdust." Emerick randomly spliced together bits of harmonium, harmonica, and calliope recordings into a cacophonous melange that filled the middle eight bars of the song.

In July 1968, Emerick left EMI studios during the stress-filled *White Album* sessions. He returned in 1969 to help the band record their final album, *Abbey Road*. Emerick would go on to win engineering Grammies for both *Sgt. Pepper* and *Abbey Road*. After the group's break-up, he became an in-demand engineer and worked with Paul McCartney, Elvis Costello, Badfinger, Art

The innovative techniques the Abbey Road engineers employed on the Beatles' recordings included sampling, artificial double tracking (ADT), multitrack recording, backward recording, and guitar feedback. George Harrison often said that the idea of harnessing feedback came when someone placed a guitar too near one of the amps; John subsequently figured out how to re-create it on stage. The buzzing feedback that opens "I Feel Fine" was the first time that effect was used on a rock record—but certainly not the last. The Beatles' experimentation with musique concrète, typically a montage of electronically modified and/or acoustic sounds, led to segments taped backward, key features of "Tomorrow Never Knows," and "I'm Only Sleeping." Adding a variety of studio-created sound effects to the music—the resonating glass bottle near the end of "Long Long Long"—was another audio trick, as was what the band called "random" mixes—

streaming a radio broadcast onto the end of "I Am the Walrus." This technique is more often referred to as chance determinism.

With Martin at the helm, the studio engineers began incorporating classical music—the string quartet on "Yesterday," classical strings mixed with guitars on "Strawberry Fields"—into the songs. The Beatles insistence on saturated sound led to the close miking of the strings for "Eleanor Rigby" and placing mikes into the bells of the brass instruments on "Got To Get You Into My Life." Even though the Beatles made the blending of rock music with orchestral music acceptable, the whole time they were at Abbey Road there was still a large Pop/Classical switch on the mixing console. In fact, there was so much tension between the two groups of engineers, they ate at separate tables in the canteen. (Of course, it was the pop music that helped pay for the classical recordings at EMI.)

Top: George, Paul and John in discussion with George Martin at Abbey Road.

Garfunkle, Cheap Trick, Big Country, and Gentle Giant, among others. He received a final, lifetime Grammy Award for Technical Achievement in 2003.

Opposite, above: Norman "Hurricane" Smith's solo career took off in the early 1970s.

Opposite, below: A diminutive Ringo Starr presents a Grammy Award to Geoff Emerick, for Best Engineered Recording—Non-Classical, on March 8, 1968.

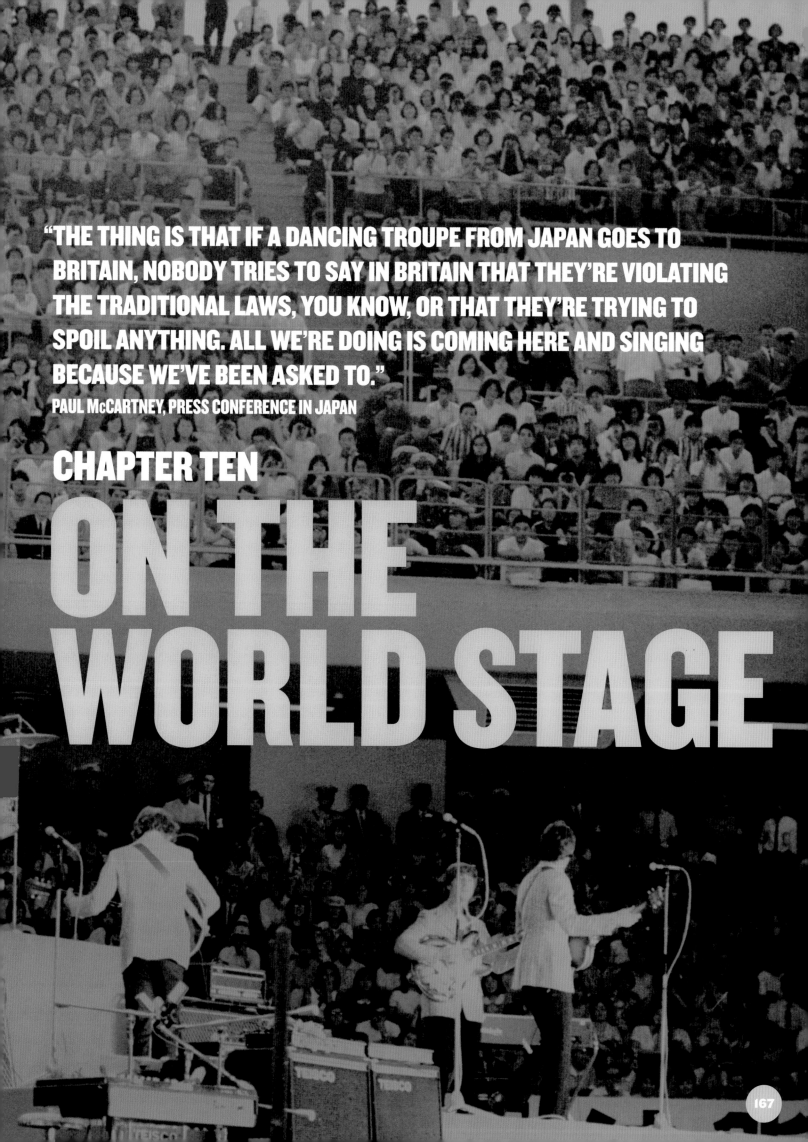

"THE THING IS THAT IF A DANCING TROUPE FROM JAPAN GOES TO BRITAIN, NOBODY TRIES TO SAY IN BRITAIN THAT THEY'RE VIOLATING THE TRADITIONAL LAWS, YOU KNOW, OR THAT THEY'RE TRYING TO SPOIL ANYTHING. ALL WE'RE DOING IS COMING HERE AND SINGING BECAUSE WE'VE BEEN ASKED TO."

PAUL McCARTNEY, PRESS CONFERENCE IN JAPAN

CHAPTER TEN

ON THE WORLD STAGE

schedule would be especially wearying. They were also trying to contend with those ongoing audio problems during live performances, issues they had yet to master.

The more the complexities of music and recording attracted the Beatles, the more difficult it became for them to replicate their music on stage. Not that it mattered overmuch; the screaming fans had increased their frenzy, if that was even possible, and blotted out most of the musical gaffes. Even so, John reportedly advised the crowd one night, "Don't listen to our music. We're terrible these days."

Partially to blame for the poor quality of the concerts was the absence of sound checks—now an industry standard—and the lack of any decent means of amplification. As the venues got larger, the fidelity grew proportionally worse. Yet the fans didn't seem to care.

A CULTURAL TREASURE

The tour would begin in Anchorage, Alaska, after which Brian had booked the group for three concerts in the Nippon Budokan Temple in Tokyo. What he didn't realize was that many Japanese considered Budokan a sanctified cultural space, where sumo wrestling, judo matches, and other traditional martial arts took place. These concerned citizens believed the Beatles were about to violate a treasured site, and protesters were already in the streets before the Beatles even arrived.

This open hostility was new to the band. Once inside their Tokyo hotel, the Beatles found themselves under heavy police guard, unable to move about. They had no chance to slip outside

Top: The Beatles pose for the press as they disembark at Tokyo International Airport, Japan, on June 29, 1966.

Bottom: Robert Whitaker documented the Beatles' World Tour in 1966. This is one of his pictures of the band performing at the Nippon Budokan in Tokyo, July 1, 1966.

Opposite: Imelda Marcos, wife of the Philippines' President, appears with her children, in October 1971.

Previous pages: Whitaker catches John and Ringo trying on kimonos.

After recording *Revolver* but just prior to its release, the Beatles set out on a summer world tour that focused on the Pacific Rim, Alaska, Japan, and the Philippines, followed by shows in India. The boys, who were not feeling very enthusiastic about touring at the time, knew this travel-heavy incognito, as they sometimes did, and sample the city. (John purportedly got past the guards and went antique hunting, flashing his money around like a swell.)

The Beatles tried to defend their presence in Tokyo during a press conference, Paul pointing out that they'd been "invited" there. But even in the world capital of polite restraint, the press insisted on asking patronizing questions. "What are you going to do when you grow up?" one reporter sniped. John retorted, "We don't wanna grow up," while Ringo shot back, "What are YOU gonna do?"

After the boys were informed that the massive rain storm that had previously hit Anchorage appeared to have followed them to Tokyo, they were asked to comment on the fact that the band was now being called the "Beatles Typhoon." John quipped, "There's probably more wind from the press than from us."

"SNUBBING" THE PHILIPPINES

If the cultural climate was awkward and restrictive in Tokyo, it got downright scary in the Philippines, where The Beatles were scheduled to play two shows at the Rizal Memorial Football Stadium in Manila. Brian Epstein had offered preferred concert seating to Philippines president (and despot) Ferdinand Marcos, his flamboyant wife, Imelda, and their children. In return, Mrs. Marcos invited the Beatles to join her family for a breakfast party at the palace the day after their concert. Epstein, who made it a policy to never accept official requests or invitations, declined the offer, explaining that the Beatles needed the day off to rest.

This snub on their part so inflamed

"WE OWN PRACTICALLY EVERYTHING IN THE PHILIPPINES."
FIRST LADY IMELDA MARCOS, WHO DID NOT OWN THE BEATLES

the first lady, that the Beatles and their support staff were ejected from their hotel and given a police escort to the airport that same afternoon. (Earlier in the day Brian had issued an apology on Philippines television, but the static during the broadcast was so bad, no one heard it or saw it.) Brian had never faced such open hostility. That morning an official informed him that he had to pay a substantial tax levy of Pesos 74,450 (almost $2,000 U.S.)—eating up all the profit from their concerts. Then, adding injury to insult, the Beatles and their entourage were physically assaulted while going through customs. The band was roughed up and Brian got punched in the face, while the roadies were kicked and pummeled. Mal Evans barely made it to the plane, blood streaming down his leg.

As unused to this sort of brusque treatment as they were, this was not the first time touring had given the Beatles cause to reflect. Once, after returning from a tour of Germany, George had received a

death threat in the mail. John often admitted he was afraid of being shot while on stage. They all had loved ones at home they would have preferred to spend their time with rather than roadies, PR people, the press, hotel clerks, bellboys, and room service staff. But touring was the law of the land for pop artists, who used concerts to promote their newest albums and singles. Not to mention, touring could be a lot more lucrative than the pennies-per-record deal most singers—including the Beatles, with their puny EMI contract—had been offered. No, it seemed touring was a necessary evil. But after a while, each member of the group began to think, "What if? Why not? Who says we have to tour to sell our records? We're Beatles, after all. We don't follow rules, we make them."

Even Paul, who was always more enamored of being on stage and performing live than his mates, occasionally wondered what it would be like to give up the stress and bother of all that traveling.

"I SUPPOSE IF I HAD SAID TELEVISION WAS MORE POPULAR THAN JESUS, I MIGHT HAVE GOT AWAY WITH IT"

JOHN LENNON, 1966 press conference

Considering all the wisecracks, rude remarks, and ill-conceived comments John Lennon made in his lifetime, it is bewildering that something he said during an interview, something that was in earnest and quite possibly true, got taken out of context and created a furor.

In March 1966, John was being interviewed by journalist Maureen Cleave for a series of articles about the Beatles' lifestyles. She'd noticed a number of books about philosophy and religion in his library at Kenwood, and so asked him his views on Christianity. John thought a bit and then replied, "Christianity will go. It will vanish and shrink. I needn't argue about that; I'm right and I'll be proved right. We're more popular than Jesus now; I don't know which will go first—rock and roll or Christianity. Jesus was all right but his disciples were thick and ordinary. It's them twisting it that ruins it for me."

Cleave's article appeared in the *London Evening Standard*, complete with Lennon's comment, and elicited no response from the public. After all, he hadn't been expressing a radical sentiment; for decades Christian clergymen in England—and around the globe—had been lamenting the falling away of the faithful and furthermore acknowledging that material things often took the place of religion.

AMERICAN BACKLASH

Five months later, when an American teen magazine, *Datebook*, splashed John's comment about Jesus across its front cover, the response from the public, especially

"WE JUST FELT IT WAS SO ABSURD AND SACRILEGIOUS THAT SOMETHING OUGHT TO BE DONE TO SHOW THEM THAT THEY CAN'T GET AWAY WITH THIS SORT OF THING."
WAQY DJ TOMMY CHARLES

in America's Bible belt, was swift and punitive. Two radio stations in Alabama and Texas immediately announced a ban on broadcasting any Beatles' records; before long many other stations followed suit. Conservative town fathers censured the band, organizing anti-Beatles rallies and record burnings. Even the Vatican denounced the quote.

Unfortunately, the band was due to tour America while this anti-Beatles revolt was taking place. When the repercussions from John's comment continued to spread, Brian considered canceling the tour. Instead he scheduled a press conference during their first stop, in Chicago—well before the tour reached the Bible belt. John reiterated that his remark had been taken out of context, that he had no grievance with Christianity or the church, and that, "I was just saying it as a fact and it's true more for England than here. I'm not saying that we're better or greater, or comparing us with Jesus Christ as a person or God as a thing or whatever it is. I just said what I said and it was wrong. Or it was taken wrong."

John apologized again and again, but in 1969 he reminded the press that he still believed what he'd said was true, that the Beatles had more influence on teens than Christ. "Some ministers stood up and agreed with it," he was quick to point out. And in truth, *America*, the Jesuit magazine, had written, "Lennon was simply stating what many a Christian educator would readily admit."

In spite of the apologetic press conference, things got tense in Memphis when the ultra

conservative Ku Klux Klan not only nailed a Beatles' album to a cross, vowing to "take vengeance," they also picketed the concerts dressed in their long robes and ominous pointed hoods. The daytime concert proceeded without a hitch, but then someone threw a firecracker onto the stage and it went off. The three other Beatles and everyone in the wings immediately looked at John. Press agent Tony Barrow remarked, "We would not at that moment have been surprised to see that guy go down."

It was no wonder Lennon often spoke of a fear of being shot while on stage. Furthermore, this series of frightening incidents— including someone taking a shot at their plane as they landed in Texas—had to have affected all the Beatles' judgment as they reached a crossroads at the end of that tour.

"I always remember to thank Jesus for the end of my touring days; if I hadn't said that the Beatles were 'bigger than Jesus' and upset the very Christian Ku Klux Klan, well, Lord, I might still be up there with all the other performing fleas! God bless America. Thank you, Jesus."

JOHN LENNON, 1978, being glib

Opposite, top: John speaks at a Beatles press conference at Heathrow Airport, July 1966.

Opposite, below: A photographer catches Paul and George (with Ringo and John behind) on the tour bus during the American tour, August 1966.

Above: The Ku Klux Klan, shown here at a rally in Atlanta, marched against the Beatles outside their concerts.

"AFTER DECIDING NOT TO TOUR, I DON'T THINK WE CARED A DAMN. WE'D BEEN HAVING MORE FUN IN THE STUDIO . . . AND THE SONGS WERE GETTING BETTER AND MORE INTERESTING."
RINGO STARR

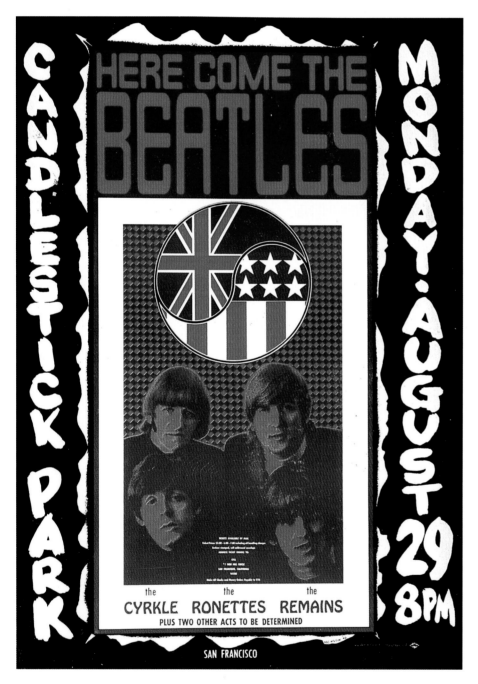

In August 1966 the Beatles embarked on their third tour of North America—where they were scheduled to play thirteen cities in the United State plus Toronto. After the press conference in Chicago, Brian prayed the fans wouldn't boycott the remaining shows. Yet even though the tour ended up being a financial success, for the first time the band played to empty seats at many of the venues, including during their second appearance at hallowed Shea Stadium, which Sid Bernstein had again arranged. It looked like John Lennon had found the precise way to slow down Beatlemania. Or perhaps some fans were simply moving on to other, "cooler" trends, as teenagers often did.

The American tour ended on August 29, 1966, with a single show at San Francisco's Candlestick Park stadium, the home of baseball's Giants and football's 49ers. The fans in attendance had no idea they were witnessing a significant milestone in the history of the Beatles. The Beatles themselves, however, had a pretty good idea this was it. Ringo later spoke of the group discussing all their touring issues and insisting that this "had got to end," while they were at the stadium, but, he added, no decisions were made until they returned to London.

Although the venue had room for 42,500 patrons, only 25,000 tickets sold. There were blocks of empty seats all around the stadium, and the promoter, Tempo Productions, actually lost money on the concert. Performing in support of the Beatles were the Remains, Bobby Hebb, the Cyrkle and the Ronettes.

Above: A poster advertises what became the last official Beatles concert, at Candlestick Park Stadium, San Francisco, August 29, 1966.

Opposite: The Beatles relax in the buffet car of a train, during their mini-tour of Germany, June 22, 1966.

According to the MC, popular KYA disc jockey "Emperor" Gene Nelson, the backstage dressing room was a free-for-all, with the press trying to get their kids into the show, Joan Baez hanging out with the bands, and a host of celebrities crowding in.

The boys hit the stage at 9:27 PM and proceeded to play "Rock and Roll Music," "She's a Woman," "If I Needed Someone," "Day Tripper," "Baby's in Black," "I Feel Fine," "Yesterday," "I Wanna Be Your Man," "Nowhere Man," "Paperback Writer," and "Long Tall Sally." There is a sort of poetic justice to the fact that the last commercial concert the Beatles played was in America, and that the final song they performed was Little Richard's homegrown R&B rocker. Rarely are roots and influences so gracefully acknowledged, even unwittingly.

"ASK ME WHY"

To anyone who understood the pressures the Beatles faced on a daily basis, the reasons for their decision to stop touring were not a huge mystery.

• They were frustrated at not being able to hear themselves playing on stage and embarrassed over the resultant subpar performances.

• They wanted to be able to play longer, more eclectic sets instead of a rigidly structured twenty minutes of their latest hits.

• They were all feeling a great weariness over life on the road.

• Naturally, they all wanted to spend more time with their families and friends at home.

• They were experiencing the natural growing apart of any youthful group as they mature and find themselves drawn to divergent pursuits and interests.

• They believed they no longer needed to tour to sell records.

• John, Paul, and George really wanted to focus on studio work, experimenting with audio equipment, and stretching the limits of the technology.

• They all felt they had enough financial security at that point to give up the lucrative tours.

There had also been disturbing incidents in different parts of the world—some people brought ailing relatives for the Beatles to touch and cure, as though they were holy men. Once, in Sydney, Australia, a woman had tossed her mentally disabled child at Paul while he rode on a truck bed in a parade. (Fortunately, he caught the child.) It was these bizarre expectations held by some of their fans that the Beatles wished to leave behind.

Brian, who visibly enjoyed all the bustle and public recognition of touring, was initially not happy with their decision. Some of his friends claim that the beginning of his mental and emotional decline coincided with this event. But his merger of NEMS Enterprises with Robert Stigwood in early 1967 somewhat belies this theory—Brian confided to a number of people that he was weary of managing the Beatles and initially wanted Stigwood to take over the reins. (It's also possible Brian didn't realize the distancing effect this lack of touring would have on his relationship with his boys until many months had passed.)

Brian Epstein started out with one lone assistant when he first managed the Beatles. But as time passed, and the band's fame increased, he hired additional staff to help him oversee their daily routine as well as their tours. Perhaps the most important members of this latter crew, were the men whose job it was to get the Beatles safely in and out of performance venues, press conferences, hotel rooms, to and from airports . . . in fact to handle any situation that required moving the Beatles from point A to point B without a trail of screaming fans.

NEIL ASPINALL

Neil Aspinall had been a schoolmate of Paul's and became involved with the Beatles via Pete Best's mom, with whom he'd had a romantic relationship. He took over the role of road manager early on, driving a van owned by drummer Best. He left his accounting job to become the Beatles full-time road manager in 1962, moving up to personal assistant the following year—leaving the driving and carrying chores to Mal Evans. Once the band stopped touring, Neil performed various jobs within the organization, some requiring his keen accounting skills. This was also true when he ran Apple Corps—his ability to make sense of both the legal and financial documentation was invaluable. Once the legal issues concerning the break-up of the Beatles were resolved in the 1990s, Neil was directed to assemble the audio

Above: Neil Aspinall escorts John and George onto the stage through a crowd of fans, during the band's relentless touring in 1963.

Opposite: Mal Evans, the gentle giant of the Beatles' support staff.

"HE SHOULD BE CONSIDERED THE FIFTH BEATLE."

GEORGE HARRISON ON NEIL ASPINALL, AT THE BEATLES HALL OF FAME INDUCTION

and video materials that would eventually become the *Anthology* series. He left Apple in 2007, and died the next year of lung cancer.

MAL EVANS

Mal Evans got his first Beatles' gig because he was a fan. A telephone engineer who worshipped Elvis, while at the Cavern Club one day on lunch break, he was immediately taken with this cocky Scouse band, whose irreverent style reminded him of the King. After the Beatles became regular headliners, George Harrison asked the manager to hire the 6'6" Evans to be a part-time bouncer at the club. Mal eventually left both his jobs to become bodyguard, roadie, and driver for the group. Big as he was, Evans had the ability to

gently but firmly move fans out of the way whenever the Beatles were in danger of being overrun. He calmed the crowds when people brought their disabled loved ones to the Beatles' hotels, believing that the band members were magically endowed with healing powers. The only punch Mal may ever threw was to knock out the broken

"Mal was a big lovable bear of a roadie."

PAUL McCARTNEY

windshield of the band's van after it was struck by road debris during a night trip from London to Liverpool. He was also the procurer of band instruments once the Beatles had become too famous to shop for themselves. When

George Harrison felt he needed a fresh sound, he would send Evans to any nearby music shop to buy a new guitar, and before he was out the door John would call out for Mal to buy him one, as well.

Mal made a cameo appearance in *Help!*, playing the burly swimmer who pops out of the ice hole and asks for directions. But for the most part he remained in the background, offering protection and comfort. Evans stayed with the group all the way to the breakup. His life ended tragically in 1976—he was fatally shot in his apartment by the Los Angeles police while waving an unloaded firearm. He had reportedly been despondent for some time after his former charges had gone their separate ways.

ALISTAIR TAYLOR

Alistair Taylor was Brian Epstein's right-hand man while he was running the NEMS store in Liverpool, and he became a key player when Brian took over the management of the Beatles. In 1962 he left Liverpool for London due to his wife's asthma, but rejoined Brian's team when Epstein and the Fabs moved to London the following year. Taylor's nickname, "Mr. Fix-it," came from his ability to solve problems—he could find cigarettes after closing time or hire a limousine at the drop of a

hat. He also devised the elaborate escape routes the Beatles were forced to take when leaving concert halls. Taylor helped Paul purchase High Park Farm in Scotland; rented the Magical Mystery Tour bus; resolved the complex copyright issues surrounding the *Sgt. Pepper* cover montage; and performed a host of invaluable tasks. Taylor became general manager of Apple Corps after Brian's death—and was among the pedestrians down on the street

"Alistair Taylor was a wonderful number 2."

TONY BRAMWELL,
Beatles' press officer

during the Rooftop Session in *Let It Be*. He later promoted Elton John and eventually retired to an historic cottage in Derbyshire, where he ran a tearoom with his wife. He also enjoyed making appearances at Beatles conventions. Taylor died in 2009.

DEREK TAYLOR

Derek Taylor was working as a newspaper reporter and theater critic when the Beatles came calling. Brian Epstein asked him to ghostwrite a column about the group—posing as George Harrison—for the Manchester edition of the *Daily Express*. George was not exactly pleased by what Derek wrote—and offered to collaborate with him on future columns. Taylor continued to promote the Beatles in his paper, impressing Brian with his efforts, and Brian eventually asked him to become assistant press liaison to the band. Taylor jumped at the chance, although working with

Brian turned out to be a heaven-or-hell experience. He did manage to assist Epstein in writing his 1964 autobiography, *A Cellarful of Noise*.

"Derek leaves a thousand friends."

GEOFF BAKER, Paul McCartney's press officer, on Taylor's death

Taylor got to know the Beatles well while coordinating their press conferences, and Brian soon grew jealous of Derek and began to criticize him harshly. By the end of 1964 Derek had had enough. He left NEMS, moved to Los Angeles and again found work in the music industry as a press agent—eventually signing supergroups like the Byrds and the Beach Boys. He organized the Monterey Pop Festival with Papa John Phillips in 1967 and helped boost Harry Nilsson's career by sending copies of his album Pandemonium Shadow Show to the Beatles. It was Derek who introduced David Crosby and other LA rock stars to George, who was staying at a house on infamous Blue Jay Way.

In 1968, after Brian died, Taylor moved back to England to become press officer for Apple, a shortlived gig, because the Beatles' new manager, Allen Klein, soon released him. Derek moved on to writing books about the music business, including working with George Harrison on *I Me Mine*. He also helped coordinate the *Anthology* series with the three remaining Beatles. He died in 2007, but not before he'd seen the series fully blossom into another important segment of Beatles' lore.

INSTRUMENTS OF THE MIDDLE YEARS

"WE LOVED THE BEATLES AND THEY LOVED THE BYRDS, AND WE WERE SHARING INFLUENCES."

ROGER MCGUINN, COFOUNDER OF THE BYRDS

During the mid-1960s the Beatles had a lot more disposable income, and new instruments were one of their favorites things to buy. Then again, there were always old favorites, like George's trusty Stratocaster, Rocky, that took on almost legendary status. It also didn't hurt that manufacturers—and even music stores—were quick to gift them with complementary guitars.

In 1963, George acquired a Rickenbacker 360/12 soon after he and his mates arrived in New York for the first time. It was a gift (and a second-of-its-kind prototype) from the grateful manufacturer. George single-handedly introduced the world to the high-trebled 12-string Rick in the group's first film, *A Hard Day's Night*, playing the lead on "I Should Have Known Better." Just how many future guitarists were blown away by the sound of the 360 is hard to say. It is certain that Byrds cofounder Roger McGuinn was influenced in his choice of signature guitar by George's playing. Harrison received a replacement model, which had a rounder look to the cutaways, in 1965, courtesy of a music store in Minnesota, where they Beatles were performing.

ROCKY AND FRIENDS

In 1965, John and George each received a 1961 Fender Stratocaster, in Sonic Blue, courtesy of their manager, who insisted that they be the same color. John fiddled with his a bit, most notably on "Nowhwere Man," but George's Strat (called

"Rocky") became one of his regular studio guitars at the time, making its appearance on several LPs and, most famously, on the "I Am The Walrus" video. For the filming he'd used day-glo red and lime-green paint, and "some of [wife] Pattie's sparkly green nail varnish" to give the guitar a psychedelic look. It was on this same guitar that George used a volume pedal while playing and singing "I Need You" in the film *Help!* He may not have been the first guitarist to use one, but, like his Rick 360 guitar, the song served as an introduction to many fans (and guitarists) who were not aware of the device. The pedal was also used on "Yes It Is," the B-Side of "Ticket To Ride." John had to lever it up and down by hand, because George hadn't yet learned to play and ride the pedal with his foot at the same time.

JOHN'S SIGNATURE AXE

In 1966 John purchased an Epiphone Casino, a thinline, hollow-bodied electric guitar with light-brown sunburst coloring. This would become his regular guitar once he put down the Rickenbacker, which

Above: Rocky, George Harrison's 1964 Fender Stratocaster guitar.

had become shopworn. George, like John, bought himself a Casino, a red sunburst model with a Bigsby tremelo bar, which he (and John) used extensively during their second Asian tour. This actually made a total of three Casinos, since Paul had been using a 1962 Epi (a reversed right-handed model, of course) in the studio all along to play his electric guitar solos. The Casino would become the only guitar model used by all three Beatles. Paul had continued with his Hofner bass

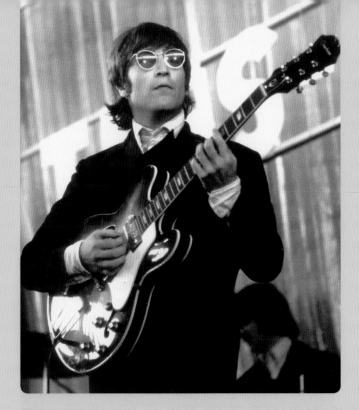

throughout the mid-1960s in concert, but he, too, wanted something with more punch while recording in the studio, especially for nailing that throbbing Motown beat. He was given a Rickenbacker bass direct from the California factory in 1965, which he used when he needed a big bottom on a song, which the Hofner couldn't quite manage. The extra thump the Rick provided would define him as a superior bassist.

George wasn't done yet. He got himself a Gibson SG Standard in 1966. Though he used it on several *Revolver* tracks and, most notably, on the video the group filmed for "Hey Bulldog," he never toured the States with it. He later gave it to Pete Ham of Badfinger. After Pete died, his brother kept it, until it was sold at auction in 2004 for over $550,000. It is currently on display at the Rock and Roll Hall of Fame in Cleveland.

Above, and bottom left: John and George perform at the Ernst Merck Halle in Hamburg with their Epiphone Casino guitars in June 1966. George's Epiphone has a Bigsby Vibrato attached.

Below, center: Paul's Rickenbacker bass guitar.

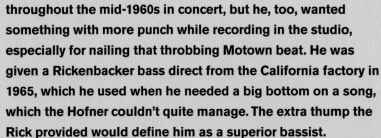

In May 2013, a 1966 custom-made Vox guitar with a Beatles' pedigree created by Mike Bennett and Dick Denney sold at auction at the Hard Rock Cafe for $408,000. The distinctive mahogany axe had been played by George Harrison during takes for "I Am the Walrus" and by John Lennon on a promo video for "Hello, Goodbye." It was then given by Lennon to "Magic" Alex Mardas.

"ONE OF THE GREAT PENALTIES THOSE OF US WHO LIVE OUR LIVES IN FULL VIEW OF THE PUBLIC MUST PAY IS THE LOSS OF THAT MOST CHERISHED BIRTHRIGHT OF MAN'S, PRIVACY."
MARY PICKFORD

CHAPTER ELEVEN

BEATLES IN PRIVATE

Domestic Arrangements

Above: Astrid Kirchherr, Maureen Cox, and Pattie Boyd sit in the stalls of the Scala Theatre during the filming of *A Hard Day's Night*, 1964.

Right: Paul's girlfriend Jane Asher had a flourishing TV career when she first met him at the age of 17.

Below: John and Cynthia onboard the Beatles' flight to New York, February 7, 1964. They put on smiling faces for the press, but their marriage was imperiled by John's long absences, his neglect of Julian, and his affairs with other women.

Opposite, top: John plays with Julian by the pool at Kenwood in 1967.

Opposite, bottom: John rests in the garden at Kenwood in 1967.

Previous pages: John, Julian, giant panda and teddy bear, also at Kenwood in 1967. Compare with p. 77.

The Beatles probably would have been quite happy to remain in London, but when the fan encroachment and stress of touring got too much for John, George, and Ringo, they all moved out to what was called the "stockbroker belt," in the London suburb of Surrey. Here, wealthy businessmen—or rock stars—could escape from the bustle of London, into the peaceful serenity of mock-Tudor mansions with restful landscaping, and still be within a short commute of the city. Paul, alone, opted to remain in his gated, detached home in St. John's Wood.

By now each of the Beatles had a serious partner, wives in three cases, a steady girlfriend, Jane Asher, in Paul's case. But there were also plenty of rumors of Beatle indiscretions, after gigs or after an evening of clubbing. It was never easy being a Beatle consort and the women were often relegated—with the exception of Jane Asher, who had an active career as an actress—to the sidelines, if not actually to the background. In the case of John and Ringo, some of this sequestering of family was due to their children. Neither famous father wanted their offspring to become fodder for the rabid British tabloids, and so family life typically occurred behind closed gates or high walls.

In 1964, when the fan presence outside his flat in Emperor's Gate, Brompton, grew too annoying, John Lennon moved his wife and son to an estate called Kenwood in the suburb of Weybridge, Surrey. The pseudo-Tudor house cost John £20,000 (about $30,000) and he paid another £40,000 (about $60,000) for renovations done by Brian Epstein's contractor, Ken

Partridge. Fortunately, the move didn't impact his song-writing partnership with Paul, who claimed that during the long ride out to John's house he often came up with song ideas or new melodies.

Cynthia's "partnership" with John was less sanguine. Once again, as she had done in Liverpool during her pregnancy, Cynthia felt marginalized from John's life. She had grown up in Hoylake, Wirral, an affluent suburb across the Mersey from Liverpool. Her father had been a successful traveling salesman before his death from cancer, and when the shy, studious Cyn first started dating John, she'd considered herself his social superior. "Not the sort of boy I usually went with," she would later confess.

But now he was jet-setting around Europe and hobnobbing with other celebrities in London, and she felt unable to take her place in this world. Pattie Boyd, George's future wife, who often traveled with Cynthia and John, recalled that Cyn was of a serious nature, and that even though she enjoyed an occasional movie premiere or shopping spree, she was not the sort to indulge in a wild night of drinking, drugging, or clubbing. Plus, she had a young child at home to look after. At least she had convinced John to let her mother, Lillian Powell, come to stay at Kenwood, to help with Julian and to supply her with some company. This didn't exactly do anything for their faltering marriage—John baited her mother, calling her Lowl, in mockery of her working-class Liverpool dialect—the two circled each other like terriers.

ACID-FUELED DAYS AND NIGHTS

John, meanwhile, was slowly

"I knew then that our marriage was in trouble. We had lost communication. John was on another planet."

CYNTHIA LENNON, on John's use of LSD

moving beyond the relatively harmless highs of pot to the more disturbing hallucinogenic effects of LSD, increasingly experimenting with acid trips. He felt they opened up the creative channels of his brain, allowing him to write vivid, stream-of-consciousness songs like "Tomorrow Never Knows" and "Rain." Cynthia had tried LSD once, when a dentist friend put some in her and Lennon's coffee, and she did not enjoy it. A second attempt, some time later, gave her an unpleasant trip. John saw this lack of insight or vision on his wife's part as a flaw, while Cynthia feared that John was becoming dependent on the drug. (Friends reported that John took so much acid, he rarely had a chance to come down, which meant he also never really got that high, yet was constantly under some kind of acid influence.) Before long his and Cynthia's alienation from each other was complete and they drifted apart, each following their own pursuits. In John's case, this meant openly pursuing other women.

Paul McCartney and Jane Asher in London

While still living with the Asher family on Wimpole Street, Paul purchased a three-story detached gated house on Cavendish Avenue in St. John's Wood. He and Jane Asher moved there in March 1965. In spite of being visibly in love with her—some of his tenderest, most enduring songs, songs like "Here, There and Everywhere," were written for her—he continued to be a hound, sleeping around with chance-met female celebrities or attractive fans. If Jane knew of this, she never used it as an excuse to end their relationship. Perhaps she hoped Paul would tire of his flings and eventually develop a core of faithfulness.

It was Asher who, in 1966, convinced Paul to buy High Park Farm, in Machrihanish, Campbeltown, Scotland, so they would have a private getaway that was not constantly under siege by the press.

The couple became engaged in 1967, but there were no announcements of a forthcoming wedding. Paul still seemed to be hedging his bets. And then when Jane was offered a tour of America acting in *Romeo and Juliet* with the Bristol company of the Old Vic Theatre, she decided to accept it. Paul was upset that she would just up and go like that, but made no attempt to stop his cheating ways. When Asher returned five months later, she found their home changed, full of people and things she didn't recognize, and Paul heavily into LSD. They did travel together to India, to study with the Maharishi, but then split up for good in July 1968—after Asher came home from Bristol and found an American writer who worked at Apple, Francie Schwartz, in bed with Paul.

Schwartz insists, however, the couple had already split up when she and Paul started dating.

THE EMPEROR LENNON

Cavendish Avenue was a five-minute walk from the EMI studios, and so the Beatles often met there before or after recording sessions. Paul and John had an unusual experience there one night, when John accidentally took acid instead of an upper during the recording of *Sgt. Pepper*. Paul took him back to his home and dropped acid as well so that John would not become freaked out. It was only the second time Paul had taken the drug, a measure of his concern for John's state of mind. Paul related later that he and John sat down facing each other, something they always did when composing together, and, "We looked into each other's eyes, the eye contact thing we used to do, which is fairly mind-boggling.

"I was never the dolly-bird type. I didn't particularly like going to discotheques and sitting up till 4 AM in a haze of cigarette smoke."

JANE ASHER

You dissolve into each other . . . It was a very freaky experience and I was totally blown away." Meanwhile John had a vision of himself as the Emperor of Eternity, and Paul began to believe John truly was in charge of the world.

Paul's concern for his friend was still in evidence a year later, in 1968 during the recording of *The White Album*, when he invited John and Yoko Ono to live with him. The arrangement seemed to be working out until John found a note Paul had written: "You and your Jap tart think you're hot shit." Paul claimed it was all in

jest; John did not find it amusing, and he and Yoko shortly moved out. In Paul's defense, during that period in his life, John *was* carrying on like the Emperor of Eternity, one who had now found the Empress he had always sought.

A COUNTRY BUNGALOW

In July 1965, George purchased a large, low-slung bungalow called Kinfauns on the Claremont Estate in Esher, near Weybridge, where both John and Ringo lived. Three months later his girlfriend, Pattie Boyd, moved in with him.

The rambling one-story house had the feel of a colonial plantation house, which must have appealed to Pattie, who had been born in Somerset, but spent her early childhood in Kenya. Her father had been a Royal Air Force pilot and her mother was from a well-to-do military family. When her parents split when she was eight, her mother almost immediately remarried. Soon after, she and her new husband took Pattie's baby sister Paula and went back to England, leaving Pattie and her other two siblings in Kenya. Pattie was reunited with her mother within the year, but carried the emotional scars for years. She attended convent schools as a young teen, and eventually grew into a beautiful young woman who hoped for a modeling career. With her slender frame, long legs, large blue eyes, and sun-kissed blond hair, and in spite of slightly rabbity front teeth, she soon became a favorite of London's fashion photographers. The swinging styles that embodied Carnaby Street—miniskirts, tall boots and lacy shirts or skinny tops—looked sensational on her.

She and George were married on January 21, 1966, with Paul McCartney as best man, and spent their honeymoon in Barbados. They appeared happy to outsiders; unlike the other Beatle wives, she enjoyed the London nightlife and accompanying George to parties and openings. Yet eventually she, too, was marginalized, mainly because George's first loyalty lay with his band. He also deepened his interest in Transcendental Meditation during the Beatles' visit with the Maharishi Mahesh Yogi in India, and his search for enlightenment turned him

"We had also covered the outside of the house with graffiti. The walls had been plain white when we moved in, so we bought some cans of spray paint and spent many happy hours cheering them up."

PATTIE BOYD on Kinfauns, *Wonderful Tonight*

away from the sexual side of his marriage to Pattie. Eighteen months after their wedding, she met Eric Clapton, a blues guitarist and member of the supergroup Cream, at Brian Epstein's home. Clapton would soon fall in love with her and make no attempt to disguise his intention of taking her away from George—who happened to be his close friend.

In spite of their marital bumps, George and Pattie

remained together at Kinfauns until March 1970, when he purchased a rambling Victorian estate called Friar Park.

Top: George poses in the garden of his new home, Kinfauns, in the summer of 1965.

Above, left and right: George at Kinfauns after he and Pattie had "cheered up" the exterior.

Opposite, top: Paul meets Jane Asher at Heathrow Airport as she arrives home from a stay in America, May 1967.

Opposite, bottom: Paul with Jane and their Old English Sheepdog, Martha, outside the Golden Gates Hotel in Glasgow, Scotland, 1966.

"I'M NOT REALLY FUSSY WHERE I LIVE— PROVIDING IT'S WITH RINGO."
MAUREEN STARKEY

Above: Ringo, and his 18-year-old wife Maureen on their honeymoon in Hove, East Sussex, February 12, 1965.

Ringo had followed John's exodus from London, and in 1965 he and new wife Maureen also settled in Weybridge, in another mock-Tudor house called Sunny Heights, on the St. George's Hill Estate. Visitors sometimes commented that in spite of all the amenities—the multiple TVs, film projectors and stereos, a billiard table and go-cart track, and even a real pub called The Flying Cow, there was no drum kit in the house. Ringo would smile and say, "When we don't record, I don't play."

Maureen, also called Mitch or Mo, had been a Ringo fan back in the Cavern days and they first met outside the club when she asked him for an autograph. She had previously dated one of Ringo's bandmates from Rory Storm and the Hurricanes, Johnny Guitar. But Ringo was the one for her, and she would spend any time off from her job as a hairdresser hanging around the Cavern to watch him perform. Eventually he asked her to dance, but when they began dating, she had to keep it secret, for fear his fans would harm her. She went with him on two vacations, to Greece and to the Caribbean—which alerted the press to her presence. Ringo

jokingly introduced her as his secretary. When Ringo was struck down by a bad case of tonsillitis in June 1964, Mo remained faithfully beside him during his recovery. He proposed in January 1965 at the Ad Lib and the couple married on February 11 at Caxton Hall in Westminster. Brian Epstein was the best man, and John and Cynthia and George Harrison were all there to wish them well.

Their son Zak was born that year, and they had a second son, Jason, born in 1967, and a daughter, Lee, born in 1970.

Maureen was perhaps the most domestic of the Beatle wives, telling fan magazines she just wanted to look after "Ritchie" and cook for him. She explained that she understood the band kept late hours and she would wait up for him with a meal for when he finally came home. During the day she occupied herself with crafts, sewing, and decorating the house. In one interview she confessed, "I put sequins on an old lampshade the other day." While it's clear she was trying to come across as a happy homemaker, there is also an undercurrent of someone who was trying to make the best of an unpleasant situation. Like Cynthia Lennon, Maureen was another Liverpool girl who found herself far from home and too frequently without her man.

When Ringo bought Peter Sellers' Elstead home, Brookfield, in 1968 and moved his family there, he allowed John and Yoko Ono to live at Sunny Heights after Cynthia forced John to leave Kenwood. Ringo sold Sunny Heights in 1969.

In January 1965, Brian moved from his lodgings at Whaddon House to 24 Chapel Street, in the exclusive embassy district of Belgravia. He spent a small fortune redoing the place, making it into a space where he could entertain on a lavish scale. He became known for his parties, especially the one he held for the Beatles to celebrate the release of *Sgt. Pepper*.

And while Brian also enjoyed exploring the gay nightlife of London, with its discreet bars and private clubs (homosexual acts were still considered criminal in England), he had already fixed his sights on a new conquest, someone closer to home.

It wasn't long into their professional association that Brian fell in love with John. Not so surprising, considering that John's cheeky charisma and Teddy boy allure were always quite potent. The other Beatles surely must have realized how Brian felt, but as if by unspoken accord, never mentioned it in public. Still, in cosmopolitan London there was an active gay subculture, which Brian took part in and which he introduced to John. John's reaction to this exotic underworld should have been his usual mocking disdain, but for some reason he allowed himself to be presented as Brian's protégé.

ON THE PROWL

As a young man in search of both a father and mother figure, John may have found in Brian aspects of both parental archetypes, and so given him a certain amount of leeway. Whatever the reason, John continued to make himself available to Brian, even so far

"I was on holiday with Brian Epstein in Spain, where the rumours went around that he and I were having a love affair. Well, it was almost a love affair, but not quite. It was never consummated. But it was a pretty intense relationship."

JOHN LENNON, *All We Are Saying*, **David Sheff**

as vacationing with him in Spain shortly after Cynthia gave birth to Julian, and while there, commenting on potential partners for Epstein as the two sipped coffee in a cafe. Paul had a theory that John was being shrewd, that he went specifically to form a bond with Brian to ensure he would be treated as the leader of the group.

The question that invariably gets asked is whether or not they were lovers. Some acquaintances have confirmed this, and it could be true; John might have allowed a brief encounter under the guise of sexual orienteering. Or not. But any physical side to their friendship had little to do with the real relationship Brian had with John and the other Beatles—symbiosis.

In Brian they had found precisely what they needed—a motivated legend-builder, while the Beatles offered him his deepest desire—his longed-for ticket to fame. The arrangement had perfect symmetry. There was an enormous reciprocal commitment between manager and band at that time, and from it arose an ethic of loyalty and industry on all sides, a cabal that would propel the Beatles to unimaginable fame. Brian's longing for John might have sparked his initial efforts for the group, but he was soon fully engaged in developing all their careers. Including his own. Brian's unrequited love for John may have seemed painfully poetic for a time, but it likely faded somewhat when factored against the astonishing things he and the other four were able to accomplish as a unit.

Above: Brian Epstein relaxes at home.

"EVERY SUMMER WE CAN RENT A COTTAGE ON THE ISLE OF WIGHT, IF IT'S NOT TOO DEAR..."
"WHEN I'M SIXTY-FOUR"

Left: Ringo and Mo at their villa in Port of Spain, Trinidad, January 1966. They were there with John and Cynthia.

on each other's company and to make sure they didn't spend their R&R time working on new songs (especially Paul, who wasn't nearly as inclined to lay about as John was; he actually wrote "Things We Said Today" during that Virgin Islands vacation).

Perhaps the earliest photos of the Beatles on vacation—as opposed to working abroad—are from the May 1963 trip Paul, George, and Ringo took to Tenerife in the Canary Islands. (John and Brian, meanwhile, were staying in Torremolinos, Spain). The three were there visiting Hamburg friends Klaus Voorman—whose father owned a villa in the hills—and Astrid Kirchherr—who took photos of the boys lounging by a pool, walking along the black volcanic sand beach, and posing in an Austin-Healey Sprite. In spite of having a number-one hit in England with "Please Please Me," the three Beatles went unrecognized in Tenerife. They even offered to play a few numbers at the San Telmo Lido bar and were turned down.

Considering the blazing pace the Beatles set during their early years, it's not surprising they valued the times they were able to get away from the grind. Once Beatlemania had spread across the globe, however, it was difficult for the band to find holiday spots where their fans didn't dog them. To avoid the worst of this, they often used fake names and wore disguises when traveling.

There was one vacation in May 1964, when Brian Epstein had booked George and Pattie Boyd, along with John and Cyn, into a resort in a very remote part of Tahiti. The weather was so hot that George asked Pattie to cut his hair, so she trimmed off quite a bit. Soon after, she discovered someone on the hotel staff had

pinched his hair clippings from the wastebasket. Another time, when John Lennon and Victor Spinetti, his costar in the first two Beatles' films, went on holiday in Morocco John intended to remain incognito. According to Spinetti, it didn't work at all—whenever anyone on the street, even veiled women and urchins, saw John, they all began chanting, "Yah! Yah! Yah!"

When making travel arrangements, Brian would usually separate the foursome into twosomes: for instance, having Paul and Jane Asher accompany Ringo and Maureen to the Virgin Islands, while the other two Beatles were on the Tahiti trip. According to Pattie, Brian usually kept Paul and John apart on vacation, possibly to prevent them from overdosing

Opposite, clockwise from top left: John and Cynthia during their vacation with Ringo and Mo in Port of Spain, Trinidad, January 1966; Paul, poolside at the Deauville Hotel, Miami Beach, February 1964; a bearded Ringo relaxes in Trinidad; four Beatles in the shallows, Miami, February 1964; John and Cynthia on the beach at Port of Spain; George, poolside at the Deauville Hotel, Miami, again during the Beatles' first U.S. trip.

"I DECLARE THAT THE BEATLES ARE MUTANTS. PROTOTYPES OF EVOLUTIONARY AGENTS SENT BY GOD, ENDOWED WITH A MYSTERIOUS POWER TO CREATE A NEW HUMAN SPECIES, A YOUNG RACE OF LAUGHING FREEMEN."

TIMOTHY LEARY, COUNTERCULTURE ICON AND LSD ADVOCATE

CHAPTER TWELVE
BEATLES IN DISGUISE

"WE SPEND MORE TIME RECORDING NOW, BECAUSE WE PREFER RECORDING."

GEORGE HARRISON, 1966

By the end of 1966, when it was time to return to the studio, the Beatles were all on drugs. George Martin later discussed this situation with Paul in relation to the making of *Sgt. Pepper's Lonely Hearts Club Band*, maintaining that the group wasn't stoned all the time. "Yeah," Paul replied. "We were." (A canny fan had only to study the cover of *Rubber Soul* to suss this. The Beatles look like escapees from "ganja Friday" at Cheech and Chong's house.) Pot and Prellies notwithstanding—or, alternatively, prompting the upsurge—the band was about to carve out even fresher creative territory with their latest effort.

Once they stopped touring, the Beatles discovered how much they enjoyed hanging out in the studio, tinkering with the latest technologies, and trying out experimental treatments on new material. It became clear, after the *Anthology* outtakes were released, that John and Paul were rarely self-conscious about presenting snatches of new songs or partial melodies to the others. George claims he never stood up to Paul or John to demand special consideration for his own compositions, not until "While My Guitar Gently Weeps" on *The Beatles*, but even he occasionally tried out his songs in front of them during this period.

The atmosphere at that time, before the band began to champ at the bit

that held them back as individual artists, must have been akin to a group of teammates or soldiers who had been rubbing along comfortably for years. Acceptance, patience, curiosity, a familiarity with each other's foibles and the good grace to overlook them—these were the qualities that made the Beatles unafraid to improvise with older material or trot out new efforts. They also no longer had the stress of being trapped together in hotel rooms, limos, and backstage. Now, if they came together, it was because they chose to. The frequent exception being when micro-manager Paul contacted the others while they were lazing about to remind them of songwriting or recording obligations. Ringo told tales of relaxing beside the pool with John and George, and hearing the indoor phone ring. "It's Paul!" they all piped in.

THE MAKING OF *SGT. PEPPER*

Considering the Beatles' fierce work ethic, pumping out seven U.K. albums and twelve hit singles in five years, it was no surprise that when they went on a brief hiatus after *Revolver*, skeptics insisted that the Fabs had lost their mojo. Or even that they were breaking up. But the group was simply percolating, giving ideas and concepts free rein and a chance to expand into actual songs.

Finally, the vision behind the new collection began to coalesce.

Paul had had a brainstorm, while flying home from Kenya, that it would be good for the band to lose their identities. "We were fed up with being Beatles," he said in 1984. "We really hated that fucking four little mop-top boys approach. We were not boys, we were men. It was all gone, all that boy shit, all that screaming, we didn't want anymore, plus, we'd now got turned on to pot and thought of ourselves as artists rather than just performers."

So an idea began to grow, that the band members could submerge themselves in a make-believe group. "We would make up all the culture around it and collect all our heroes in one place," Paul added. For the name, he wanted something that sounded like an old-fashioned medicine show, and he came up with *Sgt. Pepper's Lonely Hearts Club Band*. "Just a word game really," he said. Apparently Paul had once asked Mal Evans what the little packets in cafes marked S and P were, and Evans replied, "Salt and pepper." "Sergeant Pepper?" Paul shot back playfully. The words had stuck in his head and so were handy when he needed a clever name for this band.

IN THE STUDIO

It was during the making of this album that the Beatles became obsessed with technical experimentation, calling on the staff at Abbey Road for more and

The Beatles

FabFact

The final version of "Strawberry Fields Forever" was created by George Martin combining two takes of the song recorded in two different keys and speeds—an amazing feat considering the equipment and technology of the time—but this version still did not meet Lennon's high expectations.

Above: Paul during the *Sgt. Pepper* sessions. Refreshed after their four-month break, the Beatles gathered at Abbey Road Studios on the evening of November 24, 1966, to begin recording their new album. The first track they worked on was John's "Strawberry Fields Forever."

Previous pages: The cover of *Sgt. Pepper's Lonely Hearts Club Band*, 1967.

"*Sgt. Pepper* is Paul after a trip to America and the whole West Coast long-named group thing was coming in. You know, when people were no longer the Beatles or the Crickets—they were suddenly Fred And His Incredible Shrinking Grateful Airplanes, right? So I think he got influenced by that and came up with this idea for the Beatles."

JOHN LENNON

more audio innovations. The band employed nearly every musical resource at George Martin's command, including calliope music and a full orchestra. As a result, individual songs bore the influence of the music hall, the symphony hall, psychedelic rave-ups, and intimate bistros. But it was the effect of the album as a whole that was so remarkable. It just sounded new . . . and novel . . . and unique, and felt, in some intangible way, unlike

anything that had come before.

Abbey Road became more than just a studio during these sessions. In Studio Two, George set up a meditation room with incense and soft lighting for his recording of "Within You, Without You," and played the sitar seated on a carpet with several Indian musicians.

Two evocative "Liverpool location" songs, the off-kilter and haunting "Strawberry Fields Forever," composed while John was in Spain

on the set of *How I Won the War*, and Paul's chipper hometown homage, "Penny Lane," were to have been the pillars of the album. But EMI was demanding a Christmas single, and George Martin knew both songs had chart-topping potential. So they were cut from the album, and released as a single . . . and proceeded to cancel each other out to the extent that neither powerhouse track made it to number one. Martin still speaks with regret of the decision to release them together.

"IN MY MIND I WAS MAKING A PIECE OF ART RATHER THAN AN ALBUM COVER. IT WAS ALMOST A PIECE OF THEATER DESIGN."
PETER BLAKE

The Beatles knew they had created something unique with this album and they wanted a cover that reflected all the originality captured on the vinyl. Pop artist Peter Blake was commissioned to design the gatefold jacket, with its startling cover montage, which had been created in accordance with the Beatles' concept of "people we like." Blake explained to the band that he wanted to capture the feeling that they had just finished a concert in the park, and that the figures around them had been in the audience.

Excited fans pored over the cover photo by Michael Cooper, trying to identify all the celebrities. Among the notables represented are Bob Dylan, Edgar Allan Poe (later mentioned in "I Am the Walrus"), Albert Einstein, wax models of the Beatles and Diana Dors, Sonny Liston, T. E. Lawrence, Shirley Temple, Tom Mix, Aleister Crowley, Sir Robert Peel, Sri Mahavatar Babaji, Lenny Bruce, Stan Laurel, Oliver Hardy, W. C. Fields, Fred Astaire, Aubrey Beardsley, Aldous Huxley, Lewis Carroll, James Joyce, G.B. Shaw, H.G Wells, Dylan Thomas, Dion, Marilyn Monroe, Tony Curtis, Tyrone Power, Marlene Dietrich, Marlon Brando, Karl Marx, Stuart Sutcliffe, and Johnny Weissmuller as Tarzan.

The LP came with an insert—a set of *Sgt. Pepper* cardboard cutouts, which included a moustache, a picture card, some sergeant stripes, 2 badges, and a stand-up emblem. The inner cover featured a close-up shot of the Beatles in uniform, and, for the first time in pop music, the lyrics to all the songs were printed on the back cover. It was also the first album to use the run-out groove, leaving the needle clattering on the track.

The inner sleeve was also the first to be designed by Seemon and Marijke, aka, The Fool.

The whole cover project cost multiple thousands of pounds, shocking EMI, who considered a £75 (about $125) photo shoot their top end.

SETTING A MILITARY TREND

The donning of the candy-colored Victorian-style satin uniforms for the cover shoot must have rankled John a bit—he was quite done with jumping through promotional hoops. Or maybe he accepted it as a fun bit of pantomime—he was always keen for a bit of dress up.

It is also interesting to note that even though the Beatles were no longer bound by Brian's edict to wear similar outfits, in many photos from this period, they are still sporting identical fashion statements: Edwardian suits, colorful scarves, Indian tunics, funky jewelry, facial hair. It was as if they found some comfort in conformity, even if they were only conforming to each other. These sartorial choices went beyond merely following the current clothing trends, since fashion in England was then a mix of boho, retro, space-age modern, ethnic, and even Wild West. One can almost imagine them calling each other up to coordinate their wardrobe choices, like middle school teens, before meeting at Abbey Road.

Naturally, the custom-made bandleader costumes the Beatles

> "It seemed obvious to us that peace, love and justice ought to happen . . . we recorded *Sgt. Pepper* to alter our egos, to free ourselves and have a lot of fun."

PAUL McCARTNEY

wore became templates for street clothing in a matter of days. Army-Navy stores—which incidentally, never carried hot pink or lemon yellow satin tunics—became the go-to shops for anything military or pseudo-military: piped jackets, capes, greatcoats, frogged cadet "blouses," medals and insignia, and genuine 13-button naval bell-bottoms in boiled wool (possibly

the itchiest garment to come along since the demise of the medieval hair shirt). Movie costumes or fancy dress uniforms fetched premium prices in Soho shops. Even the most sedate fan, one who eschewed the all-out *Music Man* look, likely included a medal or military insignia on the front of his Chesterfield just to show solidarity.

FabFact

John Lennon requested cutouts of Adolf Hitler, Mohandas Gandhi, and Jesus Christ for the *Sgt. Pepper* cover. He was voted down on all counts, though the cutout of Hitler was actually made.

Above: "It was twenty years ago today . . ." The outer sleeve of the 20th Anniversary Edition of *Sgt. Pepper* on compact disc, from 1987.

OPPOSITE: The clothing boutique I Was Lord Kitchener's Valet had branches on Carnaby Street and Portobello Road and was a principal source of military-style fashion for swinging Londoners.

> "With *Sgt. Pepper*, the Beatles held up a mirror to the world. And in this looking glass the world saw a brilliant reflection of its kaleidoscopic 1967 self. It saw not the shambolic and often absurd cavortings of the hippie movement, but its perfect image—an elegant ideal; not the sordid gutterland of drug addiction, but the intriguing possibility of creative substance abuse."
>
> GEORGE MARTIN, 2006

FabFact

The morning after *Sgt. Pepper* was completed, the Beatles made their way to the Chelsea flat of Mama Cass Elliot, where they proceeded to broadcast an acetate of the album from her open windows, serenading her neighbors with the songs that would, within the year, become the anthems of the era.

It's difficult to assess the impact of the album in a continuum, even though hundreds of pages have been written about its effects on the music industry, the popular culture, and the world. The simple truth is, when people first heard the album and were set back on their heels by its sheer amazingness, they were in a completely different mindset and cultural atmosphere than those who heard it ten, twenty, or thirty years on. The early listeners felt the greatest impact, simply because the remnants of the musical past that were about to be scattered like ashes still existed in their world. Later fans hadn't experienced the trends that had gone before, so they had little idea of how mightily *Sgt. Pepper* recast the mold. This is not to say that more recent listeners cannot appreciate it or understand the album's place in pop music history. It is no fluke that the good *Sergeant* regularly tops radio polls for Best Album. Even the self-consciously hip writers of *Rolling Stone* magazine voted it number one in their 2003 poll of the 500 Best Albums of All Time.

According to Paul, *Sgt. Pepper* was partially inspired by the music Brian Wilson crafted for the Beach Boys' *Pet Sounds*. (Paul believed "God Only Knows" might have been the best pop ballad ever written, praise indeed from the man who penned "Yesterday.") *Sgt. Pepper* would go on to influence other rock concept albums such as Van Morrison's *Astral Weeks*, the Moody Blue's *Days of Future Past*, Pink Floyd's *Dark Side of the Moon*, and numerous "story-album" offerings from progressive rock groups like Yes; Emerson, Lake and Palmer; King Crimson; and Genesis. A point can be made for *Sgt. Pepper*, with its internal narrative of "made-up" characters, also influencing rock operas like the Pretty Things' *S.F. Sorrow* and the Who's *Tommy*.

Perhaps the best sleight of hand performed by this LP was how

SGT. PEPPER'S LONELY HEARTS CLUB BAND

RELEASED JUNE 1, 1967

(Songs by Lennon–McCartney, unless specified):

Side One:

1. SGT. PEPPER'S LONELY HEARTS CLUB BAND
2. WITH A LITTLE HELP FROM MY FRIENDS
3. LUCY IN THE SKY WITH DIAMONDS
4. GETTING BETTER
5. FIXING A HOLE
6. SHE'S LEAVING HOME
7. BEING FOR THE BENEFIT OF MR. KITE

Side Two:

1. WITHIN YOU WITHOUT YOU (Harrison)
2. WHEN I'M SIXTY-FOUR
3. LOVELY RITA
4. GOOD MORNING GOOD MORNING
5. SGT. PEPPER'S LONELY HEARTS CLUB BAND (REPRISE)
6. A DAY IN THE LIFE

"A DECISIVE MOMENT IN THE HISTORY OF WESTERN CIVILIZATION."

KENNETH TYNAN, CRITIC, ON *SGT. PEPPER*

the very disparate songs, from foot-tappers like "When I'm Sixty-four" to profound tracks like "A Day in the Life," managed to blend together so seamlessly. But the point of commonality was, and is, that everything on the album was hugely entertaining, offering—much like Ed Sullivan's variety show—something cheery, something silly, something dazzling, something insightful, and something for the ages.

There was another unexpected aspect to the work, in that it didn't contain any adolescent love songs. Not one. If the Beatles wanted to prove their newfound creative maturity to the world, to display their evolving personae as artists, this was certainly a very good start.

SIGNIFICANT STATISTICS

Sgt. Pepper sold a quarter of a million copies in Britain during its first week of release, and by the end of June had topped 500,000 sales. (It didn't sell its millionth copy until April 1973, however, six years later.) It went straight to number one on the U.K. charts and dominated the top slot for the next 23 weeks.

In America, the LP spent 15 weeks at number one on the Billboard 200 and went on to win four Grammy Awards. It is still in the Top 10 albums of all time worldwide and is the top-selling album of all time in the United Kingdom.

In 2003, the album was added to the National Recording Registry by the U.S. Library of Congress, which called it "culturally, historically, or aesthetically significant."

Above: Pop artist Peter Blake, who created the celebrity cover for *Sgt. Pepper*, poses in a suitably artistic setting.

Opposite: Overawed schoolkids are amazed to see the Beatles, in their extravagant costumes, promenading by the boating lake in Hyde Park, London, May 18, 1967.

"LIFE FINDS ITS PURPOSE AND FULFILLMENT IN THE EXPANSION OF HAPPINESS."

MAHARISHI MAHESH YOGI

Top: A photo of Maharishi Mahesh Yogi, the Indian mystic, by the Ganges in India, 1966.

Bottom: George and Ravi Shankar attend a 1967 press conference.

Pattie Boyd Harrison had become interested in Eastern philosophy during the 1966 trip she and George made to India, where he went to study the sitar with Ravi Shankar. When she learned that the Maharishi Mahesh Yogi, a prominent Indian guru and proponent of Transcendental Meditation, would be speaking at the London Hilton that summer of 1967, she convinced George to attend with her. It hadn't been difficult—after studying with Shankar, George began a love affair with all things Indian. He also wanted to explore alternative forms of enlightenment, including Transcendental Meditation. George later wrote that he'd attended the talk in hopes of receiving a mantra from the guru, a "password to another

world." The Harrisons, along with John Lennon, Paul McCartney, and Jane Asher, sat spellbound while the Maharishi spoke.

After the event, the diminutive guru granted the Beatles an audience with him, where they grew even more impressed with his message and his calming presence. When the Beatles discovered he would be holding a seminar in Bangor, Wales, the following day, they determined to go. They even convinced Ringo, whose wife had just delivered their son, Jason, to come along.

By this point, all four Beatles were in a state of flux. Money, drugs, sex, popularity, and power were not turning out to be the cure-all for the ills in life that bring on anxiety, depression, or confusion. Each of the young men was to some extent seeking a deeper meaning, a better understanding of the complexities of life. It must have been heartening for them to believe that someone out there might actually have the answers they sought.

TRANSCENDENTAL DEEP MEDITATION

The guru, whose birth name was believed to be Mahesh Prasad Varma, later achieved the honorifics Maharishi . . . and Yogi as an adult. He became a devoted disciple of Swami Brahmananda Saraswati, whom he knew as Guru Deva, until his death in 1953. The Maharishi then lived in the Valley of the Saints in the Himalayas, where he developed his theory of Transcendental Deep Meditation. He helped to establish the Spiritual Regeneration Movement

in 1957 with the purpose of educating people in simple forms of meditation and a "spiritual, holistic approach to knowledge."

Contrary to what some people believed at the time, the Maharishi was not some visionary figure that suddenly appeared to the Beatles in a halo of light. He'd been a familiar TV personality, according to Paul, who had often appeared on Granada's current events shows—a giggling little man who was traveling "seven times around the globe to save it." But now, in addition to instructing the Beatles in TM, it seemed he had an agenda for how they, with their limitless fame, could help him open TM centers throughout England. As Ringo later said, "I think he realized that these boys could get his message across really fast."

The Beatles traveled to Bangor by train, along with Mick Jagger, Marianne Faithful, and Donovan. Cynthia Lennon, however, missed the train, being held back by

"THE IMPORTANT THING IS THIS: TO BE ABLE, AT ANY MOMENT, TO SACRIFICE WHAT WE ARE FOR WHAT WE COULD BECOME."
MAHARISHI MAHESH YOGI

police who thought she was an exuberant fan. If there is any clear demarcation point, where her path and John's diverged, it might be there, with this literal and symbolic separation, where he rides off to seek new, transfigurative experiences and she remains trapped at home and sadly unenlightened.

The London celebrities spent two days at the seminar, forced to sleep in classrooms due to their last-minute decision to attend. Still, the mood was mellow and upbeat, like "summer camp" according to Paul, and at last the Maharishi gave each of them his or her own personal mantra— the words or syllables that the student of meditation utters in an

attempt to create transformation.

But the peaceful vibe was shattered when a phone call came from Brian's aide, Peter Brown. Something unthinkable had happened. Brian Epstein was dead. After their initial shock, the four Beatles quickly turned to the teachings of the Maharishi—relying on his words even after such a short acquaintance—and reassured themselves by agreeing that Brian was simply passing into the "next phase of his spiritual journey."

Above: The Maharishi Mahesh Yogi (foreground) and the Beatles attend the Transcendental Meditation course in Bangor, North Wales, on August 27, 1967.

Left: Cynthia Lennon leaves London's Euston Station in tears, after not being allowed on the train to Bangor with the rest of the Beatles' party.

"WELL, HE WAS ALRIGHT. I'VE FOUND OUT SINCE, OF COURSE, THAT HE WASN'T QUITE AS HONEST TO US AS HE MADE OUT."
JOHN LENNON

The Beatles trusted him right from the start, and only rarely questioned why there wasn't more money coming their way. During the early days of Beatlemania, whenever the press corps kidded the band about being millionaires and having disposable incomes, they always looked slightly bewildered, as though they couldn't figure out if the press was making up these tales of supposed riches or if their manager was keeping them in the dark. During one interview, when George Harrison was asked what he intended to do with all his money, he shot back, "What money? We don't see any of it." Then he added, in reference to Brian, "But do you see the car he drives?"

This exchange is troubling. The Beatles were not stupid, just naive—they'd never even bothered to read their early contracts with Brian. So why was there such a great disparity between their fabulous careers and their nebulous incomes? Did Brian honestly think they wouldn't start asking pointed questions about their funds somewhere along the way, like, how they could be the biggest band in show business and still be making peanuts? One possible reason for the Beatles not pressuring Brian was that when they'd started out with him the average working man, someone like George's father, was making ten pounds a week. Initially, any sum more than that seemed like a fortune to the boys.

During the mid 1960s, Brian Epstein was kept very busy supervising the Beatles' careers, as well as promoting the other groups he represented. NEMS Enterprises was responsible for all the Beatles' tour bookings, requiring Brian to act as promoter, booking agent, and manager. Plus, he was often called upon to appear on TV or radio or to write articles on behalf of the band. To the casual observer, he certainly seemed to be earning his twenty-five percent of the Beatles' income.

Brian had started out his managing career with a certain amount of idealism, and the notion that he wanted only good things for his "lads." He even paid for his own flights when he traveled with the band, because he didn't consider himself part of the entourage. But over time his noble vision and good intentions grew skewed. It turned out Brian was not as scrupulous as his genial, "Let's shake on it," manner would indicate. He got greedy and began to channel more and more of the group's money into his own coffers.

"I AM THE BAGMAN"

In 1964, when it became clear that the fame machine wasn't going to give out any time soon, Epstein asked accountant James Trevor Isherwood to set up a company to collect the Beatles' revenue from the PRS—Performing Rights Society. This led to the formation of Lenmac. Isherwood later confessed his surprise at learning that Brian was not only receiving a twenty-five percent cut of the Beatles' gross income—as opposed to the standard ten percent—but he was also deducting his office and staff expenses, phone calls, and travel and entertainment costs from the band's earnings.

In order to conceal some of his income and lower his taxes, Brian began to shake down the eager promoters who booked the Beatles, insisting they pay him "hidden fees"—in cash—on the night of the concert. He then carried this money in a brown paper bag. Maybe Brian felt he had the right to "make hay" when the opportunities arose—after all, when his contract with the Beatles came due for renewal in September of 1967, his cut would go down to ten percent and NEMS would no longer get a portion of the performance fees.

Above: Brian, in happier times, with "his boys" in their Paris hotel room, January 16, 1964.

Opposite: Brian Epstein shares drinks at an event with friend—and client—singer Cilla Black.

"WHAT HAPPENS TO MY LIFE? . . . SHOULD I GO BACK TO SCHOOL AND LEARN SOMETHING ELSE?"
BRIAN EPSTEIN, AFTER THE BEATLES STOPPED TOURING

Brian felt aimless and superfluous when he no longer had his band's tours to oversee. "What do I do now?" he asked his friends. NEMS Enterprises was also in trouble; the demand for Brian's stable of Liverpudlian acts was waning as the Mersey beat fell out of favor.

A chronic insomniac, Brian began to increase the number and variety of drugs he took . . . Preludin, marijuana, then stronger amphetamines, and even heroin. He also suffered from a serious addiction to gambling, unable to stay away from the baccarat or chemin de fer tables at the exclusive Curzon House. Paul, also a member of the private club, witnessed Brian repeatedly losing thousands of pounds a night. During the recording sessions for *Sgt. Pepper* in 1967, Epstein was purportedly away on holiday. In reality, he had admitted himself to the Priory Clinic in Putney in an attempt to get clean. He left the clinic for the album's launch party, and then promptly checked back in again. When Brian's father died in July 1967, his precarious grip on his crazily spinning world began to slip. His mother Queenie openly expressed her concern over his mood swings to his friends and other family members.

BANK HOLIDAY

On August 24, 1967, Epstein invited his assistant Peter Brown and NEMS chief executive Geoff Ellis to join him for the Bank Holiday at his East Sussex country home, Warbleton. But when the group of young men, probably hustlers, Brian had also invited failed to appear that Friday, he drove back alone to London in a snit. When he called Brown from Chapel Street the next day, he sounded groggy. Brown reported that the young men had eventually shown up, and he suggested that Brian take the train down to Warbleton rather than drive. Epstein said if he decided to come he would phone Brown to let him know which train he'd be on. Brown and Ellis waited in vain for that phone call.

Epstein's butler Antonio had not heard a peep from Brian since Friday, and by Sunday he was quite worried. He phoned Brian's assistant, Joanne Newfield, who rushed over to Chapel Street. When she couldn't rouse Brian through his locked bedroom door, she phoned Brown, who suggested she contact his doctor, John Galway, and ask him to come to the house. Antonio and Galway managed to break down the door, revealing Brian lying dead on the bed, wearing pajamas, and surrounded by his correspondence.

The Beatles, who were in Wales with the Maharishi Mahesh Yogi, were devastated by the news. Brian's confidantes claimed he knew he was losing his hold over the band . . . especially John, and he feared this guru was a new threat. There were even some who claimed that if the Beatles had never gone to Wales, Brian would not have been in such an agitated state that weekend.

"INCAUTIOUS OVERDOSE"

While there was also speculation in the press that Brian committed suicide (there had been earlier, half-hearted attempts), the official verdict was accidental death—from the combining of six Carbitral sleeping pills with alcohol. The coroner determined that Brian's tolerance for Carbitral had become so high over time that six pills would not necessarily have been a lethal dose. It was the addition of alcohol, he concluded, that proved fatal.

Much has been written about Brian Epstein's failings as a manager: his habit of keeping his bands on a shoestring allowance, the unconscionable merchandising

arrangement he approved for the Beatles, and the cripplingly stingy contract he agreed to with Parlophone (from the all copies of "She Loves You" that sold, the bands' earnings amounted to about £800 (about $1,200) each, followed by his questionable financial practices and the brown bag incidents. The Beatles definitely got wind of it all . . . in time. Years later, John Lennon was quoted as saying, "He knew what he was doing; he robbed us."

Yet one thing remains evident. In spite of Brian's initial dislike of the pop music scene, his financial bungling, and his later greed, somehow it all turned out okay for his boys. Through his efforts the Beatles were able to find the right music producer, the right engineers, the right tour promoter, the right American TV showcase, the right movie director, and most importantly,

the right audience. Would all this have been possible if Brian were the wrong manager? Who can say? In the cosmic continuum, as George Harrison no doubt believed, sometimes when things are meant to happen, they happen.

Top, and above: The Beatles—Ringo, George, John, and then Paul, below—are shown during the aftermath of Brian Epstein's death.

Opposite: When the Mersey Sound declined, Brian began to siphon money from the Beatles.

the heels of their greatest triumph, the transcendent *Sgt. Pepper*.

Magical Mystery Tour featured a cast of middle-class tourists on a bus trip—a lampoon of the popular British charabanc tours that specialized in mysterious destinations—with the four Beatles playing passengers. Ringo gets the most screen time as a young man accompanied by his whining, zaftig aunt . . . shades of Paul and his annoying grandfather in *A Hard Day's Night*. The movie contains outdated music hall routines (Victor Spinetti's gibberish-spouting army sergeant), random conflicts (a spontaneous race between the bus, a bicycle, a Mini Cooper, and a Rolls Royce), and humor at the expense of little people, heavy people, and women.

One definite plus should have been the musical interludes with songs

> "John and I remembered mystery tours, and we always thought this was a fascinating idea: getting on a bus and not knowing where you were going. Rather romantic and slightly surreal!"

PAUL McCARTNEY, *Many Years from Now*, Barry Miles

As both the instigators of and the standard-bearers for the 1960s revolution of ideas, sounds, and images, the Beatles must have felt tremendous pressure not to fail. Back in Liverpool none of that mattered—if you screwed up, you shrugged it off and swaggered on. But after achieving international fame, they knew stakes were now so much higher, that their every effort fell under the microscope of critical scrutiny. No matter that they had lost their driving

Above: A profile portrait of John during *Magical Mystery Tour*, September 14, 1967.

wheel with the death of Brian Epstein, they would continue to be judged by a different, higher standard than other entertainers.

Still, no entity can sustain success or popularity for years and years without a misstep. And so the Beatles met what some considered their Waterloo in the form of a loosely organized, comedy-oriented TV program filmed at Paul's instigation in September 1967. It was to have been a romp, but it ended up a raspberry. The timing was unfortunate, coming as it did on

by the Beatles—"Fool on the Hill," "Blue Jay Way," etc.—but while these are certainly worthwhile to listen to, several segments seem self-indulgent (Paul rolling his eyes in close-up "alone on the hill" is especially grating). Sadly, the songs barely make up for the long, unfunny comic bits.

THE NOT-SO-MERRY PRANKSTERS

Paul's inspiration for the story came from the antics of author Ken Kesey and his band of Merry Pranksters, who traveled America in a funky, painted bus. (According

to Tom Wolfe, author of *The Electric Koolaid Acid Test*, LSD and other drugs played a large part in why the Pranksters were so Merry.) Like Kesey, Paul and his fellow Beatles had also been experimenting with hallucinogens and so he decided they should share the insights of their acid trips with their fans via a TV film that would combine their far-out, surreal acid experiences with a cozy and comical British travelogue offering burlesque interludes. Logic comes to a screeching halt at this bizarre fusion. As Neil Aspinall later said, "If Brian had been alive it might have been made but it would never have gone out."

Mystery Tour fans insist this production, even more than the two previous films, inspired the concept of the music video, and it's true that the colorized lenses used on "Flying" and the light show in "Blue Jay Way" were intriguing and innovative. Sadly, when the film debuted on December 26, Boxing Day, the BBC broadcast the program in black-and-white—so that the color-filtered scenes simply looked gray and murky. The public, who had settled down for a nice bit of holiday fun with the Beatles, was not amused. (To be fair, much of the British populace was without color TVs at that time, so the Beatles ought to have factored that in when art directing the tinted scenes.)

Paul actually went on the telly the next day to apologize. "We don't say it was a good film," he conceded. "It was our first attempt. If we goofed, then we goofed. It was a challenge and it didn't come off. We'll know better next time." But the damage had already been done. Music's golden boys had proven to have feet of clay—and ears of tin when it came to gauging the public's taste.

"The bigger they are, the harder they fall. And what a fall it was . . ."

JAMES THOMAS, *Daily Express,* 1967

Top: The Fab Four relax on Plymouth Hoe while shooting *Magical Mystery Tour* on the Devon coast. Perhaps the best that could be said about the project was that they all appeared to be having a good time during the production.

Above: The Beatles pose together in a publicity shot for *Magical Mystery Tour*, September 12, 1967. They were rarely shown together in the film, except when performing their songs.

MAGICAL MYSTERY TOUR

EXTENDED PLAY SINGLE
RELEASED DECEMBER 8, 1967

(All songs Lennon–McCartney,
unless specified):

1. **MAGICAL MYSTERY TOUR**
2. **YOUR MOTHER SHOULD KNOW**
3. **I AM THE WALRUS**
4. **THE FOOL ON THE HILL**
5. **FLYING** (Lennon–McCartney–Harrison–Starkey)
6. **BLUE JAY WAY** (Harrison)

Left: The cover art from the *Magical Mystery Tour* extended play single was also used on the American album.

Opposite, counterclockwise from top: A gallery of photos from the *Magical Mystery Tour*: Paul and Ringo pass the time before the start of the journey; George, in Newquay; Ringo demonstrating his soccer skills to members of the coach party; Paul, with musician and poet Ivor Cutler, who played Mr. Bloodvessel. The Scottish eccentric was a favorite of John's.

THE "FAIRGROUND" ALBUM

The Beatles recorded the album for the most part in April and May 1967, not long after they wrapped *Sgt. Pepper*. Paul reminisced that the songs went back to his and John's youthful summer days, full of carnivals, sideshows, and seaside vacations—"Very much in our fairground period," he said. The British double EP, issued on December 8, featured only the six songs from the program. In America, where EPs did not compute, Capitol—against the Beatles' wishes—released a full-length LP that also offered the 1967 non-album singles "Penny Lane," "Strawberry Fields Forever," "Hello, Goodbye," "Baby You're A Rich Man," and "All You Need Is Love."

Fortunately the record received a much better reception than the BBC program. Critics agreed the album was "worth buying," although *Rolling Stone* offered a one-line review by John Lennon:

"There are only about 100 people in the world who understand our music." John's opinion notwithstanding, *Magical Mystery Tour* was nominated for a Grammy for Best Album of 1968 and stayed at number one on the U.S. charts for eight weeks. The American LP became a valued companion piece to *Sgt. Pepper*, like a marginally less entertaining but still endearing younger sibling.

Beatles' fans often claim that if *Sgt. Pepper* was the pot album, then *Magical Mystery Tour* was the acid album. The bizarre cover, again featuring the foursome in costume—this time wearing furry animal outfits complete with face-obscuring masks—bears this out. In terms of concept, this cover appears a bit over the top, with the Beatles so completely shrouded as to be almost unrecognizable. The logical progression from this point would be a cover where the Beatles have disappeared completely, one with no image at all, but of course such a thing was out of the question . . .

LOVE ACROSS THE PLANET

Our World, the first live, international TV broadcast via satellite took place on June 25, 1967. The Beatles—representing the United Kingdom—contributed a live version of "All You Need Is Love," written specifically for the event and aimed at the war-torn sections of the globe. A host of celebrity friends joined them in the chorus. The broadcast included Maria Callas and Pablo Picasso and was watched by 400 to 700 million people.

Above: The Beatles represented their country during the *Our World* broadcast.

205

"I LET PEOPLE MAKE REMARKS ABOUT ME, BUT IT DOESN'T TOUCH ME, ALL THOSE REMARKS."
MAHARISHI MAHESH YOGI

In February 1968, the Beatles decided to travel to the Maharishi's remote retreat in Rishikesh, a beautiful area at the base of the Himalayas, where the Ganges runs from the mountains across the plains to Delhi. The Beatles were "off LSD and other drugs" now and into spiritual enlightenment,

as they'd announced at a press conference before their trip. They'd told the yogi, they explained to the reporters, that after only two days with him they knew Transcendental Meditation was the answer they'd been seeking.

The participants in this pilgrimage included John and Cynthia Lennon,

Paul and Jane Asher, George and Pattie Harrison and her sister Jenny Boyd, Ringo and Maureen Starkey, folk singer Donovan, Mike Love of the Beach Boys, and actress Mia Farrow and her sister Prudence. The group had gone there intending to take a course meant for instructors of

"I wrote quite a few songs in Rishikesh and John came up with some creative stuff. George actually once got quite annoyed and told me off because I was trying to think of the next album. He said, 'We're not fucking here to do the next album, we're here to meditate!' It was like, 'Oh, excuse me for breathing!'"

PAUL McCARTNEY, *Many Years from Now*, Barry Miles

Transcendental Meditation. But when the celebrities announced their desire to simply deepen their meditation skills, the Maharishi, never one to miss the main chance, indulged them.

In spite of all the smiling faces in the many photo ops with the holy man, the Beatles felt an odd restraint. As Paul recollected to John in a scene from *Let It Be*, the two would sneak away from the main group, and confess that being there felt a bit like being back in school. Yet John should have been the one crying out the loudest for some kind of emotional outlet or spiritual relief. His marriage was all but over, he had distanced himself from his son while avoiding any personal time with his wife, and, yet again, someone he loved had died unexpectedly . . . and under dramatic circumstances. John even went up in a helicopter with the yogi, hoping he would impart some cosmic insights. All John got was an aerial view of the compound.

As it turned out, *this* diminutive Asian mystic was not destined to become John's salvation.

"SEXY SADIE, WHAT HAVE YOU DONE?"

Ringo left first, unable to stomach the food at the camp. Paul, who'd only intended to stay for a short time, left next. Of the four Beatles, only John and George remained now to sit at the feet of the master. But after John heard from his pal Magic Alex that the guru had been making advances toward one of the young women, he'd had it. He and George packed up and headed off to Delhi in their car. On the way, John began composing a bitter song, "Maharishi," about his experiences in Rishikesh and his sense of betrayal. After George convinced him to tone it down and rename it, the backlash ballad became "Sexy Sadie."

In spite of the bad vibes that resulted from the trip to the retreat, both George and Paul remained devotees of meditation. There was another plus—John had stopped taking LSD while there and the result was a renewed burst of creative energy, which he seemed to share with Paul and George. The three came up with at least thirty new songs while in India, composed mostly on acoustic guitars. They included: "Dear Prudence," written for Mia Farrow's sister who insisted on meditating in her room, "Bungalow Bill," "Why Don't We Do It in the Road?," "I'm So Tired," and "Mother Nature's Son." While they were at the retreat together, folk singer Donovan had schooled John on his own method of fingerpicking, which Lennon would later use on both "Dear Prudence" and "Julia."

In May 1968, after all the Beatles were back in England, twenty-three of these songs were polished and demo-ed at George's bungalow in Esher. Many of them would form the building blocks of the Beatles' next major work.

Top: John strums his guitar during the Beatles' retreat at Rishikesh, India.

Opposite: The Beatles and their wives at Rishikesh with the Maharishi Mahesh Yogi, March 1968. The group includes Ringo and Maureen, Jane and Paul, George and Pattie, Cynthia and John, Beatles roadie Mal Evans, and Beach Boy Mike Love.

"WE'RE IN THE HAPPY POSITION OF NOT NEEDING ANY MORE MONEY. SO FOR THE FIRST TIME, THE BOSSES AREN'T IN IT FOR PROFIT. WE'VE ALREADY BOUGHT ALL OUR DREAMS. WE WANT TO SHARE THAT POSSIBILITY WITH OTHERS."

PAUL McCARTNEY, MAY 1968 PRESS CONFERENCE TO LAUNCH APPLE CORPS

CHAPTER THIRTEEN
APPLE CORPS

"OUT OF HIS DEPTH, A BEATLE MIGHT COMMANDEER A ROOM AT SAVILE ROW, STICK TO CONVENTIONAL OFFICE HOURS AND PLAY COMPANY DIRECTOR UNTIL THE NOVELTY WORE OFF."

ALAN CLAYSON AND SPENCER LEIGH, *THE WALRUS WAS RINGO*, (2003)

Even before Brian Epstein died, the Beatles knew they needed to find more efficient ways of safeguarding their wealth from the punitive rates of the Inland Revenue. They also recognized that one manager was no longer capable of overseeing all their far-reaching interests. The Beatles were a conglomerate now, no longer just a band. The best thing, they agreed, would be to go into business for themselves and try to manage their own financial and corporate affairs.

In early 1967, when their accountants told them that they had two million pounds to either invest or lose to the government in taxes, the band created Beatles and Co., which replaced Beatles Ltd., their initial tax shelter. Now each Beatle would own five percent of the new partnership, and the other eighty percent of their revenue (excepting songwriting royalties) would go into a corporation and thus be taxed at a lower rate. In spring 1968, this multimedia corporation would be christened Apple Corps.

While Brian, ever the retailer, initially imagined the corporation as a tool for marketing Beatles' merchandise and paraphernalia in a series of stores, "like Woolworth's" he was reported to have said, the band decided they wanted to take a broader approach. As John Lennon explained, "We decided to play businessmen for a bit because we've got to run

Left: Entrepreneur Robert Stigwood with Ahmet Ertegun, President of Atlantic Records, at Stigwood's party for Eric Clapton in 1974.

Opposite: The Bee Gees, with Robert Stigwood, their manager, in the background, at Hamburg airport in Germany, 1968.

Previous pages: The Apple Tailoring store on the King's Road, Chelsea, shown in 1968, was owned by Apple Corps, and run by designer John Crittle.

our own affairs now. So we've got this thing called 'Apple' which is going to be records, films, and electronics—which all tie up." Eventually the divisions of Apple Corps would include Apple Records, Apple Electronics, Apple Films, Apple Studios, Apple Music Publishing, Apple Overseas, Apple Publicity, and Apple Retailing.

THE STIGWOOD MERGER

In January 1967 Brian Epstein insisted he was growing weary of all his managerial responsibilities. The truth was probably more related to the Beatles' decision to stop touring, something Brian had always looked forward to. Nevertheless, he decided he would seek a partner to help him run NEMS Enterprises, someone who could manage the Beatles and his other groups for him. He found a likely candidate in Australian Robert Stigwood, a former

theatrical agent, who had, along with Joe Meeks, become England's first maverick record producer. He had also been affiliated with EMI, and had successfully promoted the supergroup, Cream.

Stigwood was already friends with Brian, and when Epstein approached him about a merger, he gladly accepted. Everyone else on Brian's side was shocked and bewildered by this decision. When Brian announced to the Beatles that Stigwood would now be managing them, Paul threatened that thereafter the group would only ever record "God Save the Queen" and "sing it out of tune." John responded with a rhetorical question to Stigwood, "We don't know you. Why would we do this?" Brian compromised by retaining the Beatles for himself and giving his new partner the balance of his artists.

> "He was in every way the first British music business tycoon, involved in every aspect of the music scene, and setting a precedent that was to become the blueprint of success for all future pop entrepreneurs."

SIMON NAPIER-BELL, rock manager, on Robert Stigwood

Stigwood was not only a notorious spendthrift, he had a reputation as an abrasive control freak. His high-handed behavior soon put Brian off and had valued NEMS staff members ready to abandon ship.

A TAKEOVER THREAT

Brian Epstein died while Apple was still being structured, and his loss sped up the need for the Beatles to take control of their finances. Paul suggested that Clive Epstein, now managing director of NEMS Enterprises, come aboard with them. But, according to Paul, Clive feared the Beatles were "wild men" who would squander all his money.

Not long after Brian's death, the band learned that Robert Stigwood was angling to buy NEMS Enterprises outright to gain control of the Beatles and their catalog. Fortunately, when the actual incorporation of Apple was finalized, they were safe from outside predation. And with the

band no longer in the NEMS fold, Stigwood backed off, leaving to form his own company, the Robert Stigwood Organization. (Stigwood would later take unwitting revenge on the group for eluding him by linking their music with his abysmal production of *Sgt. Pepper's Lonely Hearts Club Band*, possibly the worst movie musical ever made.)

In December 1967, Brian's assistant Alistair Taylor—and a longtime friend to the Beatles—was asked to become Apple's general manager. Taylor posed as a "one-man band" for a magazine ad that encouraged hopeful artists and performers to apply at Apple's Baker Street office. The ad ended with the tagline "This man now owns a Bentley." The lure must have worked; as George Harrison later said, "We had every freak in the world coming in there." Some of them actually received seed money for their endeavors and most were never heard from again.

THE BIRTH OF A LOGO

The bright green, Granny Smith apple that became instantly recognizable as Apple Corps' logo was taken from a painting by surrealist Rene Magritte. While one of Magritte's most famous paintings, *Man in a Bowler Hat*, shows a businessman with a large green apple where his head should be, it wasn't the source of the inspiration. Paul McCartney, who loved Magritte, ended up purchasing one of the artist's lesser paintings called *Le Jeu de Mourre*, of another green apple with "Au Revoir" written on it in script. It was this work that inspired the company's logo. The green apple image was also used on the LP labels, whole on side one, and halved on side two. For some recordings, such as *Let It Be*, the apple was colored red, in this case to identify the album as a United Artists (as opposed to a Capitol Records) release.

In February 2007, Apple Inc., the computer conglomerate, officially took possession of the Apple Corps logo after a long trademark dispute— but agreed to lease it back to the entertainment company. At the time, Steve Jobs said: "We love the Beatles, and it has been painful being at odds with them over these trademarks. It feels great to resolve this in a positive manner, and in a way that should remove the potential of further disagreements in the future."

The Apple Bites Back

Right: Jenny Boyd, Pattie Harrison's sister, co-managed the Apple Store along with John Lennon's childhood chum, Pete Shotton. Alas, many of the employees felt free to walk off with the merchandise, which helped to speed the store's demise.

Opposite, center, and bottom: Before and after—the Dutch art collective, The Fool, touch up the mural they created on the facade of the Apple Store in Baker Street. Unfortunately, no permits had been granted, and the artwork was painted over by order of the city council.

Opposite, far right: Dutch design collective The Fool consisted of, from left Marijke Posthuma and her husband Simon, Barry Finch (foreground), and artist Josje Leege, May 15, 1968.

> "We had, like, a thousand people that weren't needed. But they all enjoyed it. They were all getting paid for sitting around. We had a guy there just to read the tarot cards, the *I Ching*. It was craziness"
>
> **RINGO STARR,** *The Walrus Was Ringo*, **Clayson and Leigh (2003)**

Apple started out strong and went on to be declared the most successful record company of 1968.

But behind the scene things were not rosy. As they had done with *Magical Mystery Tour*, the Beatles believed that good intentions guaranteed a positive outcome. Once again they didn't factor in their lack of appropriate background or training. They had no business skills (back in the early days, Stuart and Pete were the closest thing they had to business managers), no experience in running anything or supervising anyone, no idea how to prepare a plan of operation or a financial forecast. But this didn't trouble the Beatles. Apple was meant to rise above any mere business; it would furnish a haven for artists, a think tank, a fertile environment where new voices and new ideas would flourish. All on their dime.

In spite of the Beatles' philanthropic attitude and genuine hopes for finding and funding new talent, within two years Apple Corps was hemorrhaging money. At board meetings the band members appeared naive and unprepared. And they were certainly not acting like bosses—the employees at Apple Corps were out of control, using company funds to purchase drinks and drugs, make long-distance calls to friends, and enjoy expensive meals on the town.

Finally, former road manager Neil Aspinall temporarily took over the reins at Apple, injecting some order and discipline into the chaos. (In 1969, when the Beatles brought Allen Klein aboard as their manager, he became chairman of Apple Corps. The no-nonsense Klein jettisoned much of the office deadwood and got things running smoothly for a time.)

APPLE SUBSIDIARIES

THE APPLE STORE

In December 1967, Apple Retailing gave birth to the Apple Store, managed by John's friend, Pete Shotton and Pattie Boyd's sister, Jennie. Paul wanted it to become an artsy boutique, "a beautiful place where beautiful people can buy beautiful things." Instead, it became the first ship in the Beatles' fleet to run aground. The brilliant Dutch art collective, The Fool, had been commissioned to paint a dazzling psychedelic mural across the facade, but no one from Apple had bothered to ask for permits. After a legal battle with the local zoning board, the striking mural was ordered painted over. This moral and artistic defeat made the Beatles lose much of their interest in the store. Pilferage and theft were also rife, with both staff and customers blithely carrying off clothing and accessories. When the shop closed in July 1968, after losing nearly £250,000 (almost $400,000), Paul announced that the goods inside would be given away for free. It appears the London public had anticipated him on that decision.

"If they'd protected it and the painted wall was there now, they would be saying, 'Wow, look at this. We've got to stop it chipping off.'"

GEORGE HARRISON on The Fool's mural in Baker Street

FabFact

On July 31, 2008, the BBC program *Newsnight* projected a copy of the original mural onto the building that now stands where the boutique stood, in honor of the fortieth anniversary of the shop's closing.

APPLE SCRUFFS

Once the Beatles actually had a home base in London—the various Apple Corps buildings at Baker Street, Wigmore Street, and finally Savile Row—it was inevitable that female fans would start congregating there. George Harrison first used the phrase to describe these girls who regularly haunted Apple or Abbey Road Studios hoping to meet or speak with a Beatle—and then immortalized them with a song. (Scruff is British slang for someone who appears unkempt or dirty.) Paul invited two Abbey Road scruffs, Lizzie Bravo and Gayleen Pease, to come inside and sing background on "Across the Universe." John donated the version they made to a UK charity album, and it also appears on *Past Masters*. Paul, famously, had several scruffs climb into the window of his second-floor bathroom (hence the song) and raid his closet. In 1985 former scruff Carol Bedford published a memoir, *Waiting for the Beatles*.

"HELLO, I'M ALEXIS. I WOULD LIKE TO SAY HELLO TO ALL MY FRIENDS AROUND THE WORLD AND TO ALL THE GIRLS AROUND THE WORLD AND TO ALL THE ELECTRONIC PEOPLE AROUND THE WORLD. THIS IS APPLE ELECTRONICS."

MESSAGE FROM MAGIC ALEX'S NOTHING BOX

Above: Peter Asher (left) and Gordon Waller of Peter and Gordon perform on *Hullabaloo* at NBC's Studio 8-H, New York, March 30, 1965. The Beatles made Peter Asher—Jane's brother—head of A & R at Apple.

Top right: Paul signed Mary Hopkin after Twiggy phoned him and alerted him to the talented Welsh singer.

Opposite, top row, left to right: James Taylor, Billy Preston, and Badfinger were three of the earliest Apple Records hitmakers.

Opposite, below: Ravi Shankar, George's sitar instructor—and close friend—was also signed by Apple Records.

APPLE RECORDS

Of all the divisions of Apple Corps, its record label seemed to have the best instincts for backing successful ventures. (And after all, who knew more about the creation and production of pop music that these four guys?) The Beatles' novel approach to recruiting and their inclusive interest in different genres resulted in a mixed bag of artists, with the label eventually encompassing folk singers, rock and rollers, jazz musicians, world music, and even classical compositions by British composer John Tavener.

"Those Were the Days" was released as Apple Catalogue 2. The position of Apple 1 went to a record made for Maureen Starkey's 22nd birthday as a gift from Ringo, a parody of the Rodgers and Hart classic called "The Lady Is a Champ." Rewritten by Sammy Cahn, it was sung by none other than Frank Sinatra.

Mary Hopkin

Sixties supermodel Twiggy had been watching the TV show *Opportunity Knocks* one night and was so impressed by a young female contestant, she called Paul McCartney and told him to turn on the show so he could hear this "remarkable" singer. The performer in question, a petite Welsh blonde with a crystalline voice, was Mary Hopkin. Paul, likewise impressed, sent Peter Asher—his former attic mate turned chart-topper and now head of Apple A & R—to Wales to sign her. Paul already had a song in mind for his new protege, a lilting drinking song with lyrics by Gene Raskin (and a Russian melody, no less)—"Those Were the Days." The August 1968 single became a top-10 hit on both sides of the Atlantic and helped launch Apple Records in style.

"IT WAS QUITE FAST AND QUITE SIMPLE."
PETER ASHER, ON SIGNING JAMES TAYLOR TO APPLE

James Taylor

Peter Asher was also responsible for signing a young American folk singer named James Taylor. Taylor became one of the seminal figures of the singer-songwriter movement of the 1970s, and would remain a welcome presence in pop music for decades. Early songs such as "Fire and Rain," "Sweet Baby James," and "Something in the Way She Moves" (which inspired George Harrison to write "Something") were richly poetic and deeply felt . . . yet performed with a springy, spritely energy.

Badfinger

Mal Evans, the Beatles' former road manager, brought a Welsh group called the Iveys aboard the Apple Express in 1968. They charted in the United States with a minor hit, "Maybe Tomorrow," and then seemed destined for obscurity. Peter Asher recalled someone remarking that the Iveys was a wimpy name and Neil Aspinall came up with Badfinger, which everyone agreed was much groovier. With a new name and renewed energy, the band proceeded to chart internationally with a series of hits, including "Come and Get It" "No Matter What," "Day After Day," and "Baby Blue." Two of the band's members, Pete Hamm and Tom Evans, also penned the ubiquitous Nilsson hit, "Without You."

Billy Preston

Preston, an American R&B keyboard icon, has the distinction of being the only outside performer credited on a Beatles' record—the label on the "Get Back" single reads "The Beatles with Billy Preston." He performed with them on *Abbey Road* and *Let It Be*, and is also featured in the latter film. His first LP for Apple was named after one of his hit songs, *That's The Way God Planned It*. As a performer at George Harrison's 1971 Concert for Bangladesh, Preston set the house rocking.

Ravi Shankar

After Apple took over distribution of Howard Worth's *Raga*, a documentary about George Harrison's good friend, sitar player Ravi Shankar, George struggled to get both the film and album released. It was in June 1971, while they were prepping the *Raga* album in Los Angeles, that he and Shankar made plans for the Bangladesh UNICEF concert in New York's Madison Square Garden—the first ever benefit concert by world-renowned pop musicians.

"The mixing console was made of bits of wood and an old oscilloscope. It looked like the control panel of a B-52 bomber."

DAVE HARRIES, EMI Engineer on the first Apple Studios, designed by Magic Alex

Right: George Harrison, and Pete Ham of Badfinger sit at the mixing desk of the refitted Apple Studios in Savile Row.

Below: Fame, ever fickle, eluded Jackie Lomax, in spite of having George Harrison as his producer.

Jackie Lomax

Singer-guitarist Jackie Lomax, another Merseysider who had been briefly managed by Brian Epstein, was taken under George Harrison's wing after Brian died. George signed him to Apple and worked closely with him on his recordings. Lomax's records never caught fire with the public, however, and he eventually did session work with Eric Clapton, Jeff Beck, Nicky Hopkins, and Leon Russell.

Modern Jazz Quartet

This four-decade mainstay of the jazz scene, whose goal was making their bluesy bebop style of jazz accessible to the masses, recorded two notable albums for Apple—*Under the Jasmin Tree* and *Space*, the latter produced by Peter Asher. A combo CD was issued in 2010 with a bonus track— MJQ's version of "Yesterday."

APPLE FILMS

In spite of getting off to a rocky start with *Magical Mystery Tour*, Apple Films went on to produce one hit movie, *Yellow Submarine*, and several outstanding documentaries, *Let It Be*, *Concert for Bangladesh*, and *Born to Boogie*.

APPLE ELECTRONICS

With the best of intentions, the Beatles put John's "electronics whiz" friend Yanni Alexis Mardas, aka Magic Alex, in charge of this division, expecting he would revolutionize consumer electronics. Unfortunately, Alex's designs, such as an apple-shaped radio,

were impractical and expensive. Although he applied for more than a hundred patents, he received none; all his impressive gadgets were simply modifications of previously patented devices. Mardas was dismissed in 1969 when Allen Klein took over. (To be fair to the flaky Alex, he accurately predicted voice-activated phones and caller ID.)

APPLE STUDIOS

When Apple's headquarters moved to No. 3 Savile Row, the Beatles now had space for their own recording studio in the building's basement. The first incarnation of Apple Studios, designed by Magic Alex, was unworkable, however, and required a refit costing $1.5 million dollars. Trusted Abbey Road engineer Geoff Emerick oversaw the new installation. The finished space included all the bells and whistles (literally) with an echo chamber and the latest recording and mastering facilities capable of producing mono, stereo, and quadraphonic tapes or discs. It became a favorite haunt

"THERE I AM IN THE STUDIO AND THERE ARE THREE BEATLES WATCHING ME. THAT CHOKED UP MY THROAT A BIT."

JACKIE LOMAX

of the Apple artists and was also utilized by Harry Nilsson, Nicky Hopkins, Wishbone Ash, Stealer's Wheel, and Marc Bolan. The studio closed officially in May 1975.

CODA

In spite of years of turmoil, failed starts, and administrative turnovers (Neil Aspinall unofficially headed the company from 1970 to 2007), Apple Corps managed to remain in business. In 2010, *Fast Company* magazine voted Apple the second most innovative company in the music industry—primarily due to the release of *The Beatles: Rock Band* video game and the remastered Beatles catalog.

Above: The Modern Jazz Quartet made two well-received albums for Apple—*Under the Jasmin Tree* and *Space*.

Left: Crowds line up to get into the Beatles' Apple Store on Baker Street, on its final day, July 31, 1968. Whatever stock hadn't been shoplifted was given away.

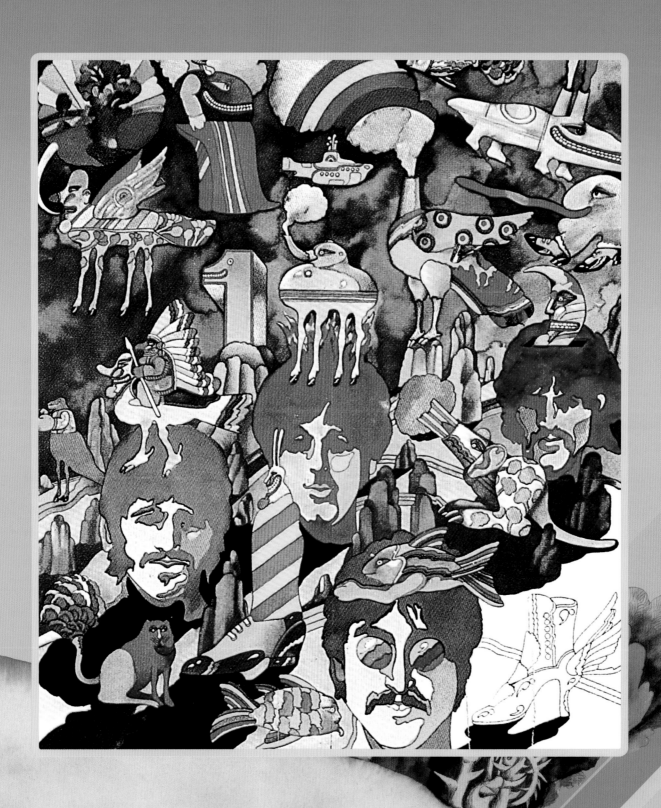

"I SAY IN SPEECHES THAT A PLAUSIBLE MISSION OF ARTISTS IS TO MAKE PEOPLE APPRECIATE BEING ALIVE AT LEAST A LITTLE BIT. I AM THEN ASKED IF I KNOW OF ANY ARTISTS WHO PULLED THAT OFF. I REPLY, 'THE BEATLES DID.'"
KURT VONNEGUT

CHAPTER FOURTEEN
ABBEY ROAD: THE LATE SIXTIES

"YOU'RE OLD ENOUGH TO KNOW BETTER..."
"CRY BABY CRY"

Even though they were no longer touring, the Beatles found their personal lives keeping them busy as 1967 gave way to the new year. Paul and Jane Asher became engaged in December and John was briefly reunited with his estranged father. The meeting did not go well and John never saw him again.

In 1966 John had met an avant-garde Japanese/American artist named Yoko Ono in the Indica gallery, and intrigued by her cerebral manner and unique notions of conceptual art, allowed her to keep in touch with him.

John and Yoko made their first public appearance as a couple in June 1968, followed in August by Cynthia Lennon's accusation of adultery against John. In mid October John and Yoko were arrested on drug charges while leasing Ringo's flat in Montagu Square. In early November, John and Cynthia were divorced.

By July, Jane Asher had broken off her engagement to Paul—partially based on finding him in bed with Francie Schwartz. But Paul already had his eye on another woman, a lanky blond photographer he'd

met in March 1967 at a Georgie Fame concert at the Bag O'Nails. American divorcee Linda Eastman was on assignment in London to photograph rock musicians, and agreed to go out with McCartney afterward to see Procul Harem at the Speakeasy. He met her again at Brian Epstein's home, at the launch party for *Sgt. Pepper*.

Linda Eastman came from a prominent New York family— her father was a high-powered entertainment attorney and her mother was the daughter of retailer Max J. Lindner of Cleveland.

Previous pages: Inset, a detail of the poster for the Italian release of *Yellow Submarine*; The background is an animation cel of a landscape from the film.

Although she had little training in photography, Eastman possessed a good eye and a strong sense of composition. After taking a series of impressive photos of the Rolling Stones during a yachting party on the Hudson River, she became the official photographer for the Fillmore East—and gained a reputation as a smart, fun-loving groupie. Her portfolio eventually included music legends like Grace Slick, Jimi Hendrix, Bob Dylan, Eric Clapton, The Who, The Doors, The Animals, Simon & Garfunkle, and Neil Young.

After Linda returned to New York, Paul met up with her while he and John were there to do public relations for their new endeavor, Apple Corps. In September 1968 he asked her to return to London to be with him. She eventually agreed and flew to England with her daughter Heather and moved in with Paul at his home in Cavendish Avenue.

George's and Ringo's personal lives were not without problems, but they weren't acting them out in public or offering the tattler-fodder provided by their two fellow Beatles. At least not yet . . .

Professionally, the Beatles had a hit single in March 1968 with "Lady Madonna," although it did not reach number one in America. The big event for fans came that summer, with the July release of *Yellow Submarine*, the Beatles first animated feature film, with a soundtrack that would follow in January 1969.

Opposite, left: John and Yoko descend the tiny spiral staircase to the basement at Robert Fraser Gallery in Duke Street, during the opening of his art exhibition "You Are Here," July 1, 1968.

Opposite, right: Cynthia Lennon stands outside the Royal Courts of Justice on November 8, 1968—the day her divorce from John was finalized.

Top: Paul holds Julian Lennon, during the Beatles' jaunt to Greece. John browses in the background.

Bottom: Photographer Linda Eastman talks to Paul McCartney during the press launch of *Sgt. Pepper*, held at Brian Epstein's house in Chapel Street, May 19, 1967.

Top and above: Animation cels from the *Yellow Submarine* film are highly prized by collectors.

> "I think that one of the nice things about the *Yellow Submarine* movie is that it seems to be perennial. People enjoy watching from each generation. And it was like the Beatles themselves. You know the Beatles seem to find a new audience each time another generation comes along."
> **GEORGE MARTIN**

The Beatles had not been anxious to commit to another film after the drubbing *Magical Mystery Tour* received, but when approached with the idea for *Yellow Submarine*, they assumed an animated film featuring their songs would fulfill the three-movie requirement of their contract with United Artists—and get the studio off their backs. (Unfortunately UA did not see things the same way and maintained the band still owed them a third film.)

Directed by George Dunning, the film had an original story by Lee Minoff, based on the song by John Lennon and Paul McCartney. The screenplay ended up requiring four coauthors: Minoff, Al Brodax, Jack Mendelsohn, and Erich Segal—who would go on to write 1970's monster bestseller, *Love Story*.

Even though the press reported that the Beatles were dubbing the voices of their characters, film actors vaguely mimicking each Beatle actually did the voiceovers. The Beatles' only participation in the filming was a live-action portion near the end, which was supposed to have psychedelic effects added. Lack of time and budget resulted in the Fab Four standing in front of a blank wall.

The plot of the film follows the Beatles as they help to rescue Pepperland, home of Sgt. Pepper's Band, from the music-hating Blue Meanies. Each member of the Beatles is introduced by a scene that references his perceived personal mystique: Ringo is a genial, philosophical soul; John transforms from a freakish Frankenstein monster by drinking a potion, George is seen as a mystic being serenaded by sitars, and Paul emerges from a room full of loud applause carrying a bouquet.

MAKING THE ALBUM

Paul McCartney explained that the song "Yellow Submarine" came into his head while he was lying in bed one summer night in 1966 and thinking about composing a children's song. It was immediately clear to him that Ringo should sing it. Not that the other Beatles didn't enter into the spirit of the actual recording with gusto—to create the various "submariner" sound effects, John blew through a straw into a pan of water to produce the sound of bubbles, George swirled water in a bucket, Paul and John spoke through tin cans to mimic the sound of orders being given, while Terry Condon and John Skinner of Abbey Road Studios dragged

YELLOW SUBMARINE
RELEASED JANUARY 13, 1969 (U.S.)
RELEASED JANUARY 17, 1969 (U.K.)
(All songs Lennon–McCartney, unless specified):

Side One:

1. YELLOW SUBMARINE

2. ONLY A NORTHERN SONG (Harrison)

3. ALL TOGETHER NOW

4. HEY BULLDOG

5. IT'S ALL TOO MUCH (Harrison)

6. ALL YOU NEED IS LOVE

Side Two:
GEORGE MARTIN ORCHESTRA:

1. PEPPERLAND

2. MEDLEY: SEA OF TIME/SEA OF HOLES

3. SEA OF MONSTERS

4. MARCH OF THE MEANIES

5. PEPPERLAND LAID WASTE

6. YELLOW SUBMARINE IN PEPPERLAND

Selections by the Beatles plus original film music.

chains through water in a bathtub to simulate ocean waves. Finally, the vocals were sped up slightly to give the song a unique sound.

The song was recorded on May 26 and June 1, 1966, and required five takes to complete. It first appeared on *Revolver* and then again on the movie soundtrack along with the previously released single, "All You Need Is Love."

Two new songs, "All Together Now" and "Hey Bulldog," were recorded for the film. "Only a Northern Song," went back to the *Sgt. Pepper* sessions, while "It's All Too Much" had never been attached to any specific project. The songs were all restricted to side one; side two featured the orchestral score George Martin composed for the film. A number of other songs used in the film, including "Eleanor Rigby," "Nowhere Man," and "Sgt. Pepper's Lonely Hearts Club Band," had appeared on previous albums.

The album charted in both England and America, climbing to number 2 in the U.S. Still, many people, including the Beatles, considered the LP to be something of a hodge-podge, with its collection of random songs taken from various studio sessions.

Above: Cover of the *Yellow Submarine* LP release.
Left: The 1969 Corgi Toys model of the Yellow Submarine, as seen in the movie. Corgi, a U.K. company, specialized in marketing models from popular film and television series, such as *James Bond*, *Batman*, and even *The Monkees*. Today, their model of the Yellow Submarine, complete with figures of John, Paul, George, and Ringo, commands a high price amongst both die-cast toy collectors and serious Beatles fans.

"IT'S A RETURN TO A MORE ROCK AND ROLL SOUND. WE FELT IT WAS TIME TO STEP BACK BECAUSE THAT'S WHAT WE WANTED TO DO. YOU CAN STILL MAKE GOOD MUSIC WITHOUT GOING FORWARD. SOME PEOPLE WANT US TO GO ON UNTIL WE VANISH UP OUR OWN B-SIDES."

PAUL McCARTNEY, 1968

Above: The 45 rpm single "Hey Jude." It is the band's most successful single.

There is little doubt this band produced any record as welcomed or as inviting of criticism as their first double LP. Called simply, *The Beatles*, it soon became known as *The White Album* because of its stark monochromatic cover.

After the masterful *Sgt. Pepper*, and yet another number one single, "Hello, Goodbye," the Beatles had followed up with lesser offerings: *Magical Mystery Tour*—enough said—and a decent single, "Lady Madonna," that nevertheless failed to top the charts. Of course, the skeptics were quick to point out that the Beatles were now past their prime and in a sad decline.

The band put these rumors to rest with the powerful one-two punch of their new single—featuring Paul's "Hey Jude" backed by John's "Revolution." "Jude," a seven-minute-plus opus, rose to the top of both the British and American singles charts and stayed there in the U.S. for a record-tying nine weeks. The first release from the Beatles' new Apple Records label, it would become the Beatles' most successful single ever, with worldwide sales over $5 million by the end of 1968 and $7.5 million by October 1972.

Naturally, the Beatles hoped for a follow-up album that would match the wild popularity of "Hey Jude," but as they were preparing to enter the studio in May 1968, a feeling of alienation began spreading among them. The truth was, these lads were maturing and their individual interests were drawing them in different directions. Four separate personalities were now itching to move beyond the restrictions of their youthful musical brotherhood. Two members in particular were perishing to get out from under the long shadow of their famous songsmith "leaders" and carve out their own territory in the industry.

Drugs had also drifted back into their lives after India; marijuana certainly, and experimentation with heroin in the case of John. John had also introduced his new paramour, Yoko Ono, into the mix, insisting she attend their recording sessions. As Paul later commented on her habit of perching on the equipment during rehearsals, "We were always wondering how to say, 'Could you get off my amp?'"

Now for the first time, the Beatles were honing their material alone, in isolation, rarely seeking out the cross pollination from the others that had always marked their efforts. George Martin complained that he was often required in three different studios by three different Beatles. Paul ended up recording four songs, "Martha My Dear," "Wild Honey Pie," "Mother Nature's Son," and "Blackbird," without any of his bandmates; John's "Julia" was also a solo effort. (Lennon expressed a particular hurt that he hadn't been included in the Paul/ Ringo recording of "Why Don't We Do It in the Road?" because it was such a "John" kind of song.)

The resultant album offered thirty relatively uncomplicated songs with the signature of the individual composer stamped clearly upon each one. Only sixteen of the cuts actually featured all four Beatles.

"*The White Album* was the tension album. We were all in the midst of the psychedelic thing, or just coming out of it. In any case, it was weird."

PAUL McCARTNEY, 1987

Above: Paul at a formal function, sometime in 1968.

Right: George and John chat at the launch of the Apple Tailoring store in Chelsea on May 23, 1968.

"Whatever else it is or isn't, it is the best album they have ever released and only the Beatles are capable of making a better one. You are either hip to it, or you ain't."

JAN WENNER, *Rolling Stone*, **December, 1968**

The album soared immediately to number one in Britain, spending seven weeks in that position, even during the traditionally slow Christmas season. Dethroned for a week by *The Best of the Seekers*, it then popped back to the top for one more week. Overall, it remained on the charts for twenty-four weeks. In America *The Beatles* hit number one after three weeks, spent nine weeks in that position, and accumulated a total of 155 weeks on the Billboard 200. The Recording Industry of America considers it the band's bestselling album with 19-times platinum status. It is the tenth best-selling album of all time in the United States.

The Beatles' popularity never seems to waver; it continues to figure at the top end of album polls. It was ranked the tenth greatest album of all time by a 1997 English poll conducted by HMV, Channel 4, the *Guardian* and Classic FM. It placed at number seventeen on *Q* magazine's 1998 list of the 100 Greatest British Albums and at number seven on the same list in 2000. In 2001, the VH1 Channel named it the 11th greatest album; in 2003 *Rolling Stone* magazine ranked it number ten of the 500 Greatest Albums. *Time* magazine

THE BEATLES

RELEASED NOVEMBER 22, 1968
(All songs Lennon–McCartney, unless specified):

Side One:

1. BACK IN THE U.S.S.R

2. DEAR PRUDENCE

3. GLASS ONION

4. OB-LA-DI, OB-LA-DA

5. WILD HONEY PIE

6. THE CONTINUING STORY OF BUNGALOW BILL

7. WHILE MY GUITAR GENTLY WEEPS (Harrison)

8. HAPPINESS IS A WARM GUN

Side Two:

1. MARTHA MY DEAR

2. I'M SO TIRED

3. BLACKBIRD

4. PIGGIES (Harrison)

5. ROCKY RACCOON

6. DON'T PASS ME BY (Starkey)

7. WHY DON'T WE DO IT IN THE ROAD?

8. I WILL

9. JULIA

Side Three:

1. BIRTHDAY

2. YER BLUES

3. MOTHER NATURE'S SON

4. EVERYBODY'S GOT SOMETHING TO HIDE, EXCEPT ME AND MY MONKEY

5. SEXY SADIE

6. HELTER SKELTER

7. LONG LONG LONG (Harrison)

Side Four:

1. REVOLUTION 1

2. HONEY PIE

3. SAVOY TRUFFLE (Harrison)

4. CRY BABY CRY

5. REVOLUTION 9

6. GOOD NIGHT

FabFact

The album's original title was meant to be *A Doll's House*, after the brooding Henrik Ibsen play. The idea was scrapped when the band Family came out with *Music in a Doll's House*. After the title *The Beatles* was suggested, the band actually had to go back over their albums and make sure that name hadn't been used before.

Opposite, above: Pop artist Richard Hamilton in his Highgate studio, London, 1970. On the wall behind him are two works by the artist Rita Donagh.

Opposite, below: This well-used copy of *The White Album* displays its individual serial number–0553635.

chose it as one of the Top 100 Albums of All Time in 2006. And in 2013, *Entertainment Weekly* proclaimed it number twelve in its 100 All-Time Greatest Albums poll (where *Revolver* reigned as number one and *Sgt. Pepper*, to the outrage of fans, did not even place).

THE UN-COVER

The cover of *The Beatles*, its bland whiteness relieved only by an embossed title and serial number on the right side, was startling and novel—and a natural progression on the devolutionary scale that went from Beatles in costume to Beatles in disguise to now, finally, Beatles in absentia. (Not far down the line, on *Abbey Road*'s cover, they would be dressed like four unrelated pedestrians—or as the "Paul Is Dead" crowd maintained: the gravedigger, the deceased, the undertaker, and the holy man—no longer even bothering to wear similar "bonded" attire.)

The concept of using a spare white cover was the brainchild of pop artist Richard Hamilton. He suggested that after the visual excesses of the two previous covers, a minimalist approach might be a relief. It was also his idea to give the covers serial numbers, like limited-edition print runs. After a number of embellishments were considered and discarded—a coffee stain, a green apple smear—the all-white version was approved.

The gatefold cover also contained extra goodies—a foldout poster featuring the song lyrics and a photo montage, again designed by Hamilton, as well as four head shots of the Beatles by John Kelly, which became de rigueur decor for dorm rooms across the globe.

"**We got the first four. I don't know where mine is, of course. Everything got lost. It's all coming up in Sotheby's I imagine. John got 00001 because he shouted loudest. He said, 'Baggsy number one!' He knew the game, you've gotta baggsy it.**"

PAUL McCARTNEY, *Many Years from Now*

INSTRUMENTS OF THE LATER YEARS

"I believe I love my guitar more than the others love theirs. For John and Paul, songwriting is pretty important and guitar playing is a means to an end. While they're making up new tunes I can thoroughly enjoy myself just doodling around with a guitar for a whole evening."

GEORGE HARRISON

Above: George Harrison's 1959 Gibson Les Paul Standard guitar in cherry finish, nicknamed 'Lucy'. It was given to him by Eric Clapton in 1968.

Into the late 1960s, John was still using his Epiphone Casino for most of his electric recordings. If it looks like a different model in some photos, that's because John had painted it, which he discovered muted the sound. So he had the surface sanded down to the original maple and revarnished. George did the same thing to "Rocky," saying the natural finish allowed the guitar "to really breathe." Paul experienced a similar muting of his Rickenbacker bass after he, too, added paint to the body during the *Magical Mystery Tour*. Like the others, he had his guitar sanded down and varnished. Of all the firsts the Beatles achieved, this has to be the oddest—the most refinished guitars.

COMPOSING IN INDIA

When John and Paul went to the Maharishi's retreat in Rishikesh, India, they each brought along a Martin D-28—Paul's a proper left-hand model—which they used to compose a number of the songs for *The White Album*. John switched to a Martin because—no surprise—he'd painted over his Gibson and messed up the sound. From then on, the D-28 became his main acoustic guitar, most notably heard on "Julia."

George's 1957 Les Paul ("Lucy") also had quite a history. After being used by several renowned axmen, it came into the possession of McCoy's guitarist Rick Derringer, who changed its original Classic Gold finish to

red. Then, dissatisfied with the new sound, he sold it to a New York guitar store, where Eric Clapton found it and gave it to George. When George came to Eric's home to ask him to play on "While My Guitar Gently Weeps," Clapton didn't have a guitar. As he explained, "I had just gotten into the car with him. So he gave me [Lucy] to play." Lucy was later stolen, and then auctioned off by mistake in California, before being returned to George.

George upgraded his acoustic sound with a Gibson J-200 Custom, which he used on *The White Album* and beyond. George switched his Strat in the final days for a custom-made Telecaster, which he used, along

"THAT MACHINE CAN DO ALL SOUNDS AND ALL RANGES OF SOUNDS— SO IF YOU'RE A DOG, YOU COULD HEAR A LOT MORE."

JOHN LENNON, ON THE MOOG, *ANTHOLOGY*

with Lucy, on the *Let It Be* sessions, including the rooftop concert.

Ringo remained faithful to his Ludwig drums. The only change he made was near the end, when he switched to the Hollywood model, in champagne gold.

TICKLING THE IVORIES

From the beginning, keyboards remained an important part of the Beatles' music, especially as they searched for instruments to enhance their evolving sound. Several early tracks featured the Hammond LT-3 organ, most notably "Mister Moonlight." The Vox Continental Organ, played by John Lennon at Shea Stadium, was designed to be

portable, as was the Hohner Pianet, which can be heard on the *Help!* tracks "Another Girl" and "The Night Before." The Pianet sounded like a Fender Rhodes set an octave higher.

The harmonium, a large, venerable, foot-powered organ, was used to create sound effects on "Being For the Benefit of Mr. Kite." When Billy Preston came to Abbey Road—at George Harrison's request—to play keyboards on the *Let It Be* album, Mal Evans brought in an electric Fender Rhodes piano, a portable keyboard favored by jazz musicians. that would end up on many 1970s jazz fusion albums.

Perhaps the band's most unusual keyboard was the Moog synthesizer.

George Harrison brought in a portable model called the IIIp. It didn't even come with a manual, and he joked that the inventor probably didn't even know how everything worked. George played it on *Abbey Road's* "Maxwell's Silver Hammer," "Here Comes the Sun," and "Because." The Moog also provided the white noise on "I Want You (She's So Heavy)." Many musicians again followed George's lead, and the Moog became a mainstay of progressive rock albums throughout the seventies and beyond.

Above, left: John, Ringo, and Paul rehease at two pianos during the *Sgt. Pepper* sessions in early 1967. George chats in the background.
Above right, and top right: The distinctive Vox Continental Organ, played by John at Shea Stadium.

"IT WAS HELL MAKING THE FILM *LET IT BE.* EVEN THE BIGGEST BEATLE FAN COULDN'T HAVE SAT THROUGH THOSE SIX WEEKS OF MISERY. IT WAS THE MOST MISERABLE SESSION ON EARTH."

JOHN LENNON, 1970

CHAPTER FIFTEEN
THE FINALE

"My cut of the movie would have been different. And I'm sure John's cut at the time would have been different—and Paul's cut. I thought there was a lot more interesting stuff than (director) Michael Lindsay-Hogg put in."
RINGO STARR

Paul came up with the idea of making a "restorative" album as a result of the discord generated during *The Beatles* sessions. He felt that if the band could return to their Cavern roots—writing and recording songs that they could then perform in a concert—all would be well. The concert could then be filmed and released as a movie, a companion piece to the album. Apple Studio's head Denis O'Dell suggested filming the rehearsals as well, for a "Beatles At Work" TV special.

The band had planned to call the album and film *The Beatles Get Back*, as in "getting back to the magic of their early days," but with the release of the "Get Back" single in April 1969, they decided to use a different song for the title—*Let It Be*. The irony was that as the amity in the band deteriorated and the infighting increased, not a one of them wanted to "let it be."

Michael Lindsay-Hogg was brought aboard to direct, a logical choice who had started out on

the TV pop music show *Ready Steady Go!* and recently directed an unaired special, *The Rolling Stones Rock and Roll Circus*. Lindsay-Hogg had an interesting personal background. The son of actress Geraldine Fitzgerald and the natural son of actor Orson Welles, he was the legal heir of Sir Edward Lindsay-Hogg, 4th Baronet—and would ascend to his father's title in 1999. Michael had romantic relationships with both Jean Marsh of *Upstairs, Downstairs* fame, and American socialite Gloria Vanderbilt, and his former wife, Lucy Mary Davies, married Lord Snowdon after his divorce from Princess Margaret.

COLD AS ICE

The film sessions began at Twickenham Film Studios on January 2, 1969, but the cold, cavernous sound stages proved too unwelcoming for the band. The movie set shifted to the relatively small basement studio at Apple Headquarters on Savile Row. Unfortunately the building's heating system was too noisy for filming and had to be turned off in the studio. The Beatles ended up feeling cramped, chilly, and cranky.

At one point, the film portrays Paul and George, still at Twickenham on January 6, discussing George's guitar riff on "Two of Us," Paul being quietly, doggedly critical while George seems frustrated

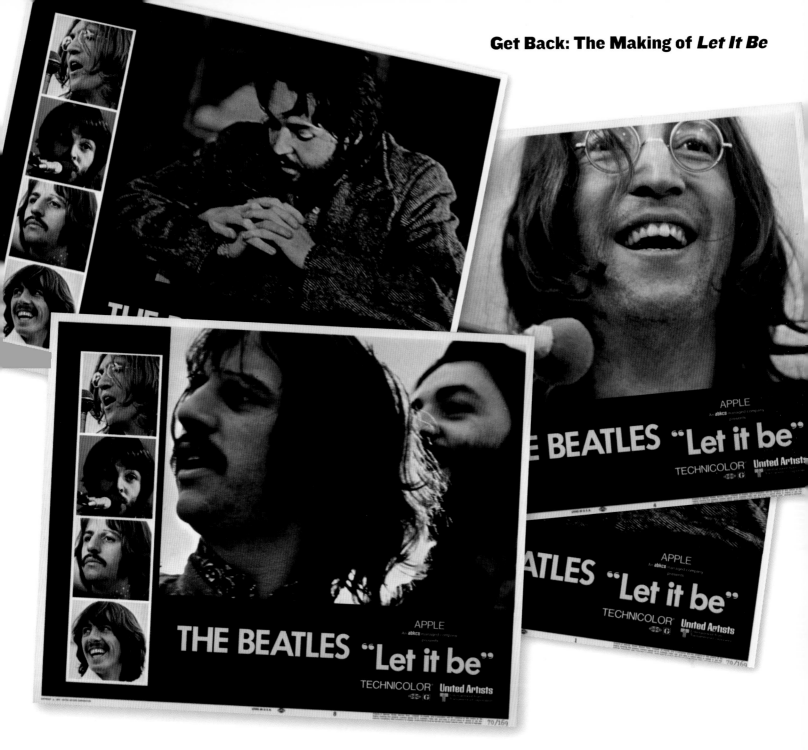

"IF THAT BOY DIES, YOU'RE GOING TO COP IT."
PAUL McCARTNEY, *LET IT BE*, WARNING A SOUND ENGINEER ABOUT GEORGE'S HOT MICROPHONE.

and put upon. "I'll play, you know, whatever you want me to play," George says, "or I won't play at all if you don't want to me to play. Whatever it is that will please you . . . I'll do it!" What the film doesn't show is George telling the band he was finished and walking out on them. He proceeded to go home and write "Wah Wah."

At a meeting on January 15,

Harrison agreed to return, his proviso being that the band scrap their plans for a major concert and that the rehearsals move to Apple Studio. The other members agreed, and since the concert was a nonstarter, they decided to expand the rehearsal footage into a film. Their accountants approved this idea—the band had already plowed considerable money into the project—plus, it would fulfill their

film contract with United Artists. There was one hitch, however. The sessions were recorded in 16mm and needed to be enlarged to 35mm for movie screens, with the result that the framing in the film version was wrong. It had to be adjusted so that the Beatles heads were not cut off in certain scenes.

Above and opposite: Movie poster and lobby cards for the *Let It Be* movie.

Previous pages: John and Yoko, in December 1968.

235

The film concludes with a live concert on the roof of Apple Headquarters. The four Beatles, all their stresses apparently left behind in that arctic basement studio, come together for one final rousing performance, the last they would ever give in public as a group. There was John, the steel-rimmed intellectual in Yoko's fur coat, like a Russian dissident on the lam from the gulag; George, lean and hungry in a black fur parka; Paul dapper in a dark suit, warmed only by his exertions on the Hofner; and Ringo, the Edwardian dandy in his wife's red mac—flailing merrily behind them all. And finally, Billy Preston grinning and intense on the electronic keyboard, like the guest at Thanksgiving dinner who makes the squabbling family mind their manners.

They played for forty-two minutes—including multiple versions of "Get Back," "Don't

Let Me Down," and "Dig A Pony." They also sang "I've Got a Feeling," and "One After 909," mixed in with some fooling around at the microphone with "I Want You," "Danny Boy," "God Save the Queen," and "A Pretty Girl Is Like A Melody."

Workers on their lunch hours, secretaries, and city gents, stopped below to listen, as did all the neighbors, who opened their windows or went up onto their roofs. Near the end of the set, the police calmly rang the downstairs bell and politely insisted that the concert stop because it was disrupting street traffic. The Beatles expressed disappointment over receiving just a "warning." They'd have liked it better if they had been hauled off to jail for disturbing the peace, and, as Paul later said, it would have furnished a "great ending for the movie— 'Beatles Busted on Rooftop Gig!'"

The film was released in May 1970, and came out on VHS and Laserdisc format in the early 1980s. It eventually became unavailable in any format (except for bootlegs), and fans still anxiously await the release of an authorized DVD. The movie earned the Beatles an Academy Award for Best Original Song Score.

While subsequent viewings of the film reveal that the sessions were not as acrimonious as they seemed the first time fans watched in shock—and saw their beloved lads sniping and sparring—*Let It Be* still possesses an aura of discord. Some of it was surely spurred by the stolid presence of Yoko Ono, who sits cipher-like next to John in most

shots, barely responding to the creativity flowing around her. There is one cringe-worthy scene of her appearing to climb over the drum kit in order to crouch beside him while he mans the snare during a run-through of "Octopus's Garden."

MAKING THE ALBUM

The production of the soundtrack was no less fraught with turmoil than the film itself. George Martin and independent producer Glyn Johns each prepared a mix of the album, but the Beatles were not satisfied with either version. When the criticisms from the band turned personal, Martin refused to work with them any longer. Johns tried remixing the album, still to no avail, and when he walked out, American producer, and creator of the infamous "wall of sound," Phil Spector was brought in to finish the job.

Two singles were also released during the filming of *Let It Be*: "Get Back"/"Don't Let Me Down" on April 11, 1969, and "The Ballad of John and Yoko"/"Old Brown Shoe" (Harrison), May 30, 1969. A third single, "Let It Be"/"You Know My Name (Look Up the Number)," was released on March 6, 1970.

LET IT BE

RELEASED MAY 8, 1970

(All songs Lennon–McCartney, unless specified):

Side One:

1. TWO OF US

2. DIG A PONY

3. ACROSS THE UNIVERSE

4. I ME MINE

5. DIG IT (Lennon–McCartney–Harrison–Starkey)

6. LET IT BE

7. MAGGIE MAE (trad. arranged Lennon–McCartney–Harrison–Starkey)

Side Two:

1. I'VE GOT A FEELING

2. ONE AFTER 909

3. THE LONG AND WINDING ROAD

4. FOR YOU BLUE (Harrison)

5. GET BACK

Opposite: It was so cold on top of the Apple Corps building during the rooftop session that John wore Yoko's fur coat and Ringo put Mo's raincoat on over his suit.

FabFact

An alternate version of the LP, *Let It Be . . . Naked*, was released in 2003. It strips away a lot of Phil Spector's instrumental treatments and also uses different versions of some songs.

> "I don't like people explaining albums. The only way you can explain it is to hear it. You can't really use words about music, otherwise we'd do a talking album. The album is the explanation, and it's up to you to make sure what you want of it. There is no theme to *Abbey Road*. There never is a theme to any of our albums, although some people saw one in *Sgt. Pepper*."
>
> PAUL McCARTNEY, 1969

After enduring rocky recording sessions with both *The White Album* and *Let It Be*, George Martin had to be seriously coaxed into working with the Beatles on their next album. According to Martin's recollections in 1994, Paul rang him up and said, "Look, you know, what happened to *Let It Be* is silly. Let's try to make a record like we used to. Would you come and produce it like you used to?" Martin replied, "Well, I'll produce it like I used to if you'll let me." Paul then contacted John, George, and Ringo in February 1969 to bring them aboard a new project that would become *Abbey Road*. Martin made the right choice this time. "It really was very happy, very pleasant," he said. "And it went frightfully well."

That winter into spring, the band worked loosely on the new material in conjunction with the *Let It Be* sessions, and then in April 1969 they set out to record a throwback, an album that would, hopefully, showcase them as they had once been, not as they were. It was almost as though they all suspected this was their last hurrah, and tacitly agreed to make the most of it.

FabFact

George Harrison confessed his favorite cover of "Something," which he kept in his own jukebox, was by American R&B icon James Brown.

FabFact

John called "Maxwell's Silver Hammer" more of Paul's "granny" music, and Ringo agreed, but added, "we needed stuff like that on our album so other people would listen to it."

"SOMETHING" GOOD

The finished album contained a number of significant tracks—John Lennon's pounding anthem, "Come Together"; Ringo's second composition, inspired by a trip to Sardinia, the charming "Octopus's Garden"; and two George Harrison efforts. "Here Comes the Sun," with its distinctive fingerpicking, was written in Eric Clapton's garden. "Something," which opened the album, became the song where George equaled if not surpassed John and Paul as balladeers. Originally recorded near the end of *The White Album* sessions, "Something" was George's first A-side (actually a double A-side with "Come Together"). It hit the top five in England and went on to reach number one in America. It also became—surely some vindication for the oft-slighted George—the second most covered Beatles' song after "Yesterday."

The moody "Because," influenced by Beethoven's Moonlight Sonata, featured John, Paul, and George in triple-tracked three-part harmony

Paul's major solo contribution, besides the bluesy "Oh! Darling," and the sing-along ditty "Maxwell's Silver Hammer" was his portion of the ear candy song medley—dubbed "the Long One"—that ends side two, making his voice the last one heard on the final album the Beatles ever recorded.

A few of the songs actually contained coded messages. The line "You never give me your money, you only give me your funny papers," from "Golden Slumbers" is not a reference to the comics in a newspaper; it was the disparaging term the Beatles used for all the useless notices of income they received. As George said in 1969, according to *Anthology*, "We get bits of paper saying how much is earned and what this and that is, but we never actually get it in pounds, shillings and pence." George also related that "Here Comes the Sun," was his reaction to being outdoors and not cooped up at Apple Headquarters in an endless meeting with accountants.

Paul also had a message to deliver—about how difficult things had gotten at Apple after Allen Klein began to take over. As he stated in *Many Years from Now*, "That's what 'Carry That Weight' was about: not the light, rather easy-going heaviness . . . In this heaviness there was no place to be. It was serious, paranoid heaviness and it was just very uncomfortable."

According to George Martin, the band members didn't precisely know this would be their swan song. "But," he amended, "everybody felt it was." He further admitted the Beatles weren't the only ones who needed to take a break; he was also looking forward to the release it would afford. Yet near the end, he surely thought back over the years of working with these clients—his friends now—and wondered what his life would have been like if Brian Epstein hadn't brought them around to EMI that day.

The last time the four Beatles worked together in a studio was the final overdub on "She's So Heavy."

"I liked the 'A' side but I never liked that sort of pop opera on the other side. I think it's junk because it was just bits of songs thrown together."
JOHN LENNON, 1971

"The second side of *Abbey Road* is incredible! *The White Album*, ninety-nine percent of it is very good. If I had Desert Island Discs, I'd take the *White* one or *Abbey Road*, I think. I like the boys playing together, you know. I like a group."
RINGO STARR, 1969

Opposite: George Martin and Cilla Black, discussing her single "Work Is A Four Letter Word," which he produced.

Above: John and Yoko Ono relax in the studio, probably listening to playbacks of their debut album *Unfinished Music No. 1: Two Virgins*.

> "That the Beatles can unify seemingly countless musical fragments and lyrical doodlings into a uniformly wonderful suite . . . seems potent testimony that no, they've far from lost it, and no, they haven't stopped trying."
>
> **JOHN MENDELSOHN,** *Rolling Stone*, equating *Abbey Road* to *Sgt. Pepper*

Abbey Road originally had a working title of *Everest*—based on the cigarette brand, Everest Milds, engineer Geoff Emerick smoked. The Beatles even planned to fly to the Himalayas to do a photo shoot for the cover. When that proved too daunting (read expensive), assistant engineer John Kurlander recalls someone suggested they go somewhere much closer: to the zebra crossing just outside the studio. Paul even sketched out a rough thumbnail of how the Beatles should appear. His suggestion for the title followed naturally after that—plus he was amused that it "sounds a bit like a monastery."

The cover sleeve was designed by Apple Records' creative director Kosh and featured neither the band's name nor the album's title. The cover photo—shot by freelancer Iain Macmillan and showing the Beatles striding single file along the zebra crossing near the studio—became an instant classic. Everybody, including *The Simpsons* animated TV show, parodied it. In fact, the crossing is still a favorite spot in London for tourist photo ops. Macmillan took the photo from atop a stepladder in the center of the road while a policeman help up traffic. Paul was originally wearing sandals, but took them off during the shoot. It was he who picked out the cover image from a series of six, the only one where the Beatles

appeared to be walking in time— even if they were walking away from the studio that had once been such a huge part of their lives.

CRITICAL REACTION

Abbey Road was released in England on September 26, 1969, and on October 1 in America— well before *Let It Be*, even though it was produced after the film. Although initial reviews were mixed, including complaints over the "artificial effects" on some of the tracks, many critics agreed that the Beatles had done what they'd set out to do—prove to the world that they could still write, play, and sing the heck out of a song.

It became the United Kingdom's best-selling album of 1969, the eighth highest selling of 1970, and the fourth highest selling of the entire 1960s. Three weeks after its release in America it hit the top of the charts, where it spent eleven weeks. It remained in the top 200 for 83 weeks and became the fourth best-selling album in 1970.

LEGACY

Despite those uneven reviews when it first hit, *Abbey Road* eventually came to be viewed as one of the Beatles' greatest efforts. Neil McCormack of the *Daily Telegraph* called it the Beatles' "last love letter to the world" praising its "big, modern sound." Nicole Pensiero

ABBEY ROAD
RELEASED SEPTEMBER 26, 1969
(All songs Lennon–McCartney, unless specified):

Side One:

1. **COME TOGETHER**
2. **SOMETHING** (Harrison)
3. **MAXWELL'S SILVER HAMMER**
4. **OH! DARLING**
5. **OCTOPUS'S GARDEN** (Starkey)
6. **I WANT YOU (SHE'S SO HEAVY)**

Side Two:

1. **HERE COMES THE SUN** (Harrison)
2. **BECAUSE**
3. **YOU NEVER GIVE ME YOUR MONEY**
4. **SUN KING**
5. **MEAN MR MUSTARD**
6. **POLYTHENE PAM**
7. **SHE CAME IN THROUGH THE BATHROOM WINDOW**
8. **GOLDEN SLUMBERS/CARRY THAT WEIGHT/THE END**
9. **HER MAJESTY**

of *PopMatters* online considered it "an amazingly cohesive piece of music, innovative and timeless." In 2009 *Rolling Stone* readers named it the top Beatles album; in 2012 the magazine ranked it number fourteen on their list of

"HER MAJESTY'S A PRETTY NICE GIRL, SOMEDAY I'M GOING TO MAKE HER MINE, OH YEAH, SOMEDAY I'M GOING TO MAKE HER MINE."

LAST LINE OF LAST SONG OF LAST BEATLES ALBUM

the 500 Greatest Albums of All Time. It came in at number twenty-two on *Entertainment Weekly*'s 2013 poll of the 100 Greatest Albums Ever. Although there is some dispute over placement, with some sources naming *The White Album* or *Sgt. Pepper*, most sources list *Abbey Road* as the Beatles' best-selling album.

Above: The sleeve of the 2009 Digital Remaster CD of *Abbey Road*.

"NOT BAD FOR A GARAGE BAND FROM LIVERPOOL."

LISTENER REVIEW OF THE ALBUM *1* ON AMAZON.COM

The Beatles felt strongly that including hit singles on their albums—or lifting songs from their existing albums to release as singles—was a form of bilking the public, who laid out good money to purchase their music and didn't deserve duplication (as opposed to the typical approach, where the hit single was often the only selling feature on a popular artist's LP). So their singles poured out over the years, but were not collected onto an album until 1970's *Hey Jude* appeared, featuring most non-album British singles and their B-sides: "Can't Buy Me Love," "I Should Have Known Better," "Paperback Writer," "Rain," "Lady Madonna," "Revolution," "Hey Jude," "Old Brown Shoe" (Harrison), "Don't Let Me Down," and "The Ballad of John and Yoko." It should be noted that "I Should Have Known Better" and "Can't Buy Me Love" had been Capitol singles, but their only appearance on an album in the United States had been on United Artist's soundtrack of *A Hard Day's Night*.

NUMBER ONE WITH A BULLET

Perhaps in an effort to create an album with the shortest title ever, Apple Records released *1* in November 2000. (The date marked the thirtieth anniversary of the Beatles' breakup.) It was a collection of 27 of the band's number one songs from 1962 to 1970.

Producer George Martin compiled *1* along with the three surviving Beatles. It combined tracks from both the American and British versions of *20 Greatest Hits*, with the addition of "Something." All the songs were updated for the new release, with the original analog files digitally remastered by Peter Mew of Abbey Road.

Universally well received and topping music charts all over the globe, *1* became the bestselling record of the decade in America—and the world—and remains the fourth best-selling album in the U.S. It also holds the record as the fastest-selling album of all time. In September 2011, the album was remastered and rereleased, proving once again that Beatles fans can never have too much of a good thing.

UK SINGLES — PARLOPHONE OR APPLE

TITLE	Release Date	Chart Peak	Writer	B-SIDE	NOTES
"Love Me Do"	1962	17	Paul	"P.S. I Love You"	Paul sang lead and John played harp—overdubs were not available until later on.
"Please Please Me"	1963	1	John	"Ask Me Why"	Their first number 1 hit in England (number 2 on Record Retailer).
"She Loves You"	1963	1	Both	"I'll Get You"	Begat the UK Beatlemania movement, charted 31 weeks.
"I Want to Hold Your Hand"	1963	1	Both	"This Boy"	
"Can't Buy Me Love"	1964	1	Paul	"You Can't Do That"	
"A Hard Day's Night"	1964	1	Both	"Things We Said Today"	
"I Feel Fine"	1964	1	John	"She's A Woman"	
"Ticket to Ride"	1965	1	John	"Yes It Is"	
"Help!"	1965	1	John	"I'm Down"	
"We Can Work It Out"	1965	1	Both	"Day Tripper"	Both songs hit number one.
"Paperback Writer"	1966	1	Paul	"Rain"	
"Yellow Submarine"	1966	1	Paul	"Eleanor Rigby"	First number one with Ringo singing, both topped chart.
"Penny Lane"	1967	2	Paul	"Strawberry Fields Forever"	Double A-side; both songs charted only to number 2.
"All You Need Is Love"	1967	1	John	"Baby You're A Rich Man"	
"Hello Goodbye"	1967	1	Paul	"I Am the Walrus"	
"Lady Madonna"	1968	1	Paul	"The Inner Light"	Last single released on Parlophone.
"Hey Jude"	1968	1	Paul	"Revolution"	First single on Apple; biggest-selling hit worldwide.
"Get Back"	1969	1	Paul	"Don't Let Me Down"	
"The Ballad of John and Yoko"	1969	1	John	"Old Brown Shoe"	John and Paul play all instruments, first single in stereo.
"Something"/ "Come Together"	1969	4	George/ John		Double A-side; both sides were listed in the Top Ten.
"Let It Be"	1969	2	Paul	"You Know My Name (Look Up the Number)"	

US SINGLES   CAPITOL OR APPLE

TITLE	Release Date	Chart Peak	Writer	B-SIDE	NOTES
"I Want to Hold Your Hand"	1964	1	Both	"This Boy"	The song launched the British Invasion.
"She Loves You"	1964	1	Both	"I'll Get You"	Swan version rereleased.
"Please Please Me"	1964	3	John	"From Me to You"	
"Twist and Shout"	1964	2	Russell/Medley	"There's A Place"	Their only cover song to chart Top Ten.
"Can't Buy Me Love"	1964	1	Paul	"You Can't Do That"	Flew to number 1 in two weeks.
"Do You Want to Know A Secret"	1964	2	John	"Thank You Girl"	Vee-Jay release; featured George on vocals.
"Love Me Do"	1964	1	Paul	"P.S. I Love You"	
"A Hard Day's Night"	1964	1	Both	"Things We Said Today"	
"I Feel Fine"	1964	1	John	"She's A Woman"	
"Eight Days A Week"	1965	1	John	"I Don't Want to Spoil the Party"	
"Ticket to Ride"	1965	1	John	"Yes It Is"	
"Help!"	1965	1	John	"I'm Down"	
"Yesterday"	1965	1	Paul	"Act Naturally"	Studio publicity at first claimed it was from film, *Eight Arms to Hold You.*
"We Can Work It Out"	1965	1	Both	"Day Tripper"	
"Nowhere Man"	1966	3	John	"What Goes On"	
"Paperback Writer"	1966	1	Paul	"Rain"	
"Yellow Submarine"	1966	2	Paul	"Eleanor Rigby"	The Supremes' "You Can't Hurry Love" kept "Yellow Submarine" from number 1.
"Penny Lane"	1967	1	Paul	"Strawberry Fields Forever"	The song reached number 8.
"All You Need Is Love"	1967	1	John	"Baby You're A Rich Man"	
"Hello Goodbye"	1967	1	Paul	"I Am the Walrus"	
"Lady Madonna"	1968	4	Paul	"The Inner Light"	Last Capitol single.
"Hey Jude"	1968	1	Paul	"Revolution"	First Apple single; over seven minutes long; more than six million copies sold worldwide.
"Get Back"	1969	1	Paul	"Don't Let Me Down"	
"The Ballad of John and Yoko"	1969	8	John	"Old Brown Shoe"	Side A radio play limited due to John's epithets "Christ" and "crucify me."
"Come Together"/"Something"	1969	1	John/George	"Something"	"Something" now B side; both sides hit number 1.
"Let It Be"	1970	1	Paul	"You Know My Name (Look Up the Number)"	
"The Long and Winding Road"	1970	1	Paul	"For You Blue"	Last group single; Phil Spector's overwrought arrangement put Paul off the group, for good.

"I COULDN'T PUT MY FINGER ON ONE REASON WHY WE BROKE UP. IT WAS TIME, AND WE WERE SPREADING OUT. THEY WERE SPREADING OUT MORE THAN I WAS. I WOULD'VE STAYED WITH THE BAND."
RINGO STARR

CHAPTER SIXTEEN
COMING APART

"I DIDN'T LEAVE THE BEATLES. THE BEATLES HAVE LEFT THE BEATLES, BUT NO ONE WANTS TO BE THE ONE TO SAY THE PARTY'S OVER."
JOHN LENNON

"AFTER BRIAN DIED, WE COLLAPSED. PAUL TOOK OVER AND SUPPOSEDLY LED US. BUT WHAT IS LEADING US, WHEN WE WENT ROUND IN CIRCLES?"

JOHN LENNON, *ROLLING STONE*, ISSUE 51

In 1962, the Beatles arrived on the international music scene with great fanfare, like conquering heroes. They left it like a band on the run, slipping out one by one after dark. Some fans, those who hadn't been paying attention, were shocked. Others were not surprised in the least; what they feared had come to pass. Still others felt vindicated, having been predicting the split since "Love Me Do." Most fans, though, felt a deep sadness, almost a heartache. This rare musical entity, which for many had been the blazing emblem of their youth, was no more. This titan of rock and blues and pop, whose output seemed undiminished by any current discord and whose creative energy offered the promise of many more years, if not decades, of audio diamonds, had ceased to exist.

Almost at once rumors of a reunion began circulating and would still be floating in the ether today, except for two things. As George Harrison so wryly stated, "As far as I'm concerned, there won't be a Beatles reunion as long as John Lennon remains dead." Alas, George, too, is now preventing any such thing from occurring.

The Beatles had begun drifting toward dissolution since the days of *The White Album*, each feeling a tug to pursue private goals, to work alone. John, after so many years of writing what he considered adolescent love songs,

was now enamored of Dylan-esque personal narrative. Paul, who studied musical trends like some people scrutinize the stock market, wanted to stick with the pop vernacular he loved. George was increasingly drawn to Indian music and a more cerebral lifestyle. Both George and Ringo had often been relegated to supporting roles and, rightly so, felt outside the creative loop. They wanted a voice.

BAD BROMANCE

In the studio, the band increasingly had trouble igniting the old sparks. Synergy is a tricky thing—it can't be forced, manipulated, or projected. It is either there between creative collaborators or it is not. The Beatles had for some time feared it was no longer there. It is a testament to their talent that its lack was not always evident in their recordings. Yet how sad to lose that energy they'd once shared. It's no wonder they didn't want to work together any longer, not when the magic of performing and recording had all but vanished.

What, then, had brought them to this pass? What killed all the pleasure for the Beatles when other groups, the Kinks, the Who, and

Above: Brian Epstein in the Granada Television studios, Manchester, during a recording of *Late Scene Extra*, November 25, 1963.

most notably the Rolling Stones, continued on, some even into the new millennium? A look back at the band's schedule, beginning with those early days of busing around the north of England, shows a full roster: tours; concert dates; writing, rehearsing and recording sessions; TV specials and talk shows; radio interviews, movies; documentaries; and almost weekly meetings with the press. Surely a case can be made that they were burned out and simply wanted to climb off the treadmill.

Brian Epstein had worked to keep the group a tight-knit unit during the early days, acting as mediator whenever there was friction between the members. George, in a way, also helped defuse any conflicts. He tended to back down from confrontations, and as the youngest, most impressionable Beatle, his presence sometimes kept John and Paul from blowing up, fostering a sort of "let's not argue in front of the kids" mentality. But Brian died . . . and his calming influence was gone; and George grew up . . . and soon wanted more recognition than his two bandmates were willing to accord him.

There were other factors at work there besides weariness and exhaustion, besides the desire for creative autonomy. Drugs like LSD certainly didn't help—inflating their egos while expanding their minds, making John, especially, feel like he was miles ahead of his mates in the "fookin' genius" category.

Meanwhile, a deep rift formed among them over the question of who would manage the band and

Apple Corps, and when the smoke cleared, Paul found himself the pariah. John was not blameless, inflicting his artsy, misfit girlfriend on his fellow Beatles. Oddly, she among all the factors that led to the breakup attracted the most blame . . . maybe because it was easier to fault an actual person than an amorphous managerial dispute or a struggle for creative equality.

FabFact

On Ringo Starr's 1973 album, *Ringo*, the other three Beatles appeared, but not on the same tracks.

Above: George Harrison was keen to begin producing his own songs, especially after a fertile time spent with Bob Dylan and The Band.

Previous pages: The Beatles, probably taken at Wapping during their "Mad Day Out," Sunday, July 28, 1968.

"YEA, THOUGH I WALK THROUGH THE VALLEY OF THE SHADOW OF DEATH, I WILL FEAR NO EVIL ... FOR I AM THE BIGGEST BASTARD IN THE VALLEY."
MOTTO ON ALLEN KLEIN'S DESK

As the attempted takeover of NEMS by Robert Stigwood proved, the Beatles in any shape or form were a hot property. Allen Klein, who managed Sam Cooke and the Rolling Stones, was known in the music industry as the man who could shake the money tree until gold rained down. He must have thanked his lucky stars when John Lennon appointed him his financial advisor in 1969 after Brian's death.

The son of immigrants from Budapest, Klein had graduated from Upsala College in New Jersey and started working as an auditor for a record company as well as freelancing as a bookkeeper for several celebrities. When Klein and his business partner wife

met Bobby Darin at a wedding, he promised the singer he could audit his books and gain him an extra $100,000 in royalties. Darin agreed, and Klein unearthed enough overdue payments to make good on his promise. It wasn't long before record companies began to fear him and his discerning eye.

After John brought him aboard, Klein at once assessed the whole Beatles empire. Clive Epstein had been running the "shop" at Apple, while Paul was acting as artistic director, but there was no one to make business decisions for Apple or move the band forward financially. Like a seasoned jockey, Klein saw his opening and he went for it. He made a proposal to the

whole band—he would manage them without a fee, taking only a commission on any money he earned for them. If Apple failed, he wouldn't get a cent.

Initially, Klein seemed like a godsend. He immediately negotiated a new contract with EMI, making sure his illustrious clients finally got their due—the highest royalties ever paid an artist up to that point. His concession to the label was permission to finally issue compilations, something Brian had refused EMI. He also had the band release "Something"/"Come Together"—both tracks from *Abbey Road*—as a single in October 1969. (The Beatles typically did not lift singles from albums but issued them as standalones.) This move alone garnered so much income for the band that they were able to return to the Get Back (*Let It Be*) album, which had been shelved in December.

Klein also got Apple running more smoothly and kicked out the freeloaders and the hangers on. His take-no-prisoners style, however, won him few friends among the Beatles' close circle, especially when he fired their longtime associate Alistair Taylor.

IN-LAWS AND OUTCASTS

The infighting over management started after Paul married Linda Eastman in March 1969. Her father, Lee Eastman, was a prominent entertainment attorney, and so Paul thought it made sense for the Beatles to put their trust (a bit shaky now after Brian's sticky fingers had been revealed) in an experienced show business lawyer, instead of the slightly shifty Klein. The other Beatles disagreed.

Paul's attitude was viewed as disloyal . . . and of course his bandmates feared that he would get preferential treatment if their manager was Paul's father-in-law, Lee, or his brother-in-law, John (similar to the way the other Beatles disliked it when John Lennon traveled with Brian Epstein or played up to his vanity). Paul, who had always been much more of a unifying, father figure to the band than purported leader John, was now considered a turncoat. Even "little brother" George stood against him.

Meanwhile, Dick James, who

owned controlling shares of the Lennon-McCartney catalog through Northern Songs, grew anxious over the bickering and open hostility among the band members. As a result he and his partner, Northern Songs co-chairman Charles Silver, sold their shares to Britain's Associated Television (ATV) without giving the Beatles or Klein a chance to counter-bid. No amount of finagling could gain back the publishing rights to John and Paul's songs from ATV's head, the powerful Sir Lew Grade. (In 1985 ATV sold its catalog to American pop legend Michael Jackson, who had, once upon a time, been encouraged by Paul McCartney to invest in music publishing.) The most powerful, prolific, and popular songwriting team of

the second half of the twentieth century now no longer owned their own songs. It was a travesty.

Opposite, left: Allen Klein.

Opposite, right: John and Yoko in December 1968.

Top: Paul McCartney, the last Beatle bachelor, wed Linda Eastman at the Marylebone register's office on March 12, 1969.

Bottom: Paul and Linda enjoy a drive through London four weeks before their wedding.

"Oh, Yoko"

"The Beatles were a group made up of four very complex men— my small hand could not have broken those men up. They broke up because they'd reached an end; but in doing so they all created wonderful new beginnings."

YOKO ONO

There is one person who still takes a lot of heat for causing the break up—Yoko Ono, John Lennon's mistress and eventual wife. She made herself a handy target for potshots, in spite of no real evidence that she willfully separated John from the group. As Paul himself explained John's emotional abandonment of his bandmates—the two were simply in that early flush of love, when John only had eyes for his new darling. Yet there is no underestimating the amount of vitriol hurled at her during the period of the

breakup, and even though over time she evolved into a respected "wise woman" of the arts, those ill feelings still crop up among fans.

One reason for Ono's vilification was that she never attempted to make herself sympathetic to the public. Nor did she attempt to befriend the other Beatles or their partners. Once she and John became a couple, they presented themselves as a bonded unit, to the point of dressing alike and wearing their hair the same way (rather like a throwback to the early

Beatles of Brian's creation). You wanted one, you also got the other. And far and away it was John people wanted, making tag-along Yoko into the original Mini Me.

Born with the bluest blood in Japan, to a Samurai family with interests in banking, Yoko spent the early part of World War II in America, but when her father's bank transferred him to Saigon, the rest of her family returned to Japan. There, as John had, she suffered horrible war-related deprivation, even having to beg

composer Toshi Ishiyanagi, Ono wed American jazz musician and art promoter, Anthony Cox, in 1962. (One version of their story is that he had heard of her in New York and tracked her down to a mental institution in Japan, where her family had placed her after a suicide attempt.) They were married again in 1963, when it turned out her divorce from Ishiyanagi was never finalized. Their daughter Kyoko was born in August 1963. The marriage proved to be a mistake, but the couple, who still performed together, stayed married for the sake of their careers.

While Ono had gained a name for herself in American conceptual art circles, she also alienated a lot of influential people with her constant self-promotion. Ono claimed her hardscrabble years during the war had made her aggressive and gave her a deep understanding of what it meant to be an outsider. Seemingly nothing daunted Yoko, who crashed avant-garde parties and private showings, haunted the offices of art gods like Ivan Carp, and was considered by some to be a gallery gadfly. The negative feelings she generated within this insular world kept Ono from having many of her truly original ideas accepted, allowing white male artists to appropriate her concepts and earn the accolades.

> **"Yoko became an important person in the New York avant-garde. People came from long distances to attend the performances. They were the most interesting things going on."**
>
> **JOHN CAGE, composer, on Ono's art career in America**

for food to feed her siblings. She returned to the exclusive Gakushuin School in 1946, attending classes with the future emperor, Akihito. After two years as the first female philosophy major at Gakushuin University, Ono left to rejoin her family, now living in Scarsdale, NY.

NEW MENTORS

She began attending Sarah Lawrence College, but was much more interested in all the avant-garde "happenings" taking place in the New York City art scene, much to the dismay of her family. Ono soon began to perform her own unique brand of conceptual or performance art—for instance, setting a painting on fire or having show attendees cut her clothing off her—operating out of the Tribeca loft of La Monte Young while being mentored by John Cage.

After a six-year marriage to

Opposite: John and Yoko confer after sharing a meal at the Apple offices in London, 1969.

Above: Yoko Ono sits with her second husband—American film producer, art promoter, and jazz musician Anthony Cox—and their daughter Kyoko Chan Cox, circa 1965.

"You know the song: 'Those wedding bells are breaking up that old gang of mine.' Well, it didn't hit me till whatever age I was when I met Yoko . . . The old gang of mine was over the moment I met her."

JOHN LENNON, *All We Are Saying*, **David Sheff**

Left: John and Yoko outside the Robert Fraser Gallery, at the launch of his show there in July 1968.

"I ALWAYS HAD THIS DREAM OF MEETING AN ARTIST WOMAN AND FALLING IN LOVE."

JOHN LENNON

In 1966 Ono and Cox with baby Kyoko embarked for England, to attend an important conceptual art gathering in London called The Auto-Destructive Art Symposium. Such were Yoko's powers of persuasion that she managed to get the event's organizer to put them up in his home. That was where Yoko heard about the Indica Gallery in Mason's Yard, St. James's, which was a favorite haunt of the London underground. She first met Paul there, who, after hearing her ideas on conceptual art, suggested she talk to John, who was "into all that avant-garde stuff."

When she and John did meet, on November 7, 1966, it was the day before the opening of her conceptual art exhibit "Unfinished Paintings and Objects" at the Indica. John was instantly intrigued by her and they continued to stay in touch— including corresponding during the Beatles' India retreat—until 1968, when, with Cynthia away on holiday in Greece, the two spent a night recording music at Kenwood and then became lovers.

Many who knew Lennon were staggered by this choice. This was John, after all, who'd always wanted a Bridget Bardot, not an Asian conceptual artist with a childlike voice and a mane of untamed hair. Those familiar with Yoko, on the other hand, were probably less surprised. At no time had she ever pretended to be anything other than a woman on a mission to gain fame, acclaim, and an artistic platform. To Yoko, John Lennon must have seemed like her own personal trifecta.

THE GADFLY

Yoko's bulldog tenacity and imperviousness to insults combined to make her the one thing none of the Beatles, least of all John, could tolerate: an insinuating, self-impressed climber. In spite of this, he was totally devoted to her, allowing her privileges with the band that no woman had ever been given. In the anti-Ono camp there is a theory that John purposely inflicted Yoko's irritating "gadfly" presence on his bandmates to drive a further wedge between himself and the other three. Well, what else were fans to think? John invited her into the studio without the other Beatles' permission, while she made no attempt to be cordial or gracious, but rather had the effrontery to give the band suggestions about their recordings, comments no doubt received with astonishment and great bile on their part.

At one point in the film *Let It Be*, Paul reminds John of their trip to India, of seeing him walking so humbly with the Maharishi. "It just wasn't you," Paul points out several times, and the viewer gets the feeling Paul is not referring to John with the guru, but to John with Yoko.

If it was true that John used Yoko to pry him loose, he should have waited. What came to light soon after John quit was the not-surprising revelation that Paul, George, and Ringo were also unhappy with many aspects of the band. Meanwhile, the bitter resentments engendered by the grating presence of Yoko increased professional enmities, left lasting emotional scars, and, ultimately, were probably not even necessary for John's liberation. So while she might not have broken up a band that was teetering on the edge of dissolution, she, wittingly or not, damaged longtime friendships and removed most of

FabFact

According to Geoff Emerick in his *Here, There and Everywhere*, Yoko often seemed oblivious to her effect on others. Once, when she woke up from a nap in the studio, she wandered over to George Harrison's personal pack of biscuits and took one. George saw this and cried out, "That bitch!" John fought back, but could do little to defend his wife's actions, mainly because he was similarly obsessive about the food he brought to the studio.

"The Beatles were fantastic. They left their mark. But a hundred years from now, it's Yoko Ono the world's going to remember, and not John Lennon or the Beatles."

CHARLOTTE MOORMANI, performance artist, *New York Times*

THE ONO CYCLE

Apple Records. ● in association with Tetragrammaton Records. ⌀ T-5001   May 1968. Made in Merrie England.

During 1968 and 1969, Lennon found himself divided between his obligation to the Beatles' studio efforts and production of the three experimental albums he created with Yoko, *Unfinished Music No. 1: Two Virgins* (notorious for its full-frontal nude cover shot), *Unfinished Music No. 2: Life with Lions* and *Wedding Album*. The couple formed the Plastic Ono Band in 1969, and released *Live Peace in Toronto 1969*. John also changed his name to John Ono Lennon on April 22, 1969, in a rooftop ceremony at the Apple Headquarters.

Above: The back cover of *Unfinished Music No. 1: Two Virgins* featured a slightly less scandalous nude photo of John and Yoko, from the . . . rear.

John's previous support system, making it necessary for him to turn to someone else—to her.

After the couple emerged from their protest rally honeymoon, he appeared to have taken on aspects of her persona—he was deep now and cerebral, an artiste with a conscience instead of an angry rocker. And while this cloak of antiwar activism eventually came to fit him well, initially onlookers wondered where the waggish, care-for-none John had gone.

Yet Yoko was only one of many factors that affected the band's state of mind during these end times. It was clear from comments made by George Martin that they had already been spinning apart in a widening gyre for several years. So it seems perplexing, in light of this, that so few people in the music business and the press or in the Beatles' fan base had even the slightest charity for Yoko. After all, John had finally found his wife-mother-sister-soulmate, and he felt fine . . . "like winning the pools." Shouldn't that have earned some props for the missus? Apparently it did not.

"THE BEATLES IS OVER, BUT JOHN, PAUL, GEORGE, AND RINGO ... GOD KNOWS WHAT RELATIONSHIP THEY'LL HAVE IN THE FUTURE. I DON'T KNOW. I STILL LOVE THOSE GUYS! BECAUSE THEY'LL ALWAYS BE THOSE PEOPLE WHO WERE THAT PART OF MY LIFE."

JOHN LENNON

Things finally came to a head in September 1969. *Abbey Road* was completed in August, and a month later John officially announced his departure from the band to Paul, Ringo, and a few close friends at Apple Headquarters. He'd made up his mind on September 12, before flying off to perform with the Plastic Ono band at the Toronto Rock and Roll Revival. A week later, after having a rousing time performing on his own in Canada, he attended the meeting and told them he was through. (If the other Beatles were initially skeptical, it might have been because not long before that a drugged-out Lennon had called a meeting at

Apple to announce that he was the "Second Coming of Christ.") The band pleaded with him to keep the news a secret, which he did.

Paul made the official announcement that he was leaving the group in April 1970, via press release, after the debut of his first solo album. His dissatisfaction had peaked when he first heard Phil Spector's elaborate version of "The Long and Winding Road," a track Paul envisioned as a simple ballad. When he asked Klein to remove the cloying harp music, he refused. That had been the last straw for Paul.

MAKING IT LEGAL

Then, on December 31, 1970, Paul dropped a bombshell—he initiated a lawsuit against the other three Beatles and Apple, demanding that the band's contractual partnership be legally dissolved. He further stated that he refused to be represented by Allen Klein and that he had not received an audited account of Apple's books since it was founded in 1967. He also asked that a court-appointed receiver monitor Apple Corps during the suit and that Klein be charged with mismanagement of funds. (Never mind that Klein was actually making money hand over fist for the Beatles, Paul still didn't trust his methods.)

Paul's logic behind bringing the suit was that if the Beatles were never going to tour or perform concerts or record again, there was no reason for them to remain bound together as a legal entity. The court case dragged on for four years, and the band was not officially dissolved until January 1975.

Eventually Klein proved himself to be a thief. The Rolling Stones had fired him in the late 1960s, but not before he transferred the rights to their pre-1970 song catalog to himself. With the Beatles, he weathered the break up and went on to help George Harrison set up the Concert for Bangladesh to benefit UNICEF. Klein supposedly mishandled some of the money that was meant to go to the children's charity, and he was further suspected of diverting funds from the live album. He ended up under investigation by the IRS. When he'd abetted George in keeping Yoko Ono from performing at the concert, he alienated John Lennon, who fired him. Klein then sued Lennon, Harrison, and Starr for $19 million. In 1977 he was awarded $4 million in damages.

Klein's misdeeds came to light too late to vindicate Paul. Meanwhile, Lee and John Eastman's careful handling of Paul's finances increased his holdings and investments, until he became one of the wealthiest people in show business. So Paul got the last laugh, one surely overshadowed by a great sense of loss.

Considering John, George, and Ringo had already started working on solo projects before Paul's lawsuit, they appeared to have their futures roughly blocked out for them. At least professionally. Emotionally was a different story. Not unlike a divorce, the emotional impact of this separation—especially after so many years together on the roller coaster, sharing the creative highs, the critical lows, and the labyrinthine complexities of great fame—could not be calculated or anticipated. It could only be experienced.

Paul retreated to his remote farm in Scotland, George to his home in Esher and subsequently to an eccentric's estate, Friar Park. Ringo would base himself first in England and then Los Angeles. John would leave Britain behind and seek a haven in a place that had once welcomed him with open arms and screaming fans—New York City.

"THEY HAD AN UNPRECEDENTED EFFECT ON MUSIC AND CULTURE, GLOBALLY. THEY CHANGED THE WAY MUSIC WAS MADE, HOW IT WAS HEARD, AND THE SENSE OF WHAT IT COULD ACCOMPLISH..."

JOE LEVY, *BILLBOARD* EDITOR, 2013

Opposite: John and Yoko, in 1969, appear stressed by the high tension before the official break up.

Above: "All Those Years Ago"... George in pensive mood, onstage at the Cavern in 1962; Ringo posed at his Ludwig drum kit, late 1963; and Paul and John, backstage at the Finsbury Park Astoria, London, during the band's Christmas Show residency, on December 30, 1963.

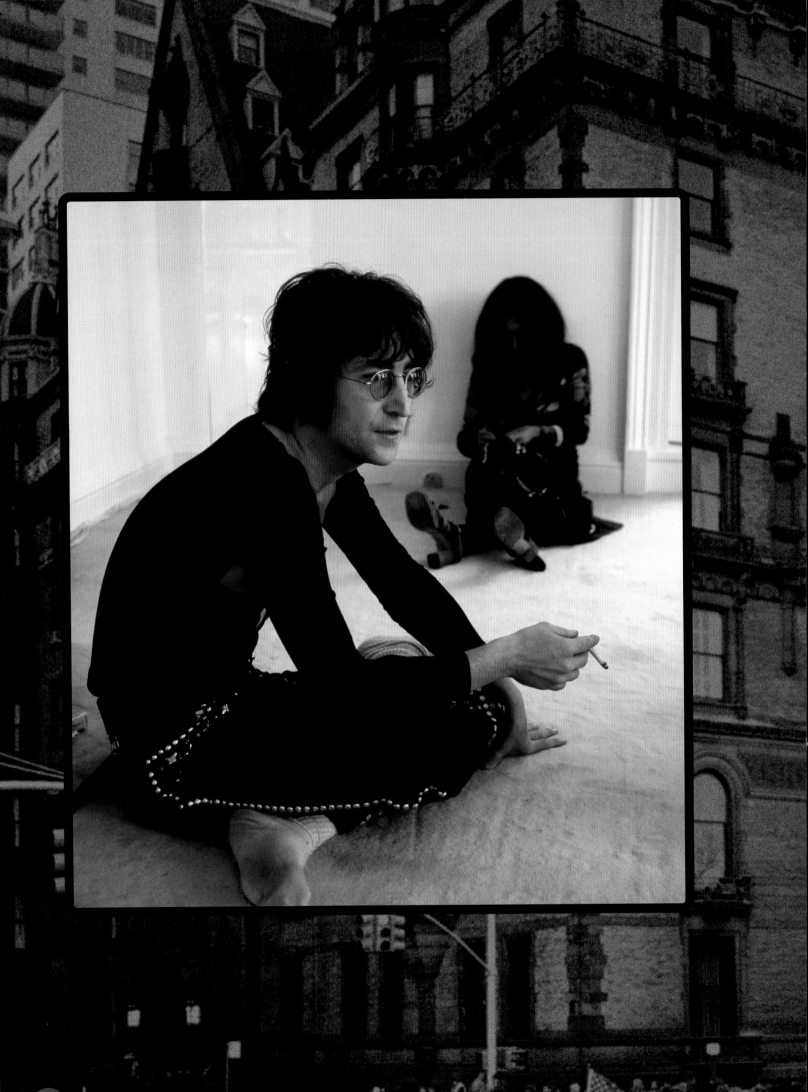

"MY LOVE OF NEW YORK IS SOMETHING TO DO WITH LIVERPOOL. THERE IS THE SAME QUALITY OF ENERGY IN BOTH CITIES."

JOHN LENNON

CHAPTER SEVENTEEN

JOHN LENNON: SOME TIME IN NEW YORK CITY

Bed Peace, Hair Peace

"I learned everything from her . . . It's a teacher-pupil relationship. That's what people don't understand. She's the teacher and I'm the pupil. I'm the famous one, the one who's supposed to know everything, but she's my teacher. She's taught me everything I fucking know."

JOHN LENNON, interviewed three months before his death

John Lennon left the Beatles like some teenage version of himself flinging out of Aunt Mimi's house—simmering with resentment over real and imagined slights—in this case slights leveled against him and Yoko both. That he had thrust her up and into the faces of the other three, that she had shown no appreciation over this privilege, did not matter to him. He wanted out, and he had generated enough animosity from his mates, with Yoko, with his ego, with his LSD and his heroin, with the alterations to his persona, to ensure an unchallenged departure. The downside of this ploy was a level of resentment and pain sufficient to fuel his anger for years, resulting in forays into primal scream therapy and other experimental "healing" techniques.

When John fell in love with Yoko, he told boyhood friend Pete Shotton it was like being a teenager again,

that feeling of being unable to think of anyone but that person, be with anyone but that person. What he hadn't counted on was Cynthia returning from a vacation in Greece and walking in on him and Yoko, both in bathrobes, in the parlor of Kenwood.

Cynthia sued John for divorce on August 22, 1968 (a countersuit to his original suit against her for adultery!) and it went through in November. After Yoko's divorce from Tony Cox was finalized, she and John planned to get married on the ferry from England to France. When that proved impossible, they wed on the island of Gibraltar on March 20, 1969. The ceremony took place only eight days after Paul married Linda Eastman—almost as though John needed to steal his former best friend's thunder.

John and Yoko spent their honeymoon in Amsterdam, creating a "bed-in" for the press with the duel themes of "Go to Bed for Peace" and "Grow Your Hair for Peace." They then duplicated this effort in Montreal, at the Queen Elizabeth Hotel, after the United States denied them entry. It was there John recorded the antiwar song, "Give Peace a Chance," from his bed with many of his friends joining in. These celebrated bed-ins, with their goal of generating a worldwide war protest, resulted in one of the most powerful counterculture anthems ever written *and* a conceptual

art masterpiece—proving to skeptics, who believed Yoko Ono would be the end of John Lennon, what happens when two bright, singular talents combine their areas of creative expertise.

Some years later, he and Yoko initiated an antiwar poster campaign—large handbills that said WAR IS OVER, IF YOU WANT IT appeared all around the world, including a billboard in New York's

"I had to survive this for Julian. I couldn't afford to crumble: I had to be strong, do what was best for him. I could fight the divorce, but that would get horribly messy . . . I would countersue for divorce, citing his adultery with Yoko."

CYNTHIA LENNON

Times Square. While the press belittled their sentiments, making light of their message and their medium, Yoko Ono still insisted they were having an impact. In the world of conceptual art, she explained, "You haven't succeeded unless half the people walk out."

TITTENHURST PARK

After their war-protest honeymoon, the newlyweds settled down at Tittenhurst Park, a 72-acre Georgian estate in Berkshire.

"Vampire-woman-sucks-life-out-of-man-who-enjoys-every-minute-of-his-destruction."

GEOFFREY STOKES, music critic, *The Village Voice*, **"The Infantilization of John Lennon"**

Following the unofficial breakup of the Beatles in 1970, John and Yoko produced an album, *John Lennon/Plastic Ono Band*, and released it to critical acclaim. No longer required to pen juvenile love songs or sing along to Paul's music hall ditties, John was free, finally, to emulate long-time idol Bob Dylan and express the things that moved him and that mattered to him. His experiences with primal scream therapy also gave his solo work a raw edge that had just begun to emerge in his final efforts with the Beatles.

Opposite: John and Yoko promote their "bed-in for peace" in an Amsterdam hotel room on March 25, 1969—shortly after their wedding. They went on to re-create the protest in Toronto, where they would record "Give Peace A Chance."

Above, left: John at Tittenhurst, July 1971.

Above, right: In December 1969, John and Yoko arranged for a series of large antiwar posters to appear in twelve major cities worldwide—including this billboard in New York's Times Square.

Previous pages: Inset, John and Yoko at Tittenhurst, July 1971; Background, crowds gather outside the Dakota in New York , shortly after hearing the news that John had been killed.

The new album contained the poignant, autobiographical "Mother" and John's pseudo-anthem "Working Class Hero" (at which Aunt Mimi scoffed, pointing out that he'd been raised "anything but working class"). The single "Instant Karma!" (Lennon)/"Who Has Seen the Wind" (Ono) also charted well, as did John's "Power to the People," with its "Instant Karma"-like chanted chorus. Lennon's next album in 1971 did not fare so well with the critics, but it did contain one of his finest, most accessible songs, the title track "Imagine."

John and Yoko remained at Tittenhurst until August 1971, when Yoko suggested they move to New York to escape the continuing fallout from the breakup of the Beatles. They lived at first in the St. Regis Hotel, then in a series of apartments until, after a break-in at their Greenwich Village flat, they found a more secure location at the massive and historic apartment building, The Dakota, on West 72 Street and Central Park West.

It was here that John became acquainted with leftwing activists Jerry Rubin and Abbie Hoffman, who convinced him and Yoko to perform at a rally for John Sinclair, jailed for ten years for selling two joints to a cop. As

"PART OF ME SUSPECTS THAT I'M A LOSER, AND THE OTHER PART OF ME THINKS I'M GOD ALMIGHTY."
JOHN LENNON

a result of this and other rally performances, John produced an album with Yoko in June 1972, *Some Time in New York City*. The double LP, featuring a 2-sided Live Jam, consisted of protest songs, political anthems, and a number of songs by Yoko. Many critics panned it, some claiming the couple were "patronizing the issues"—and the public.

"Brian Epstein had stopped us from saying anything about Vietnam or the war. And he wouldn't allow questions about it. But on one of the last tours, I said, 'I'm going to answer about the war. We can't ignore it.' I absolutely wanted the Beatles to say something about the war."

JOHN LENNON

Left: John and Yoko get some help from a police officer as they try to work their way through the crowd after leaving the Immigration Office on Broadway, New York, May 12, 1972.

As a result of his outspoken criticism of the United States' policies regarding the war in Vietnam, in 1972 John Lennon found himself singled out as an undesirable alien by President Richard Nixon and his henchman, FBI Director J. Edgar Hoover. A campaign of open surveillance and wiretapping ensued, causing John to develop deep paranoia, which he often spoke of to the press and during TV interviews. On March 23, 1973, the U.S. Immigration Department served John with a deportation order, demanding that he leave the country within sixty days; that he was ineligible for admission to the United States based on his 1968 misdemeanor conviction for cannibis possession in London.

John and Yoko hired immigration lawyer Leon Wildes to defend him; Wildes frankly told the couple they were probably going to lose. Still, he went ahead with a plan of action—wearing the government down by appealing every order

to leave, hoping the feds would eventually tire of the case and the mounting expense and go away.

Lennon, meanwhile, continued to vocally oppose the war, appearing at anti-war concerts or speaking at marches, where he quoted Gandhi and Martin Luther King Jr. And in spite of his claim of hating violent solutions, he and Yoko went on TV talk shows with Black Panther Bobby Seale and radical Angela Davis. These appearances with the major polarizing figures of the era were light-years away from his days clowning in Hamburg or doing silly pantomime at the Christmas Show. He wasn't yet thirty, but he had clearly assumed the mantle of the dedicated "peace-nik" agitator.

JOHN AND MAY IN L.A.

In the midst of all this tension, while John was recording *Mind Games* in 1973, he and Yoko agreed to a trial separation. Some of the pressure she felt was due to her inability to locate her daughter,

Kyoko, whom Anthony Cox had abducted in late 1971. At Yoko's suggestion, John traveled to Los Angeles that summer with May Pang, a beautiful young Chinese American who was his and Yoko's personal assistant and production coordinator. While there, they rented a beach house and lived together in merry disarray with Harry Nilsson, Ringo Starr, and drummer Keith Moon of the Who. John got drunk and caroused with Nilsson nearly every day; he became so disruptive at the Troubadour in West Hollywood that he was thrown out twice. He also attempted to record an album of rock and roll classics with Phil Spector, until the notoriously flaky producer disappeared with the tapes after a car accident.

Lennon and Pang returned to New York in 1974, moved into a penthouse apartment on East 52nd Street, while John recorded the chart-topping *Walls and Bridges*. The LP included Lennon's only solo number-one hit (the other Beatles

"AT NIGHT HE LOVED TO CHANNEL–SURF AND WOULD PICK UP PHRASES FROM ALL THE SHOWS. ONE TIME, HE WAS WATCHING REVEREND IKE, A FAMOUS BLACK EVANGELIST, WHO WAS SAYING, "LET ME TELL YOU GUYS, IT DOESN'T MATTER, IT'S WHATEVER GETS YOU THROUGH THE NIGHT."
MAY PANG, ON THE ORIGIN OF THE SONG

Above: May Pang, the Lennons' personal assistant, was more or less chosen by Yoko to look after John during the couple's 1973 trial separation. John and May hit the West Coast and ended up cavorting with Harry Nilsson, Keith Moon, and Ringo.

FabFact

It was May Pang who encouraged John to reach out to Julian, and then to Paul, while both former Beatles were on the West Coast. John and Paul played together for the last time at the Los Angeles Hit Factory studio in 1974. Even though the session included Stevie Wonder and Harry Nilsson, the resultant recording was so bad that a bootleg of the session was released as *A Toot and a Snore in '74.*

already had theirs), "Whatever Gets You Through the Night"—with an assist from rising star Elton John—as well as the haunting "#9 Dream." Julian, who had reunited with his father in Los Angeles after a four-year separation, played the drums on the cut, "Ya Ya." Lennon would appear with Elton John at the latter's Thanksgiving concert in Madison Square Garden—Lennon had promised to show up there and sing if "Night" hit number one, which it did.

When Al Coury, a vice president at Capitol Records recovered the Spector tapes, John was able to complete his oldies album titled appropriately enough, *Rock 'n' Roll.* As much as he'd enjoyed experimenting at Abbey Road, in his heart he'd always yearned to re-create those early Sun or Chess disks. Released in February 1975, the album, supported by the single "Stand by Me," met with some flak—critics called it "a step back"—but it reached number six on the American and U.K. charts and was eventually certified gold in both countries. The cover featured Jürgen Vollmer's picaresque portrait of greaser John lounging in a Hamburg doorway.

John returned to Yoko in early February 1975; both were determined to make their marriage work. They decided to try again for a child, in spite of doctors'

warnings of fertility problems, and Yoko soon discovered she was pregnant. John was overjoyed. But the INS still had him in their sights, threatening him with deportation even after Nixon was forced to resign from office for covering up the Watergate break-in (and made his bizarre, smiling-and-waving exit onto Marine One). John finally learned that the government had dropped its case against him—citing a miscarriage of justice—on his 35th birthday, the same day Yoko was in the hospital giving birth birth to their son, Sean Taro Ono Lennon.

KYOKO GOES MISSING

Although Yoko Ono was awarded full custody of her daughter after her divorce from Anthony Cox, Cox abducted Kyoko in 1971, when she was eight, and took her "underground." He eventually became a born-again Christian and raised his daughter, renamed Rosemary, in the Church of the Living Word. He and Kyoko left the church in 1977, but Kyoko and her mother were not reunited until 1994. Since then they have reestablished a relationship.

"MUM WAS MORE ABOUT LOVE THAN DAD. HE SANG ABOUT IT, HE SPOKE ABOUT, BUT HE NEVER REALLY GAVE IT, AT LEAST NOT TO ME AS HIS SON."

JULIAN LENNON, *THE TELEGRAPH,* DECEMBER 2011

Top: John holds Julian in a rare fatherly pose.

Bottom: After his birth, Sean Lennon became the center of his father's universe.

John was held transfixed by his cherubic new son, this child who had been "planned," as he once pointed out, unlike Julian, whom John professed to love but had often neglected emotionally. John soon turned away from the demanding world of composing and recording, determined to focus on this miracle child. Yoko, meanwhile, took over the reins of John's business affairs, including the numerous lawsuits against him, working out of their office on the main floor of the Dakota. (This "house-husband" arrangement, with John raising the baby while Yoko took care of the family's business, was the same dynamic she'd created with Anthony Cox and Kyoko.)

Whatever John's demons had been in the past, this new, diminutive presence in his life seemed to be going a long way toward eradicating them. And so what if, as some critics pointed out, John entered the "father business" like he had the "music business," with an eye to increasing his popularity? It didn't make him less of a loving parent.

HEY, JULES

Unfortunately for Julian Lennon, due to his father's touring commitments with the early Beatles (and, back then, a certain disdain for family life) John had not been able to express the same level of devotion to his first son. Still, according to Cynthia Lennon, even though John might be on tour, he always returned to little Julian. After the Lennon's divorce, however, John moved to America with Yoko, making it difficult for him to see his son. "But," Cynthia added, "there was constant contact . . . always constant. There were phone calls. There were presents. There was as much as John could do at the time. I think that in many interviews that Julian's had all that comes across is love, and he had a marvelous relationship even though it was at a distance . . . but slowly it built up and it was really building up beautifully before he lost his father. It's a great tragedy because they would have been great pals, and they would have jammed together and had a wonderful time."

The truth was, John almost always chose Beatles over family, and during the divorce had chosen Yoko over Cynthia and Julian. It was not surprising that at times the boy felt Paul McCartney was closer to him and bore more affection for him than his own father. During those ragged days, Paul even wrote a song to cheer him up, "Hey, Jules, don't make it bad . . ." which, of course, became the hugely popular, "Hey

"You don't really miss anything specific. You just miss them breathing, just being there. I miss the way his skin felt, the sound of his voice. Him tucking me in at night."

SEAN LENNON, 1998, *New York* magazine, on missing his father

Jude," and set the whole world to chanting, "Naa . . . naa . . . naa . . . na-na-na-na." That was probably small solace to Julian at the time.

A MUSICAL HERITAGE

Julian Lennon went on to become a musician in his own right, releasing his debut album *Valotte*. in 1984. It climbed to number seventeen on the Billboard 200 chart and hit number twenty in the United Kingdom. before going platinum. The single, "Too Late for Goodbyes," hit number six in the United Kingdom, number five on the *Billboard* Hot 100 and number one on the Adult Contemporary chart. A second single, "Valotte," only reached 55 in England, but in America it hit number two on the Billboard Mainstream Rock chart. Julian's follow-up album, *The Secret Value of Daydreaming*, went gold.

Today, Julian, who recently turned

fifty and resembles an open-faced, less-angular version of John, represents a number of charities, including the Prince's Fund and the Lupus Foundation, as well as his own humanitarian effort, the White Feather Foundation.

Julian still has ambivalent feelings about John, who left him out of his will, forcing his son into a protracted court battle until an undisclosed settlement was reached. When asked recently what he'd learned from John, Julian shot back, "How not to be a father." Fortunately, he always had his mum there, rooting for him and supporting him. A strong-willed woman taking care of business, just as John's Aunt Mimi had done, but in Cyn's case, offering much more love and acceptance.

It was almost a given, considering his parents, that Sean Lennon, who also bears an uncanny

resemblance to his father, would chose a career in music. He sings and plays guitar and has an interest in experimental rock, as well as folk, alternative, and indie rock. In the mid-1990s, Lennon toured as a bass player with Cibo Matto. His first solo album, 1998's *Into the Sun*, resulted in a single, "Home," and a music video that received extended play on MTV. Since 2008, he has performed as Ghost of a Saber Tooth Tiger with Charlotte Kemp Muhl. In 2011, Sean recorded the American-language version of the songs for the title character in *A Monster in Paris*, a French animated film.

Sean Lennon is also an activist who supports his mother in her many charitable efforts for Amnesty International, Autism Speaks, The Gorilla Foundation and a number of other worthy causes.

Top left: Julian Lennon photographed in December 1984, around the time his hit album *Valotte* was released.

Center: Julian as he appears today, still displaying an uncanny resemblance to his father.

Right: Sean Lennon took part in the fiftieth anniversary of the Beatles' first visit to the U.S., including an appearance on *The Late Show With David Letterman* with the Flaming Lips.

"After John passed away, my grief showed in my face. I knew that was not good for our son, Sean, so one day I looked in the mirror and tried to make myself smile. At first it looked made-up, and I thought, 'Ugh, will this be good enough?' But with practice, it felt more natural, and eventually my whole body started to smile—I think that's how I saved myself."

YOKO ONO

Three weeks after the release of *Double Fantasy*, on December 8, John was doing a *Rolling Stone* magazine cover shoot—at home—with his neighbor, the award-winning photographer Annie Liebowitz. Lennon, as usual, insisted on Yoko being photographed with him. The result of Liebowitz's inspired shoot was a tender, vulnerable photo of a naked John in fetal position tucked up against a clothed Yoko. (In 2005, the American Society of Magazine Editors ranked it the top magazine cover of the past forty years.) After Liebowitz left, John gave a three-hour interview to DJ Dave Sholin of San Francisco's RKO Radio. At the end of the session, John summed up, "I consider that my work won't be finished until I'm dead and buried and I hope that's a long, long time." Then he and Ono headed out to the Record Plant Studio, where they were mixing their next single, Yoko's song "Walking on Thin Ice."

As John and Yoko waited for their car service, several fans approached the couple asking for autographs. One of them, a stocky young man, handed John his copy of *Double Fantasy*. "Do you want it signed?" John asked, then scribbled his signature as the fan, Mark David Chapman, nodded. Another fan, amateur photographer Paul Goresh, captured the moment with his camera.

John and Yoko spent several hours at the studio, then hurried home so that John could say goodnight to Sean. It was approximately 10:50 p.m. when they got to the Dakota, and John and Yoko got out on 72nd Street instead of inside the building's private courtyard. The doorman, a former CIA agent, Jose Sanjenis Perdomo, later reported seeing Chapman waiting in the shadows of the arched entryway.

FIVE BULLETS

After John and Yoko passed him, Chapman stepped forward, assumed a crouched combat stance, and quickly fired five hollow-point bullets from a Charter Arms Undercover .38 Special revolver, four of them plowing into Lennon's left shoulder and back. John cried out, "I'm shot! I'm shot!" as he staggered up to the reception area. (Some witnesses claim it was Yoko who cried, "John's been shot!") The night porter, Jay Hastings, seeing the severity of the wounds and all the blood, immediately called the police. Perdomo, meanwhile, had disarmed Chapman, who then peeled off his coat and hat—presumably to prove he had no other weapons—and sat on the curb thumbing through a copy of *The Catcher in the Rye*.

The police rushed Lennon to nearby Roosevelt Hospital in the back of a squad car, and he was able to make some response when they asked if he was John Lennon. Shortly after that he lapsed into unconsciousness. He arrived at the ER with no pulse, and the doctors and nurses worked on him for more than 20 minutes, including open-heart massage, before they were forced to give up.

ACCOSTING JT

Mark David Chapman had compiled a whole list of celebrities he intended to kill after John Lennon, including Johnny Carson, Walter Cronkite, Jacqueline Kennedy Onassis, and Elizabeth Taylor. On December 7, Chapman grabbed singer James Taylor in the 72nd Street subway station, near the Dakota, and, according to Taylor, "The guy had sort of pinned me to the wall and was glistening with maniacal sweat and talking some freak speak about what he was going to do . . . how John was interested, and he was going to get in touch with John Lennon." At the time, Taylor was merely rattled by the incident; he had no way of knowing how close he'd come to John Lennon's future assassin.

label, Geffen Records, shows a woman aged and made haggard by the last in a line of personal tragedies—the miscarriages she suffered with John, the abduction of Kyoko, and now the murder of her husband before her eyes.

STUNNING NEWS

That night and the next morning, the world reeled at the news. John's death became a seminal moment for many, akin to the John F. Kennedy assassination or Neil Armstrong's walk on the moon, when individuals recalled precisely where they'd been and what they were doing when the event took place.

People wept openly, and wondered what the world had come to, when pop entertainers became fodder for assassination. Was it a measure of how thoroughly John's politicization had affected his music, that he was made a target by a delusional young zealot . . . as though he were a world leader, a controversial activist, or a holy man? Perhaps he was all three, in the sense that his followers were global, many of his songs advocated radical activism, and that he freely preached a philosophy of pacifism and non-violence. And while he had never set himself up to be the sort of bloke who died for his beliefs, there was much of the Christ-like martyr in the "misunderstood genius" pose he'd adopted since his youth.

Chapman's bullets had shredded the aorta and its branches. Lennon's cause of death was noted as hypovolemic shock brought on by the loss of more than eighty percent of his blood volume.

In a bizarre coincidence, as Lennon was pronounced dead, numerous witnesses, including his surgeon, reported that "All My Loving" began playing on the hospital's PA system.

Chapman was a security guard who lived in Honolulu, Hawaii.

He'd had a difficult childhood, including delusional episodes of being the "king" of the little people who lived in his bedroom walls, and had recently been drawn into the born-again Christian movement. His motivation for the shooting was never made clear, although theories ranged from obsessive idol worship (as in, if he killed Lennon he could become Lennon) to religious rage over Lennon's "We're bigger than Jesus" comments. Whatever his grievance against the former Beatle, Chapman had already made one aborted attempt to kill John that October, actually getting as far as New York before flying home. But on the night of December 8th he succeeded . . . and put an end to a troubled, extraordinary, legendary life.

Yoko Ono, near hysteria, asked the hospital not to announce John's death to the press until she could get home and tell Sean herself. Photos of her being escorted from the hospital by a consoling David Geffen, head of the Lennons' new

"THERE WAS A TREMENDOUS INTIMACY IN EVERYTHING JOHN LENNON DID, COMBINED WITH A FORMIDABLE INTELLECT. THAT IS WHAT MAKES HIM A GREAT SINGER."

JACKSON BROWNE, ON *ROLLING STONE*'S TOP 100 SINGERS

People across the globe deeply mourned the loss of John Lennon the Beatle and John Lennon the man. Over time, he had become more than just a rock and roll performer—he was the dreamweaver, as he'd once phrased it, the key spirit behind a now-departed age.

Over the next day or two spontaneous memorials sprang up in many major cities, in Liverpool and London, certainly, even behind the Iron Curtain, in places like Mala Strana Square in Prague. In New York City, grieving fans gathered outside the Dakota along Central Park West, holding up peace signs and messages of condolence, clasping flowers and lit candles, singing and swaying together with tears running down their cheeks. There were young children, teenagers, adults, even seniors, in fact the same collective demographic that had watched John and the Beatles first perform on *Ed Sullivan* so many years earlier. When several fans committed suicide out of grief, Yoko issued a message of consolation to all those mourning John's death, ending with, "When something like this happens, each one of us must go on."

Paul McCartney spent the day after the shooting in the studio, his natural haven. Ringo called on Yoko in person, while George Harrison issued a statement of grief, saying, "I am stunned. To rob life is the ultimate robbery." In 1981, George released his musical tribute to John, "All Those Years Ago," which featured Paul and Ringo, the first time the three of them sang together since 1969. Paul's plaintive song for John, "Here Today," appeared in 1982 on *Tug of War*. In 2012, Bob Dylan memorialized his friend with "Roll on John" on the *Tempest* album.

STRAWBERRY FIELDS

In 1985 the City of New York dedicated the section of Central Park directly across from the Dakota to Lennon's memory. Called Strawberry Fields, it was a place John had often walked with his family. Many countries donated trees to the serenely landscaped site, which also includes three Dawn redwoods that are expected to top a hundred feet and will be visible from many places in the park. The city of Naples, Italy, donated a beautiful circular mosaic with the word "Imagine" at its center. Fans and wellwishers often place flowers, candles, instruments, and similar mementos there. Memorial gatherings for other departed performers, including George Harrison, have occurred at the treasured spot.

CAREER ASSESSMENT

John Lennon felt so insecure about his singing voice that he had George Martin employ double tracking on most of his cuts. (Although double tracking normally involves a singer performing along with their own recording, for a bigger, richer sound, the Abbey Road engineers figured out how to do the same thing in one take using variable-speed recorders; they called this automatic double tracking or ADT.) Yet Lennon possessed one of the most evocative and recognizable voices in rock or pop music history. His flinty baritone worked equally well for teen-dream love songs, raucous rock and roll numbers, psychedelic anthems, and thoughtful ballads . . . and his complex harmonies with Paul McCartney were one of the Beatles' hallmarks.

Lennon provided both lead and rhythm guitar for the Beatles, as well as playing mouth organ, piano, drums, and, on occasion, the tea chest bass. As his prowess as a musician grew, he incorporated new guitar techniques into his music, including slide guitar and a distinctive fingerpicking method he learned from folk singer Donovan.

Lennon was voted number 5 in the *Rolling Stone* poll of the 100 Greatest Singers (The First Lady of Soul Aretha Franklin scored number one); "Imagine" was voted number one in *Rolling Stone*'s poll of the 10 Greatest Solo Beatles Songs; Lennon also came in at number 7 in their list of the Top Ten Rock and Roll Rebels.

"PAUL WAS ALWAYS MORE INTERESTED IN MUSIC, PER SE, WHEREAS JOHN WAS MORE INTERESTED IN WORDS, PER SE."
GEORGE MARTIN

As a songwriter John had few equals, and only one peer—his partner Paul McCartney. Even though it became clear over time that the "Lennon-McCartney" brand represented more individual efforts than a true collaboration, their ability to fill in the gaps for each other when necessary and their healthy sense of competition kept them sharp and prolific.

Lennon's honors include: an MBE in 1965; posthumously, a 1982 Grammy for Album of the Year, *Double Fantasy*, and a Grammy Lifetime Achievement Award in 1991. Among many memorials, Lennon has been honored with a bronze statue in a Havana park and the Imagine Peace Tower on an island outside Reykjavik, Iceland. In 2002, Liverpool renamed its airport Liverpool John Lennon Airport and adopted the motto, "Above us only sky."

Top: John, at a press conference at Heathrow airport on his return from honeymooning with Yoko, April 2, 1969.

Above, left: Fans commemorate the twenty-fifth anniversary of John's death at the Imagine memorial in Strawberry Fields, Central Park, December 8, 2005.

Bottom: John's mosaic memorial, a gift from the city of Naples, Italy, at Strawberry Fields.

"NOTHING PLEASES ME MORE THAN TO GO INTO A ROOM AND COME OUT WITH A PIECE OF MUSIC."
PAUL McCARTNEY

CHAPTER EIGHTEEN
PAUL McCARTNEY: MULL OF KINTYRE

Lovely Linda

> **"We spend so much time together, because that's how we like it. I never used to go on girls' nights out, even at school. And Paul has never liked going out for a night with the boys, either."**
>
> **LINDA McCARTNEY**

When Linda Eastman first met Paul in May 1967, it was two years after her divorce from geologist John Melville See Jr., and, in spite of her reputation as a party girl, she had started looking for someone to settle down with and help raise her daughter, Heather. Therefore she was naturally cautious about forming a serious attachment with someone as flighty as this particular Beatle was reputed to be. Then again, years earlier she had joked to friends in America that someday she was going to marry Paul McCartney—so his presence in her life might have seemed preordained. Eventually she allowed herself to be courted in earnest, and by October 1968, she and Paul were living together at Cavendish Avenue.

For his part, Paul was surprised to discover that his "Lin" took as much pleasure from the beauty and simplicity of nature as he did. He later claimed she taught him how to relax . . . how to just "wing it" and not always need to be in control. It was also clear that some of the same things that drew John to Yoko—finding that rare, autonomous woman with a mind of her own working in a creative field—attracted Paul to Linda. Those days of groping groupies and casual flings were now behind both Beatles—at least for the time being.

FAMILY MAN

That December, shortly after Linda had moved in with him, Paul proposed to her while they were on holiday in Portugal. The two were wed on March 12, 1969, at the Marylebone Registry Office, with Paul's brother and Mal Evans in attendance. Afterward, the couple set off on a two-week honeymoon in New York. Linda was already pregnant with their first child, and after a trip to Corfu, she and Paul and Heather began spending time at High Park Farm in Scotland. Mary Anna McCartney, named for Paul's mother, was born in London on August 28, 1969.

Baby Mary, the peek-a-boo cherub

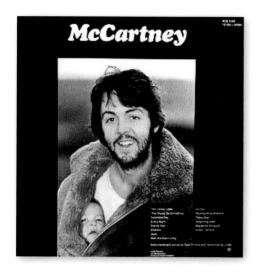

shown on the back cover of the McCartney album, was followed by Stella Nina in 1971 and James Louis in September 1977. (Paul had already officially adopted Heather in 1969.) Initially the place Paul went to grieve over the disintegration of the Beatles, rustic High Park Farm soon became the cozy family home that Paul and Linda created together. For years he retreated to this patch of Scottish coastline with his small clan—to tend the animals, tromp the countryside, and to pose for Linda's camera cavorting with his kids.

Based on Paul's relationship with Julian Lennon—and to some extent his function inside the Beatles—he possessed a strong paternal streak,

"She loved the fresh air and the freedom and the privacy of the countryside . . . She was just a great person to hang out with: very funny, very smart and very talented."

PAUL McCARTNEY, on Linda

and his own children appeared to fill him with joy and offer him a sense of completion. He relished their company so much, in fact, he even took them touring in the mid-1970s, when he and Linda began a new phase of their life together—as rock music's royal couple.

FACES OF AN ERA

As a photographer with access to the inner realms of pop music, Linda had been fortunate to capture on film many of the music industry personalities that molded the 1960s. These photographs were later exhibited in more than 50 galleries internationally, as well as at the Victoria and Albert Museum in London. In 1993, she published a book of her work from that time entitled *Linda McCartney's Sixties: Portrait of an Era*. Another example of her work is the sleeve photo from Paul McCartney's and Michael Jackson's single, "The Girl Is Mine."

Above: Paul and Linda arrive at Heathrow airport London from the USA, with two-year-old daughter Mary, March 1971.

"AT THE END OF THE BEATLES, I REALLY WAS DONE IN FOR THE FIRST TIME IN MY LIFE. UNTIL THEN, I REALLY WAS A KIND OF COCKY SOD."
PAUL McCARTNEY

Top, left: Paul and Linda attend a party a few weeks before their wedding.

Top, right: Paul and a pregnant Linda dance together during the launch party for Wings.

Above: Paul and Linda at the 1971 Grammy Awards. Paul collected the award for Best Original Score Written for a Motion Picture or a Television Special on behalf of the Beatles for *Let It Be*.

Opposite: Paul's second album, *Ram*, got off to a rocky start with critics, but eventually many reevaluated the work and some even labeled it the "first indie pop album."

In the fall of 1969, while the Beatles were in the process of breaking up, Paul was nearly despondent. For one thing, he was losing the only job he had ever known, the thing that had given him security and a sense of identity. It also hurt that he, who had always kept the band's welfare foremost in his thoughts, was now being vilified by his mates for refusing to let the somewhat shady Allen Klein handle his career.

Linda encouraged him to keep writing and composing, especially the sort of songs that had always appealed to him. He no longer had to tamp down his own tastes or risk John's scathing commentaries about "granny" songs. Paul later acknowledged what a great help Linda was to him during this period of loss and depression, how she became a significant part of the healing process.

The family retrenched at the Scottish farm for a few months, where Paul's creativity at last began to return. After the family's return to London in late December, he began laying down tracks at Cavendish Avenue, starting with "The Lovely Linda." The result was his first solo album, *McCartney*, wherein he played all the instruments and sang harmony with his wife. The recordings, with their home-studio origins, all had the raw, unsophisticated sound that Paul loved—and had insisted on in the "Get Back" tracks.

SHOOTING THE MESSENGER

Perhaps the final battle of the Beatles' breakup was played out during this time. Paul expected his album to drop on April 17, but *Let It Be*, the album and film, as well as Ringo's LP, *Sentimental Journey*, were all slated by Apple for release around that time. Also, the *Hey Jude* album had dropped in America only the month before. So John and George, as directors of Apple, arranged a June debut date for Paul's album, and Ringo offered to carry the message to him at home. Paul was so incensed by this "three-against-one" maneuver that he "went crazy" and threw Ringo out of his house.

Then, a week before the LP's drop date, on April 10, McCartney issued a press release in the form of a self-interview that implied he was leaving the Beatles (i.e., in the interview he could not say whether his break from the group was "permanent or temporary"), leading to reports that the band was finished. And while John had actually quit the previous September, he had not gone public with the news

> **"Maybe John was right. Maybe the Beatles were crap. The sooner I get this album out and get it over with the better."**
>
> **PAUL McCARTNEY**

at the band's request. Now John was furious that Paul had been the one to make the official announcement, especially since he had founded the group, not Paul. Looking back, Paul conceded, "I was not a popular bunny."

Unfortunately, the McCartney LP got lost in the "Beatles Break Up!" hysteria that inevitably became the favorite chew toy of the entertainment media. Yet the album did furnish one bright beacon to light the way for Macca's future endeavors, the luminescent, "Maybe I'm Amazed." Beatle Paul couldn't have done any better.

SOLDIERING ON

Paul should have enjoyed his new freedom, but he still struggled to find his footing. He'd thought true collaborators for years, Paul still missed being able to bounce ideas and tunes off his old friend.

> **"When I write, there are times—not always—when I hear John in my head . . . I'll think, OK, what would we have done here? . . . and I can hear him gripe or approve."**
>
> **PAUL McCARTNEY**

creating *McCartney* was hard, but it had been made while he was still technically a Beatle, when the fallout from the breakup hadn't yet assaulted him. Now, especially after he'd initiated a lawsuit to dissolve the Beatles' partnership, the flak grew increasingly worse and he was taking hits from fans and the other Beatles. And even though he and John had not been

As a result, he worked closely with Linda on his next record, *Ram*, which was recorded during the early days of Paul's legal battle. This time Paul brought in other musicians to round out his sound— guitarists David Spinozza and Hugh McCracken, and drummer Denny Seiwell—who would reunite with Paul in Wings. *Ram* was released on May 17, 1971, to less-than-

flattering reviews, although one of the LP's three singles, "Uncle Albert/Admiral Halsey," hit number one in America. As time passed, the LP managed to redeem itself with the critics, some calling it the "first indie pop album," others insisting it was "earthy, domestic, and honest." Today it is considered a herald of the singer/songwriter movement that swept the popular music scene in the 1970s.

FabFact

In March 1971, just prior to the release of *Ram*, Paul had his first hit single with "Another Day," which peaked at number 5 in the U.S. and number 2 in the U.K.

"Paul persuaded me to join the band. I would never have had the courage otherwise. It was fun at the beginning. We were playing just for fun, with Paul's group."

LINDA McCARTNEY

friend Denny Laine, the guitarist/vocalist who'd been part of the early Moody Blues and sung lead on their monster hit, "Go Now." Paul had a special reason for choosing Wings as the name of his new group—during the difficult birth of the McCartneys' second child, Stella, both Linda and the baby had been in danger, and as Paul prayed for their safety, a pair of wings appeared to comfort him. The band's first album, *Wild Life*, aimed for that raw sound Paul craved, and partially achieved it by using first takes of the recordings on eight of the tracks. Unfortunately, the completed album, which some critics believed was purposely "second-rate," did McCartney's solo career no favors. (It did eventually go gold, however.)

In February 1972, guitarist Henry McCullough was added to the lineup and the band set out, crowded into a van, to play a series of gigs at British universities. (Imagine the surprise of a pub manager when a bloke who looked and sounded suspiciously like Paul McCartney asked him if his "band" could come in and play a few sets.) Paul made sure no Beatles songs were part of the play list—he wanted to establish Wings as an entity quite apart from the Fabs. This warm-up tour was followed by Wings Over Europe, with the band (and Paul's family) touring smaller Continental venues in a brightly painted double-decker bus.

Top: Linda and Paul smile during a break in the 1973 *Red Rose Speedway* tour.

Above: A Wings photocall in November 1972.

In 1971, Paul decided to form a band, one that could slip in and out of small clubs and halls, honing its sound, just as the Beatles had done back in the early days. Since the notion of being separated from Linda for the length of a tour seemed unthinkable, Paul convinced her to join the band. He coached her on the keyboard, and tried to teach her to sing harmony. (Linda admitted years later that critics of her singing had been right, that on the early Wings LPs she was sadly off key.)

In addition to Linda, Paul recruited drummer Denny Seiwell, who'd played on *Ram*, and longtime

CLIMBING TO THE TOP

That same February, the band released the single "Give Ireland Back to the Irish," which, no surprise considering its anti-British Union sentiments, was banned on the BBC. Still, it went on to hit number sixteen in the U.K., and reached number one in Ireland and Spain. Later that year, the single "Hi, Hi, Hi" made the Top Ten in America and, in spite of being banned by the BBC—this time for supposed drug references—still hit the Top Five in England. At the end of 1972 Paul, with Wings, reunited with George Martin and recorded the theme song to the latest James Bond adventure, *Live and Let Die*. The single not only morphed into a mega-hit, it became part of Paul's lifelong concert repertoire.

In April 1973 the band, now billed as Paul McCartney and Wings, hit its stride with their second album, *Red Rose Speedway*. Recorded in Los Angeles and London, the LP reached number one on the Billboard 200 and launched the single, "My Love," which reached number nine in Britain, but topped the charts in America. During May and June the band embarked on a successful tour of Great Britain.

Although many Wings sidemen came and went through the years, the only musician who stuck with Paul and Linda was Denny Laine. By the time Wings went into the studio to record *Band on the Run* in the late summer of 1973, the group had lost Seiwell and McCullough. Undaunted, the three remaining members flew to the EMI studios in Lagos, Nigeria, and laid down the tracks—with some help from Ginger Baker and others. Released in December, the album achieved widespread critical and public acclaim. It reached number one in both England and America and contained three hit singles: the title track, "Jet," and "Helen

Wheels." It seemed as if the specter of the Beatles's massive success would never again trouble Paul.

After the 1974 stand-alone hit single, "Junior's Farm," 1975 saw another well-received album, *Venus and Mars*, supported by two popular singles: "Listen to What the Man Said" and "Venus and Mars/Rock Show." In between stops of their 1975–76 Wings Over the World Tour—encompassing Australia, Europe, America, and Wembley, England—the band recorded *Wings at the Speed of Sound*, which produced two American top hits, "Silly Love Songs," and "Let 'Em In." The United States portion of the tour also resulted in a live triple album, *Wings Over America*, which prompted a stirring concert version of "Maybe I'm Amazed" to hit the charts. In 1977, a reduced Wings (due to the departure of Jimmy McCulloch and Joe English) recorded "Mull of Kintyre," a bagpiped paean to the McCartneys' beloved Scottish coast; it swept the international music scene and became Wings' only number one single in Britain (and ended up as the best-selling single in United Kingdom history).

STADIUM GIANTS

As successful as the band's albums became, the Wings tours were almost historic in terms of both press coverage and the attendance of their fans. Wings grew into one of the most popular "stadium" bands—like Journey and Boston, groups that had been inspired by the music of *Abbey Road*. Wings sold out wherever they played and made news everywhere they went. Being a former Beatle had turned out to be a plus for Paul, and not the liability he originally feared it would be.

Altogether, Wings put out seven studio albums—the final two were 1978's *London Town* and 1979's *Back to the Egg*—and nearly thirty singles, many of which charted in the top ten. The band broke up in the early 1980s; Denny Laine left after Paul revealed, in the wake of John Lennon's shooting, that he would no longer tour out of concern that the same fate might befall him.

Top: Paul and Linda in 1972, the year Wings recorded the mega-hit James Bond theme song "Live and Let Die."

"RAVI SHANKAR NOT ONLY OPENED MY EYES TO MORE SPIRITUAL MUSIC, BUT HE HELPED ME TO LOOK INWARD SO I COULD FIND OUT WHO I REALLY AM."

GEORGE HARRISON, *BILLBOARD* CENTURY AWARDS, 1992

CHAPTER NINETEEN

GEORGE HARRISON: IN THE MATERIAL WORLD

"THE BIGGEST BREAK IN MY CAREER WAS GETTING INTO THE BEATLES .... THE SECOND BIGGEST BREAK SINCE THEN IS GETTING OUT OF THEM."

GEORGE HARRISON

now and he was determined to make the most of it. In addition to Dylan and The Band, who inspired the song "All Things Must Pass," Harrison also found himself influenced by Delaney Bramlett—after a short stint performing with Delaney and Bonnie and Friends—who taught him the slide guitar technique he used on "I Dig Love," and by Billy Preston—whose music inspired the gospel-based "My Sweet Lord" and "What Is Life." The song "Awaiting on You" expressed Harrison's fascination with meditative chanting, while "Ballad of Sir Frankie Crisp (Let It Roll)" was dedicated to the Victorian builder of George's new home, Friar Park.

TRIPLE TREAT

The album, which was released November 27, 1970, consisted of four sides of recorded songs— replete with themes of spiritual growth, many of them accompanied by George's loosey-goosey slide guitar—and one LP called *Live Jam*. The recording incorporated producer Phil Spector's notorious Wall of Sound and featured backup musicians Bobby Whitlock, Jim Gordon, Carl Radle, Bobby Keys, Jim Price, and Dave Mason, all affiliated with Delaney and Bonnie; Eric Clapton; Ringo Starr; John Barham; Badfinger; Pete Drake;

After the breakup, George definitely had the most to prove in terms of solo output. He'd been waiting for a chance to show the world what he could do as a songwriter when not restricted to a few "charity" spots per Beatles album, and so set to work almost immediately with a backlog of material he'd been collecting since 1966.

During a 1968 visit with Bob Dylan in Woodstock, NY, George discovered that jamming with Dylan and his backup group, The Band, allowed him a freedom of expression he'd rarely felt with the Beatles. George knew he longed to reexperience that same sense of autonomy in the studio, yet he also hesitated to show disloyalty to his own band. By the end of 1969, however, it was clear the Beatles were drifting apart.

Production on George's new album, *All Things Must Pass*, started at Abbey Road in April 1970, days after Paul McCartney announced his departure from the Beatles. George's "road ahead" was clear

Above, left: George sits with members of a Hare Krishna sect in August 1969.

Billy Preston; Hamburg mate and bass guitarist Klaus Voorman; and keyboardist Gary Wright.

Both the critical and public reaction to the album surely surpassed Harrison's wildest expectations. It was hailed by critics as a masterpiece, and Harrison's talent as a songwriter and performer was duly lauded. The album rocketed to number one on countless charts around the world, lingering there for months, and eventually went multiplatinum. Many critics and fans consider it the finest of all the Beatles' solo efforts. It went on to win the 1973 Grammy for Album of the Year and also exposed Indian-

influenced music to the widest audience it had ever reached.

The album resulted in two singles, "My Sweet Lord" which became a worldwide hit and the biggest-selling English single of 1971; and "What Is Life," a top-ten hit in America that went to number one in Europe (and was the U.K. B-side of "My Sweet Lord").

All Things Must Pass vindicated George, proved he was no lightweight, and gave him a place in the limelight he'd likely always deserved. But it also set up an impossibly high expectation from the public, one that was to haunt George for the rest of his life.

Subsequent indifferently-received albums—*Dark Horse, Extra-Texture (Read All About It), Gone Troppo,* and *Cloud Nine,* were reminders that he hadn't lived up to his debut album, and even successful LPs like *Living in the Material World* or *Thirty-three and 1/3* came up short by comparison. He was cursed, as Orson Welles had been after creating *Citizen Kane,* by peaking practically out of the gate.

CODA: It has been officially announced that *All Things Must Pass* is to be inducted into the legendary GRAMMY Hall of Fame in 2014—during the 40th anniversary of that institution's founding.

"**Wagnerian, Brucknerian, the music of mountain tops and vast horizons . . .** "
BEN GERSON, critic, *Rolling Stone*

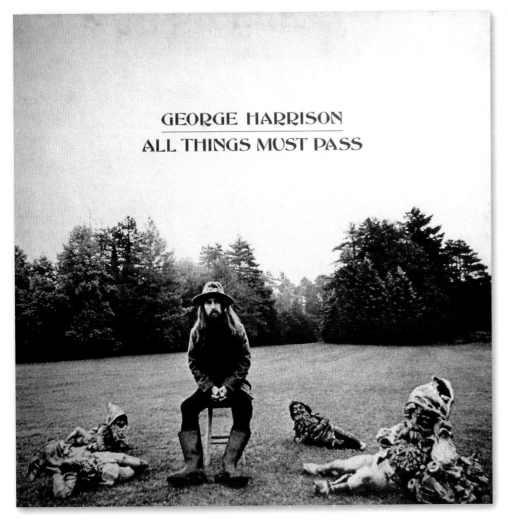

THE COVER

Barry Feinstein's puckish cover shot featured George, attired like a nineteenth-century farm laborer, relaxing among a quartet of garden gnomes. It was George's idea to have the three LPs placed in a box rather than in a triple gatefold cover, and he hired designer Tom Wilkes to construct the hinged cardboard container. It proved effective but ungainly—or as Apple staffer Tony Bramwell recalled, "It was a bloody big thing . . . You needed arms like an orangutan to carry half a dozen."

Left: The front cover of *All Things Must Pass*, George's triple-album solo release after the breakup of the Beatles.

Previous pages: Inset, George in the studio around the time of "My Sweet Lord."

"IT IS A DREAM ON A HILL AND IT CAME, NOT BY CHANCE, TO THE RIGHT MAN AT THE RIGHT TIME."

DEREK TAYLOR

Top: George felt a a great emotional connection to the landscape—the trees, shrubberies, grottoes, statuary, and follies—of Friar Park. A favorite occupation was relocating the ponds and other water features, to the amusement of his son, Dhani.

Above: A hand-tinted postcard of Friar Park, circa 1910.

1970 was also a significant year for George in terms of his private life. He and Pattie left behind the funky domain of Kinfauns and moved into a rambling old pile in Henley-on-Thames called Friar Park. Some time earlier, George had heard that the home of an eccentric Victorian lawyer, Sir Frank Crisp, was scheduled for demolition. Interest piqued, he looked into it and discovered a storybook property—a 120-room Gothic revival manor with extensive gardens, and numerous follies and water features. He immediately saw enormous possibilities in the derelict estate, including space for a state-of-the-art studio, and knew he had to own it.

George quickly set up a full recording studio, which he called FPSHOT (Friar Park Studio, Henley-on-Thames), and put out the welcome mat to all his musical friends and connections . . . and to many female fans, of whom he apparently never tired.

"I WENT STRAIGHT TO THE TOP OF THE HOUSE AND LOWERED THE FLAG BEARING THE OM SYMBOL THAT GEORGE HAD BEEN FLYING FROM THE ROOF AND HOISTED A SKULL AND CROSSBONES INSTEAD. THAT MADE ME FEEL MUCH BETTER."

PATTIE BOYD, ON FINDING GEORGE WITH MAUREEN STARKEY, *WONDERFUL TONIGHT*

Meanwhile, George's marriage to Pattie was fragmenting. It was hard to believe the attractive, trendy couple of the press photos—the wry, dapper Beatle and his adorable, fashionable wife—were not ideally suited. But they were having the same problems as any two spouses who were being drawn in different directions. After George devoted himself to the study of Vaishnavist Hinduism and felt the need to elevate himself spiritually, he began to withdraw from his wife sexually. (Oddly, his newfound beliefs did not keep him from shagging other women, including Maureen Starkey.)

"LAYLA"

Pattie at first tried to emulate George's deep devotion, hoping to find peace and solace in meditation, but eventually realized she did not have the same dedication to it as he did. He avoided her during the daytime, spending endless hours in the studio with friends and hangers-on. After he invited a number of Hare Krishnas and their families to occupy one wing of the house—purportedly to help with the restoration of the grounds—Pattie claimed she rarely saw him alone. If she'd thought she would get him to herself after the Beatles split, she soon discovered his new solo career occupied him almost as much as his obligations to the band had. Near the end of their marriage he was also increasingly under the influence of alcohol and cocaine.

There was another complication: George's close friend, blues guitarist Eric Clapton, made no attempt to disguise how much he desired Pattie, to the point of writing her one of the most impassioned love songs of all time, "Layla." He recorded the tune with his band, Derek and the Dominoes, and it became a massive and abiding hit single. While George sometimes denied that "Something" had been written for Pattie, Eric wanted the whole world to know how he felt about "L"—as he called her. He even dated her sister Paula, out of frustration at not being able to woo Pattie herself.

Pattie eventually began an affair with Eric, but when he became addicted to heroin she returned to George. It soon became clear, however, that between her husband's meditation, his fixation with the studio, and his addictions and frequent depression the marriage could not mend. She and George separated in 1974 and divorced in 1977. Eric cleaned up and reunited with Pattie, and George accepted his presence in her life. When she and his friend were married in Arizona on March 27, 1979, he actually attended the wedding. This happy event was the closest the Beatles came to reuniting—Harrison, McCartney, and Starr all played together during the reception. John Lennon chose not to attend.

"George used coke excessively, and I think it changed him . . . it froze his emotions and hardened his heart."

PATTIE BOYD

Top: George, Pattie, and Ravi Shankar in August 1972. George and Ravi spent long months organizing the Bangladesh concerts, but the end result—enlisting other celebrities to raise funds and publicizing the plight of millions of refugees—made all that effort worthwhile.

Bottom Pattie and Eric Clapton attend the premiere of the rock opera *Tommy* in London, March 1975.

Bangladesh

> "... there are no politics involved. What is involved is starving children and for once, relief through thirty-five musicians who should represent the feeling of anyone who loves their music."
> **BILLBOARD**

Bangladesh is a small country that lies along the fertile Bengal delta. Originally part of India, it was partitioned in 1947 and became the eastern sector of the newly created country of Pakistan. After many years of discrimination and political neglect from Pakistan in the western sector, East Pakistan strived for independence through national activism and civil disobedience . . . and finally achieved it in 1971 by winning the Bangladesh Liberation War. The country was already reeling, however, from the effects of the massive Bhola cyclone, which had struck in 1970. News sources estimated that more than half a million Bengalis had died as a result. Then in the spring of 1971, heavy flooding added to the country's woes. Refugees from the cyclone, the flooding, and the punitive atrocities of the war continued to pour into India, creating a nightmare scenario of more than seven million displaced Bengalis facing starvation and the outbreak of cholera.

George first learned of the plight of these people in 1971 from his good friend, Bengali Ravi Shankar. Shankar kept George updated on the dire situation while the two were working in Los Angeles on the soundtrack of the film *Raga*. George even wrote a song, "Miss O'Dell," which alludes to the corrupt Indian officials who kept aid shipments of rice from getting to the refugee camps. He and Shankar finally determined to do something—to find some way to raise money for the refugees and to increase public awareness of what was happening halfway across the world. George realized that as an internationally known and respected musician he had the power, as few others did, to rally entertainment figures to come together for a benefit concert.

It took him nearly three months to set it up (with the aid of the same Chris O'Dell, his music assistant and a former Apple

Top: George and Bob Dylan share the stage at the Concert for Bangladesh at Madison Square Garden on August 1, 1971. It was Dylan's first live performance in five years.

Left: George and Ringo perform during the concert. John Lennon had agreed to appear without Yoko, but after a spat with his wife he dropped out and flew to Paris.

Opposite, above: A view of the vast Madison Square Garden arena. Over the two concert performances the assembled band played to more than 40,000 people.

staffer), but eventually the plans for a two-concert show to be held at Madison Square Garden on August 1 fell into place.

The performers included Bob Dylan—his first live appearance in five years, Ringo Starr, Eric Clapton, Billy Preston, and Leon Russell, as well as Harrison and Shankar and an impressive backup ensemble that included the Beatles' old friend Klaus Voorman.

They played to a total of 40,000 people and in the end, the concert raised approximately $243,000 for U.N.I.C.E.F., enabling the U.N. to aid children in Bangladesh as well as those facing starvation in the Horn of Africa.

The subsequent live triple album, released that winter by Apple Records (after settling disputed rights' issues with Capitol and Columbia), went on to become a bestseller—in spite of a high price tag—in both America and England, and it garnered the

"WHEN I DID BANGLADESH, I SPENT A COUPLE OF MONTHS, EVERY DAY AND NIGHT, ON THE TELEPHONE, TRYING TO TRICK PEOPLE INTO DOING IT AND MAKING A COMMITMENT. NOWADAYS, YOU PHONE SOMEBODY UP, AND IT'S AN ACCEPTED PART OF LIFE THAT EVERY SO OFTEN YOU GIVE SOMETHING TO CHARITY."
GEORGE HARRISON

Grammy for Album of the Year. The distinctive packaging was designed by the same team that had created *All Things Must Pass*, Camouflage Productions partners Tom Wilkes and Barry Feinstein.

The effect of the Concert for Bangladesh—the first-ever rock and roll fundraiser—cannot be understated. Ultimately, it became part of George's legacy to other celebrities, the concept

that one influential person can make a difference, and that not just the individual performers but also the people who attend, who man the phones, and who call in pledges are key parts of the process. Bangladesh formed the template for other superstar benefit concerts, such as Farm Aid, Live Aid, Live 8, We Are the World, the Concert for New York City held after the attacks of 9/11, and the Concert for Hurricane Sandy.

Olivia and Dhani

"They each had so much material of their own, too much to be contained. It had to spill over. For George, it was perfect timing. I'm sure John and Paul felt the same because they made albums right after the Beatles broke up."

OLIVIA HARRISON, about the timing of the Beatles' split

Harrison created his own recording label, Dark Horse Records, in 1974. After that he had frequent business dealings with A&M Records in L.A., his label's parent company, and there was one particular female staff member he often spoke to on the phone. He thought she had a nice voice and decided he wanted to meet her, so in 1977 he flew to L.A. to see her in person. Her name was Olivia Trinidad Arias, an attractive, dark-haired woman of British/ Mexican heritage, who was born in Mexico City and had grown up in Southern California. Olivia and George soon began dating, things got serious, and they were married in 1978 at the registry office in

Henley-on-Thames, a month after the birth of their son, Dhani.

More down-to-earth than Pattie Boyd, Olivia took a great interest in Friar Park. She enjoyed working on the grounds alongside George, helping him restore the once-elaborate gardens and landscape the many scenic vistas. (George's two older brothers, Peter and Harry, were groundskeepers there.)

Olivia also aided George on his global quest for privacy, or as she put it, his desire "to get as far away as he could." After the couple built a haven on the Hawaiian island of Maui, the search continued until they fell in love with Australia.

There they designed a primitive cliff-top compound on Hamilton Island—"pristine and stunning"—the site recommended by George's good friend, Formula One racing legend Jackie Stewart. They called it Letsbeavenue (from the comedy line, "Let's be havin' you.") Near the end of his life, George also purchased a luxe mountain villa in the Swiss canton of Ticino, with breathtaking views of Lake Lugano and the Swiss Alps.

Olivia, like her husband, also involved herself in various charities and humanitarian causes. In 1990 she, along with Beatles wives Linda McCartney, Barbara Bach, and Yoko Ono, founded the Romanian Angel Appeal to help the multitude of children living in deplorable conditions in Romanian orphanages. That same year, the Appeal released a fundraising album called *Nobody's Child*, which featured songs donated by Elton John, Billy Idol, Van Morrison, Paul Simon, the Bee Gees, Eric Clapton, Ringo Starr, George Harrison, Traveling Wilburys, Mike and the Mechanics, Duane Eddy, Stevie Wonder, and Smokey Robinson, among others.

WITH THE WILBURYS

During the late 1970s, after the birth of Dhani, George turned to a softer, more contemplative sound with the album, *George Harrison*.

1981's *Somewhere in England*—featuring the Lennon homage "All Those Years Ago," a reworking of a song written for Ringo—was released after John's murder. And 1982 saw the forgettable, *Gone Troppo*, and a triumphant comeback album, *Cloud Nine*, which went platinum and contained a rollicking cover of James Ray's foot-stomping "Got My Mind Set on You."

In 1988 George found himself in a position to perform with his own custom-designed group, as Paul McCartney had done with Wings. George had initially arranged for several of his favorite musicians—Bob Dylan, Tom Petty, the Electric Light Orchestra's Jeff Lynne and the legendary Roy Orbison—to come together in Dylan's garage to record a B-side for a new Harrison single. The song they laid down, "Handle with Care," turned out so well that George asked the group to record a whole album. The result was *Traveling Wilburys Vol. 1*, one of the most entertaining, upbeat LPs to hit the airwaves since the Fab Four first cut *Please Please Me*. The album went triple platinum, and "Handle with Care," "End of the Line," and "Tweeter and the Monkey Man" all got heavy airplay. The album won a Grammy for Best Rock Performance by a Duo or Group.

A second album, *Traveling Wilburys Vol. 3*—regarding the numbering, George said "let's confuse the buggers"—was recorded after the sudden death of Roy Orbison. It contained a dedication to "Lefty Wilbury," Orbison's alter-ego on the first album.

Opposite, left and top: Olivia and George were an attractive, soulful couple—reflecting their interest in humanitarian causes.

Top, right: Terry O'Neill's 1987 portrait of George and his son Dhani was taken in London.

"It's horrible to lose your dad. But day by day I miss him more as a mate. He was my best friend in the whole world."

DHANI HARRISON, *Here Comes the Son*, Nigel Williamson

DHANI HARRISON

George was a doting father who, according to Dhani, wanted to share everything with his only son. That naturally included his music. But Dhani also recalled one time during his childhood when "Uncle" Ringo schooled him on the drums, and the loud noise so frightened the boy that he never drummed again. Dhani studied visual arts at Brown University in Rhode Island, but chose to become a musician after a brief career as an aerodynamicist. Dhani collaborated with his father on his final album, *Brainwashed*, and coproduced it with Jeff Lynne after George's death. The album went on to earn a Grammy nomination.

Dhani made headlines in the fan magazines in June 2012 when he wed blond, long-haired model-turned-psychologist Sólveig 'Sola' Káradóttir, who looked at first glance very much like his father's first wife, Pattie Boyd. The wedding, which was held in the garden amphitheatre at Friar Park, ended up being a "very Beatles affair"—both Paul and Ringo attended and Stella McCartney designed the embroidered wedding gown.

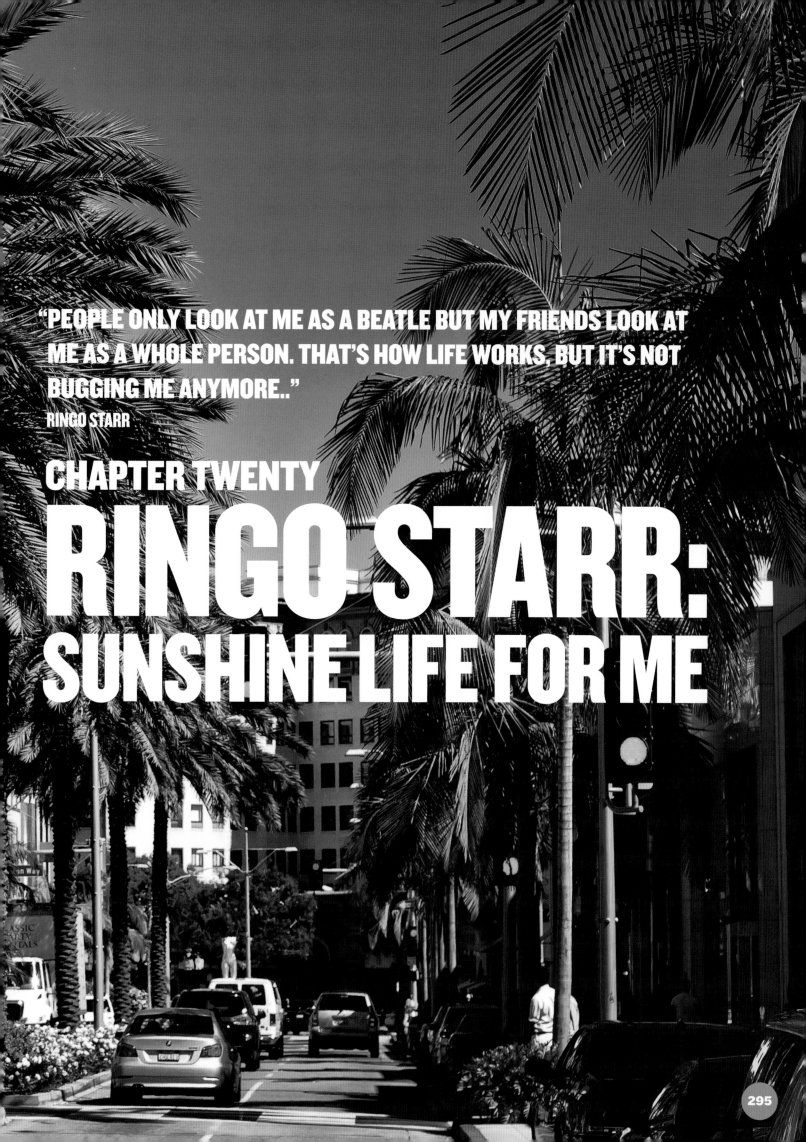

"PEOPLE ONLY LOOK AT ME AS A BEATLE BUT MY FRIENDS LOOK AT ME AS A WHOLE PERSON. THAT'S HOW LIFE WORKS, BUT IT'S NOT BUGGING ME ANYMORE.."
RINGO STARR

CHAPTER TWENTY

RINGO STARR: SUNSHINE LIFE FOR ME

"WHAT WILL I DO WITH MY LIFE NOW THAT IT'S OVER?"
RINGO STARR, AFTER THE BREAKUP OF THE BEATLES

Ringo Starr—he of the steady beat and easy-going demeanor—seemed the least likely of the Beatles to become an emotional wreck after the breakup of the band. Yes, there had been that one eruption of anger and frustration during *The White Album* sessions, when he'd fled to sunny Sardinia, but he'd come home without rancor and afterward spoke of enjoying the studio experience once the band was together again. His

good nature and relaxed manner were legendary. He also seemed to understand, better than his mates, that the life of a rock band was finite, and he often spoke to the press about what he would do when the Beatles ceased to exist.

Unlike the other Beatles, Ringo had a close-knit family of four—wife Maureen, and kids Zak, Jason, and Lee—to keep him occupied once his responsibilities to the Beatles ended. When John and

Yoko moved out of Tittenhurst Park, Lennon's country house in Berkshire, to head for America, Ringo bought the estate in 1973 and relocated his clan there from Brookfield. He rechristened Ascot Sound Studio, which Lennon had built on the grounds, Startling Studios and launched into the making of solo albums with gusto. It wasn't long before Ringo began hitting the charts with both albums and singles.

Yet, in spite of all the distractions, Starr was deeply grieved by the demise of his old life. It was as though he had lost the spiritual turbine that not only drove his drumming, but charged his heart as well. His drinking increased and he became verbally abusive at home. He also began a series of meaningless affairs, as if cheating on Mo could restore his sense of identity or self esteem. His children, as much as he loved being a dad, were not filling the gap in his life; and making music alone, or with an occasional assist from one of his old Liverpool chums, just wasn't the same.

MAUREEN'S HEARTACHE

Eventually the marriage broke up. He and Maureen separated in 1975—but not before Mo engaged in a brief fling with George Harrison. Ringo rationalized that it was better a Beatle than "someone you don't know," but John was scandalized that one of his mates could be so predatory, "almost incestuous," least of all George. The couple were divorced on July 17, 1975, on the grounds of infidelity based on Ringo's affair with an American model named Nancy Lee Andrews.

Maureen was nearly crushed by the failure of her marriage, and she found herself set adrift with few survival skills, no knowledge of money or taxes or even how to live life on her own. "I'm as thick as two short planks," she confessed during a post-divorce interview. Depression soon overcame her, and according to Cynthia Lennon, she attempted suicide by running her motorcycle into a brick wall. Mo survived, but afterward required reconstructive surgery on her face.

"I've lived through a lot, and I've learnt a lot. I'd say I'm a happier person these days. I'm happy with my life now. I've learnt to be contented. I've matured."

MAUREEN STARKEY, post divorce from Ringo

The white knight who came to her rescue was a man called Isaac Tigrett, the founder of the Hard Rock Cafe restaurant chain and the House of Blues. He and Maureen first met in 1976, and married in 1989; they had one daughter, Augusta. When Maureen was diagnosed with leukemia in the early 1990s, she received the most up-to-date treatment, including a bone marrow transplant from her son, Zak. In spite of it, Maureen Starkey Tigrett died on December 30, 1994, surrounded by her family. Ringo, too, was at her bedside.

The song "Little Willow" on the 1997 album *Flaming Pie* was a tribute to her and her children by Paul McCartney, who had known Mo since the Beatles' Cavern days.

FabFact

The cover shot of the *Hey Jude* LP was taken in the doorway of Tittenhurst Park during John's tenure there. (Ringo would buy the estate in 1973.) John and Yoko's "his and hers" album covers for the Plastic Ono Band were also shot there.

Opposite: Ringo and Maureen meet the press during their honeymoon in Hove, February 1965.

Above: Ringo and Maureen at Heathrow airport, February 1970. Ringo's badge refers to the film *The Magic Christian* in which he starred alongside Peter Sellers.

Previous pages: Ringo was never at a loss for words in front of a press microphone, and many of the Beatles' more memorable quips came from him.

HITTING HIS STRIDE

His third album, 1973's self-titled *Ringo*, became a pop classic and featured three hit songs: "It Don't Come Easy," "Photograph," and "You're Sixteen." Little Ritchie was on a roll. And not just in the music side of things. The previous year he'd directed his first film, a documentary on Marc Bolan's glam band, T-Rex, called *Born to Boogie*. During that period he also appeared in *200 Motels*, Frank Zappa's cult film; *That'll Be the Day*, a David Essex drama about early rock and roll; and *Son of Dracula*, Nilsson's vampire spoof.

During the Beatles' heyday, Ringo's bandmates had always been willing to lend him a hand when it was "Starr-time" in the recording studio. And even though George Harrison helped work out the melody on Ringo's second composition, "Octopus's Garden," George allowed Ringo all the credit. On two later collaborations, however, Ringo made sure George received his due—for his contributions to the hit singles "It Don't Come Easy" and "Photograph." The other three Beatles continued to support Ringo's efforts, offering tunes, studio input, or accompaniment until John's death in 1980. Ringo's *Rotogravure*, his fifth solo LP, would be the last album on which all four Beatles were involved.

In 1972 he scored his biggest single in the United Kingdom, "Back Off Bugaloo," which climbed to number two. In 1974, he scored with "Oh My My" and "Only You," and 1978 he covered Hoyt Axton's "No, No Song" with Nilsson

> **"Ringo took his chance well and his homely lugubrious voice suited those typically maudlin country songs like a charm. It's one of the best Beatle solo albums."**
>
> **BOB WOFFINDEN**, *The Beatles Apart*, summing up *Beaucoups of Blues*

While he often received little credit for his mostly lightweight tracks on the Beatles' albums, Starr, like George Harrison, got a taste of sweet vindication after the breakup, in this case becoming the first of the band's members to score seven consecutive Top Ten singles.

Ringo's song selection formula was simple—give people what they like. He'd understood that about Paul's "granny" songs, even if sometimes John did not. For March 1970's *Sentimental Journey*, his first solo release, Starr assembled a collection of the Tin Pan Alley standards that had been his earliest musical influences. He told the press, "I did it for my Mum." The album got only fair notices but managed to sell half a million copies.

That fall his second album, *Beaucoups of Blues*, riffed on Ringo's country and western numbers for the Beatles; Starr traveled to Nashville to record with session legend Pete Drake. This LP was such a departure from the schmaltz of *Sentimental Journey* that the critics didn't know what to do with it, though some felt Starr's voice was more suited to this genre than to retro classics. It only charted to 65 in America (35 on the C&W charts) and not at all in England.

singing backup and it became one of those ubiquitous radio hits. Ringo continued to produce solo albums of varying quality every few years, one highlight being 1981's *Stop and Smell the Roses*.

BARBARA BACH: A PARTNER FOR LIFE

Even before his marriage ended, Ringo had begun spending time on the West Coast of America, where he romped in Malibu with John Lennon and Nilsson during the former's "Lost Weekend" in the mid-1970s. Lennon and Nilsson had connected through their heavy drinking and their crazy dares, but Starr and Nilsson actually became close friends. Ringo was even best man at Nilsson's third wedding in 1976.

And then in 1980, Ringo began filming on the lightweight comedy *Caveman* and tumbled hard for his beautiful costar, Barbara Bach. Starr says he fell in love with her across an airline counter as her boyfriend was dropping her off at the airport. Bach, in spite of her exotic features and sultry green eyes, was born in humble Queens, NY, and became an actress after a successful stint as a model. When she played opposite Roger Moore in 1977's *The Spy Who Loved Me*, she ascended to that rarified cinema pantheon known as the Bond Girl.

She and Ringo were married in April 1981. (Bach was divorced from businessman Augusto Gregorini with whom she had two children, Francesca and Gianni.) It was clear Barbara and Ringo shared a deep commitment to each other, one that was strengthened

when they survived a serious car crash together. But they also shared something less savory—they were both, they would acknowledge later, alcoholics. It took a drunken episode seven years into the marriage, where Ringo says he nearly killed his wife with his fists, to scare them both into serious rehab.

After undergoing successful treatment in 1988, the couple became regulars on afternoon talk shows and late night variety programs; Ringo was hilarious trying to remain deadpan on

Saturday Night Live (*SNL*) while Billy Crystal's Fernando repeatedly told Barbara, "zhou look mah-vellous." Starr was also the only one of the Beatles to actually host SNL.

Opposite: Ringo rubs elbows with Elton John and Marc Bolan at the *Born to Boogie* premiere on December 14, 1972. Starr directed the documentary film about Bolan's band, T-Rex.

Top: Ringo, Harry Nilsson (center), and Who drummer, Keith Moon, attend the West Coast premiere of *That'll Be The Day* in which Ringo and Moon had roles. Ringo had a long-term love affair with America's West Coast and often partied out there with other music celebrities.

Bottom: Actress Barbara Bach possessed an exotic beauty that attracted Ringo from their first encounter.

"I'VE SAID THIS OVER AND OVER AGAIN, BUT I LOVE BEING IN A BAND."
RINGO STARR

In another ironic twist, Ringo ended up forming a rock group that outlasted the lifespan of the Beatles and Wings put together. Ringo Starr and His All-Starr Band have remained a rock music fixture for more than two decades.

Ringo appeared to be keeping a low profile after the release of *Old Wave* in 1983; his career seemed to have stalled and he was also having increasing problems with alcohol. Then in 1989, after his successful rehab, producer David Fishof approached Ringo with the idea of creating a supergroup that would feature a rotating roster of the best musicians in the business, based on their availability to tour. Ringo, as a well-respected musician and former Beatle, would become the lure that drew performers to the group and the glue that would hold them all together over the years. "I had been thinking the same thing,"

Starr recalled. "So I went through my phone book, rang up a few friends and asked them if they'd like to have fun in the summer." The friends who said "yes" included former Eagle Joe Walsh, Clarence Clemons and Nils Lofgren of Bruce Springsteen's E Street Band, Levon Helm and Rick Danko of The Band, as well as Roger Hodgson, Dr. John, Billy Preston and session drummer Jim Keltner.

A SMORGASBORD OF SOUND

The All-Starr Band's 1989 maiden tour resulted in Ringo's first live album—and enough good vibes for Starr, Walsh, and Lofgrin to decide to do it all again. They reassembled, with some personnel changes, for another tour in 1992, then Ringo took the show on the road ten more times, including an extended tour in 2012–2013.

It was soon clear how well-connected Ringo was in the industry—the cream of the music biz turned out to tour with him. Other luminaries who became All-Starr Band recruits or guest performers over the years included Garth Hudson, Todd Rundgren, Dave Edmunds, Nick Lowe, Burton Cummings, Harry Nilsson, Randy Bachman, Mark Farner, Felix Cavaliere, John Entwhistle, Steven Tyler, Mark Rivera, Peter Frampton, Gary Brooker, Jack Bruce, Simon Kirke, Ginger Baker, David A. Stewart, Dave Mason, Eric Carmen, Andy Summers, Ray Davies, Roger Hodgson, Ian Hunter, Howard Jones, Greg Lake, Sheila E., Colin Hay, Paul Carrack, John Waite, Billy Squier, Richard Marx, Edgar Winter, Rod Argent (formerly a Zombie during the British Invasion), Hamish Stuart, Gary Wright, Rick Derringer, Richard Page, Steve Lukather, and Gregg Rolie. The 2010–2011 Tour featured one guest appearance by Paul McCartney, who played bass on "Birthday."

The typical format of an All-Starr concert was engineered to please fans both old and new. Ringo would perform hits and more recent material followed by several Beatles' songs and, interspersed with his numbers, various other band members would re-create memorable moments from their own careers. As Ray Shasho, reviewer for the *Clearwater Times* in Florida, wrote of the 2012 Tour: "The band appeared and sounded like a finely tuned racing machine, with engines revved and in immaculate condition . . . There wasn't one shining star this evening . . . just a galaxy filled with all-starrs."

THE STARR KIDS

During the first All-Starr tour, Zak Starkey performed as a guest drummer, then during the 1992 and 1995 tours, Zak was an actual member of the band. This wasn't nepotism by any means—Ringo's eldest child had carved out a legitimate career as a drummer from the time he was a teen.

By age ten, Zak had taught himself the drums by playing along with the records of his favorite bands. Even though Ringo bought his son a champagne sparkle Ludwig kit when he was eleven, he did not give the boy much encouragement— and at most two lessons—mainly because he hoped his son would avoid a show business career and become a doctor or lawyer. But the apple doesn't fall far from the tree . . . and Zak's future was preordained. At age twelve, he received a white-and-gold Premier kit from his godfather, the Who's manic percussionist, Keith Moon (though no real drumming lessons there either) and was soon performing with a punk garage band, the Next. Eventually, Zak began hauling Moon's kit around Britain like any other apprentice drummer, and ended up sitting in with the reformed Spencer Davis Group in the early 80s. From the mid-1990s on, Zak was playing with the Who on tour, including the post 9/11 benefit Concert for New York in 2001. Roger Daltry and Pete Townsend concurred that Starkey—a fierce power drummer— was the best match for their band since the death of Moon nearly 20 years earlier. In 2004, Zak began playing with pop phenomenon, Oasis, although he continued to tour with The Who, two highlights being the halftime show at 2010's Superbowl XLIV in Miami and the

closing ceremonies of the London Summer Olympics in 2012.

Jason Starkey also followed in his father's footsteps and entered the music business as both a rock drummer and road manager. He played with a number of bands, including Buddy Curtis and the Grasshoppers, the Peoples' Friend, Empire of Sponge, and—with Zak— in Musty Jack Sponge and the Exploding Nudists. Jason's career course, however, was not as smooth as his brother's, and several times he ended up in trouble with the law facing petty theft and drug charges. He eventually settled down in the United Kingdom with wife Flora and his two sons. Jason has famously been quoted as saying that having Ringo Starr as his dad was, "a total pain."

Daughter Lee Parkin Starkey was born to Ringo and Maureen only months after the Beatles split up. An early fan of the punk/ Goth scene, she held a number of mundane jobs. Then in the late 1980s she and friend Christian Paris opened Planet Alice, a boutique that specialized in

vintage clothing from the 1960s, in the Portobello Road in London. When her mother moved to Los Angeles after marrying Isaac Tigrett, Lee relocated the store to Melrose Place. After the boutique closed, Lee returned to London, but stayed involved in fashion design. Then, a year after her mother's death from leukemia in 1994, Lee herself was diagnosed with a brain tumor. Surgery in Boston and radiation therapy appeared to stem the disease, but in 2001 the tumor returned. After successful treatment, Lee once again became involved in the world of fashion. She and her boyfriend, Beady Eye bassman Jay Mehler, are the parents of triplets Ruby, Jakamo, and Smokey. Lee, who keeps a low profile, is sometimes seen at Zak's concerts, at Stella McCartney's runway shows, and at charitable events.

Opposite: Ringo takes center stage during a performance of his All-Starr Band in 2012, a show that featured Todd Rundgren, former Toto guitarist Steve Lukather, and Santana keyboardist Gregg Rolie.

Above: Ringo's kids Zak (Drummer for the Who and Oasis), Lee, and Jason, attend their mother Maureen's 1989 wedding to Isaac Tigrett.

The Hip Elder Statesman of Rock

> "I don't collect any memorabilia. I wish I'd have kept everything I had. But who knew you had to keep it? Just gave it away. And we lost so much and we didn't look after a lot of it. I believe Paul's got everything he ever had, but I lost a lot of mine."

RINGO STARR

Ringo has continued to pop up on talk shows or in the pages of *Rolling Stone*, looking older, yes, but somehow more distinguished, as if he had finally grown into that hound-dog face. As a youth, he'd always maintained a dapper appearance and even now could give sartorial tips to other Golden Age rockers.

He and Barbara enjoy traveling together . . . and to facilitate this, they maintain homes in Los Angeles and Monte Carlo (Ringo craved sun and surf ever since the Beatles' early visits to Miami) as well as a getaway in Colorado, and a 17th-century English manor house near the village of Cranleigh. The Starkeys currently spend most of their time in Monte Carlo, where they are residents, and in the United States.

In the mid-1990s, Ringo reunited with Paul and George, overdubbing material onto a demo of a 1977 John Lennon song, "Free As a Bird." It hit the airwaves in 1995—the first true Beatles single in 25 years—and became a Top Ten hit. The following year the three collaborated again and had a hit with "Real Love," another Lennon song.

Ringo has quipped regarding Paul, "We're the only two remaining Beatles, although he likes to think he's the only one." The affection between them was apparent as the two sparred in 2007 during a Larry King interview at the opening of *The Beatles LOVE* by Cirque du Soleil in Las Vegas. Ringo continues to work with Paul, as well as the widows of John and George, to oversee the Beatles' legacy. In a 2011 interview in the *Daily Mail*, Starr revealed that he had been with Yoko Ono and Olivia Harrison in Iceland for a celebration marking what would have been John's 70th birthday. He also pointed out that his wife Barbara and Yoko were good friends and that, "We're all OK together." Yoko had previously performed at Ringo's own 70th birthday party at Radio City Music Hall, while Paul feted him by singing the Beatles' "Birthday."

In 2008, Starr released *Liverpool 8*, for which he cowrote all of the tracks including the poignant title song. Some critics considered it a worthwhile comeback vehicle.

CAREER ASSESSMENT

It is pointless to argue Ringo's merits as a drummer. Over the years he has continued to impress his advocates and leave his detractors cold. Yet perhaps there is one opinion that carries more weight than all the others, the opinion of the producer who worked with Starr the longest, (and who had him temporarily replaced during the Beatles' first recording session)—Sir George Martin. Martin wrote of him in *All You Need Is Ears* (1979): "I did quickly realize that Ringo was an excellent drummer for what was required. He's not a technical drummer. Men like Buddy Rich and Gene Krupa would run rings around him, but he is a good solid rock drummer with a steady beat, and he knows how to get the right sound out of his drums. Above all, he does have an individual

sound. You can tell Ringo's drums from anyone else's and that character was a definite asset to the Beatles' early recordings."

Martin was correct—the greatest tribute to Ringo's distinct signature as a drummer might be that a fan hearing only the drum track from most Beatles' hits would immediately be able to identify the song.

Ringo Starr's honors and awards include:

• 1965 – MBE awarded by Queen Elizabeth II
• 1984 – a minor planet discovered in August by Brian A. Skiff, was christened 4150 Starr in his honor
• 1988 – Inducted into the Rock and Roll Hall of Fame as part of the Beatles
• 2010 – honored with a star on

"We are good friends. We don't live in each other's pockets, but if we're in the same country, we get together. He's singing and playing on my latest album and I played on several of his. We're just pals. We're the only two who've experienced all this who are still here."

RINGO STARR, on Paul McCartney, *Daily Mail*

Hollywood's Walk of Fame near the other three Beatles at North Vine Street in front of the Capitol Records building
• 2013 – became a Commandeur of the Ordre des Arts et des Lettres

FabFact

In a 2011 poll, *Rolling Stone* readers voted Ringo Starr the fifth greatest drummer of all time. This elevated standing was no doubt partly due to how the remastered Beatles' recordings showcased his skills in a way that the vinyl LPs had not. As Starr himself said, "The remasters are great—because you can hear the drums. The drums are up, brother."

Opposite: Ringo Starr and his All-Starr Band perform at Hard Rock Live! in Florida in 2012. Ringo never lost his zest for performing live—or for pleasing his audiences.

Above: Ringo and actress Barbara Bach celebrate their wedding day, April 27, 1981. The ceremony took place at Marylebone Registry Office, and guests included George and Olivia Harrison, Paul and Linda McCartney (holding James), and Bach's son Gianni.

CHAPTER TWENTY-ONE

ROCK ON: THE BEATLES' LEGACY

The Beatles' Legacy

Even though the band broke up in 1970 and was officially dissolved in 1975, in many respects the Beatles are as visible in the present as they ever were. There have been stage productions, conferences, conventions, newsgroups and web sites devoted to them, as well as numerous Facebook pages and even a popular video game. The Beatles have been featured in special editions put out by popular magazines like *Life*, *People*, and *Rolling Stone*, while biographies or memoirs from those who knew them well appear frequently. Movies like *Backbeat*, *Nowhere Boy*, and *I Want to Hold Your Hand*, hark back to the early days, and documentaries cover everything from Fab Four press conferences to John's U.S. deportation issue, to John and Ringo's crazy, poignant relationship with Harry Nilsson. Martin Scorsese lent his fine sense of detail and atmosphere to *George Harrison: Living in the Material World*. Even Las Vegas got into the act with *The Beatles LOVE*, an extravaganza from Cirque du Soleil.

The Beatles' music continued to circulate long after the dissolution of the band . . . and with the arrival of the 1995 *Anthology* package— comprising a new audio collection, a TV miniseries, and a coffee table book—fans were invited behind the scenes to experience outtakes, ad libs, and rehearsal sessions.

When it comes to entertainment in any form—reissued and remastered CDs, movies, documentaries, TV shows, video games, reference books, photo albums, and biographies, stage shows, conventions, and tribute bands—it seems the Beatles' Liverpudlian luster never dims.

Above: Director Martin Scorsese accompanies Olivia Harrison to the U.K. premiere of his *George Harrison: Living in the Material World*, at BFI Southbank, London, October 2, 2011.

Above, right: Cirque du Soleil's *The Beatles LOVE*, during *The Night That Changed America: A Grammy Salute To The Beatles* at the Los Angeles Convention Center on January 27, 2014.

Clockwise, from above: Neil Innes and Eric Idle's Beatles parody, *The Rutles*, from 1976; *The Beatles LOVE* by Cirque du Soleil at The Mirage Hotel & Casino, Las Vegas, June 27, 2006; Ringo and Sir Paul launch the XBox 360 game *The Beatles: Rock Band* in Los Angeles, California, June 1, 2009; *The Beatles: Rock Band* and the Beatles' digitally remastered albums go on sale in the U.K. at HMV Oxford Street, London, September 2009

Above, and above, right: Studio portraits of the Monkees, in Los Angeles, California, 1967.

Previous pages: Inset, the Monkees, 1967; Background: Visitors walk along the hallway to the theater for *The Beatles LOVE* by Cirque du Soleil in Las Vegas, 2006.

THE MONKEES

In 1965, Screen Gems TV executives Bob Rafelson and Bert Scheider came up with the idea for a teen-oriented series called *The Monkees*. It would feature a quartet of fun-loving young musicians trying to become stars—not unlike the careers of the world-renowned Beatles. After a major casting call, the studio hired American actors Mike Nesmith, Peter Tork, former child star Micky Dolenz (Micky Braddock of Circus Boy), and British stage actor Davy Jones. Seasoned songwriters like Tommy Boyce and Bobby Hart, Neil Diamond, Gerry Goffin and Carole King were hired to pen hits for them. After the 1966 debut of the show, which offered madcap plots, wacky humor, and upbeat musical interludes, *The Monkees* became a must-see for the under-20 set. The group actually toured— they could all sing and even play to some extent—and their acting chops helped convince fans that they were a genuine band.

From the start, songs like "Last Train to Clarksville" and "Daydream Believer" charted well, and the band even began to write their own material. Just like the real Beatles, however, each member wanted the group to go in a different direction. Although the show only lasted two seasons, the band also made a film, *Head*, in 1968. But by then their fame had run its course . . . until the series got a new life on cable TV in the 1980s, and the children of the original fans made their music popular again. In 2012 Mike Nesmith, who'd walked away from the Monkees more than once— even while touring—reunited with his bandmates after the untimely death of Davy Jones, and toured with them as a tribute to Jones.

Over time it became clear that these Beatles' copycats had actually left their own mark on music history.

THE FEST FOR BEATLES FANS

The breakup of the Beatles did not alter the deep devotion of their fans. Conventions dedicated to the group subsequently sprang up in both the United States and overseas. The most popular American gathering, originally called Beatlefest, is now known as the Fest for Beatles Fans. Started in New York in 1974 by Mark Lapidus—with the blessing of John Lennon—it offered a place to view Beatles-related performers, purchase memorabilia, and donate money to help a designated charity. It still exists for all these purposes. Both Yoko Ono and George's sister Louise Harrison sponsored charities to which attendees could contribute.

Fans experience all things Fab at these conventions—movies, concert clips, interviews, artwork

> "THE *ANTHOLOGY* WAS VERY GOOD FOR ME BECAUSE IT REMINDED ME OF THE BEATLES' STANDARDS AND THE STANDARDS THAT WE REACHED WITH THE SONGS."
> PAUL McCARTNEY

from both fans and Beatles' friends such as Klaus Voorman and Astrid Kirchherr, panel discussions, and trivia contests. Some attendees dress up in collarless jackets or satin *Sgt. Pepper* tunics, ready to perform in a "Battle of the Bands," often with instruments identical to those used by the Beatles.

In the collectibles' marketplace, vendors sell records, books, magazines, T-shirts, buttons, jackets, artwork, and artifacts from the original British Invasion. One of the rarest finds, the original "butcher" cover from *Yesterday and Today*, has been valued at $10,000. But the Fest's biggest draw is the guest performers: Peter and Gordon, Donovan, Neil Innes of the Rutles, and Denny Laine of Wings are just a few of the celebrities who have attended Fests in the last forty years.

BEATLEMANIA ON BROADWAY

"Beatlemania," the name the press gave to the frenzy that affected young female Beatles fans in the mid-1960s, became the title of a 1977 Broadway revue. *Beatlemania* featured four sound-alike and look-alike performers who impersonated the band members. Audiences loved it! From a distance—and with a little imagination—the actors appeared to be credible facsimiles of the originals.

Beatlemania opened in the spring, and played for almost eighteen months, before the Beatles'

lawyers stepped in and closed it down. After a financial settlement with Apple Corps was reached, however, the show took to the road, playing venues across America. A 1981 movie called *Beatlemania* featured the cast of the show and boasted, "Not the real Beatles, but an incredible simulation."

MORE BEATLES ON BROADWAY

The new millennium saw the advent of not one but two Beatles' shows on the Great White Way— *Rain: A Tribute to the Beatles on Broadway*, was a concert-format musical that ran from fall 2010 through summer 2011. *Let It Be*, a 2012 London hit that grossed more than $14 million, opened in New York in July 2013. It featured more of a biographical story line, as look-alike musicians traced the Beatles' history while playing their hit songs. Unfortunately, the American version did not live up to its backers' expectations and closed in September 2013. (The play was also sued by the producers of *Rain*, who claimed *Let It Be* borrowed heavily from their show.) Happily for fans, *Let It Be* settled with the producers, and is scheduled to begin a North American tour in 2014–2015.

ANTHOLOGY

The *Anthology* project, a mid-1990s collaboration among the three surviving Beatles, followed the band's history through its

members' eyes and offered a rare glimpse behind the scenes in the studio. The total package consisted of a series of documentaries, a three-part audio collection, and a coffee table book.

The film series, initially comprising six hours of footage, took nearly five years to complete and contained voiceovers from all four Beatles. It aired over several nights in fall 1995 on ITV in England and on ABC in America—and won the Grammy for Best Music Video—Long Form.

The three audio collections (each containing three LPs or two CDs) offered previously unreleased material, plus outtakes and demos. When *Anthology 1* was released in 1995, it sold 450,000 copies in one day, a record that still stands. The next two versions came out in 1996. Klaus Voorman designed all three sleeves, which consisted of a collage of Beatles covers and posters that formed a continuous mural when placed together.

The impressive, oversize *Anthology* book was released in 2000 and featured interviews with the band (culled from the documentaries or incorporating fresh material) and insights from key players, as well as dazzling spreads brimming with rare photos. Perhaps the definitive chronicle of the band's genesis, the book quickly shot to the top of the *New York Times* bestseller list in the United States.

"MY GRANDKIDS ALWAYS BEAT ME AT *ROCK BAND.* AND I SAY, 'LISTEN, YOU MAY BEAT ME AT *ROCK BAND,* BUT I MADE THE ORIGINAL RECORDS, SO SHUT UP.'"

PAUL McCARTNEY

THE BEATLES: ROCK BAND

When it was time for Harmonix, developer of the popular *Rock Band* play-along video game, to create their third release, they turned to the music of the Beatles. The resulting 2009 version featured simulations of all four Beatles in different iterations of their careers, including noteworthy live performances. The game had the approval not only of Apple Corps, but also of Paul, Ringo, Yoko Ono, and Olivia Harrison. Dhani Harrison acted as liaison between Apple and Harmonix, while Giles Martin, George Martin's son, oversaw the production of the music in a modern, multitrack format.

THE DEFINITIVE REMASTERS

With the advent of 1988's *The Beatles Box Set*, fans were finally able to purchase the band's digitally formatted catalog in a single set, with a choice of LP, cassette, or CD. More recently, a team from Abbey Road led by senior engineers Allan Rouse and Guy Massey worked for four years to prepare the definitive digital version of the catalog. Since some purists feel that digitalizing early recordings "squashes" the dynamics of the music, the team offered a "faithful to the source" box set with the mono versions of most albums, and a stereo version reworked for the sensibilities of modern

listeners. Fortunately for the team, the Beatles' precious analog master tapes have been carefully archived and maintained by EMI.

Both box sets were released September 9, 2009, the same day that *The Beatles: Rock Band* hit the shelves. *The Beatles: The Original Studio Recordings* (stereo version) went on to win the 2011 Grammy for Best Historical Album. In 2012, to the delight of old-school fans, the set was also offered in vinyl.

SPECTACLE:
Cirque du Soleil's *The Beatles LOVE*

In 2006, the Montreal-based theatrical company Cirque du Soleil debuted *LOVE*, a Beatles extravaganza presented in its own theater at the Mirage Resort in Las Vegas. The show, which was conceived in cooperation with Apple Corps—and based on an earlier idea by George Harrison—tells the story of the Beatles through music, dance, and acrobatics in a fanciful circus setting. Written and directed by Dominic Champagne, the musical directors were Sir George Martin and his son, Giles Martin. In 2007, to celebrate the one year anniversary of *LOVE*, Paul and Ringo joined talk show host Larry King in Las Vegas. The former Beatles bantered playfully with each other before they were joined by Yoko Ono and Olivia Harrison.

AWARDS AND HONORS:
The Rock and Roll Hall of Fame

In 1988, the Beatles were inducted into the Rock and Roll Hall of Fame by fellow British rocker Mick Jagger. Paul McCartney, involved in a lawsuit against the others, chose not to appear at the New York City event, so it was Ringo and George who stepped up to accept the honor. After a standing ovation, Ringo joked, "You can sit down; I'm going to be here for hours," and then ribbed the Hall of Fame for labeling the Beatles "a pop group." George offered heartfelt thanks to Lead Belly, Little Richard, and the other seminal American musicians who had influenced the Beatles, and laughingly admitted that the group "got a bit bigger than any of us expected." Then Yoko, along with John's two sons, approached the microphone. Yoko assured the audience that John would have been there to celebrate; Julian Lennon thanked his father and the three surviving Beatles for inspiring him and so many others. After young Sean Lennon remarked that he was up there for "doing nothing," Ringo retorted, "We're all doing nothing. Give us the prize and let's get home!"

The Beatles found themselves in exalted company that year—the other inductees for 1988 were the Beach Boys, the Drifters, Bob Dylan, Berry Gordy Jr, Woody Guthrie, Lead Belly, Les Paul, and the Supremes.

Afterword

"I must confess, when the Beatles finished around about 1970, I thought, 'OK. We've done jolly well,' I didn't honestly think I'd still be talking about them thirty or forty years later. I thought interest would gradually peter out. But it does seem—and I've gotten quite used to this—each generation, as it comes along, finds Beatles music out for themselves. And I'm grateful for that. If anything, it was the epitome of British music in the last century."

GEORGE MARTIN

The places where the Beatles lived and worked and performed and the people who were close to them all had a profound effect on their music, and the band, in turn, had a reciprocal uplifting effect on many of their haunts and associates.

PLACES

Liverpool became a popular tourist destination soon after Beatlemania spread across the globe like a tuneful pandemic. Today the city, which is a designated UNESCO World Heritage Site, offers a host of cultural events and venues, with more museums and art galleries than any English city outside London.

Beatles'-related attractions abound: In Liverpool take a "Ferry Cross the Mersey" or buy a ticket for the official Magical Mystery Tour, a two-hour bus trip that visits Penny Lane, Strawberry Field, and the Beatles' childhood homes, while a guide supplies details about the band's early days. The award-winning Beatles Story Experience is a museum with two sites: Albert Dock and Pier Head. It houses an amazing collection of Beatles memorabilia and offers a 3-D and 4-D musical experience.

The National Trust now owns Aunt Mimi's home, Mendips, and Paul's teenage home at 20 Forthlin Road;

look-ins are a must for visiting fans. The Epstein family home at 27 Anfield Road, now the Epstein House Hotel, features a Beatles' museum focused on Brian's life and career. The Casbah Club, that early Beatle hangout, is open for tours with Pete Best's brother.

On Penny Lane, the street sign was stolen so many times, the city now paints the street's name on the corners of buildings. The bright red, wrought iron fence of Strawberry Field Orphanage still draws visitors.

Ringo Starr's birthplace, a small terrace house in Dingle, had been marked for demolition along with 400 other Victorian-era homes, part of Liverpool's never-ending urban renewal. But in 2012, the house—along with 15 others—was saved by the City Council, giving locals a chance to renovate the historic properties.

The Cavern Club, which closed in May 1973, was reopened by Liverpool F.C. player Tommy Smith in 1984, utilizing 75 percent of the original site. In 1999 Paul McCartney revisited the club to perform his final gig of the year and publicize his new record, *Run Devil Run*. In *Across the Universe*, a movie homage to the Beatles, early shots of an unnamed music club were actually filmed at the Cavern.

Nearby on Mathew Street, leaning against a brick pillar outside the Cavern Pub, stands a life-size bronze sculpture of John Lennon, the hipshot pose resembling Jürgen Vollmer's famous 1961 photograph. Every year fans by the thousands photograph each other with one arm draped casually over John's shoulder.

Paul still owns his London house on Cavendish Avenue as well as a home in Peasmarsh, East Sussex. Unfortunately, after the death of Linda, Paul paid fewer and fewer visits to their beloved Hill Park Farm in Scotland, and he recently released the caretakers.

The EMI Studio in St. John's Wood, known as Abbey Road (and officially renamed since 1970), is still popular with discerning musicians. A threat from property developers in 2009 resulted in the government granting the building English Heritage Grade II listed status, making it illegal to perform any exterior alterations. EMI still has plans to sell the building, however, leaving its fate to be determined.

Apple Corps, once a fixture of exclusive Savile Row, is now located at 27 Ovington Square, in London's equally tony Knightsbridge district.

Carnaby Street, which continues to be a major London tourist draw,

became a pedestrian mall in 1973.

Outside London, the Kenwood estate that John Lennon bought for £20,000 in 1964 recently went on the market for nearly £14 million. Sadly, the Harrisons' hip bungalow, Kinfauns, was torn down in the early 2000s. Friar Park remains home to Olivia Harrison, George's widow. The historic estate of Tittenhurst Park, which passed from John to Ringo, was sold for £5 million in 1988 to the president of the United Arab Emirates.

PEOPLE

George Martin was inducted into the Rock and Roll Hall of Fame on March 15, 1999.

The previous year, Martin decided it was time to say goodbye to music producing. But before he "stealed away," he wanted to make one last very personal album. The result was *In My Life*, a collection of Beatles songs he had produced, now interpreted by a variety of different artists, including Robin Williams, Celine Dion, Goldie Hawn, and Phil Collins. In the documentary on the making of the album, Martin comments on his decades in the music business, "If you turn me upside down, you will see notes falling out of my ears."

Peter Asher, Paul's attic mate on Wimpole Street, and half of

the hit-making duo Peter and Gordon, successfully managed both James Taylor and Linda Ronstadt, and became a notable record producer in the United States. Asher reteamed with Gordon Waller in 2005 to perform occasional concerts; Waller passed away in 2009.

Jane Asher, still an attractive redhead, continues to act in British television and movies and has become, famously, a baker of exquisite cakes.

Cynthia Lennon has written two books on her life with and without John—*A Twist of Lennon* (1978) and *John* (2005)—and continues to make herself available to interviewers and biographers.

Julian Lennon, a musician and photographer, released *Everything Changes* in 2011, his first album in thirteen years. He is active on the Internet and can be followed on Facebook.

Yoko Ono remains the powerhouse behind John's interests and, in addition to keeping his memory alive, she—along with Sean Lennon—supports many philanthropic institutions.

The Beatles left a legacy of rebirth, regeneration, and increased revenue streams for their hometown, spurred a cultural renaissance in England and many parts of the world; and brought tax dollars to their adopted countries. It was all as it should be—the "lads" enriching the places that so often inspired and shaped their music. But, ultimately, their greatest gift to the world was their enduring catalog of songs and melodies, some borrowed, some unwittingly copied, some composed on the fly, others evolving over many years . . . but most of them the direct offspring of those driving sounds of the early 1960s that traveled across the Atlantic Ocean from the United States, with a shake, rattle, and roll.

"THE BEATLES WERE JUST FOUR GUYS THAT LOVED EACH OTHER. THAT'S ALL THEY'LL EVER BE."
RINGO STARR

"THE BASIC THING IN MY MIND WAS THAT FOR ALL OUR SUCCESS THE BEATLES WERE ALWAYS A GREAT LITTLE BAND. NOTHING MORE, NOTHING LESS."
PAUL McCARTNEY

"THE BEATLES WILL GO ON AND ON."
GEORGE HARRISON

"WE RECKONED WE COULD MAKE IT BECAUSE THERE WERE FOUR OF US. NONE OF US WOULD'VE MADE IT ALONE, BECAUSE PAUL WASN'T QUITE STRONG ENOUGH, I DIDN'T HAVE ENOUGH GIRL-APPEAL, GEORGE WAS TOO QUIET, AND RINGO WAS THE DRUMMER. BUT WE THOUGHT THAT EVERYONE WOULD BE ABLE TO DIG AT LEAST ONE OF US, AND THAT'S HOW IT TURNED OUT."
JOHN LENNON

I'll be there when all your dreams are broken;

To answer your unspoken prayer.

When the little things you're doing

Don't turn out right,

Don't you worry, darlin', I'll be there.

"I'LL BE THERE," BOBBY DARIN
final song of the night at the Cavern

Beatles Bibliography: Book and Film References

BOOKS

A Cellarful of Noise (1964); Brian Epstein; Doubleday

In His Own Write (1964); John Lennon; Simon & Schuster

A Spaniard in the Works (1965); John Lennon; Simon & Schuster

The Beatles: the Authorized Biography (1968) Hunter Davies, McGraw-Hill

Apple to the Core: The Unmasking of the Beatles (1972); Peter McCabe and Robert D. Schonfeld; Martin Brian and O'Keefe Ltd.

All You Need Is Ears (1979); George Martin; St. Martin's Press

A Twist of Lennon (1980); Cynthia Lennon; Avon

Lennon (1987); Ray Coleman; McGraw-Hill

The Complete Beatles Recording Sessions (1988); Mark Lewisohn; Hamlyn (reissued by Sterling in 2013)

Tell Me Why: A Beatles Commentary (1988); Tim Riley; Knopf

The Lives of John Lennon (1988); Albert Goldman; William Morrow & Co

Revolution in the Head: The Beatles' Records and the Sixties (1994); Ian MacDonald; Fourth Estate

Beatle!: The Pete Best Story (1994); cowritten by Pete Best and Patrick Doncaster; Plexus Pub.

With a Little Help from My Friends: The Making of Sgt. Pepper (1995); George Martin and William Pearson; Little Brown

and Co. (Released in Great Britain as *Summer of Love: The Making of Sgt. Pepper* by Pan Books)

Shout! The Beatles and Their Generation (1997); Philip Norman; Mjf Books

Paul McCartney: Many Years From Now (1997), Barry Miles, MacMillan

The Beatles Anthology (2000); The Beatles; Chronicle Books

The Ultimate Beatles Encyclopedia (2000); Bill Harry (publisher of Mersey Beat); Mjf Books

I, Me, Mine (2002); George Harrison; Chronicle Books

Hard Nights: My Life in Liverpool Clubland (2004 rev. ed.); Roy Adams; Cavernman Publications

A Hard Day's Write: The Story Behind Every Beatles Song (2005); Steve Turner; Carlton Books, Ltd.

The Beatles: The Biography (2005), Bob Spitz; Little, Brown and Co.

John (2005); Cynthia Lennon; Crown

Here, There and Everywhere: My Life Recording the Music of the Beatles (2006); Geoff Emerick and Howard Massey; Gotham

Wonderful Tonight: George Harrison, Eric Clapton, and Me (2007); Pattie Boyd; Crown Archetype

The Fifth Beatle: The Brian Epstein Story (2013); Vivek Tiwary, Philip Simon, Andrew C. Robinson, and Kyle Baker; Graphic novel from Dark Horse

Lennon: The Man, the Myth, the Music—The Definitive Life (2011); Tim Riley; Hyperion

The Beatles in Hamburg: The Stories, the Scene, and How It All Began (2011); Spencer Leigh; Chicago Review Press/Omnibus Press

The Beatles in Liverpool: The Stories, the Scene, and the Path to Stardom (2012); Spencer Leigh; Chicago Review Press/Omnibus Press

Tune In: The Beatles: All These Years, Vol. 1 (2013); Mark Lewisohn; Crown Archetype

How the Beatles Changed the World (2014); Martin W. Sandler; Walker Childrens

GENERAL BEATLES REFERENCES

"Beatles Reunion in Las Vegas" video (2007); to commemorate the first anniversary of *The Beatles LOVE* in Las Vegas; *Larry King Live*

"The Beatles Overtake Their Idols" (2013); Forrest Wickman; Slate.com

"How the Beatles Went Viral" (2014); Steve Greenberg; *Billboard*

"Why the Beatles Are Still the Best" (2014); Mitch Albom; *Detroit Free Press*

WEB REFERENCES

beatlesbible.com
thebeatles.com
beatlesnews.com
beatlemoney.com
beatlesfans.com
beatlelinks.net
dmbeatles.com
onabbeyroad.com
beatlesnumber9.com
applerecords.com
beatlesthroughtheyears.com
beatleswiki.com
beatlesinterviews.org

Left: The Beatles perform in a color still taken during the shooting of *A Hard Day's Night*, March 1964.

BEATLES FILMOGRAPHY

(Title, release date, director, and studio or production company)

Films Starring the Beatles:

A Hard Day's Night (1964); Richard Lester; United Artists

Help! (1965); Richard Lester; United Artists

Magical Mystery Tour (1967); The Beatles; BBC

Yellow Submarine (1968); George Dunning; United Artists and King Features Syndicate

Let It Be (1969); Michael Lindsay-Hogg; United Artists

Documentaries:

The Beatles at Shea Stadium (1966); BBC Television

Imagine (1972); Steve Gebhardt, John Lennon, and Yoko Ono; Joko

The Compleat Beatles (1982); Patrick Montgomery; MGM

Imagine: John Lennon (1988); Andrew Solt; Warner Bros.

The Beatles: The First U.S. Visit (1991); Kathy Dougherty, Susan Froemke, and Albert Maysles

The Beatles Anthology (1995); Geoff Wonfor/Bob Smeaton; Apple Corps

The U.S. vs. John Lennon (2006); David Leaf and John Scheinfeld; Authorized Pictures

Of Time and the City (2008); Terence Davies; British Film Institute

All Together Now: Cirque du Soleil's LOVE (2008); Adrian Wills; produced by Martin Bolduc and Jonathan Clyde

The Day John Lennon Died (2010); Michael Waldman; Finestripe Productions

George Harrison: Living in the Material World (2011); Martin Scorsese; HBO

I Was There . . . When the Beatles Played the Cavern (2011); John Piper; Shiver

Beatles Stories: A Fab Four Fan's Ultimate Road Trip (2011); Seth Swirsky; Julukesy Films

Good Ol' Freda (2013); Ryan White; Tripod Media

Films About the Beatles:

The Birth of the Beatles

(1979); Richard Marquand; Dick Clark Productions

The Hours and Times (1991); Christopher Münch (writer/director/producer)

Backbeat (1994); Iain Softly; PolyGram Filmed Entertainment

Two of Us (2000); Michael Lindsay-Hogg; VH1

In His Life: The John Lennon Story (2000); David Carson; Michael O'Hara Productions and NBC Studios

Nowhere Boy (2009); Sam Taylor-Wood; Ecosse Films, Film4, UK Film Council, and Hanway Films

Lennon Naked (2010); Edmund Coulthard; Blast! Films

Films Inspired by the Beatles:

All This and World War II (1976); Susan Winslow; Visual Programme Systems Ltd.

Sgt. Pepper's Lonely Hearts Club Band (1978); Michael Schultz; Apple Corps and RSO Records

I Wanna to Hold Your Hand (1978); Robert Zemeckis; Universal Studios

The Rutles: All You Need Is Cash (1978); Eric Idle and Gary Weis; Eric Idle and Lorne Michaels

The Rutles 2: Can't Buy Me Lunch (2005); Eric Idle; Warner Bros.

Across the Universe (2007); Julie Taymor; Revolution Studios

Index

PAGE NUMBERS IN ITALICS INDICATE ILLUSTRATIONS

SONG INDEX

A

"A Day in the Life" 81
"A Hard Day's Night" *135*, 145
"A Pretty Girl Is Like a Melody" 237
"Across the Universe" 213
"Act Naturally" 143, 145, 164
"Ain't She Sweet" 44
"All My Loving" 101, 116, 297
"All Things Must Pass" 284–285
"All Those Years Ago" 268, 291
"All Together Now" 223
"All You Need Is Love" *9*, 165, 204–205, 223
"And Your Bird Can Sing" 164
"Another Girl" 143
"Awaiting on You" 284

B

"Baby Blue" 215
"Baby, You're a Rich Man" 165, 204
"Baby's in Black" 145, 173
"Back in the U.S.S.R." 227
"Back Off Bugaloo" 298
"Bad Boy" 164
"Bad to Me" 82
"Ballad of John and Yoko, The" ... 237, 242
"Ballad of John and Yoko, The"/ "Old Brown Shoe" 237
"Ballad of Sir Frankie Crisp (Let It Roll)" 284
"Beautiful Boy (Darling Boy)" 265
"Because" 238
"Being for the Benefit of Mr. Kite" ..59, 163
"Birthday" 300
"Blackbird" 225, 227
"Blue Jay Way" 202
"Boys" 81
"Bungalow Bill" 207

C

"Can't Buy Me Love" 113, 135, 145, 242–243
"Carry That Weight" 239
"Come and Get It" 83, 215
"Come Together" 238
"Coming Up" 264
"Cry for a Shadow" 44

D

"Danny Boy" 237
"Day After Day" 215
"Day Tripper" 173
"Day Tripper"/"We Can Work It Out" 164
"Dear Prudence" 207
"Devil in Her Heart" 99, 164
"Dig a Pony" 237
"Dizzie Miss Lizzie" 143, 145, 164
"Do You Want to Know a Secret?" ...80, 82
"Doctor Robert" 164
"Don't Bother Me" 81, 98
"Don't Let Me Down" 236–237, 242
"Don't Pass Me By" 81, 227
"Drive My Car" 164, 280

E

"Eight Days a Week" 138
"Eleanor Rigby" 158–159, 163, 223
"End of the Line" 291
"Everybody's Trying to Be My Baby" 145

F

"Fame" 83
"Fire and Rain" 215
"Fool on the Hill" 202
"For No One" 159
"Free as a Bird" 302
"From Me to You" 63, 100, 102, 164

G

"Get Back" 215, 236, 237

"Girl Is Mine, The" 273
"Give Ireland Back to the Irish" 276
"Give Peace a Chance" 258, 259
"Glass Onion" 227
"Go Now" 276
"God Save the Queen" 237
"Golden Slumbers" 238
"Good" 154
"Good Night" 81, 227
"Goodbye" 83
"Got My Mind Set on You" 291
"Got to Get You Into My Life" 159, 163

H

"Handle with Care" 291
"Helen Wheels" 277
"Hello, Goodbye" 164, 177, 204
"Hello Little Girl" 82
"Help!" 141, 143, 145
"Helter Skelter" 227, 280
"Here Comes the Sun" 238–239
"Here, There and Everywhere" 159, 182
"Here Today" 268, 278
"Hey Bulldog" 177, 223
"Hey Jude" *224*, 262, 280
"Hi, Hi, Hi" 276
"Home" 263
"Honey Don't" 81
"Honey Pie" 227
"How Do You Do It?" 68–69

I

"I Am the Walrus" 163, 176
"I Call Your Name" 82, 164
"I Dig Love" 284
"I Feel Fine" 138, 145, 163–164, 173
"I Need You" 143, 176
"I Saw Her Standing There" ... 80, 99, 116, 164
"I Should Have Known Better" 176–177, 242
"I Wanna Be Your Man" 80–82, 173
"I Want to Hold Your Hand" 80, 95, 99, 112–113, 115–116, 137, 164
"I Want to Tell You" 159
"I Want You" 237
"I Will" 227
"I'll Be Back" 138, 164
"I'll Be on My Way" 82
"I'll Get You" 80
"I'll Keep You Satisfied" 82
"I'm a Loser" 138
"I'm Down" 145
"I'm in Love" 82
"I'm Only Sleeping" 81, 159, 163
"I'm So Tired" 207
"I've Got a Feeling" 237
"I've Just Seen a Face" 143, 164
"I've Lost My Little Girl" 19–20
"If I Needed Someone" 164, 173
"Imagine" 259, 268
"Inner Light" 155
"Instant Karma!"/ "Who Has Seen the Wind?" 259
"It Don't Come Easy" 298
"It's All Too Much" 223
"It's for You" 82
"It's Only Love" 143, 164

J

"Jet" 277, 280
"Julia" 207, 225, 231
"Junior's Farm" 277, 280
"Just to Dance with You" 80
"(Just Like) Starting Over" 265

K

"Kansas City" 138

L

"Lady Madonna" 221, 242
"Layla" 287

"Let 'Em In" 277
"Let It Be"/"You Know My Name (Look Up My Number)" 237
"Let Me Roll It" 280
"Listen to What the Man Said" 277
"Little Willow" 297
"Long and Winding Road, The" 254
"Long Long Long" 163
"Long Tall Sally" 164, 173
"Love of the Loved, The" 82
"Love Me Do" 68–71, 68, 80, 112
"Love You To" 155
"Lovely Linda, The" 274

M

"Maggie Mae" 154
"Maharishi" 207
"Martha My Dear" 225
"Matchbox" 81, 164
"Maxwell's Silver Hammer" 238
"Maybe Tomorrow" 215
"Maybe I'm Amazed" 275, 277
"Michelle" 154
"Miss O'Dell" 288
"Mister Moonlight" 231
"Money (That's What I Want)" 52
"Money" 99, 164
"Mother" 259
"Mother Nature's Son" 207, 225, 227
"Mull of Kintyre" 277
"My Bonnie" 44
"My Love" 277, 280
"My Sweet Lord" 284–285
"My Valentine" 279

N

"Night Before, The" 143
"No Matter What" 215
"No, No Song" 298
"Norwegian Wood" 154–155
"Nowhere Man" 164, 173, 176, 223
"#9 Dream" 260–261

O

"Ob-la-di, Ob-la-da" 227
"Octopus's Garden" 81, 237–238
"Oh Babe (What Would You Say)" 162
"Oh My My" 298
"Oh! Darling" 238
"Old Brown Shoe" 242
"One After 909" 63, 237
"Only a Northern Song" 223
"Only You" 298

P

"P.S. I Love You" 69, 80
"Paperback Writer" 159, 173, 242
"Penny Lane" 165, 191, 204
"Photograph" 298
"Piggies" 81, 227
"Please Mr. Postman" 99, 164
"Please Please Me" 69–73, 70, 72–73, 80, 98, 100, 102, 112–113
"Power to the People" 259

R

"Rain" 181, 242
"Raunchy" 19
"Real Love" 302
"Revolution" 224, 242
"Revolution 1" 227
"Revolution 9" 227
"Rock and Roll Music" 173
"Rocky Raccoon" 227
"Roll on John" 268
"Roll Over Beethoven" 99, 164
"Run for Your Life" 80

S

"Saints, The" 44
"Savoy Truffle" 227
"Sexy Sadie" 207

"Sgt. Pepper's Lonely Hearts Club Band" 223
"She Loves You" 58–59, 81, 102, 112–113, 115
"She Loves You"/"I'll Get You" 164
"She Said, She Said" 159
"She's a Woman" 138, 145, 164, 173
"She's Leaving Home" 280
"She's So Heavy" 239
"Silly Love Songs" 277
"Slow Down" 164
"Some Other Guy" 45
"Something" 215, 238, 242, 287
"Something"/"Come Together" 248
"Something in the Way She Moves" 215
"Stand by Me" 261
"Strawberry Fields Forever" 157, 163, 165, 191, 204
"Sweet Baby James" 215

T

"Taxman" 81, 159
"Tell Me What You See" 143, 164
"Thank You Girl" 63, 164
"This Boy" 99, 112, 112, 164
"Those Were the Days" 83, 214
"Ticket to Ride" 143, 176
"Till There Was You" 102, 116
"Tip of My Tongue" 83
"Tomorrow Never Knows" ... 159, 162–163, 181
"Too Late for Goodbyes" 263
"Tweeter and the Monkey Man" 291
"Twist and Shout" 81, 102, 113, 144
"Two of Us" 234

U

"Uncle Albert/Admiral Halsey" 275

V

"Valotte" 263
"Venus and Mars/Rock Show" 277

W

"Wah Wah" 235
"Walking on Thin Ice" 266
"Watching the Wheels" 265
"What Goes On" 164
"What Is Life" 284–285
"Whatever Gets You Through the Night" 260–261
"While My Guitar Gently Weeps" 190, 226, 231
"Why Don't We Do It in the Road?" 207, 225, 227
"Wild Honey Pie" 225
"Wind Cries Mary, The" 95
"Wipe Out" 111
"With a Little Help from My Friends" 195
"Within You, Without You" 155, 191
"Without You" 215
"Woman" 265
"Working Class Hero" 259
"World Without Love" 82

Y

"Ya Ya" 260–261
"Yellow Submarine" 81, 222–223
"Yes It Is" 164, 176
"Yesterday" 82, 143, 163–164, 173
"You Can't Do That" 80–81, 164
"You Like Me Too Much" 143, 164
"You Really Got a Hold On Me" 99, 164
"You're Going to Lose That Girl" 143
"You're Sixteen" 298
"You've Got to Hide Your Love Away" ..143

GENERAL INDEX

A

Arias, Olivia Trinidad. *See* Harrison, Olivia
Abbey Road 81, 163, 229, 238–*240, 241,* 248
Abbey Road Studios *54–73, 56–61, 63 71,* 151–165, *163,* 191, 218–231
Adams, Roy 40
Ali, Muhammad *117*
All Things Must Pass 284–*285,* 289
Amsterdam, the Netherlands 258
Animals, The 124–*125*
Anthology ...165, 175, 190, 239, 306, 308
Apple Corps 102, *208*–217, *211, 213, 236,* 239
Apple Electronics 216
Apple Films 216
Apple logo 211
Apple Records 214–216, 224
Apple Studios 216–217, 234
Apple Store, The *208,* 212, *213, 217, 225*
Apple, Inc. 210
Arias, Oliva Trinidad. *See* Harrison, Olivia
Asher, Jane 61, 95–96, 159, *180, 182*–183, 186, 196, *201, 206,* 220, 311
engagement to Paul McCartney 182
Asher, Peter. *See Peter and Gordon*
Aspinall, Neil 102, *174,* 212, 215, 217
Astoria Theatre, Finsbury Park 102

B

Bach, Barbara *299,* 302, *303*
Back to the Egg 277
Badfinger *215*
Bailey, David *88,* 89
Bambi Kino 36
Bangladesh 288–289
Beach Boys. *See* Wilson, Brian
Beatlemania 71, 77, 96, 104, 106–*107,* 172,186, 198, 280, 307, 310,
in U.S. 116, 120, 124, 138, *148*
Beatlemania 307–308
Beatles '65 .... 138, *139,* 164, *165*
Beatles and Co. 210
Beatles Box Set, The 309
Beatles Christmas Show, The *103*
Beatles for Sale 138–*139,* 164
Beatles: Rock Band, The 217, *306,* 309
Beatles Second Album, The . 99, 164, *165*
Beatles VI 164
Beatles, The 72
Beatles' Recording Sessions, The 157
Beaucoups of Blues 298
Beaulieu, Priscilla 149
Bedford, Carol 213
Bee Gees, The *211*
Belgravia 185
Berkshire, UK. *See* Tittenhurst Park
Bernstein, Sid *114*–115
Berry, Chuck *16*
Best, Pete *27,* 52, 62, *64–65,* 85, 310
early life 26
ousting from the Beatles 64–65
Black, Cilla *43,* 83, *198,* 199, 238, *239*
Blake, Peter 192, *195*
Bolan, Marc *298*
Born to Boogie (movie) 216, *298*
Bowie, David 83, *281*
Boyd Harrison, Pattie. *See* Boyd, Pattie
Boyd, Jenny *212*
Boyd, Pattie *131,* 153, 158, *180,* 181–183, 196, *206,* 212, 286–*287*
early life 183
marriage to George Harrison 183
divorce from George Harrison 287
marriage to Eric Clapton 287
Brainwashed 291
Bravo, Lizzie 213
Brodax, Al 222
Byrds 96, 126, 135, 154–155, 158, 175–176, 293
Byrne, Nicky 104, 106

C

Candlestick Park *172*
Capitol Records 58, 71, 73, 98–99 112–113, 115, 134, 138–139, 143 164–165, 204, 242, 261, 289, 303
Carnaby Street 90, *91,* 183, 192
Carnegie Hall *114, 117*
Casbah, The 26, 64
Cavern. *See* Liverpool
A Cellarful of Noise 175
Chapman, Mark David 266–267
Chiswick House, West London 159
Cirque du Soleil's *The Beatles LOVE* 309
Clapton, Eric 226, 231, 238, *287, 306*
Clay, Cassius. *See* Ali, Muhammad
Cleave, Maureen 170
Cloud Nine 285, 291
Club Noreik, South Tottenham 96
Complete Beatles Recording Sessions, The 138
Concert for Bangladesh (movie) . 216, 289
Concert for Bangladesh (the concert) *289*
Coury, Al 261
Cox, Anthony *251,* 258, 261–262
Cox, Maureen. *See* Starkey, Maureen
Cox, Kyoko Chan *251,* 261–262
See also Ono, Yoko

D

Dakota, The. *See* New York City
Dark Horse 285
Dark Horse Records 290
Davis, Angela 260
Devlin, Johnny 136
Donovan *126,* 206
Double Fantasy 264–266, *265*
Dunning, George 222
Dylan, Bob. 136–*137,* 259, 284, *288,* 289

E

Early Beatles, The 73, 164
Eastman, Linda. *See* McCartney, Linda
Easybeats, The 126, 127
Ecce Cor Meum 278
Ed Sullivan Show, The 104, 116–117, *118–119*
Elgar, Sir Edward *57*
Emerick, Geoff *162*–163, 226, 253
EMI Recording Studios. *See* Abbey Road Studios
Emperor's Gate, Knightsbridge 94, 180
Epstein, Brian 41, *48*–53, 64–65, 69, 71, 76–80, 82–83, *94,* 98–99, 103–104, 106, 112, 114–115, 124, 130–131, 133, 137, 140, 149, 153, 161, 169, 171–175, 183, *185*–186, 198–202, *198–200,* 210–211, 216, 220, 239, *246,* 247–248
Epstein, Clive 211
Epstein, Harrie 48
Epstein, Queenie 48, 52, 200
Ertegun, Ahmet *210*
Evans, Mal 102, 174–*175, 206,* 207, 215, 272
Extra-Texture (Read All About It) 285

F

Fab Four 48
Fairfield Halls, Croydon *100*
Fest for Beatles Fans 307–308
Flaming Pie 278, 297
Flick, Vic 135
Flowers in the Dirt 278
Fool, The 212, *213*
Forthlin Road 21
Foy, Jim 52
Friar Park *286–287,* 290, 292

G

Gandhi 260
Gaumont Cinema, Doncaster, England *78*
Geffen, David *267*
Geffen Records 267
Gentle, Johnny 26
George Harrison 290
George Harrison, Living in the Material World 293
Gerry and the Pacemakers *37, 53, 101*
Giles, Martin 308
Give My Regards to Broad Street (movie) 278
Gone Troppo 285, 291
Goons, The *62*
Grosse Freiheit 31

H

Hamburg, Germany 28–37, 28, 31, 34–35
"Exis" 35–36
Bambi Kino 36
Grosse Freiheit *31*
Indra Club *28,* 30, *31,* 32
Kaiserkeller, The 32
St. Pauli 30
Top Ten Club *24, 34,* 36, 41, *45, 65*
Hamilton, Richard 228–*229*
Hard Day's Night, A *128–130,* 131–136,*132–135,* 164, 176, 202
movie still *130*
Harrison, Dhani 290–*291*
Harrison, George (personal life)
early life *22–23*
marriage to Pattie Boyd 183
divorce from Pattie Boyd 287
marriage to Olivia Trinidad Arias 290
birth of son 290
death 292
Harrison, Harold 22
Harrison, Louise 22
Harrison, Olivia *290*–293, *303, 306*
Harrison, Pattie. *See* Boyd, Pattie
Harry, Bill *51*–52
Help! 94, *140–143,* 144, 153, 164, *165,* 176
Hendrix, Jimi 95
Hey Jude *224,* 242, 274
Hockney, David *88,* 89
Hoffman, Abbie 259
Holly, Steve 281
Hoover, J. Edgar 260
Hopkin, Mary *83, 214*
Hulanicki, Barbara *88*
Hutchins, Chris 149

I

I Me Mine 175
India 196–197, *206*–207
Rishikesh *206*–207
Indra Club *28,* 30, *31,* 32
Instruments
Early years 84–*85*
Middle years *176–177*
Later years *230-231*
Into the Sun 263
Introducing . . . The Beatles 73, 99, 164

J

James, Dick *71*
Jobs, Steve 210
John Lennon/Plastic Ono Band 259
John Lennon's Jesus Controversy 170
John, Elton 260, 298
Jones, Tom *281*
Juber, Laurence 281

K

Kaempfert, Bert 44
Kaiserkeller 32
Kelly, Freda *79*
Kelly, John 226–227, 229
Kennedy, Jackie *110*
Kennedy, President John F. *110*–111
Kenwood 180–*181,* 252, 258
Kinfauns 180, 182–*183*
King Jr., Martin Luther 260
Kinks, The *124*
Kirchherr, Astrid 33–35, *34, 36,* 37, 46, *47, 180,* 186
engagement to Stuart Sutcliffe 36
Kisses at the Bottom 278–279
Klein, Allen 175, 212, *248*–249, 254
Koschmider, Bruno 30, 36
Kramer, Billy J. and the Dakotas *53,* 112, *126-127*

L

Laine, Denny 277, 281
Leege, Josje 212, 213
Lennon, Alfred 18
Lennon, Cynthia 18, 19, 21, 24–25, *78–79,* 94, *180,* 181, *186,* 187, *197, 206 220,* 258, 262
Lennon, John (personal life)
early life 18
marriage to Cynthia Lennon and birth of Julian 78–79
departure from the Beatles 254
divorce from Cynthia Lennon 258
marriage to Yoko Ono 258
birth of Sean Lennon 261
shooting and death 266–267
Lennon, Julia *18*
Lennon, Julian 79, 94, *178, 181, 221,* 258, 261–263, *262–263*
Lennon, Sean *262–263*
Lester, Richard 123, 131–133, 137 140–141, 143
Let It Be (Broadway show) 308
Let It Be . . . Naked *237*
Let It Be 154, 207, 216, 231, 233–238, *234–235,* 237, 252
Lewishohn, Mark 157
Liebowitz, Annie 266
Linda McCartney's Sixties: Portrait of an Era 273
Lindsay-Hogg, Michael 234
Live Jam 284
Live Peace in Toronto 1969 253
Liverpool, England 10–27, *10–15,* 257, 302, 310
Casbah, The 26, *64*
Cavern 37–53, *38–40, 42–43, 50,* 83
Forthlin Road 21
Madryn Street 11
Mendips *18,* 76
Scotland Road 41
St. Peter's Church 21, 51
Toxteth 40
Liverpool Oratorio 278
Living in the Material World 285
Lomax, Jackie *216*
London *86*–91, *94*–107
See also Abbey Road Studios
Astoria Theatre, Finsbury Park *103*
Belgravia 185
Carnaby Street 90, *91,* 183, 192
Chiswick House, West London 159
Club Noreik, South Tottenham 96
Emperor's Gate, Knightsbridge ... *94,* 180
Fairfield Halls, Croydon *100*
Montagu Square *94*–95,
Prince of Wales Theatre *102*
St. John's Wood *182*
Tiles, Oxford Street 96
UFO Club, Tottenham Court Road *97*
Whaddon House, Knightsbridge *94*

Index

London Town 277
Los Angeles Hit Factory Studio 261
Love 309
Love Story 222

M

Madryn Street 11
Magic Alex. *See* Mardas, Yanni Alexis
Magical Mystery Tour 58, 164–165, *202–205,* 212, 216, 222, 231
Mahesh Yogi, Maharishi *196–197, 206*–207
Majestic Theatre, Birkenhead, England *74, 92–93*
Manchester Apollo theater *77*
Making of Sgt. Pepper, The 60
Many Years from Now 239
Marcos, Ferdinand 169
Marcos, Imelda *169*
Mardas, Yanni Alexis *216*
Martin, George 52–*53,* 59–64, *60, 63,* 68–72, 73, 77, 89, 98–99, 121, 131–133, 136, 138, 143, *155,* 162–*163,* 190–192, 196, 222–223, 225–227, 237–*238,* 242, 253, 268–269, 277, 302–303, 309
MBE *152–153*
McCartney *273*
McCartney II 278
McCartney, Heather 272, 273, 281
McCartney, James 278, 303
McCartney, Linda 220–*221, 249,* 258, 272–279, *272–274, 276–277,* 281, *303*
  early life 220–221
  meeting Paul McCartney 220
  marriage to Paul McCartney 249
  birth of children 272–273
  death 278
McCartney, Mary 20, 272, 273, 278, *281*
McCartney, Michael 20, 21
McCartney, Paul (personal life)
  early life *20–23*
  departure from the Beatles 254
  marriage to Linda Eastman 272
  birth of children 272–273
  marriage to and divorce from Heather Mills 279
  marriage to Nancy Shevell 279
McCartney, Stella 273, 276, 278, *281,* 291
McGuinn, Roger. *See* Byrds
Meet the Beatles! 98–*99,* 115, *164*
Memory Almost Full 278
Mendelsohn, Jack 222
Mendelsohn, John 240
Mendips *18,* 76
Menuhin, Yehudi *57*
Merchandising, the Beatles 104, *105–107, 148*
Mersey Beat (newspaper) 49–*51*
Mew, Peter 242
Mills, Heather 279
Mind Games 260
Minoff, Lee 222
Modern Jazz Quartet 216, *217*
Mods *41*
Monkees, The *304, 307*
Montagu Square *94*–95
Montreal "Bed-in" 258
Moody Blues *126, 127*
Moon, Keith 260, *299*
Murray the K 116, *117,* 126, 144

N

NEMS Enterprises 48–50, 52–53, 106, 198–200, 211, 248
New 278
New York City *256*–260
  Carnegie Hall *114, 117*
  Dakota, The 256–257, 259, 262, 266–269, *267, 269*
  East 52nd Street 260
  Plaza Hotel 116
  St. Regis Hotel 259
  Strawberry Fields 268, *269*
  Times Square 258–*259*
Nicol, Jimmie *136*
Nilsson, Harry 260–261
Nippon Budokan *168*
Nixon, President Richard 260
No. 3 Abbey Road. *See* Abbey Road Studios

O

O'Dell, Chris 288
O'Dell, Denis 234
Ono, Yoko 47, 95, *220, 225, 232, 236,* 237, *239, 248, 250*–255, *250–254, 256, 258*–269, *260, 265, 267*
  early life 250–251
  meeting John Lennon 220
  birth of son 261
  marriage to John Lennon 258
Orbison, Roy *101,* 291
Our World 9, *205*
Owen, Alun 132

P

Pang, May 260, *261*
Partridge, Ken 180–181
Past Masters 213
Pease, Gayleen 213
Peter and Gordon 82–*83,* 95, 126, *127, 214*
Petty, Tom *293*
Pink Floyd *97*
Pipes of Peace 278
Plastic Ono Band 253, 254
Plaza Hotel 116
Please Please Me 69, 73, 83, 99, 164
Pop Goes the Beatles 103
Powell, Cynthia. *See* Lennon, Cynthia
Presley, Elvis 18–*19,* 22, 104, 106, 111, 115, 120, 123, 130–131, 141, *149,*
Preston, Billy *215, 236*
Prince of Wales Theatre 102
Princess Margaret 102
Produced by George Martin 61

Q

Quant, Mary *78, 88,* 89–90
Quarrymen *19,* 21, 23, 43
Queen Elizabeth Hotel 258
Queen Elizabeth, the Queen Mother *102*–103

R

Rain: A Tribute to the Beatles 308
Ram 274–*275*
Rebels, The 22
Red Rose Speedway 276–277
Residences *94–95,* 180, *181,* 182–*183,* 252, 258, 260, *286*
Revolver 47, 151, 157–*160,* 161, 163–164, 168, 177, 190, 223, 229
Rigg, Diana *88,* 89
Ringo 247
Ringo Starr and His All-Starr Band 300–301, *300, 302*
Rishikesh 206–207
Rock and Roll Hall of Fame 309
Rock 'n' Roll 261
Rockers *41*
Rolling Stones *82, 124,* 125
Rotogravure 298
Rubber Soul 59, 79, 81, 154–155, *156,* 157–158, 164, 190
Rubin, Jerry 259
Run Devil Run 278
Rutles, The (movie) *306*

S

Sassoon, Vidal *88,* 89
Scorsese, Martin 293, *306, 306*
Scotland Road 41
Searchers, The *37*
Secret Value of Daydreaming, The 263
Seekers, The *126*
Segal, Erich 222
Seiwell, Denny 276–277
Sentimental Journey 298
Sgt. Pepper 58–59, 81, 153, 161, 163–164, 175, *188,* 189–191, 190–195, *193,* 211, 229
Sgt. Pepper's Lonely Hearts Club Band See Sgt. Pepper
Shankar, Ravi *155, 196*–197, *215,* 283, *287*–288
Shapiro, Helen *100*–101
Shea Stadium *144, 145, 146–147,* 172
Shenson, Walter 132
Sheridan, Tony 30, *44*
Shevell, Nancy *279*
Shirelles, The *17*
Shotton, Pete 212, 258
Silver Beatles *22,* 23, 25–26
Sinclair, John 259
Smith, Mimi 18, 70, 76, 258–9
Smith, Norman "Hurricane" *162*
Some Time in New York City 259, 264
Something New 164
Somewhere in England 291
Spector, Phil 237, 254, 260
Springfield, Dusty 124–*125*
St. John's Wood *182*
St. Pauli 30
St. Peter's Church 21, 51
St. Regis Hotel 259
Starkey Tigrett, Maureen. *See* Starkey, Maureen
Starkey, Jason *301*
Starkey, Lee *301*
Starkey, Maureen 95, *180,184, 186, 206*–207, 208, 214, 287, *296–297,* 301
  marriage to Ringo Starr 152
  births of children 184
  divorce from Ringo Starr 297
  marriage to Isaac Tigrett 297
  death 297
Starkey, Richard. *See* Starr, Ringo
Starkey, Zak *301*
Starr, Ringo
  early life *33, 66–67*
  joining the Beatles 64–65
  marriage to Maureen Cox 152
  births of children 184
  divorce from Maureen 297
  marriage to Barbara Bach 299
Stigwood, Robert *210–211,* 248
Stop and Smell the Roses 299
Storm, Rory and the Hurricanes 32–*33, 66,* 67–*68*
Strawberry Fields 268–*269*
Studio Two. *See* Abbey Road Studios
Sullivan, Ed *115,* 116, 118–119, *123,* 144
Sunny Heights 184
Surfaris, The *111*
Surrey, England 180–*181,* 184, 252, 258
Sutcliffe, Stuart *22,* 23, *24,* 26, *27, 34,* 35, *36, 45–46,* 51, 63, 84, 192
  early life 25–26
  engagement to Astrid Kirchherr 36
  departure from the Beatles 46
  death 46–47

T

Taverner, John 214
Taylor, Alistair 50, 211, 175, 249
Taylor, Derek 175
Taylor, James *215*
Tempest 268
Thank Your Lucky Stars *70,* 71
That Was The Week That Was *88*
Them *126*
Thirty-three and 1/3 185
Thomas, Chris 226
Tigrett, Isaac 297
Tiles, Oxford Street 96
Times Square 258–*259*
Tittenhurst Park 256, 258–259
Tokyo, Japan 166–167, 167–169
  Nippon Budokan *168*
  Tokyo International Airport *168*
Toot and a Snore in '74, A 261
Top Ten Club. *See* Hamburg, Germany
Toxteth 40
Traveling Wilburys 290–291
Traveling Wilburys Vol. 1 291
Traveling Wilburys Vol. 3 291
Troubadour, West Hollywood 260
Tug of War 268, 278
Twiggy *91,* 214

U

UFO Club 97
Unfinished Music No. 1: Two Virgins 239, *253*
Unfinished Music No. 2: Life with Lions 253

V

Valotte 263
Van Morrison *126*
Vee Jay Records 99, 112
Venus and Mars 277
Vollmer, Jürgen 33–*35,* 36, 47
Voorman, Klaus 33–*34,* 161, 285

W

Waiting for the Beatles 213
Waller, Gordon. *See* Peter and Gordon
Walls and Bridges 260
Warhol, Andy *122,* 123
Waters, John 41
Wedding Album 253
Whaddon House, Knightsbridge 94
White Album, The 81, 161, 163, 224–229, *227–229*
White, Ron 52
Who, The 41, *124*
Wild Life 276
Wildes, Leon 260
Williams, Allan 26, *27,* 32, 40, 51, 67
Wilson, Brian 157, 194
Wings 276–278, *276–277,* 281
Wings at the Speed of Sound 277
Wings Over America 277
With the Beatles 73, 82, *98,* 102, 112, 164
Wonder, Stevie 261

Y

Yellow Submarine 216, *218*–230, *222–223*
Yesterday and Today 59, 164, *165*

Z

Zombies, The 126, *127*

Designer Duncan Youel would like to thank Mark Naboshek, Bill Harry, Rod Davis, Ulf Krüger, Alex Mertsch, and Glenn Gass, and offer a special mention to Jennifer Jeffrey at Endeavour London Ltd (www.endeavourlondon.com) for her help with picture research at Getty.

Author Nancy Hajeski would like to acknowledge Duncan Youel and the art and editorial support team for their unflagging efforts on this book, and Richard T. Hajeski and David Vanderheyden for their research assistance.

This book is dedicated to Beatles fans everywhere . . . and considering that in 2008 NASA beamed "Across the Universe" into deep space, I literally mean *everywhere*.

Beatles memorabilia, pictures and background imagery courtesy of the following individuals and organizations: Shutterstock: 4-5, 28-29, 30-37, 38-39, 103, 128-129, 149, 150, 151, 152, 152, 163, 178, 188, 189, 232-233, 233, 282-283, 294-295; **Sean Moore Collection** 6, 105, 106, 107, 148, 190, 219, 222, 226-227; **The Quarrymen, Les Kearney**: 19; **Alexander Mertsch, www.bsights.de**: 28, 32, 35; **Mark Naboshek Collection**: 44, 51, 68, 104, 105, 106, 107, 139, 191, 223; **Liverpool Records Office, City Engineers**: 49; **Bill Harry www.triumphpc.com/mersey-beat**: 51; **Duncan Youel Collection**: 72, 98, 139, 142, 156, 160, 193, 204, 223, 241, 273, 275, 285; **Glenn Gass** 94, 95; **Steve Clarke, www.theanalogdept.com**: 229; **www.vintagevibe.com**: 231; **psychedelic-rocknroll.blogspot.co.uk**: 231; **Ericka Gray Photography www.gustfront.com**: 270-271; **henleyonthames. org**: 286; **Pictures courtesy of Getty Images as follows: AFP**: 269tl, 306tl; **Dave Benett**: 290r; **Blank Archives**: 80r, 137r, 224, 253; **John Bulmer**: 250; **CBS Archive**: 115, 116l, 118, 187br; **John Downing**: 88ml, 88br; **Frank Edwards**: 299t; **Tony Evans**: 88bl, 195; **Gamma-Keystone**: 23b, 178, 181, 207; **Gamma-Rapho**: 109, 141; **Getty Images**: 10-11, 13, 14, 16t, 20, 21, 23t, 27b, 30, 37tr, 40, 41, 42b, 43b, 57, 62, 63t, 66, 67, 70, 75, 78r, 79b, 80l, 88tl, 91, 92, 97l, 101t, 102r, 103l, 110, 124tl, 125m, 126t, 126br, 127bl, 127tr, 127tl, 136, 152, 155, 162, 170, 173, 182, 184, 185, 197, 199, 200, 201, 203b, 205ml, 205mr, 205bl, 205tl, 206, 212, 213tr, 213c, 213b, 214r, 215tm, 215b, 216tl, 217b, 220l, 221, 225b, 236, 237, 238, 243, 248l, 248r, 249t, 251, 254, 255tl, 257r, 259r, 262, 263, 267t, 269tr, 269b, 270, 272, 274b, 276b, 277, 284, 287, 294, 296, 297, 305, 306tr, 306mr, 307b, 311, 313, 320; **Guitarist Magazine**: 54; **Dave Hogan**: 281ml, 281bl, 281br; **Imagno**: 142t; **Clodagh Kilcoyne**: 177br; **David Livingston**: 279; **Andrew Maclear**: 208, 252; **Larry Marano**: 300, 302; **New York Daily News**: 120, 121, 145t, 144, 146, 267b, 288l, 289;

New York Historical Archive: 114b; **Michael Ochs**: 5, 9, 22, 33, 38, 50, 63b, 83b, 99, 108l, 117tl, 122t, 125t, 127br, 129, 130, 134b, 135, 137l, 140t, 145b, 148br, 163, 165tl, 165br, 165tr, 171, 188, 191, 214l, 244, 247, 261, 265b, 304, 306ml, 307t, 315; **Terry O'Neill**: 58, 59, 71, 124r, 286r, 291, 299b, 303; **John Phillips**: 306b; **Popperfoto**: 41t, 53, 76, 79t, 86, 88mr, 102l, 116r, 117tr, 117m, 123, 124, 126bl, 140b, 153, 169, 175, 180m, 180b, 192, 196t, 198, 249b, 273b, 274t, 293b; **Michael Putland**: 210, 215tr, 216l, 256l, 259l, 276t, 281tl, 292, 298; **Redferns**: 111, 149r; **Fiona Adams**: 255tr; **Howard Barlow**: 281tr; **Cummings Archive**: 196b, 273tr; **Phil Dent**: 56; **Jeremy Fletcher**: 61b; **GAB Archive**: 16, 60, 83t, 133, 134t, 172, 174, 218, 282; **Gems**: 162t; **Charlie Gillett Collection**: 19t; **Mark & Colleen Hayward**: 18, 43t, 64, 77b, 78l, 82, 96, 117b, 186, 187tl, 187mr, 187bl, 219, 222, 231l, 258; **Ivan Keeman**: 125b; **Ulf Krüger/K&K**: 24, 27t, 31, 34b, 37tl, 45, 46, 47, 85r, 177t, 177bl, 211l; **Chris Morphet**: 229t; **Petra Niemeier/K&K** 143; **Nigel Osbourne**: 85l, 176, 177m, 230; **Ellen Piel/K&K**: 34t, 37; **David Redfern**: 100l, 113, 154r, 202, 203t, 217t, 225t **John Rodgers**: 48, 220r; **Max Scheler/K&K**: 42, 180t; **Gilles Petard**: 17; **Jürgen Vollmer**: 35tl, 36; **Andrew Whittuck**: 97; **Val Wilmer**: 255b; **Jack Robinson**: 215l; **Sankei Archive**: 168t; **SSPL**: 12, 122b; **Bob Thomas**: 112, 232, 246; **Time & Life Pictures**: 15, 88tr, 94, 187tr, 187ml, 194, 239, 265t, 288t, 301; **TS Productions**: 65; **Underwood Archives**: 260; **United Artists**: 128, 132; **V&A Images**: 44l, 61l, 77t, 101, 127ml; **Michael Ward**: 131; **Robert Whitaker**: 150, 154l, 158, 159, 166, 167; **WireImage**: 114t, 205tr, 293t; **Andy Wright**: 100r; **Vinnie Zuffante**: 290l

Overleaf: The Beatles take a break from their rehearsals for the Royal Variety Performance at the Prince of Wales Theatre, with coffee after lunch at the Mapleton Hotel. November 4, 1963.